D1065471

FUG YOU

FUG YOU

{ *An Informal History of the Peace Eye Bookstore, the Fuck You Press, The Fugs, and Counterculture in the Lower East Side* }

Ed Sanders

DA CAPO PRESS

A Member of the Perseus Books Group

Poem by Elin Paulson, courtesy of Leif Grund.

Ted Berrigan, "Despair Poem"; comments on flyer for Tuli Kupferberg's 4 May 1966 reading at the Folklore Center; quote from Berrigan letter after d. a. levy died, courtesy of Alice Notley.

Works by Charles Olson published during his lifetime are copyright © the Estate of Charles Olson. Previously unpublished works by Charles Olson are copyright © University of Connecticut Libraries. Introduction to Peace Eye, and "Act in Creation/Arouse the Nation," used by permission.

Text of "Firing Line" courtesy of Firing Line (Television Program) Broadcast Records, Hoover Institution Archives, Stanford University.

Phil Ochs, a verse from "The Marines Have Landed on the Shores of Santo Domingo," courtesy of Michael Ochs © 1968 Barricade Music, Inc.

Quote from article by Tuli Kupferberg, used by permission of Samara Kupferberg.

Designed by Jeff Williams
Set in 13 point Arno Pro by the Perseus Books Group

Library of Congress Cataloging-in-Publication Data

    Sanders, Ed.
    Fug you: an informal history of the Peace Eye Bookstore, the Fuck You Press, the Fugs, and counterculture in the Lower East Side / Ed Sanders. — 1st Da Capo Press ed.
        p. cm.
    Includes index.
    ISBN 978-0-306-81888-2 — ISBN 978-0-306-81943-8 (e-book)
    1. Sanders, Ed. 2. Peace Eye Bookstore. 3. Fuck You Press. 4. Fugs (Musical group) 5. Underground press publications—New York (State)—New York. 6. Counterculture—New York (State)—New York—History—20th century. 7. Lower East Side (New York, N.Y.)—Intellectual life—20th century. I. Title.

PS3569.A49Z46 2011
306'.1—dc23
[B]

2011037017

Published by Da Capo Press
A Member of the Perseus Books Group
www.dacapopress.com

Da Capo Press books are available at special discounts for bulk purchases in the U.S. by corporations, institutions, and other organizations. For more information, please contact the Special Markets Department at the Perseus Books Group, 2300 Chestnut Street, Suite 200, Philadelphia, PA 19103, or call (800) 810-4145, ext. 5000, or e-mail special.markets@perseusbooks.com.

10 9 8 7 6 5 4 3 2 1

Dedicated to the presidency of Robert Kennedy, to the spirit of the
Great Be-In in Golden Gate Park, to the enjoyment of freedom,
to the quick advance from four- to sixteen-track recording,
to peace and love and sharing the largesse, to all those groped
by J. Edgar Hoover in the silent halls of Congress, and to a Nation
that could invent the wah wah pedal.

Let other pens dwell on guilt and misery.
—Jane Austen, *Mansfield Park*, chapter 48

It all coheres...
—Sophocles, *Women of Trachis*,
Pound translation

but why tell all just because Tell tells you to tell
—*1968, A History in Verse*, about being on
William Buckley's *Firing Line* with Jack Kerouac

Of course, facts rarely work themselves
into any kind of symmetry.
—Richard Drinnon, *Facing West:
The Metaphysics of Indian-Hating
and Empire Building*

These Fragments I have shored against my ruins
—T. S. Eliot, "The Wasteland," l. 431

When the mode of the music changes
the walls of the city shake.
—Tuli Kupferberg adapted (and considerably improved)
from Damon of Athens, ca. 460 B.C.

I was trying with all my might to make
of myself "a potent social force."
—Maxim Gorki, *One Autumn Night*

"In America you can say anything you want
—as long as it doesn't have any effect."
—Paul Goodman

CONTENTS

THANKS

⟨◊⟩

The author wishes to give thanks for research help to Steve Clay of Granary Books for helping locate good copies of some of my publications. Also my gratitude to Steve Clay for reading through my archive material at NYU Fales Collection, and to Marvin Taylor, director, the Fales Library and Special Collections at the Elmer Holmes Bobst Library at New York University, for clean copies of the *Marijuana Newsletter*.

Thanks to Michael Basinski, curator, the Poetry Collection, at the Library, University at Buffalo, SUNY, and to James Maynard, assistant curator, the Poetry Collection, for copies of my notebooks from the early 1960s and for information from the Harvey Brown archive. Thanks to Melissa Watterworth Batt, Curator of Literary, Natural History, and Rare Book Collections at the University of Connecticut Libraries, for helping the author's research during a visit and for providing copies of items in the author's archive in the Rare Book Collection.

Thanks to old friends Duncan McNaughton and Tom Clark for outstanding recollections; to excellent artist Ann Leggett; to Jan Herman for archival material relating to the banning of "The Hairy Table" from the NEA anthology in 1970; to Mike Boughn for material on the life and times of Harvey Brown; to Richard Alderson for his recollections on the recording of The Fugs at Impact Sound in New York City, 1966–1968.

My gratitude to Timothy D. Murray, librarian and head, Special Collections Department, University of Delaware Library, for good copies of the withdrawn edition of *APO-33* by William S. Burroughs. Thanks to Beth Reineke for research help; to Terrence Williams for memories of Lawrence, Kansas, in 1965; to Bobby Louise Hawkins for The Fugs footage from Placitas; to Kim Spurlock for help on the Neal Cassady chronology; and to George Kimball, Jim Fitzgerald, and Ben Schafer.

Thanks to the microfilm department at the Sojourner Truth Library at SUNY New Paltz, and at the library at Vassar College in Poughkeepsie, New York. Thanks to the Smithsonian Center for Folklife and Cultural Heritage for information on the early history of The Fugs.

Thanks to Stan Cornyn, former VP of Reprise Records, and coauthor (with Paul Scanlon) of *Exploding: The Highs, Hits, Hype, Heroes, and Hustlers of the Warner Music Group*, for going out back of his house to his archive barn and sharing some Fugs documents.

FROM THE AUTHOR

⁕

As the years described in this book whizzed by, I believed most fervently that the roots of revolution were going to lift the concrete away from the field of truth, after which Bread and Roses and the utopian place I called Goof City would grow up afresh in a warless world—Goof City on the hill, Goof City in the Lower East Side, Goof City shining.

I was raised in a little farm town called Blue Springs in western Missouri, which, when Dwight Eisenhower's Interstate Highway System connected it to greater Kansas City beginning in the late 1950s, saw most of its farms, forests, and orchards turned into bedroom subdivisions. After a year at Missouri University in Columbia, I hitchhiked to New York City in the summer of 1958 to attend New York University, where I had a vague concept at first of becoming a rocket scientist (it was the era of the Mercury Program), but switched to Greek and Latin after a couple of semesters.

I soon was enmeshed in the culture of the Beats as found in Greenwich Village bookstores, in the poetry readings in coffeehouses on MacDougal Street, in New York City art and jazz, and in the milieu of pot and counterculture that was rising each month. There was the impact of the Happenings and of the moral fervor of the civil rights movement. Also of great allure was the underground movie scene traced by Jonas Mekas in his weekly columns in the *Village Voice*.

I was very impressed with the images of ancient Egypt and began experiments in utilizing hieroglyphic-like elements in my own writing. The visual aspect of intelligence was increasing during the television and movie era; children born after World War II had higher visual intelligences. The Eye was in the ascendency, and the mode of the music, thanks to the rise of advances in music technology, was changing also.

That fact would help lead me to joining the Mimeograph Revolution, studying Egyptian hieroglyphics, founding an avant-garde singing group called The Fugs, and helping to form another strange political group called the Yippies.

The culture of the Lower East Side—with its very affordable, rent-controlled apartments—and the general affordability of the larger culture opened up great vistas of possibility. I realized that the Nation's future was "up for grabs," as if some Deity had tossed a cultural basketball up for many millions to seize and dribble toward their home hoop. Hence my adoption of the phrase "Total Assault on the Culture," inspired by William Burroughs.

The daily flow of news affected our art, and I have tried to bring some of the details of the broader political reality into the tapestry of recollection. Some could isolate themselves from it, but the news of the war in Southeast Asia, for instance, was an incessant drum beat jarring our concentration on Beauty and Creativity, beginning around the fall of 1963 and lasting through the decade and beyond. In many ways they were the Drums of Doom that prevented the Great Society from continuing from the great Medicare and Medicaid legislations of 1965, say, toward universal health care.

But other events, too, blocked the rise of paradise—the Birmingham bombing, Freedom Summer, Selma, the use of napalm and defoliants in Vietnam, the Gulf of Tonkin Resolution, teach-ins, the Watts Riots, God Is Dead, the banning of LSD, and on and on. Then, in 1967, public discussion that the CIA had killed Kennedy—could that be true? Folk rock, Pop Art, Summer of Love, communes, the Revolution, sex forever, riots in Newark, the Tet Offensive, revolutions in theater and dance, Martin Luther King and Robert Kennedy, Chicago, Woodstock, Nixon, Chappaquiddick, the Moon Walk, the Moratoriums, Altamont, cults that kill, oh Lord, like Poe's "Scoriac River that restlessly rolls."

In attempting to enact "Total Assault on the Culture," I undoubtedly did some things and promoted some concepts about which I feel remorse and sometimes even shame. My regrets or memoirist anguish do not rise to the level of Hardy's *Mayor of Casterbridge* or those, say, of Thomas Carlyle. But I sure made some errors during my years that cannot be blamed on chromosome damage, erotomania, hunger for what they called in my Midwest youth "spermatum nirvanum," vodka, pot, paraquat, psilocybin universe-wandering, anarcho-socialism, or excessive Protestant mean streak.

There are many names associated with this story. During these years I met thousands of people while working on various projects, from antiwar demonstrations, benefits for lots of causes, The Fugs, the music scene, the art scene, the publishing scene, Chicago and the Yippies, and the byways of rock and roll, managers, agents, and perpetrators of all kinds. In this tracing of those years, I no doubt left out those who ultimately will be seen to have more importance to this tracing than I have indicated. My apologies that they have been underreported on these pages.

Sequencing the time stream is sometimes difficult. I'm now in my seventy-first year of "quiet desperation," and I apologize for the "gaps" in my recollections. The shopworn adage "If you lived fervently in the 1960s, how could you possibly remember them?" becomes an actual fact when trying to weave a tapestry of the past. Like, exactly what was the date that artist and filmmaker Harry Smith—the first night I met him—threw Aleister Crowley's *Book of Lies* into the tall porcelain urinal at Stanley's Bar?

Just as in my book-length biographical poem about my longtime friend, *The Poetry and Life of Allen Ginsberg*, I chose to pass over some things in silence, not to be so judgmental, to let certain matters sleep unto the supernova of the sun. In addition, I have decided not to settle any scores in my recollections. I was sometimes imperfect in my behavior toward others, tending at times toward arrogance and egotistical smugness.

I will not claim to have been an integral part of much of anything in the tale of these years—but I was an experimental participant. I know that I was convinced there'd be Vast Change as I sped through the Kennedy, Johnson, and early Nixon years. Accordingly, I surged through the decade on my own little missions, many of them of little importance now, but then I strutted through the time track, daring to be part of the history of the era.

In this book of remembrances I decided not to drain to its dregs the urn of bitter memory, to paraphrase Shelley's famous line. I have chosen to accentuate the energy, the wild fun, the joyful creativity, and the schemes of

Better World derring-do and to consign as much bitterness and bad memories as possible to the halls of darkness.

My parents raised me not to be a whiner, so I've done my best to avoid being a whining former rock and roller and countercultural icon whose "Total Assault on the Culture" turned out to be composed, at least in good part, of woof tickets. Even though a good number of our Dreams turned to ashes, these years still pulse in my psyche with their wonderment, fun, creativity, eros, visions of human betterment, and, yes, total assault on the culture.

ED SANDERS
Woodstock, New York

FUG YOU

The Glories of the Early '60s

◦◦◦◦◦

In the fall of 1963 Allen Ginsberg mailed me a poem called "The Change," which he'd just created while riding on the Kyoto-Tokyo express train in Japan. On the train he had broken down and wept while writing that he was on a new path now, that he had returned to his body after the ecstatic years following the 1948 vision (alluded to in "Howl") in which he had heard the ghostly voice of William Blake chanting the poems from *The Songs of Experience* beginning, "Oh Rose, Thou Art Sick" and "Ah, Sunflower, Weary of Time" in an apartment in Spanish Harlem. From 1948 through half of 1963 he had obeyed the implications of his Blake visions, searching for personal Illuminations and Ecstasy. But now, after a spiritual journey to India and Japan, he was determined to live in his own body, not seek Visions so much, and settle into a loving mammaldom with all other fellow suffering beings. I published "The Change" at once in *Fuck You/ A Magazine of the Arts*, an issue I printed just after the assassination of John Kennedy, a murder that was beginning to shriek in our minds and would keep shrieking for years to come.

When Allen mailed me his visionary poem, I was in the midst of my final two semesters at New York University, studying Greek and Latin. In my spare time I studied Egyptian. On the benches of Washington Square Park, near the NYU main building, during the warm months I began to set two Blake poems, "The Sick Rose" and "Ah, Sun-Flower," to melodies. I was inspired by Allen's having heard Blake himself chanting those very poems in an apartment in Spanish Harlem, some fifteen years before. I also came up

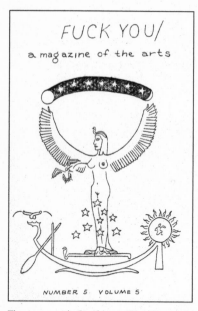

FUCK YOU/
a magazine of the arts

NUMBER 5   VOLUME 5

The issue with Ginsberg's "The Change"

with a melody for "How Sweet I Roamed from Field to Field," one of Blake's earliest works of genius, written as early as age eleven. These songs provided the kernel of identity for the founding, a year later, of The Fugs.

The year 1963 was an important one for me. City Lights published my *Poem from Jail*, written in 1961 after I had attempted to swim aboard a Polaris submarine during its commissioning in Groton, Connecticut, and conduct a peace vigil atop its missile hatches. I had a kind of rebel renown as the publisher of *Fuck You/ A Magazine of the Arts*, which I had begun in early '62. In a "Secret Location in the Lower East Side," I printed around five hundred copies of each issue on a mimeograph machine on colored paper and gave almost all of them away free.

POEM
FROM
JAIL

Ÿ

Ed Sanders

FUCK YOU/ A MAGAZINE OF THE ARTS
EDITED, PUBLISHED & PRINTED BY ED SANDERS
AT A SECRET LOCATION IN THE LOWER EAST SIDE,
NEW YORK CITY, U.S.A.

A Secret Location in the Lower East Side, number 1, February 1962.

The Mimeograph Revolution

There were other mimeograph presses around the country, and some were beginning to call it the Mimeograph Revolution. Out in Cleveland a young poet named d. a. levy began Renegade Press, utilizing a combination of mimeo and letterpress. By 1963 I believed in the spark, the *iskra*, that the revolutionaries of Russia early in the twentieth century talked about. I believed that the *iskra* could or would somehow burst out of a poetry café on

Second Avenue or inspire a network of minds and sweep America to Great Change. Or even that a network of mimeographs steadily publishing, coast to coast, city to town to bookstore to rebel café, could help a nonviolent revolution to blossom forth in full bread and roses glory!!!

The Founding of My Magazine

I founded *Fuck You/ A Magazine of the Arts* in February 1962 after a bunch of us, mostly friends from the *Catholic Worker*, went to see Jonas Mekas's *Guns of the Trees* at the Charles Theater on Avenue B. I was there mainly because the ad for the film in the *Village Voice* stated that my hero Allen Ginsberg was in it. For years I had avidly read Jonas Mekas's weekly *Voice* column, "Movie Journal," which mainly focused on the struggles and delights of the world of underground films.

I sensed from reading Mekas's weekly columns that he was a person of great generosity and communality of spirit. That is, it wasn't all Me! Me! Me! as in so much of the avant-garde. I thought he had a genuine will to help other filmmakers thrive and survive. I later learned that Mekas had paid for the printing of Jack Smith's film *Flaming Creatures*.

Mekas had just founded the Film-Makers' Cooperative and lived nearby on Twelfth Street, although I didn't know that while I was watching *Guns of the Trees*. The Lower East Side in those years was a Do-It-Now zone, and you knew maybe only a snippet of someone's history or scene, if anything at all. All I knew is that the first thing I read each week in the *Voice* was "Movie Journal."

I was particularly fascinated by the appearance of Allen Ginsberg as a narrator in the film. I had not yet met Ginsberg, although I had memorized "Howl" when I was still in Missouri in 1957, and I had seen him at Beat/New York School readings, such as one in November 1959 where he read at the Living Theater with Frank O'Hara. Wow. As I

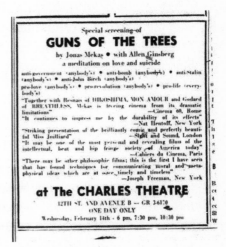

Ad in the *Village Voice* for the screening of *Guns of the Trees*, February 14, 1962. Beat-up image from microfilm at Vassar Library.

"All those groped by J. Edgar Hoover in the silent halls of Congress," dedication, early issue, *Fuck You/ A Magazine of the Arts*

sat fascinated in the Charles Theater that February night with my pals, I never could have dreamed that the author of "Howl" and "Kaddish" would become a close friend.

At one point in *Guns of the Trees* Ginsberg chanted one of his poems with the sentence "I dreamt that J. Edgar Hoover groped me in a silent hall of the Capitol." It was a fragment that opened up such huge vistas of possibility in my mind! I transformed the fragment into the dedication for my soon-to-be-published magazine.

Jonas and Adolfas Mekas and the Film-Makers' Cooperative

Just as Allen Ginsberg was born in New Jersey in 1926 (and not near the Dniester River in Russia) because the pogroms in the Russian Pale, first in the 1880s and later around the time of the Kishinev pogrom of 1904, drove his mother's and father's families to the American Dream, so, too, were Jonas Mekas and his brother, Adolfas, driven from Lithuania to the United States, this time in their case by the Nazis. In the early 1940s Jonas and Adolfas put out a mimeographed anti-Nazi newspaper, cutting stencils on a typewriter in a woodshed behind their house in Semeniskiai in Lithuania. Later they escaped from a German slave labor camp.

In 1949 they arrived in the United States, where both of them became filmmakers. In 1955 Jonas founded the magazine *Film Culture*. In the fall of 1958 he began his very influential weekly column, "Movie Journal," in the *Village Voice*. In the summer of 1960 the Mekas brothers purchased some out-of-date film stock and began their feature-length film *Guns of the Trees*. Jonas wrote the script.

Mekas formed the Film-Makers' Cooperative in early 1962 after another film distribution operation refused to screen a film by Stan Brakhage, *Anticipation of the Night*. The Film-Makers' Cooperative practiced no censorship at all, and 75 percent of the rental fees for showing a film went directly to the filmmaker. And so in early 1962 the Charles Theater on Avenue B near Twelfth Street began showing underground films. Some of us from nearby streets eagerly attended.

Across the street was Stanley's, a packed bar frequented by poets, civil rights activists, filmmakers, painters, and oodles of others from the nearby rent-controlled buildings. After *Guns of the Trees* my friends and I adjourned to Stanley's for conversation and fun. Inspired by the film, I announced that evening that I was beginning a magazine and I solicited manuscripts. The name I tossed out among the revelers made them laugh. It had been in my mind a number of years.

Typing a Wild Magazine at the *Catholic Worker*

In those years I was active in the peace and Ban the Bomb movements. I volunteered at the Committee for Nonviolent Action located on Grand Street, and a number of my friends were on the staff of the *Catholic Worker* newspaper or did other volunteer work for the Worker at its House of Hospitality on Chrystie Street, which is a southern extension of Second Avenue. They were antiwar Catholic pacifists who lived a life of voluntary poverty. Sometimes I watched them hold prayer circles on the second floor on Chrystie Street.

A few of them wrote for the *Catholic Worker*, and some of them at night worked the streets of Greenwich Village to get donations in exchange for issues. It was understood that because of their lives of voluntary poverty, they were allowed to use some of the donations for their personal needs, such as a few 25¢ quart bottles of Rheingold beer (my crowd's drink of choice), which they might take back to their pads, or even use the quarter for a mug of dark beer at Stanley's.

The Catholic Worker provided the best lunch imaginable—beautiful chunks of homemade bread and a healthy soup that worked wonders, especially for someone who might have had too many vodkas at Stanley's the night before. I sometimes had lunch there and now and then picked up clothes or shoes from the free clothes bin on the second floor.

I was, of course, aware of Catholic activist Dorothy Day, her presence at the *Worker*, and her writing, which I could sense was sometimes stunningly good. Her hair was white, and her facial expression was somewhere between fierce and loving. She seemed always on the road, but now and then I would spot her in the House of Hospitality at 175 Chrystie Street, where the offices and soup kitchen resided.

Staff members lived in buildings on nearby streets, and were expected to be celibate unless married. This was 1962, not that many months after the pill 🔵 became extremely common, along with the diaphragm, among damozels of the left.

There were all kinds of legends about Dorothy Day on people's lips— that she had had a wild youth, that she had been the model for Marcel Duchamp's 1912 painting, "Nude Descending a Staircase," which turned out not to be true. She had been born in 1897 and would have been around fourteen or fifteen at the time of the painting.

Many of us were undergoing wild-youth times ourselves, and the thought that someone who would soon be touted as material for sainthood had had wildness during her salad days was soothing and inspiring at the same time.

She had founded the *Catholic Worker* newspaper back in the spring of 1933 and somehow kept it going. I'd heard over 100,000 copies of each issue were printed. Dorothy Day also led the creation of a series of Catholic Worker Houses of Hospitality around the nation. I learned that she had written for *The Masses*, that great and ultracreative magazine that had vigorously opposed America's participation in World War I and that Woodrow Wilson had crushed out of existence with indictments for sedition and raids.

By 1962, her sixty-fifth year, Day had taken part in demonstrations against mandatory civil defense/nuclear war drills, during which sirens forced New York City residents once a year to go into underground shelters or at least to get off the streets. Her credentials for doing good were almost overwhelming.

The day after watching Ginsberg chant poetry in *Guns of the Trees*, I typed the first issue of *Fuck You/ A Magazine of the Arts* on a *Catholic Worker* typewriter, on the third floor, on mimeograph stencils that I borrowed. I also borrowed from the *Worker* a few reams of flecked, colored paper called Granitex. The first issue was a beautiful light green; subsequent issues were in various shades of red. Some pages were flecky gray, and a few were blue or near-chrome yellow.

On February 19, a Monday, I went to a typewriter store on Second Avenue, and for $36 plus change I purchased a small Speed-o-Print mimeograph machine and some printing ink, which I poured into the open top of the printing drum.

In the first issue I published two excellent poems by Jean Morton, then on the *Catholic Worker* staff. In the "Notes on Contributors," I wrote, "Jean Morton—a mad stomper for the Catholic Worker. Jean is a word-machine and her many secret notebooks will cleave out about ten feet of leather-bound library space of the future."

While I was typing the stencils for the first issue, my friend Nelson Barr quickly wrote a "Bouquet of Fuck Yous," which I drew by hand on the stencil, using a stencil-cutting stylus I found in the desk I was sitting at. I noted in the

Ticket to the Mimeograph Revolution. My small Speed-o-Print mimeo, $36.06, February 19, 1962, able to fit nicely on the porcelain bathtub cover in my kitchen at 509 East Eleventh Street.

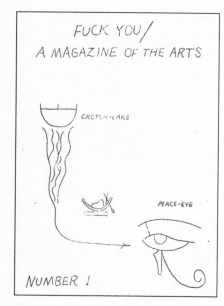

The cover of the first issue of *Fuck You/ A Magazine of the Arts*, drawn by stylus on stencil, February 1962.

typed "Notes on contributors," "(Barr's) Bouquet of Fuck Yous was written as this went to press. Composition time: 43 seconds. Place: 3rd floor, Catholic Worker."

An Egyptian Vision

I was writing a series of poems involving several Egyptian hieroglyphs—the Eye of Horus, which I called Peace Eye, and the small, single-person Egyptian boat found as a hieroglyph on thousands of funerary texts, which I identified with D. H. Lawrence's "Boat of Death." I was not normally very religious, but one afternoon a few months previous I had seen the side of a skinless cow's face, with large eye staring, in the window of a meat store on Second Avenue (not far from where I soon purchased my Speed-o-Print), which gave me a kind of Egypto-poetic religious moment. Since the 1940s in Missouri when my mother would name and describe the constellations and stars in the summer sky, I had been looking for a schematic that would describe the universe. Once in New York I went from studies in Hindu/Indian/Upanishad texts to Egyptian hieroglyphs, which by early 1962, after taking a course at the New School in the Egyptian language, I knew pretty well. After my vision in the window of the meat store, I began the works I called "The Soft-Man Poems," a kind of semireligious text inspired by William Burroughs's novel *The Soft Machine*, portions of which I had been studying in magazines, commingled with my fascination with the solar myths of ancient Egypt.

Uh oh. It wasn't long before it came to the attention of Dorothy Day that her typewriter, her stencils, her groovy green Granitex paper, and her third-floor office had been used to publish *Fuck You/ A Magazine of the Arts.* Day issued an edict that *Catholic Worker* staff members could not publish in my magazine. Most complied, but several resigned, including Jean Forest and her husband at the time, Jim Forest, soon to be a longtime prominent antiwar activist and writer.

I published issue number two a few weeks later, featuring a poem by Jim. He had been managing editor of the *Catholic Worker* and later on wrote biographies of Dorothy Day and Thomas Merton. I wanted no quarrel with Dorothy Day, whose power and worth were right there in her columns, in the soup line, in the clothing bin, in the tireless activities against war, and in her passion for social justice, so I published an editorial in the next issue:

```
    EDITORIAL        EDITORIAL        EDITORIAL

        SEVERAL STAFF MEMBERS OF THE CATHOLIC WORKER WERE STOMPED
OFF THE WORKER SET AS A RESULT OF PUBLISHING IN FUCK YOU/ A
MAGAZINE OF THE ARTS OR AS A RESULT OF CONTINUED ASSOCIATION
WITH ITS EDITOR. DOROTHY DAY, THE HEAD STOMPER AT THE CATHOLIC
WORKER, HAS SUCCOMBED TO THE JANSENIST DIALECTIC AND FLICKED 4
PEOPLE OFF THE SET THERE. THIS OUTBURST OF CALVINISTIC DIRECTIVES
SEEMS TO US NOT IN THE SPIRIT OF ANARCHY, NONVIOLENCE, & THE VIEW
OF CHRIST IN EVERY MAN. HOWEVER, WE UNDERSTAND THE NEED OF THE
GRAND OLD LADY OF CATHOLIC PACIFISM FOR A CLOSED METAPHYSICAL
SYSTEM WHERE THERE ARE NO DISTURBANCES SUCH AS FUCK YOU/ A MAGAZINE
OF THE ARTS, ETC. THEREFORE, IN FUTURE ISSUES OF THIS MAGAZINE
WE SHALL REFRAIN FROM ANY MENTION OF THE CATHOLIC WORKER TO SAVE
MISS DAY FROM ANY MORE METAPHYSICAL DISTRESS. IF ANY OF THE MAD
GROPERS LEFT AT THE WORKER WANT TO PUBLISH IN FUCK YOU/ A MAGAZINE
OF THE ARTS ALL MANUSCRIPTS SHOULD BEAR THE NOTATION: "APPROVED BY D.D."

                    YOURS IN CHRIST, THE SEXUAL LAMB,

                        ED SANDERS

    EDITORIAL        EDITORIAL        EDITORIAL

        WELL WELL WELL! THE EDITOR & THE ENTIRE EDITORIAL BOARD
OF FUCK YOU/ A MAGAZINE OF THE ARTS WERE STOMPED INTO HART ISLAND
WORKHOUSE FOR 15 DAYS AS A RESULT OF THE NONVIOLENT SIT-DOWN IN
FRONT OF THE NEW YORK OPERATIONS OFFICE OF THE ATOMIC ENERGY
COMMISSION AFTER KING JOHN ANNOUNCED ATMOSPHERIC TESTING. THE
JUDGE WAS A PRICK AND AFTER THE PACIFISTS REFUSED TO ASS-KISS,
WAVE THE FLAG, OR PROMISE NEVER TO COMMIT CIVIL DISOBEDIENCE
AGAIN HE WENT BERSERK AND FLICKED THEM IN FOR 15. IN JAIL THE
OFFICIALS GAVE THEM THE ROYALTY SCENE BECAUSE EVER SINCE ALLEN
HOFFMAN GOT ALL THESE GUARDS FIRED AT RIKERS ISLAND WHILE HE WAS
IN ON A CIVIL DEFENSE PROTEST CHARGE, THE NEW YORK DEPT OF CORRECTION
HAS BEEN PARANOIAC ABOUT PACIFISTS. THIS TIME THE FUZZ OUTDID
THEMSELVES HOWEVER, PROVIDING EVERYTHING EXCEPT BOOZE AND SNATCH.
A LOVELY LOVELY 15 DAYS.
```

Several staff members of the *Catholic Worker* were stomped off the *Worker* set as a result of publishing in *Fuck You/ A Magazine of the Arts* or as a result of continued association with its editor. Dorothy Day, the head stomper at the *Catholic Worker*, has succombed to the Jansenist Dialectic and flicked four people off the set there. This outburst of Calvinistic directives seem to us not in the spirit of anarchy, nonviolence, and the view of Christ in every man. However, we understand the need of the grand old lady of Catholic pacifism for a closed metaphysical system where there are no disturbances such as *Fuck You/ A Magazine of the Arts*. Therefore, in future issues of this magazine we shall refrain from any mention of the *Catholic Worker* to save Miss Day from any more metaphysical distress. If any of the mad gropers left at the *Worker* want to publish in *Fuck You/ A Magazine of the Arts*, all manuscripts should bear the notation, "approved by D. D."

Yours in Christ, the Sexual Lamb,

Ed Sanders.

I vowed not to mention the *Catholic Worker* in future issues, and I didn't. In a way Dorothy Day reminded me of my own mother, Mollie, who had passed away when I was a senior in high school in Missouri. My mother was very religious, taught a Sunday School class for high schoolers, and was very liberal on many issues, except she was a bit puritanical. Mollie would almost certainly have sided with Dorothy Day.

The same month, February 1962, that I typed those first stencils at the *Catholic Worker*, I joined writers Grace Paley and Bob Nichols, and others, to help found the Greenwich Village Peace Center, located in a storefront on West Third Street between Bleecker Street and Sixth Avenue. Meeting Grace Paley and Bob Nichols was a big inspiration. I helped varnish the floors, helped set up shelves to prepare the opening of the Peace Center, and was invited by the Board of Directors to serve as chair of the "Nonviolent Peace Action Committee."

A Sit-In at the Atomic Energy Commission

On Friday, March 3, President Kennedy announced that if the Soviets did not sign a permanent cheat-proof test-ban treaty before the end of April, he would resume the testing of nuclear weapons in the air. A bunch of peace activists, including some of my pals from the *Catholic Worker*, had already planned to conduct a sit-in at the New York branch of the Atomic Energy Commission (AEC) if Kennedy announced U.S. tests. (I had been arrested at the Russian Mission to the United States a few months earlier when the Soviets conducted open-air nuke explosions.)

The sit-in was scheduled for Monday. The weekend was spent preparing and printing the leaflets and notifying demonstrators. Two leaflets were written. One was a fact sheet for those committing civil disobedience that recommended serving jail sentences rather than posting bail or paying fines. The other leaflet, to be handed out at the sit-in, explained its purpose, decried atmospheric tests, urged workers to quit their jobs at the AEC, and urged everyone not to pay taxes for nuke-puke. The peace groups pursued the doctrine of "openness and truth"—that is, of informing the police and AEC officials of exactly what was going to take place. They sent out announcements to the press.

Monday morning was a bitter, windswept day. The New York Atomic Energy Commission was located at 376 Hudson Street on the lower west side of Greenwich Village near the piers. Before the demonstration the police had erected a ring of gray barricades around the entrances.

That morning I awakened nervous, meditating about the impending confrontation. I washed with meticulous care because I recalled all too well the shabby treatment I had received from a police officer who had noted my murky feet during my arrest at the Russian Mission. Ever thereafter I had always Spic-and-Span'd myself prior to any demonstration. I didn't eat.

As I walked from the Secret Location on East Eleventh, I recalled how that very weekend there had been demonstrations in Times Square where club-wielding police on horses had ridden up on the curb into a large crowd packed on Father Duffy's traffic island—and the blood had dripped from the whacked skulls.

When I arrived at the AEC, there was that strange electric aura that always seemed to occur just prior to civil disobedience. The bitter cold, the throngs of police, the pickets, the barricades, the weird intelligence agents with movie cameras, the traffic oozing extra slowly by, the reporters, the nervous protest leaders—all combined both to thrill and to terrify. I spotted a few of my friends, most of them from the *Catholic Worker*, already sitting behind the barricades outside the front door. They waved and soon I, too, had slipped through the blocking legs of the police and under the gray boards, silently nodding to those already sitting.

I sat with my knees bunched up and my arms locked around them. I could see the supporting picket line move slowly in a large oval, signs hoisted against Kennedy's nukes. We were warned by a police captain to move from the door or we'd be arrested. Then it began.

There was a quick engine roar as an arrest wagon backed up to the sit-in. Two detectives with food-bloated faces, thick dark blue overcoats, and narrow-brimmed felt hats double-nabbed me, one to a shoulder, sucking me out of the close hem-in of the barricades and toward the police van, half drag, half carry. Then it was a heave-ho scene, and I was plopped aboard.

Not all of the thirty or so demonstrators who were arrested "went limp"—as they termed a totally relaxed arrest posture. Some walked to the wagon instead. The argument was that going limp created violence because it tended to anger the gruff, huffing police haulers.

When the van was full, the back door was locked and we were driven away to the New York Criminal Courts Building at 100 Centre Street. Those jammed aboard sang numbers one, two, and three on the arrested-pacifist Hit Parade: "We Shall Overcome" and "Down by the Riverside," with a little satiric "God Bless America" thrown in.

For the next five hours we were treated to the criminal justice stockyards, herded along with the hordes of sullen unfortunates arrested that day in New York City. Finally we were placed in a "holding tank" packed with the accused, located just outside the courtroom. There was a parade back and forth of legal defense aides with scribbled clipboards trying to assist the poor.

After a seemingly endless chain of mumbling confrontations with the judge, many of which seemed to be drug related, the docket numbers and names of the pacifists were moan-droned by the bailiff as they were herded into the room and the arresting officers lined them up in front of the judge, a dour scowler with curtains of chin blubber dangling.

The first thing to be noted in standing before the judge was that the big brown N in the motto IN GOD WE TRUST, high on the wall behind him, had fallen off. The judge flashed some red onto his face when one of my co-arrestees, lining up with the others in front of the bench, refused to face the judge but rather insisted on facing the spectators. "I refuse to recognize the existence of these proceedings," he announced.

The gavel-whacking judge admonished the supporters in the front row to shut up. The judge then launched into a cold-war lecture that culminated in the old "You'd never get to do this in Russia—you'd be sent to Siberia." Then he gave the one not facing him, because of his noncooperation, notice of bail of $500, but the others he released on their own recognizance. All defendants were charged with discon—disorderly conduct. Those who had gone limp were given additional charges of resisting arrest. The august red face set a date for pleading of March 23, 1962, 10:00 AM. "And be on time!" the judge admonished.

Our pro bono attorney was Ernst Rosenberger. Five years later he would serve as my American Civil Liberties Union (ACLU) attorney, successfully defending me against my arrest for publishing *Fuck You/ A Magazine of the Arts*.

On March 23 most of us pled guilty to disorderly conduct in exchange for the dropping of resisting-arrest charges. I and a few others (including *Catholic Worker* friend Jim Forest and future Fugs manager Nelson Barr, who was a regular contributor to *Fuck You*) were sentenced to ten days at the Hart Island Workhouse. Then we were escorted back into the bowels of the Tombs (the nickname for the New York City Criminal Courts building) to be fingerprinted.

I was opposed to the FBI fingerprint storage system, and I knew that the New York City fuzz would flash my prints right down to DC for the big file. I notified the guards that I was not going to cooperate with fingerprinting and was astounded at the commotion this seemed to cause.

My refusal convinced the jail officials that they might have some sort of Pretty Boy Floyd on their hands. Aha, they rubbed their hands, smilingly knowingly, aha, a criminal! They told me they were going to take the prints by force, and still I refused.

Then they sent me to see a prison psychologist, the purpose presumably to determine if I might get violent while resisting the printing. I assured the officer that I would be totally nonviolent but that I'd have to be carried to the print room.

When I was dragged into the room, the officer seemed to assume that I was going to cooperate, even after I fell several times from the chair into a limp heap on the floor. The officer picked up my limp right hand, the fingers dangling in desuetude. The officer rolled a smush of ink across the smooth desktop with a roller. Then he blacked my fingers and placed them on a fingerprint card. "Roll your fingers," he ordered. "I'm sorry," I replied. "I can't cooperate. I don't believe in fingerprinting."

The cop cursed. He grabbed a finger and pressed it onto the card, trying to roll my finger himself. But the card was too smudged to use. "C'mon, cooperate!" he hissed. I contemplated deliberately twitching my fingers with each attempt, but I didn't really want to get beaten up by a bunch of guards. I ruined four fingerprint cards before the set was finally complete, by which time a superior officer was waiting in the room, his carotid pulsing rapidly on a florid neck above a tight white collar bearing golden adornments. Mr. Florid Neck grabbed the finger card and raced away to run the prints. "Aha! Now we'll check *you* out right away!"

A few minutes later a gray school bus with barred windows drove the fresh prisoners up through the Bronx and then to a ferry that slowly thrashed through Long Island Sound to Hart Island. I told prison officials I was a journalist and a poet and hinted that I might write an article about jail conditions. Apparently the prison staff assigned someone to check this out because I was approached three times while on Hart Island and was asked things like "How's the article coming along?" and "How are they treating you? Be sure and send us a copy of the article."

We were processed into the citadel, after which there was a nude stroll through a milky-hued footbath and a check for cooties. At the clothes bin we were given some stiff black shoes, loose jeans, blue shirt, towels, and thick green overcoat. Never in my life had such a negative rush of immediate boredom stormed my soul.

The Death of Bennie Paret

I used to see boxer Emile Griffith, sporting a beret, walking on Times Square. Sometimes he would come into the cigar store where I worked the night shift. He was a popular figure on the street and was well recognized.

The night of my second day on Hart Island, March 24, 1962, there was a televised fight for the welterweight world championship between Bennie "Kid" Paret and Emile Griffith. It was a grudge battle. Kid Paret, a former Cuban sugar-field worker brought to temporary riches via face-punch, had been the champion. Emile Griffith took away the crown in early 1961 by a knockout. Paret then recaptured the crown on July 30, 1961, in a hotly disputed decision. An angry feud developed. Rather than fading gracefully into retirement, Paret was pressed from all sides to continue his career and a further face-punch was arranged. The jail dorm was totally silent and dark save for the tube. The dorm guard sat with feet on the desk, watching the fight. The convicts sat on their bunks and stared. During the early rounds Griffith seemed the casual winner. In the twelfth round Paret was snuffed.

Griffith backed Paret into the corner ropes. Bash. Paret fell against the padded corner brace, his head and upper body jutting at an angle outside the ring. Then there were twenty quick bashes on Paret's face and head: *baf, baf, baf, baf, baf, baf, baf, baf, baf, baf, baf, baf, baf, baf, baf, baf, baf, baf, baf, baf.* The referee stood staring. The dormitory was staring. Everybody was staring. In Miami the fighter's wife watching the battle on TV screamed, "Stop it! Stop it!"

The final scene for the TV-starers showed Paret bent back, eyes closed, loose light-colored trunks with wide stripes down the side, his kidneys pressed against the corner padding, his left arm hanging defenseless at his side, his right arm still cocked but skewered to the side. Griffith was still bashing.

Finally, at 2:09 of the twelfth round, the referee, Ruby Goldstein, yelled, "Hold it!" and threw his arms around Griffith to prevent further hits. Griffith was loath to stop and made a lunge or so to continue—then subsided. And Paret slid down to a crouch, his knees askew. The lowest of the three parallel ring ropes was hooked under his right shoulder, his arm still jutting upward in a fighting posture.

He was in a coma. They removed his mouthpiece—and carried him away. In a few minutes the TV announcer mentioned that Paret had been given last rites. He was taken to Roosevelt Hospital, where a doctor gave him "chances of recovery one in ten thousand."

Shortly thereafter the guard switched off the TV. Lights out. No conversation. I lay stunned in the gloom and spat out the side of the bunk, as if a *ptooey!* could exorcise what I had just seen. I didn't know whether to pray for Paret or to fall into a frothing rage at the so-called art of boxing. I made a personal vow that if there ever were an actual revolution and if I were ever in an orb of power over the People's Bureau of Athletics, then I'd try to ban boxing.

On my bunk I tried to pray for the injured boxer. A few days later the poor man died. But I couldn't get the fight out of my mind. It echoed with the *baf baf baf baf baf baf* and the bloodlust roar and the tense blood-stare silence of the dormitory.

I served my ten days at the Hart Island Workhouse, where I began writing the Times Square poems that would appear in a couple of years in my book *Peace Eye*. A fictional account of the AEC sit-in is in the story of the same name in *Tales of Beatnik Glory*.

An Unself-Confident Egomaniac

I was chasing what Ezra Pound called "the white stag of fame." I was certainly not alone in that chase. During my years in the Lower East Side

Hunter Thompson called me at home when he was promoting his book on the Hells Angels and Terry Southern was assiduous in promoting himself; Allen Ginsberg raced into the offices of the *New York Times* demanding it review *Howl and Other Poems* back in 1956.

I guess I was one of those unself-confident egomaniacs that Jack Kerouac alludes to in the opening lines of *The Subterraneans.* I sent copies of *F.Y.* to Pablo Picasso, Samuel Beckett in Ussy-sur-Marne, Nikita Khrushchev, Jean Paul Sartre, Charles Olson in Gloucester, Fidel Castro in Cuba, and Allen Ginsberg care of an American Express office in India (Ted Wilentz of the 8th Street Bookshop had given me Allen's address). I also sent the magazine to Edward Dahlberg, Gary Snyder, Robert Duncan, and others. As I roamed around the bars, galleries, and coffeehouses of lower New York City, I gave away thousands of free copies of my publications.

Samuel Beckett, I once read, showed someone the *F.Y.* I had mailed to Ussy-sur-Marne, but he never sent me text to publish.

I took part in the Nashville-Washington Walk for Peace from late April into early June. The summer of 1962 I resumed working the 5:00 PM to 2:00 AM shift at the cigar store on Forty-second Street, and I continued writing a sho-sto-po, or short story poem, about Consuela and her adventures on Times Square, inspired by an actual person and filled with my researches into ancient Egyptian language and religion.

That summer I met a wild young guitarist from Bucks County, Pennsylvania, named Steve Weber. He was the only guy I spotted on Avenue A those months barefoot, playing a guitar with all kinds of stickers and small pieces of artwork glued to it. I noticed his mother showed up now and then to check on her son, but she left him to his explorations. Three years later Weber would play electric guitar for the early Fugs.

Two friends, John Harriman and Paul Prenske, opened the Cantina of the Revolutions on East Ninth Street near Avenue C. It was a place to hang out that summer of '62. You paid what you could for homemade soup and coffee.

The Charles Theater and Ron Rice's *Flower Thief*

I continued hanging out at the Charles Theater during 1962, handing out issues of my magazine to any and all. I'll always remember filmmaker Ron

 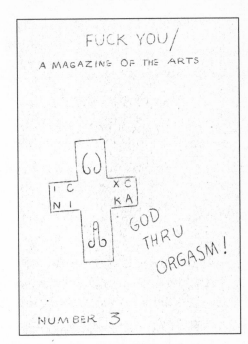

F.Y., issue number 2, April 1962, and *F.Y.*, issue number 3, June 1962

Rice in green shoes at a reception at the Charles, where his film *Flower Thief* was shown with success during the summer of 1962. Rice's movie was an inspiration for Jack Smith's *Flaming Creatures*, filmed a few weeks later. And it was an inspiration for me, publishing the early issues of *Fuck You/ A Magazine of the Arts* in my black-painted pad at 509 East Eleventh, just a few hundred feet from the Charles. And, of course, just across the street from the Charles, the cold mugs of bock beer at Stanley's.

At a party that year I saw Ron rushing in naked to toss a cat at Tiny Tim, who was performing with his ukulele. Ron seemed heroic, operating with flashes of genius in what I interpreted as voluntary poverty, the hallmark of the Catholic Worker movement and the Committee for Nonviolent Action.

Outside the Charles that summer I met legendary Beat hero Tuli Kupferberg, who was selling his magazine *Birth*. I gave him an issue of *Fuck You/ A Magazine of the Arts*, and he promised to send a poem to Box 193, Stuyvesant Station. I was very happy to meet Tuli. It was the beginning of The Fugs and a lifelong friendship. As for Stuyvesant Station, I started getting letters addressed to

A typical letter to the magazine in the '60s.

Fuck You, a Magazine of the Arts
     Box 193
       Stuyvesant Station
         NY, NY 10009

And, mirabile dictu, during the three-year history of the magazine, no one at the post office objected; they just stuck the letters in my box. I was always grateful, and to this day my opinion of the United States Postal Service is shaped toward the good.

A Polished *Poem from Jail*

Friends such as Jean Morton urged me to publish *Poem from Jail*. So finally I gulped and sent it to Lawrence Ferlinghetti at City Lights Book. To my shock, he replied in July '62, interested in publishing it. Ferlinghetti marked up the manuscript so much that I dared to recall Ezra Pound marking up T. S. Eliot's early draft of "The Waste Land" in 1931.

In the poem, I had several lines about Madame Chiang Kai-Shek:

And Madame
Chiang Kai-Shek
too old now
to fuck for the
China Lobby

Ferlinghetti would insist when he printed the poem as a book in altering the text to

And Lady

...

too old now

to fuck for the China Lobby

"You'll get sued, his soldiers will come for you," Lawrence Ferlinghetti jotted next to the lines. I heeded most of his suggestions and prepared a new manuscript, which I sent and he accepted for publication. At last I was being published where "the best minds" of my generation gathered!

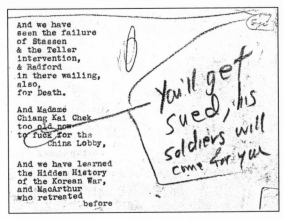

```
And we have
seen the failure
of Stassen
& the Teller
intervention,
& Radford
in there wailing,
also,
for Death.

And Madame
Chiang Kai Chek
too old now
to fuck for the
        China Lobby,

And we have learned
the Hidden History
of the Korean War,
and MacArthur
who retreated
        before
```

You'll get sued, his soldiers will come for you

Lawrence Ferlinghetti's comments on text in *Poem from Jail.*

The "Freaking" Issue of *F.Y.*

In August I put out the fourth issue of *Fuck You/ A Magazine of the Arts.* It brought to the fore the question of freakiness and insanity. At a dinner party I had attended once with George Plimpton, Robert Lowell, and a well-known New York editor, the editor had told us that "most of my friends believe that they're insane." It's true—my generation tended to view freakiness and insanity as something positive. The Latin adage *mens sana in sano corpore,* "a sound mind in a sound body," became for us *mens insana in a fucked-up corpore.*

Two events in the second half of 1962 shaped my perception for the rest of the 1960s: the death of Marilyn Monroe and the Cuban missile crisis.

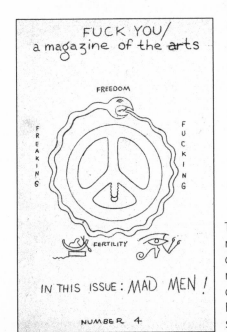

FUCK YOU/
a magazine of the arts

FREEDOM

F R E A K I N G

F U C K I N G

FERTILITY

IN THIS ISSUE: MAD MEN !

NUMBER 4

The peace sign surrounded by an ouroboros, with the surrounding words "Freedom, Freaking, Fucking, Fertility" and "in this Issue, MAD MEN!"

The Death of Marilyn Monroe

When I was in high school, the opening scene of Monroe's movie *Niagara*, with the beauty writhing in maenad-bacchic eroticism on a bed in her sleep, was one of the most charged visions I'd had up to that moment. It stayed with me right up to the news that she had passed away. Totally unknown to me at the time, across town a fairly unknown artist named Andy Warhol would soon begin a series of hand-painted portraits of Marilyn on silkscreen prints of a photo from *Niagara*.

I had watched Kennedy's birthday party on May 19, televised to a fascinated nation. Marilyn Monroe sang a bedroom-beckoning version of "Happy Birthday, Mr. President," resplendent in a clingy silver gown covered with sequins that seemed to have been grafted to her curves. Some history books aver that the star of *Niagara* had an affair with the president during these months. It's a murky cloud of Clio, the Muse of History, and something we had no inkling of as we watched Marilyn sing that night, but shortly after the famous rendition of "Happy Birthday" Kennedy cut off access from the actress, including to a special number at the White House he had set aside for her.

According to a book by reputable chronicler Anthony Summers, "Monroe would not accept that the affair was over." In an interview with Kennedy family friend Peter Lawford, he said, "Marilyn began writing these rather pathetic letters to Jack and continued calling. She threatened to go to the press."

As for Monroe, she had been in the midst of a film for 20th Century Fox called *Something's Got to Give* with Cyd Charisse, Dean Martin, and others when she interrupted the film to fly to New York City for "Happy Birthday." A few days later she came down with severe sinusitis, during which filming was delayed, and then she was fired on June 8. In the eleven weeks left to her, she worked to revive her picture so that by the day she passed away, she had won! It was to be rebegun! aided apparently by a phone call from Robert Kennedy to the head of Fox pictures.

She'd won her struggle to restart her picture and was looking ahead to new projects, one of which was a musical version of *A Tree Grows in Brooklyn*. She spoke with composer Jule Styne about the score that final week. But then on a street called Fifth Helena in Brentwood, Los Angeles, her housekeeper saw the light on in her room at midnight on August 5 and then at

3:00 AM but was hesitant to wake her because she had been having trouble sleeping. The housekeeper called Marilyn's psychiatrist, Dr. Greenson, who arrived at 3:30 to find Marilyn lying face down in death, a phone "clutched fiercely in her right hand," as he later wrote.

A swirl of rumors and variously fact-founded allegations have dust-deviled the time track since. There were her "powerful paramours"—for which read John Kennedy—and others who fucked her but "withheld their hearts"; and there was her legendary diary, with its jotted-down disclosures of Camelot. Did she die by accident when unknown people drugged her and then searched for the diary? Or was it some sort of intelligence hit to blackmail the president? What the hell was it? Or was it a self-hit from someone desperately unhappy and hungry for the long sleep of eternity, the *perpetua dormienda* that Catullus sang?

The issue whether visited the day she died has not been resolved. That weekend, according to Arthur Schlesinger's *RFK and His Times*, Robert Kennedy was in San Francisco for a meeting of the American Bar Association. He stayed with Ethel and four of their kids at a ranch in Gilroy southeast of San Francisco. A helicopter south that Saturday was theoretically possible; so, too, was the chance that he may have helicoptered out of Los Angeles late that night or early Sunday.

Marilyn Monroe's death was a blow to the nation entire. It sang a sadness and a threnody through the time track of the greater culture. Frenzied media oozathons following celebrity suicides spur self-offs. "There was a 12 percent jump in suicides in the US in the month following Marilyn Monroe's death from a sleeping pill overdose in 1962," according to a story in *New Scientist*, October 10, 2009, headlined "Media Reports of Monroe's Death Fuelled Mass Suicides."

A Party for Marilyn at Nelson Barr's

The night of Marilyn's death Nelson Barr threw a combination party and wake at his pad on the second floor at Avenue B and Twelfth, just across the street from Stanley's. It was a wild night of Rheingold beer in 25¢ quarts, pot, and more than a few pills. I wound up sleeping on the floor, I was so wasted, instead of walking around the corner to my own pad.

Elin Paulson was also at the party. She was a free-spirited young woman on the *Catholic Worker* staff. I often satirized her in my "Notes on Contributors." We were never intimate, but she had submitted some erotic poetry to the magazine, which, to my regret, I never published, partly because, even though the poetry was well worth putting to ink, it was mailed to me in a *Catholic Worker* envelope and would surely have gotten her tossed off the *Worker*. I still held the *CW* in awe, in spite of my anarcho-Egypto-bacchic persona. (The poem, still residing safely in my archive, is a testimony to eros, beginning with the words "Sex is . . ." and proceeding with a sequence of groovy, brief, hortatory lines.)

That night I spotted a marble statue, beautifully carved, that apparently had served as a fountain or had been inundated over the years. Nelson told me it had been in the apartment when he first rented it. He gave the statue to me, and I lugged it back home. I still have it, in all its exquisiteness. I've wondered for decades whether I accidentally acquired a long-lost Michelangelo!

Three weeks later I mimeographed *Poems for Marilyn*, with contributions by me, Joel Oppenheimer, John Harriman, Taylor Mead, Al Fowler, and John Keys. I read my contribution at Café Le Metro. The poem contained an ill-advised criticism of one of Marilyn's husbands, and poet Calvin Hernton yelled out, "Hey, I *like* Arthur Miller!"

The night of Marilyn statue. Is this a Michelangelo? Readers, please help me!

Since I had printed a piece by Taylor Mead in *Poems for Marilyn*, there has been the speculation that Mead might have shown it to his good friend Andy Warhol, thus providing maybe just a sliver of inspiration for the famous series of hand-adorned silkscreens of Marilyn he began shortly after her demise.

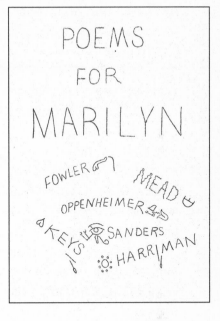

Warhol's Silkscreens

By the early 1960s Warhol had had a number of exhibitions and he was known as a skilled draftsman. In the summer of 1962 he began experimenting with silkscreening images onto painted canvas. The results were startling images that would place him at the forefront of modern art. The spirit of the aleatory, that is, of John Cage's chance operations, which Cage featured in his compositions, came into play in these early silkscreens, when talent overwhelmed technique. I was friends at the time with Warhol's assistant, poet Gerard Malanga, who told me about some of the casual and accidental silkscreen results.

Andy had a showing of his hand-painted Campbell's Soup works in Los Angeles that July, and then, just as it closed, Marilyn Monroe's housekeeper found her dead at thirty-six, a sleeping pill vial beside her. Marilyn appealed to a vast variety of Americans, from Beatnik loners to pop artists to people of power. J. Edgar Hoover, for instance, head of the FBI, had a nude photo of Monroe in his basement rec room in Washington, DC. Andy Warhol began a series of twenty-three Marilyn paintings utilizing his new technique of combining painting and screening.

Working at the NYU Purchasing Department

Warhol silkscreened the early Marilyns at just about the time I began working at the NYU purchasing department, where I monitored purchase orders for all the NYU divisions. It was a full-time job, requiring me to wear a sports coat and slacks, but I could get free tuition—useful because I wanted to continue my struggle to get a degree in Greek. My wife, Miriam Sanders, was a full-time student at NYU, studying geology. We were not yet living together, though we had been a couple since we met in Greek class back in the fall of 1958 and had gotten married in October 1961. Soon after going to work at NYU, I began taking classes again.

James Meredith

I was getting more and more into a defiant, American Bacchus state of mind. We were enjoying the fall weather, publishing and writing, reading a lot of books, and in general secretly reveling in the "rising tide of expectation" that the Kennedy administration was causing, while using our freedoms to criticize criticize criticize.

After the brilliant success of the violence-tinged Freedom Rides of the previous year, the civil rights movement was in full swing by the fall of 1962, thanks in good part to the work of Robert Kennedy's Department of Justice (DOJ) and decisions by the Supreme Court, which featured great Americans such as Earl Warren, William O. Douglas, and Hugo Black.

An air force veteran named James Meredith had been denied admission to the University of Mississippi. The NAACP took up his case in federal court; then, to the glory of time, RFK's Justice Department joined the case. In early 1962 a federal appeals court ruled that Old Miss's denial was unconstitutional. Then on September 10, just before the Cuban missile crisis, Justice Hugo Black ordered Mississippi to admit Meredith. Those of us following it in the Lower East Side were clinking mugs in jubilance in Stanley's Bar. Of course, a good number of civil rights partisans thought the Kennedys were moving much too slowly.

Thereupon Meredith twice sought to walk into Old Miss to enroll, and the governor of Mississippi himself, one Ross Barnett, blocked Meredith in person. Robert Kennedy put pressure on Barnett, threatening arrest of the governor and a $1,000 a day fine, at which he caved and Meredith gained admittance at the end of September. Another round of mugs clinked at Stanley's!

But when Meredith brought his belongings to the campus on September 13, two weeks prior to the missile crisis, a mob hurled rocks and bottles and three people died. The next day President Kennedy sent 3,000 federal troops, 400 U.S. Marshalls, and National Guardsman to Old Miss to make the point that real change was occurring.

A Spine-Chilling Speech

Then came the Cuban missile crisis. A bunch of my friends gathered around the TV set on the counter behind the bar at Stanley's, watching Kennedy's October 22 speech to the nation—one of the most fear-producing talks in hearthside history. He sketched out the missile sites in Cuba for a quiet, nervous nation of living rooms and bars and announced an air-and-sea blockade of the island, with shot-of-liquor-and-hit-of-hash-inducing sentences such as "It shall be the policy of this nation to regard any nuclear missile launched from Cuba against any nation in the Western Hemisphere as an attack by the Soviet Union on the United States, requiring a full retaliatory response upon the Soviet Union."

I prophesied a wild ride in a wild decade. "You just wait," I predicted to my table of friends. "The rest of the sixties are going to be very turbulent!" There was considerable anger at the Kennedys at Stanley's. Of course, we did not have all the behind-the-scene facts as we groused and growled, calling JFK a warmonger. We had no idea, for instance, that the Joint Chiefs of Staff were growling themselves for a first strike on Cuba without warning. And unaware for years that Chief of Staff of the Air Force Curtis Lemay, chomping on his cigar, angry that Kennedy was deciding on a blockade rather than a massive air strike without warning, complained that a blockade instead of an air attack was "worse than Munich."

People were very afraid. I know I was. I lay down a sleeping bag on a Japanese mat in my apartment. As a kind of votive tableau, I placed an oval of burning candles around my sleeping bag. Then about 3:00 AM or so I drifted to sleep. Would I wake up in other dimensions?

Later I read that Bob Dylan wrote his girlfriend, Suze Rotolo, about the same night, "Sitting in the Figaro all nite waiting for the world to end (the first nite Kennedy talked and the Russian ships were getting nearer Cuba). I honest to God thought it was all over—Not that I gave a shit any more then the next guy (that's a lie I guess) but it was interesting waiting for the bombs to fall and kill you—and it really seemed that way."

Ah, so it was, as I lay amid the burning candles, my Speed-o-Print mimeo in the distant flickers, stacks of mimeo'd magazines in the doomy gloom, prepared for the End.

The Fall of '62

I was working at NYU by day and at the cigar store on Forty-second Street during the weekends. I began experimenting with making sculptures. There was a store across the street from my apartment called H. L. Wild, which carried woodcarving supplies, and I purchased a bunch of woodcarving tools and a mallet of lignum vitae. I created a sculpture of my Peace Eye vision from a log of lignum vitae, which remains in my writing studio to this day, the only remnant of my exploration into sculpting.

I was also beginning to hang out at the Living Theater, then located on the northeast corner of Sixth Avenue and Fourteenth Street. Organized and inspired by Julian Beck and Judith Malina, the theater was a nexus for what was going on in the underground. There, in early September '62, I experienced the buzz of participating in my first benefit poetry reading! It was organized by Bonnie Bremser for her husband, poet Ray Bremser, who had just been arrested. As publisher of four issues of *Fuck You/ A Magazine of the*

The Peace Eye log.

9/6/62

Village Bulletin Board

DEADLINE: MONDAY 5 P. M.
$2 a line. $4 minimum (1)

Come to our penthouse party. Make friends from 105 Nations. Your name and address listed free. U.N. Club, Box 227-F, N.Y.C. 11. (1)

Silk Paintings, 20"x16"; $3.00. Black, gold or natural bamboo-like frame, $3.00. Choose from our 7 most popular sets: Dawn, Dream Island, Moon & Sun, Yes & No (2 panthers), Day & Night (2 warriors), Bachelor & Togetherness (3 tigers), Chinese horses & Chinese Bird. Also Buddha, 7 Black & White, 7 Classical Beauties, 5 Chinese Jade, 3 Falling Red Leaves Under Falling Waters. U.N. Club, Box 227-V, N.Y.C. 11. (1)

Open house for Ray Bremser. Living Theatre, 14th St, 6th Ave. Fri., Sat., Mon., 8 p.m. Readings, tapes: Ray Bremser. Music: Cecil Taylor. Paintings: Elaine de Kooning & Sherman Drexler. Readings: Bonnie Bremser, Julian Beck, Diane Di Prima, Ed Dorn, Herbert Huncke, Leroi Jones, Philip Lamantia, Ed Marshall, Clive Natson, Taylor Mead, Joe Oppenheimer, David Rattray, Irving Rosenthal, Marc Schleiffer, A. B. Spellman, Ed Sanders, A. Van Buskirk, John Weiners. Introduction: LeRoi Jones. (1)

Postcard brings free sample of THE BOOKLOVER'S ANSWER the bimonthly

The Ray Bremser benefit. Clippings in the author's archives.

Arts, plus just now, hot off the Speed-o-Print, the *Poems for Marilyn* anthology, I was being afforded a glimmer of underground renown. I read along with a broad cross section of poets on the New York scene, including Ed Dorn, LeRoi Jones, Philip Lamantia, John Wieners, Diane di Prima, and Herbert Huncke. Paintings by Elaine de Kooning and Sherman Drexler were on sale to benefit Bremser. Music by Cecil Taylor! Later, in the December '62 issue of *F.Y.,* I published two poems written by Ray while he was in the Tombs.

Drawing on Stencils by Flashlight

Around the time of the missile crisis, I began work on drawing and typing the stencils for a double issue of *F.Y.,* volume 5, numbers 1 and 2. I had an idea for one of the covers showing Little Orphan Annie in an erotic pose. It took me many hours to draw with various styli the image of Annie and her dog. The lights were shut off in my pad, and I drew the stencils by holding a flashlight beneath the stencil and then cutting with the styli.

The second cover was more of what I usually did: an image of Egyptian solarity and triumph. A Mayan-style sun glyph with flaming arms hovered above a solar barque with a stylized cobra head as a prow and bearing a walking cartouche with a large-eyed fish within, above which stretched an upreaching single Khepri/solar-dung-beetle claw.

A double issue of the magazine, December '62.

I was thrilled down to the anarcho-Egyptian bone that my hero Charles Olson had sent three Maximus poems to publish! But it was my "Talk of the Town" column, its heading, laboriously sketched by flashlight for one of the December '62 issues, that got me into trouble.

The Thrill of Sketching Hieroglyphs

I loved to draw Egyptian glyphs and, say, satires about the *New Yorker* onto mimeograph stencils. A few months later Ted Berrigan told me about a place that would, for about $1, burn an electronic stencil from a page of writing and drawing. But in the fall of '62 I was still laboriously cutting the images onto stencils by means of sharp styli.

The state of my Egyptian by 1962 was that I could sight-read the text on coffins at the Metropolitan Museum. There were bookstores I frequented south of Fourteenth, such as Orientalia on West Tenth, Samuel Weiser on Broadway, and a number of the famous stores on Fourth Avenue at the time, that stocked scholarly Egyptology books.

There's something thrilling about tracing a 3,000-year old papyrus or even improving an ancient sketch. I knew it as a young man drawing glyphs on mimeo stencils. I know it, too, in the years of gray—the hiero-thrill of sacred shapes.

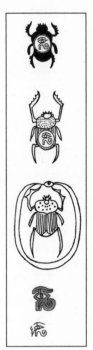

Trouble from My Editorial Notes

That late fall, after the missile crisis, I was feeling ultradefiant. I ended the "Notes on Contributors" page for volume 5, number 1 with a *cri de mimeo*:

"I'll print anything," I typed.

I had rented the two-room apartment at 509 East Eleventh Street in December 1961 for $56 a month. It was on the third floor. One room was a combined kitchen and living room. The other was supposed to be a bedroom. There were no closets, only a five-pronged clothes rack nailed to the wall in the bedroom. The rooms were tiny, and both had lumpy metal ceilings stamped with leaflike patterns in six-inch squares. I kept my Speed-o-Print mimeo resting on a porcelainized metal cover on the bathtub, which was set up in the kitchen.

I typed the mimeograph stencils. It was always a tedious chore requiring slow correction of mistakes with an erasing device and rubbery correction fluid that was brushed on the typo, blown dry with a breath-huff, and then retyped. Sometimes when I typed far past midnight by candlelight, the man next door began to pound the wall with a broom.

After I typed the stencils, I ordered a few boxes of mimeo paper. When they were delivered, I began to print the new issue. I brushed the ink on the inside of the printing drum of the small mimeograph, and I attached a stencil on the outside of the drum, smoothed it out, checked the inking, put paper in the feeding tray, and began to turn the handle to print. I did this with a feeling of elation that was just about religious. Everything was deity. I

FUCK YOU/ A MAGAZINE OF THE ARTS: PUBLISHED, PRINTED, & EDITED BY
ED SANDERS AT A SECRET LOCATION IN THE LOWER EAST SIDE, NEW YORK CITY,
USA. #5. VOLUME 1, DECEMBER 1962.

NOTES ON CONTRIBUTORS:
　　　　CHARLES OLSON/ Mad Groovy Charles Olson! The Massachusetts Stomper!
　　　　The Gloucester Bandit! The famous author of The Maximus Poems, and
　　　　numerous tractata, broadsides, & cetera.
　　　　　　　　LENORE KANDEL/ reputed to be a stunning san francisco
　　　　　　　　box. Fuck You/ 6 scheduled to feature TO FUCK WITH LOVE,
　　　　　　　　PHASE TWO.
　　　　ALL FOWLER/ anarcho-cocksucko-paedophiliac & total poet. Refuses
　　　　　　　　to gobble or ball anything over twelve years of age. Clergyman.
　　BARBARA MORAFF/ widely published poetess. One of the Four Young Lady
Fucks of the Totem/Corinth collection.
　　　　　　　　MARK SAMARA/actor & artist. A GREEN GOBBLER & Bearer
　　　　　　　　of the Peter-Basin in those lower east side Sex-fits
　　　　　　　　so whispered over by the west side hippies.
　　　　　　　　BONNIE BREMSER/ an artist & poetess. Ray Bremser's old
　　　　　　　　lady and totally fuckable.
　　　　ED MARSHALL/ the famous New Hampshire poet and dope-freak. Loves
　　　　to slip yohenbine to young boys. HELIAN HELLAN, is a recent
　　　　collection of his verse brought out by Auerhahn Press.
　　　　　　　　MILLARD FRIEDMAN/ painter. The table hustler and stein-stomp
　　　　　　　　at Stanley's Bar (12th & B). His recent paintings (Bottle
　　　　　　　　Dervishes I-LVIII) are universally banned although ONE, after a
　　　　　　　　bold editorial decision, is considering them for cover prints.
　　RON RICE/ is the preclaric mad flick-freak. Movies of his: ⸻⸻
THE FLOWER THIEF, SENSELESS, and one half retched out.
　　　　　　　　CHARLES POLANDIK/ another Polish cock to thrust into
　　　　　　　　the pile of east side lady pacifists. Painter with a
　　　　　　　　gallery on 9th St. (645 E.)
JOEL OPPENHEIMER/ poet, playwright. The Dutiful Son & The Love Bit, most
recent books. Expert marksman and authority on the Algonquian Law Hides.
　　　　　　　　JOHN KEYS/probably has balled every chick in the lower east
　　　　　　　　side. An inveterate crotch-hawk. Poet.
　　　　KIRBY CONGDON/ the evil poet. The Publishing Business' main
　　　　connection for spiritual potions, yage, yohenbine, aphrodisiacs,
　　　　& scrotal flak.
　　　　　　　　JOHN THOMAS/ a San Francisco poet. A paidopugomastikos
　　　　　　　　in the Swinburnian sense.
　　　　　　　　ED SANDERS/ Editor of Fuck You/ a magazine of the ARTS.
　　　　　　　　pacifist dopethrill psychopath. Has the Ankh symbol
　　　　　　　　tattooed on his penis.
　　　　　　　　MARY MAYO/ a fur burger supreme. Poetess. Hustles at
　　　　　　　　the Les Deux Megots on Mondays & Wednesdays.
　　　　NELSON BARR/ Religious thinker & scatophile. Peace walk
　　　　dicker. Sneaky. Duplicitous. Evil.

　　　　EDITOR'S NOTE: BARF ME YOUR FRICK DATA.
　　　　　　　　RETCH ME IN ON YOUR BABBLE VECTORS,
　　　　　　　　　　　　YOUR ARCANICS, YOUR SPEW,

　　　　　　　　　　　　　　　　I'LL PRINT ANYTHING.

adored this mimeograph machine and kept it sparkling clean. I sometimes would sit meditating on the bamboo mat, looking for hours at the Speed-o-Print sitting up on top of the bathtub.

Bodhisattva Collating Method

After all the pages had been printed, there remained the grim job of collating them. Because the magazine was usually around thirty pages in length, I could collate one whole issue at a time. I would sit cross-legged on the floor in the Bodhisattva position and nearly surround myself with three concentric semicircular rows of page piles. I worked left to right through the outer circle and then through the second half circle and finished with the last page by sweeping across the innermost row that surrounded much of my cross-legged body. I tamped each completed issue on the floor along the top and side edges to align the pages for later stapling. Slowly the pile of completed issues grew until I finally finished all five hundred.

The next and last task was when *clunk! clunk! clunk!* I stapled each copy three times along the left edge. *Whew.* Then I addressed, stamped, and mailed out as many magazines as I could afford postage for. I sent the magazine to my poet friends, to other editors, to a few easily shocked high school buddies in the Midwest, and to those I admired, such as Samuel Beckett, Edward Dahlberg, and Marianne Moore. Plus I always filled up a musette bag to hand out free copies at the 8th Street Bookshop and at the various bars, such as the Cedar and Stanley's. Stanley Tolkin would take a supply of an issue when it came out and keep copies at the bar to give out to those he knew would dig the magazine.

The Beauty of Yum

From urges unknown I started eating a strange concoction I called Yum. Yum and vitamin C, except for an occasional pierogi and sour cream feast at the nearby Odessa Restaurant, were my exclusive diet for months and months. What was Yum? Well, first I made a thick, dry two-inch bed of oats in a wooden bowl. On this I spooned two globs of Hellmann's mayonnaise. Next came generous *drip-drops* of soy sauce. Atop this mound of pure delight, I broke two fresh eggs and mixed the feast into a beige and yellow rippled blob. This was Yum. Want some?

I ate Yum every day for eleven happy months. I was always very willing to share meals of Yum with any visitor arriving at dinnertime. There was often shyness or hesitation about sharing the meal on the part of the visitor who watched the editor prepare the wet, yellow Yum-mush. Miriam, for example, and friends such as Nelson Barr were loath to enjoy the paradise of Yum.

I had never made out or even kissed Elin Paulson, but she was a pretty young poet and artist who had lived at one of the Catholic Worker apartments. She had hung out at the Cantina of the Revolutions on Ninth Street east of the park during the previous summer. She had submitted poetry to my magazine.

Yet decades later I can't help cringing at some of my editorial comments in the double issue about Elin, who had contributed some fine love poems to the issue. In the "Notes on Contributors" for volume 2 I made a strongly erotic statement about Elin. My editorial comments were very creative and occasionally not completely moored on the docks of absolute reality.

One night around midnight I was reading by candlelight when there was a knock at the door. I found myself facing an angry man with two German shepherds who was upset—very upset—over what I had written about Elin. I had known that they were seeing each other but really had not noted the seriousness of the relationship.

I could sense her passion for a loving relationship, although from a couple of the poems of hers I published, I could see she had, like many Beat/peace movement women, had a wobbly love course. Here are some sections from the poem ("With Love Still") of hers I'd just printed:

3.
I did tell you things/
& we played
our kazoos
4.
a song of love is a sad song
hi lilly
hi lilly
hi lo
a song of love is a song of woe

don't ask me how i know
5.
Someday
We
Will
Meet
Again
and
stop
wondering

Standing there nervously in the candlelit gloom of my apartment, I did feel upset with myself that someone was unhappy over what I had printed with the intention of creating pleasure. And I well understood the jealousy and upset that could be involved. So I apologized and said to the man with the dogs that most of the magazine had already been mailed out but had I known of his concern, I certainly would not have printed the editorial description.

After a few more minutes the man with the dogs left, saying as he did so that if I had not at least expressed some sort of apology, he would have beat me up. Decades later the gentleman apologized for arriving angry with the dogs.

As for Elin, she had a son, Leif, with a writer named Bruce Grund, and she moved to a commune in northern Vermont, where she lived for around forty years, painting and creating beautiful artworks of stained glass. We kept in touch by letter. She sent me some of her art, and on her passing in 2006 of cancer, I drew a glyph in honor of her.

Hands Holding Peace—
a glyph for
Elin Paulson

Meeting Harry Smith and H. L. Humes

In October 1962, just before the Cuban missile crisis and after my magazine had been mentioned by John Wilcock in his column in the *Village Voice*, I received a note from H. L. Humes, known universally as "Doc" Humes, a legendary New York novelist and one of the founders of the *Paris Review.* He wanted to get together, so we decided to meet at Stanley's Bar. The place was packed. That night artist Larry Rivers was at the bar, sitting next to Mary Nichols of the *Village Voice*.

Doc Humes and I were having a drink at a table. Suddenly he said, "There's a magician I know." He brought me to the bar to introduce me to filmmaker Harry Smith, who, amid the introductory chat, said he was working on a movie.

He liked the Eyes of Horus I had painted on my white gym socks. He had a first edition of fierce English occultist Aleister Crowley's *Book of Lies*, which in the course of a drinking evening he threw into the tall porcelain urinal at Stanley's Bar. There it resided until we left to go our separate ways. I kicked myself later for not retrieving it. He was effusive in his praise of Crowley's writing that night, saying he was a genius, although that did not prevent the toss-away of the *Book of Lies*.

I became aware of Smith's own genius at string games, and his work as a filmmaker and artist, because I visited his small apartment uptown not far from the Fifty-ninth Street Bridge and saw how his art suffused every wall.

Harry's drawing on a stencil, 1964. One of three occult stencils, from the author's archive.

He said he had gotten a grant from the Rockefeller Foundation to make a movie based on Gaston Maspero's translation of the Egyptian *Tale of the Two Brothers*. He told me he used to meditate for up to a half hour underwater, submerged in his bathtub with a cover atop it, breathing from a tube. He had a brilliant antsiness.

I had my usual satchel of *Fuck You/ A Magazine of the Arts* and gave him an issue. We became friends. Later he drew on a stencil for *F.Y.*

At first, I had only a vague idea that he was well known for his *Anthology of American Folk Music*. I quickly learned of his hand-drawn and exquisite short films. Out of deference to Harry I started reading Aleister Crowley.

Underground Films

I began hanging out on the underground film scene. It had been Mekas's *Guns of the Trees* that had inspired me to publish a mimeographed magazine, so I continued showing up at various Mekas-run film events. At a screening I met Andy Warhol. Henry Geldzahler, cu-rator of American art at the Metropolitan Museum of Art, introduced me to him. Fi-nally the inspiration of Jonas Mekas and the Film-Maker's Cooperative made me decide to acquire a 16 mm camera. I went to my friend Harry Smith for advice.

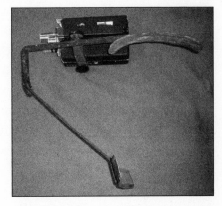

A Stedi-Rest, from my archives.

Harry urged me to purchase a so-called "battle camera, like, the kind they used filming the war." He specifically recom-mended a used Bell and Howell model 70-DE, which would be sturdy enough to withstand a few drops and bangs. I went out to search and bought one at a camera store called Willoughby's on West Thirty-second Street.

Harry also recommended that I purchase a device shaped like a large seven, called a Stedi-Rest, which greatly aided handheld camerawork. The Stedi-Rest enabled a filmmaker to avoid nervous jerks and quakes during filming. The camera was screwed into the top of the "seven," and the arms of the Stedi-Rest pushed against the stomach and on the shoulder by means of curved cushioned supports that were built on the ends of the large seven, perpendicular to the ends. With the torso supporting the camera's weight, the hands were relatively free to move about, the camera was much less likely to be dropped, and it was always more or less in position, ready to be used.

A Bell and Howell battle camera, with turret to hold three different lenses, very similar to the one I purchased

I met filmmaker Stan Brakhage at a screening at the Film-Makers' Coopera-tive and received from him a wonderful lecture on how properly to use my new Bell and Howell. Stan advised me to carry around my camera wherever I went, to forget about loading it with film for a while, and to practice ten hours a day for a few weeks "filming" things I observed, especially heavy action, like fights, crowds forming in the park, angry truck drivers, and police raids. The point, he emphasized, was to be able to stay cool under all circumstances. Stan advocated a rigorous program of physical exercise. "A moviemaker should be in as good a shape as any other athlete," he said. He should be able to twist, contort, lean slowly forward while sinking to the knees, bend backward, all the while keeping the camera exactly steady, smoothly filming the action. A cameraperson should be able to walk through a scene of grisly riot, chaos, or site of violence, the camera running, following the action in a smooth flowing riverine motion.

Help from Jonas Mekas

Jonas was very generous. He loaned his Bolex to Barbara Rubin to make *Christmas on Earth*, to Ron Rice to shoot *The Queen of Sheba Meets the Atom Man*, to Jack Smith to make *Normal Love*, and to other filmmakers. He located a source of very inexpensive film for me. I was told that the film came from the air force or perhaps the black market, that it had originally been in big rolls, and that a blind man in a darkroom had peeled off three-minute or one-hundred-foot sections. I purchased a bunch of cans. He also located a place that would develop my various film projects, some of which were spackled with balling, blow jobs, and hookahs, plus my footage of things such as the Great March on Washington and my brother's innocent Missouri wedding.

The Rise of Warhol as a Filmmaker

I agreed with Ted Berrigan that Andy Warhol was a genuine American art force. Andy Warhol started making films in the summer of '63, a series of "Kiss" films, starring a woman filmmaker and various kiss-mates. These were followed by the six-hour film *Sleep*, of a man sleeping, and *Eat*, forty-five minutes of artist Robert Indiana chowing down on a mushroom. Mekas showed these early Warhol experiments at the Gramercy Arts Theater. Mekas was cameraman for Warhol's eight-hour "study" of the Empire State Building.

Sending an Issue to Ginsberg in India

I obtained addresses of literati from Ted Wilentz, who with his brother, Eli, owned and operated the 8th Street Bookshop, then located on Eighth Street where it intersected with MacDougal Street. Ted had an apartment on the floor above the shop and used to hold regular literary soirées.

The 8th Street Bookshop was pivotal to a young poet in those days. It was at the 8th Street that I first saw a book of photos from Dachau, first met poets such as Joel Oppenheimer, first spotted Charles Olson's *Maximus Poems* and the Auerhahn Press edition of *Maximus from Dogtown—I*. It was there I monitored little magazines such as *Yugen* and *Kulchur* and where I first purchased Allen Ginsberg's epochal *Kaddish and Other Poems*.

Ted Wilentz gave me Edward Dahlberg's address, plus Samuel Beckett's and Allen Ginsberg's. I had heard Ginsberg was feeling depressed in India. I sent him an issue and asked for some poems.

The issue I sent to Allen Ginsberg in India, 1963, asking for poetry.

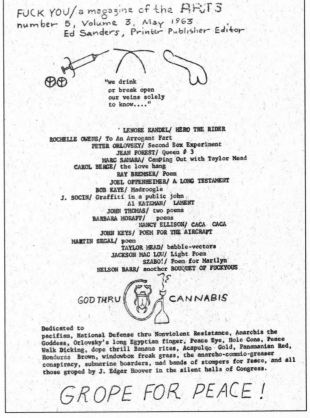

It inspired him, he later told me—for he had indeed been depressed—and helped him out of his depression. A few weeks after my letter, he sent me the poem "The Change."

While I was experimenting with underground films and publishing my magazine, I started taking classes again at New York University, where I was working in the purchasing department. As an employee of NYU, I could take courses for free. I was studying and translating Virgil's *Aeneid* with Dean Paul Culley at NYU, meeting him during my lunch hour at his office.

The Children of Birmingham

In a way 1963 was one of the most vicious years. In retrospect, I see that the dangers to the presidency should have been more than apparent. In a way JFK was surrounded by the *grrrs* of the right.

Much of the anger of the right derived from the civil rights movement, which I monitored fairly carefully from the Lower East Side. That spring there was a series of demonstrations in Birmingham, Alabama, against the almost total segregation of restrooms, drinking fountains, and public facilities. Many hundreds were arrested, including Martin Luther King, who had announced that he would lead rallies there until "Pharaoh lets God's people go."

On May 2 and 3, 1963, over a thousand children marched for freedom. They came out of the 16th Street Baptist Church two by two singing, "We Shall Overcome," with high-energy clapping. Some were as young as six. Head policeman Bull Connor unleashed biting and snarling German shepherds on the demonstrators, recalling the days of the Nazis. The world's re-

sponse was revulsion and derision. The police sprayed the children with what were called "monitor guns," contraptions that linked two hoses through a single nozzle mounted on a tripod. The guns had such force that innocent children rolled down the street as if from a flooded creek. It was a time of evil. Many in the Lower East Side community were very angry.

On May 12 John Kennedy ordered 3,000 federal troops to Birmingham. It gave us great hope to know we had a president who might actually help end segregation.

Quang Duc

On June 10, in an image of horror that stunned a generation, especially my friends in the nonviolent direction-action movement, a Buddhist monk named Thich Quang Duc, sitting in lotus position on a street in Saigon, burned himself to death as the ultimate protest against the persecution of Buddhists by the right-wing Catholic Diem regime. Between June and October seven monks, known as bonzes, burned themselves. Madame Nhu, wife of Ngo Dinh Diem's brother, liked the blazes. She called the immolations "barbecues."

The violence in Birmingham and the violence in Vietnam had an impact on the rising counterculture of the Lower East Side. It made us all the more willing to work for great change.

Al Fowler

I felt certain that I had discovered an American poetic genius. His name was Al Fowler. Fowler came to my New Year's Eve party 1961–'62 and we became friends. He was in the army, stationed in nearby Fort Jay. I gradually became aware of his talents as a poet and started publishing his work in *Fuck You/ A Magazine of the Arts*. During the magazine's thirteen issues I published twenty-seven poems by Al Fowler, including one three-pager and one five-pager.

He became famous in antiwar and pacifist circles in early '62 when the Living Theater had sponsored a World Wide General Strike for Peace, and Fowler had picketed the ferry landing leading to his army base at Ft. Jay in full uniform. He was tossed out of the army after the General Strike, and he began a career as a dealer in amphetamine. He was so good at it, he announced, that "now I can afford to be a junkie." The logic of that escaped my youthful dazzlement over his talents as a poet.

He hailed from Albany, New York, where he had composed the senior class poem in 1957 and won a National Merit Scholarship for the quality of his noggin. By the early '60s Fowler had joined a small sect, the "Free Catholic Church," and now and then sported a clerical collar, a big silver cross on his chest, and a round red anarchist button on the lapel of his frock coat. This later figured in his marginal involvement in the brouhaha regarding Lee Harvey Oswald's reported appearance in Greenwich Village prior to the assassination.

The Beginning of Filming

Meanwhile, I began shooting footage, mainly of my friends, some of which had erotic qualities. I had a bunch of ideas for films. I was concerned about

Al, who, although he had become a junkie and was fascinated with the culture of heroin, expressed a desire to kick. I wrote a film scene in which a huge "OD [Overdose] Centipede" attacked him, and then I proposed shooting footage of an Egyptian Death Barge, copied from the tombs of the Nile, sailing with Fowler arrayed in fu-

Sketches of Al Fowler by Ann Leggett. From the author's archive.

nerary splendor out into the waters between Manhattan and Staten Island.

Fowler developed a close relationship with artist Ann Leggett. Ann was a young woman with a gleam of experimentation in her eye and a talent that was undeniable. She was twenty-two and studying at the Art Students League. Though not a

Catholic, she was drawn to the Catholic Worker, where she had met Al Fowler. She had spent a few days at the House of Detention for joining with the Catholic Workers in refusing to take shelter during New York City's compulsory civil defense drill on May Day in the early '60s. In March 1963 she had an exhibition of her paintings at the Columbia University School of Architecture. She, too, was swept up in the ambience of the swashbuckling young poet from Albany. She made some memorable drawings of Fowler during those years, including one that showed him muscular and defiantly shooting up.

Then there was a murmur of trouble amid the defiance. Fowler was having more and more difficulty supporting his habit, and he was drifting into robberies. Right around the spring of '63 a customer of Al's, an NYU student I used to see at Al's apartment wearing a blue blazer with brass buttons and penny loafers, died of an overdose. It was a bugle wake-up call.

The Kick Grid

It seemed obvious that Al Fowler wanted to kick heroin, so I helped organize a bunch of our mutual friends to sit with him as he gradually reduced his heroin shots until he was free. I called it a Kick Grid, dividing the time flow into four-hour units. Years later I wrote a short story about it in *Tales of Beatnik Glory.*

Fowler lived in a building on East Ninth just off Avenue B. A group of his friends lived in the same building. One of them, let's call her Amber, had a weekly client, one of the Cassini brothers famous in the fashion business, for whom she sank to her knees as he stood in his office, and he wanted each knee to rest on his tasseled shoes, left to right, right to left, and then a blow job. It was good money. Her husband was a junkie friend of Al's named Keith. I remember seeing him quite glassy-eyed during the days of the Kick Grid.

I divided up Al's heroin supply into smaller and smaller amounts and kept the skag away from him, doling out the amounts. First Al shot up a half dose, then a quarter dose, then an eighth, then nothing. Everything went okay until Fowler became sweaty and junk sick and very uncomfortable. For the next twenty-four hours the ordeal was acute. That night was the worst. Fowler lay sweating beneath a blanket. Light hurt his eyes, so we kept the pad gloomy.

There was a contention raised in *Naked Lunch* that kickers experience a period of intense sexual desire during the turkey. This seemed to have occurred for Fowler, though I could not see for total surety in the demi-dark. Buck's County Lucy came over to visit Fowler, who was in sad shape, sobbing and sweating, his eyeglasses wet and foggy. Lucy, jean shirt tied at the stomach, put her arms around Fowler and asked if he wanted something to drink. Fowler whispered something to her and pulled her down into his rumpled lair. It was hard to view exactly because Fowler pulled his Mexican blanket over both of them. She skinnied out of her shorts and pulled aside the elastic of her panties and steered him inside her, then fell forward to kiss. It was only a matter of seconds before Fowler's junk-sick spews came forth, and he moaned thanks aplenty to his kind friend.

Later that night I awakened to hear a beating sound. What was it? It was Fowler beating his head against the wall in junk-sick agony. Fowler began to beg me for dope: "Just a little shot. Please!" Beseeching.

I gave in to Fowler, allowing him to shoot up "just a taste, man, a taste." The result was like a change from night to day, for as soon as he shot up, Fowler stopped sweating and walked around smiling and talking.

I vowed from then on, no more skag. Finally I caught him alone shooting up some skag from a secret stash under the linoleum in his living room.

During the course of the Kick Grid I'd brought my Speed-o-Print mimeo and some reams of colored Granitex paper to Fowler's pad, and I spent hours running off a hundred copies each of the first six issues of *F.Y.*

After I had discovered his secret stash of heroin under the ancient linoleum and admonished him, the Kick Grid worked to its conclusion. But it wasn't clear that he had actually kicked.

Meanwhile, I had just purchased my Bell and Howell camera and was eager to get going as an underground filmmaker. As I have mentioned, one of my first ideas for a film starred Al, whether he had actually kicked or not.

Here's the text I wrote for the scene in the Fowler movie in which the OD Centipede invades and seizes him and then his body in a Death Boat (which I intended to build) floats out from the area of the Staten Island Ferry while a chorus chants:

CLACK CLACK CLACK
the CENTIPEDE
O.D. with a hundred legs

crawls through the door
light through the window....
Death to the Reverend Fowler
to the reverend death
Slash through the door
gnashing lips the Centipede death
who takes him
over the sunrise with its leering lips
No redemption
No redemption
No redemption
from the evil and sin
no redemption
from the hate and the horror
No redemption
No redemption
The centipede
eats up the man
and the dead man knows no heat
before the sun be his
in the course of the Barge of Death
(low whisper, rising)
hustle hustle hustle hustle hustle
hustle
hustle hustle hustle
butcher butcher butcher
lift him to the lips
red blood of a slimy hate
know the frenzy
spit the blood
retch the gobble
munch the word in a Gobble
Gobble Gobble
Gobble Gobble Gobble Gobble
Gobble

Gobble Gobble

The author holding his Bell and Howell at Bobbie and Robert Creeley's house in New Mexico. Image courtesy of Bobbie Louse Hawkins.

Renting the Secret Location in the Lower East Side

In August 1963 I rented a small two-room apartment at 203 Avenue A for $27.49 a month to use as my "Secret Location" for the Fuck You Press and as a studio for the making of underground films. The apartment was located in a small back building, so it was perfect for secrecy. It had direct-current electricity, so any appliance with a motor could not be operated.

The apartment was on the second floor. Poet Clive Matson, who had told me the little pad was available, lived on the floor above me, and later writer Bonnie Bremser, then married to poet Ray Bremser, lived in Matson's apartment while Ray was serving a prison sentence.

Rent Control!

It was a rent-controlled pad! On November 1, 1943, the federal Office of Price Administration, under pressure from tenant groups, froze rents in New York City. At the end of the war tenant groups arose again to prevent unaffordable increases. Governor Thomas Dewey and Mayor William O'Dwyer of New York City imposed a system of rent control on all buildings constructed before 1947. The state legislature renewed the rent controls every three years, a system still in place in the 1960s that helped make artistic effort in New York City a thing of glory—such as my Secret Location in the Lower East Side for $27.49 a month!

"Jack Smith Decor" for the Secret Location

On Orchard Street I purchased "Jack Smith/Flaming Creatures decor"—that is, long pieces of wildly colored cloths, some gold threaded and with patterns of flowers, which I hung from all the walls of the bedroom/filming room at the Secret Location. I strung wires along the top of the walls from which I dangled the cloths to give a harem, wild-color hallucination effect. Then I attached clip-on fixtures with photofloods here and there around the room, focusing the light on the ornately covered mattress on the floor.

In the other room was my trusty Speed-o-Print mimeograph, reams of paper, and uncollated stacks of Fuck You Press publications. The compact mimeo fit nicely on the porcelainized metal bathtub cover in the kitchen.

After I moved in my stacks of magazines and publications, I wasted very little time before I began to film at the Secret Location.

A young woman named Mimi had sub-mitted some poetry to *F.Y.* She was active around the Lower East Side set, and she had volunteered to type stencils. I would see her at readings at Le Metro. One night she said she'd be at a certain place. Then she canceled. Robert Creeley had a reading, and she said, "I

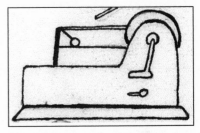

Sketch of my Speed-o-Print from an issue of *F.Y.*

want to fuck Creeley." One afternoon she and Peter Orlovksy came over to the Secret Location. Soon they were naked and balling, and I was filming.

Another film session was between poet Bill Szabo and a woman named Ellen B. I filmed them balling in my Jack Smith–esque film lair, brightly colored drapes on the wall and clip-on lights surrounding the gaudy-hued bed.

Burnt by Herbert Huncke!

One night in August 1963, just a few days after I had rented the Secret Loca-tion on Avenue A, legendary writer Herbert Huncke came in excited to the cigar store wanting to cash two checks totaling $47.50, drawn on the ac-count of Florence Barta, reputedly a girlfriend. I was tending to the constant flow of customers for cigarettes and premovie candy and was a bit dis-tracted. I cashed the checks for the fabled craggy-faced Beatnik (and later deposited them in my own account).

He said, "Could you hurry? I have a cab waiting."

And lo! the bank returned the checks to me for insufficient funds! I complained to Allen Ginsberg, who told me not to worry, that it was a Beat-era badge of honor to be burned by Huncke. He told me his own experi-ence of getting ripped off by Huncke, something about Huncke going into a house, then disappearing out the back. It was like being heckled by Gregory Corso at a reading—if it occurred, you were part of the in-crowd; the same was true with being burned by Herbert Huncke. The actual returned check can be found in the portion of my personal archive that resides at the Uni-versity of Connecticut.

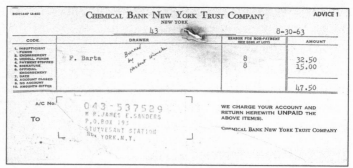

My bank statement for August '63, showing the burn by Huncke.

The Living Theater

I went to the Living Theater in the summer of '63 to use the group's typewriter to type stencils for the new issue of *Fuck You/ A Magazine of the Arts*. I remember Julian Beck's parrot squawking in the office as I typed. The Living Theater had a production of *The Brig*, and Judith Malina and Julian Beck sponsored a "Jail Poets" reading on July 23, which I took part in. *The Brig*, which depicted life in a hell-like marine corps prison, had been up and running since May. Jonas Mekas would later in the year make a film of a performance.

The Great March on Washington

I went down to DC with the Living Theater to be a part of the Great March on Washington on August 28, 1963. I brought along my Bell and Howell, plus a satchel of the freshly published issue of my magazine.

Some of those on the bus finally fell asleep, but most talked excitedly and every few minutes began singing, clapping, and stomping their feet through the long trip to DC. Over and over they sang the tunes that roused them and gave melodies to their philosophical passions: "If I Had a Hammer," "Solidarity Forever," "Ain't Gonna Study War No More," "Dona Nobis Pacem." There was a boisterous contingent who led the bus in "Cuba Sí, Yankee No," "We Shall Wear the Red and Black," and "The Internationale," that fine old song from the 1870 Paris Commune.

Pound at the Great March

As soon as the Living Theater bus landed in DC, instead of heading toward the Lincoln Memorial, I ran with my camera and satchel of the new issue of *F.Y.* to the Library of Congress. "I'd like to take a look at the Ezra Pound broadcasts," I told the librarian at the counter. I filled out the proper form and began research into what I called "The Lb Q," short for Pound Question—that is, how to deal with his anti-Semitism against the background of his undeniable talents as a poet. Not many people that Washington day really thought much about the Lb Q, but to poets in the Beat, Black Mountain, Objectivist, or Deep Image tradition, it was a serious issue. If eyes were sandpaper, I would have long ago erased the texts in Pound's collected earlier poems, *Personae*. His relentless scholarship, his mixture of tough and tender lyrics, and his love of Greek and Latin helped me become a poet.

After the war, when I was in the first grade, Pound had been indicted for treason for his anti-Semitic World War II radio broadcasts from Italy. He'd then been placed in St. Elizabeth's Hospital in DC as bonkers. There'd been a big debate among writers when Pound won the Bollingen Prize for *The Pisan Cantos* while he was in the asylum. Some said he had been a traitor for his wartime broadcasts; others said he was a great poet and his poesy separated him from the broadcasts; others said he was a silly figment of prior times and should be forgotten. In 1963 at the time of the Great March on Washington, he had long been deloonybinned and was back in Italy.

I wanted to see for myself, and I wasn't sure how soon I would return to Washington. I was brought a packet of prints of broadcast transcripts, white text on dark background, which I quickly scanned. I found to my shock that the texts were phlegmed with "kikes," "councils of kikes," and "kikettes," which were Pound's code words for Franklin Roosevelt's Cabinet:

> No one can qualify as a historian of this half century without having examined the Protocols [of the Elders of Zion] [April 20, 1943].

Talmudic Jews who want to kill off ALL the other races whom they cannot subjugate [April 20, 1942].

American lynch law had its origins in the Jewish ruin of the American South [June 15, 1942].

If you don't find a leader, you may have to wait for some kind hearted Bavarian, or Hungarian to come free you from the Jews of New York [March 6, 1942].

I said the Republicans would have all kikeria, all the kike profits out against 'em in 1944 [March 16, 1943].

For two centuries, ever since the brute Cromwell brought 'em back into England, the kikes have sucked out your vitals [March 15, 1942].

The USA will be no use to itself or to anyone else until it gets rid of the kikes AND Mr. Roosevelt [March 11, 1942].

A few minutes were more than enough. I sprinted out of the marble data center, past the Capitol, the National Gallery of Art, the Smithsonian, the White House, and the Washington Monument, eager to find my friends by the Lincoln Memorial reflecting pool.

I had never seen 200,000 people before. I located the Living Theater, and I started filming. I could hear a low-pitched, crackly noise rising from the multitude. It was my first experience with "mass-demo buzz," which came not only from the low-threated roar of the multitude but also from hundreds at the edges shout-talking for causes and distributing a vastness of leaflets, magazines, pennants, buttons, pamphlets, and broadsides for left, liberal left, civil rights, and peace groups.

I had brought with me the recent issue of F.Y., with a cover that two years and four months later would mightily offend the officer who led the raid on my bookstore. This is the

F.Y., volume 5, number 4, printed to hand out at the Great March on Washington, August 1963.

issue where, in the "Notes on Contributors," I announced, once again straying a bit from absolute reality, that I had the first fifty-three hieroglyphs of Akh-en-Aten's "Hymn to the Sun Disc" tattooed on my private parts. This would be of great, gazing interest to the police sergeant who raided my bookstore a little more than two years later. I quietly handed out some copies to friends whom I was able to locate in the hundreds of thousands by the Lincoln Memorial and the long Reflecting Pool of Truth.

Filming the Nazis

During the March I spotted a group of men scampering among the demonstrators. They would stop briefly and bend down above those who were sitting and then make strange quick jerking motions against their own noses with their hands. What was going on? The group came closer, and I saw the white circles with black swastikas on their armbands. One Nazi was making soft spitting sounds and cursing in a whisper those sitting at the Great March, his hand tracing elongated rhine-lines with two fingers pressed together.

I was very angry.

Everybody was listening to the speeches and singing, and no one wanted to be distracted. I couldn't remain passive while the hellmen of the ovens cursed those I loved. They had to be confronted. I hoisted my camera on the Stedi-Rest during Martin King's speech. King finished and the roar of a mile-wide seashell began as the ovenmen scampered away.

I thought of Ezra Pound as I filmed a minute or so of the ovenmen. Pound, who had helped me become a poet. Pound, on whom I had once relied for strength and ideas on creative rebellion. Pound, whose poetry had opened up my eyes almost as much as the poetry of Samuel Beckett, Dylan Thomas, Edgar Allan Poe, Allen Ginsberg, and Sappho. Pound, who had let me down in the Library of Congress. Soon the Nazis scampered away, and I paid attention to Martin King's final remarks.

Birmingham Bombing

A few days later, on September 15, came the bombing of the 16th Street Baptist Church in Birmingham—the very church from which the thousand children had come singing and praying back in May to begin liberating Birmingham, at least partially, from segregation. The night before some men of utter evil from the Ku Klux Klan planted a bomb beneath a magnolia bush by a window. In the morning young women in the basement of the church were getting ready for youth services upstairs. There was a blast at 10:22 AM. Four girls lay dead in their choir robes: Cynthia Wesley, Carole Robertson, Addie Mae Collins, all fourteen, and Chris McNair, eleven. The damage was terrible. A stained-glass window somehow survived; only the face of Jesus was missing.

Within months the FBI's Birmingham office identified four of the Ku Klux Klanners who had bombed these children and urged J. Edgar Hoover to present this information to the Justice Department. But Hoover blocked it, a disgraceful lack of character that demands that Hoover's name be taken off the FBI building in Washington.

We did not know that Hoover was blocking the flow of information regarding the Birmingham bombing. All we knew was that it was going unsolved. The tone for the rest of 1963, after the glory of the Great March, became garish and cacophonous.

September 7, 1963

Miriam and I took a bus to Kansas City for my younger brother Robert's wedding in my hometown, Blue Springs. We stayed in a hotel out on Country Club Plaza in Kansas City, paid for by my father, Lyle.

I brought my Bell and Howell and shot footage at the wedding reception at the Lake Tapawingo Country Club. All of the partiers, maybe fifty to

My brother Robert's wedding, with my father, Lyle, the bride, Sherry, my brother Robert, my sister, Jacqueline, and me on the far right. The occasion for one of my first underground films. From Ed Sanders collection.

seventy-five people, seemed to be bent over, doing the twist. Later I tried to remember Brakhage's advice on smooth filming as I lay, rather drunk, across the hood of the honeymoon car, my Bell and Howell 70DE battle camera whirring. I did manage to film the bride and groom as they drove away for their honeymoon.

The next morning, utterly hung over, I became a vegetarian when my father prepared steak and eggs in the hotel apartment rented for Miriam and me. It was an act of goodwill on my father's part, but I had been considering vegetarianism ever since encountering cows by the roadside the previous year on the Nashville-Washington Walk for Peace.

The Shutdown of the Living Theater

Returning to New York with the wedding footage, I was faced with the closing by the feds of the Living Theater. It was an important place in my personal world. I had heard historic poetry readings there; I had first seen Bob Dylan perform as part of the General Strike for Peace in February '62; we had tried to raise money for Ray Bremser's defense; I had typed the stencils for the recent issue of *Fuck You/ A Magazine of the Arts*; I had taken part in the Jail Poets reading, with each of us reading from the cage of Kenneth Brown's starkly beautiful play *The Brig.*

The Brig had been successfully running since May. It had attracted the attention of the federal government, which sicced the IRS on the Living Theater for unpaid taxes.

The landlord cooperated with the IRS, and one day, without notice, the Becks were locked out. That night the audience, facing a locked front door, climbed over the roof and entered the performance space through the windows for one more performance of *The Brig*. After that the production moved briefly to the Midway Theatre on West Forty-second Street.

Shortly thereafter the Living Theater split for Europe, not to return for a few years. It was a blow to the New York counterculture.

The Fall of '63

I was torn between scholarship and the American underground. The banishment of the Living Theater just made me grit my teeth and become even more determined. But there was a bewildering list of directions I could have

taken at that point. My life reminded me of a couple of lines in *Poem from Jail*—"Floodlights stagger / the sunflower," or a line from Ginsberg's "Poem Rocket," from *Kaddish and Other Poems*: "Which way will the sunflower turn / surrounded by 1000s of suns?"

A hand-drawn-on-stencil image from the "Notes on Contributors" page for the issue in which I printed Allen Ginsberg's "The Change" more or less summed up my philosopher-king stance in the fall of '63. I thought of myself as a theologian of Instant Gratification. Then came the assassination on a glary day, and instant gratification, or InGrat as I termed it later, began to get balanced by right-wing reality.

Hoping to Help the Spark of Revolution

As I have written, I believed in the spark of revolution, the *iskra,* that it could or would somehow burst out of a poetry café on Second Avenue or from the pages coming off my Speed-o-Print mimeograph in the Secret Location and sweep to rev. I was following a countertugging set of Arrows of Bewilderment.

For the moment, the Arrows of Bewilderment were winning. I had discovered Greek lyric poetry, especially the complicated metrics of Sappho. I was translating Hesiod's *Theogony* and corresponding with a number of my heroes, including Charles Olson, Allen Ginsberg, Gary Snyder, Robert Duncan, and Diane di Prima. And I was having the thrill of drawing on mimeograph stencils Egyptian hieroglyphs commingled with my own glyphs. I was making underground movies, had some good footage of the Great March on Washington, and was filming my friends here and there, including on the torrid floor mattress of my Secret Location in the Lower East Side.

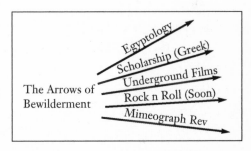

I was busy drawing stencils and gathering manuscripts for a new issue of *F.Y.,* and I, like most in the Lower East Side, was somewhat oblivious to the "rumble of the right" that historic fall. The Birmingham bombing was a clue, as was the footage of the Nazis making nose signs at those listening to Martin Luther King at the Great March.

On the political front there had been a hotline established between Moscow and Washington so that Kennedy and Khrushchev could talk each other out of any freaky propensity to wax nuke-batty. I had no idea that the right wing viewed that as appeasement and semitreason. I had no idea that the general in charge of the U.S. Air Force, Curtis Le May, viewed the resolution of the Cuban missile crisis without massive U.S. airstrikes as appeasement worse than Munich.

Much information on the larger world, even in the Lower East Side, was obtained from morning scans of the *New York Times.* I probably should have put two and two together on October 3 when well-placed writer Arthur Krock wrote a column in which he quoted a "very high official" asserting that the CIA's growth was like "a malignancy" that this official "was not sure even the White House could control . . . any longer." "If the United States ever experiences an attempt at a coup to overthrow the Government," the official went on to remark, "it will come from the CIA and not the Pentagon."

It seemed difficult, at best, to relate the outer world traced in the *New York Times* to the reality of my little world of underground movies, mimeo ink on my fingers, and coffeehouses with their wild verse. The *Times* also reported that when Ambassador to the United Nations Adlai Stevenson gave a speech in Dallas on October 24, he was spat on, jostled, and jeer-sneered by Birch-brained crackers outside the Dallas Memorial Auditorium Theater.

Meanwhile, I became friends with a young poet named Ted Berrigan. We met around the electric mimeograph at the Phoenix Bookshop at 18 Cornelia Street. Both of us used the mimeo to print our poetry magazines. He had just started a magazine called *C.* Like me, he had had trouble with the family of his future wife, Sandy, and had persevered.

Amphetamine Head

Another of my early film projects I called *Amphetamine Head—A Study of Power in America.* Since 1959 I had been studying a group of artists and bohemians known around the Lower East Side and Greenwich Village as "A-heads," amphetamine heads. They shot up amphetamine and often stayed up on A for days and days. There were plentiful supplies of amphetamine, sold fairly cheaply in powder form, on the set.

That fall I began filming *Amphetamine Head.* I decided to focus on the A-head artists, mainly painters, but there were some poets and jazz musicians as well who could be put under the banner of A. Anyone who lived on the Lower East Side and spent much time mixing with the street culture encountered A-heads. They roamed the streets, bistros, and pads compulsively shooting, snorting, or gobbling unearthly amounts of amphetamine, methedrine, dysoxin, bennies, cocaine, procaine—all of them burning for the flash that would lead to FLASH! It was almost neo-Platonic, as beneath the galactic FLASH! were subsumed the demi-flashes all urging toward FLASH!

Everybody from Washington Square to Tompkins Square called the streets "the set"—"I've been looking for you all over the set, man. Where's my amphetamine?" With a generation of folks readily present who viewed their lives as taking place on a set, there was no need to hunt afar for actors and actresses. What a cast of characters roamed the Village streets of 1963!

I'd heard rumors about a doctor giving President Kennedy shots. Uppers. It turned out, years later, that the rumors had had a basis in truth. So there was plenty of gossip at the time that the president used amphetamine and that his doctors injected him every morning. There were further speculations that the generals who met in the Pentagon war room every day planning atomic snuffs were a bit A-bombed themselves.

I was fascinated with an amph-artist named Jim Kolb, who once had stayed a few days at one of my pads. I had known him since 1960. I had observed the violence of the amphetamine heads and the raw power grabs that occurred in their glassy-eyed universe after a few months of sleeping just twice a week. If generals, corporate executives, presidents, premiers, and others were users of A, what were the implications? What if A-heads had taken over the governments of the world?

It was also commonly accepted on the set that the Germans had invented amphetamine and that the Nazis had shot up amphetamine during campaigns in North Africa in World War II, inspiring tales on the Lower East Side of futuristic battles involving fierce-breathed amphetamine humanoids, babbling shrilly like rewinding tapes, in frays of total blood. Another commonly accepted thesis was that amphetamine temporarily raised the intelligence of the user. The heads also seemed proud that A-use destroyed brain cells. One of the A-heads might shout, "I lose trillions of cells every day, man, grooo-VY!"

Amphetamine altered sex. Some under A's spell waxed unable in eros or sublimated their desire beneath a frenzy of endless conversation or art projects. Others with strong natural urges experienced this: that the erogenous areas became extended under A to include every inch of bodily skin. Men could not easily come, and women loved it forever. The image of amphetamine-driven Paolos and Francescas writhing for hours on a tattered mattress was humorous but true.

I became aware that some of the A-heads were talented artists. One of the problems was the high destruction ratio of their art. Most of it was abandoned or lost in the endless succession of evictions from apartments. When they first occupied a new pad, they sometimes proceeded to turn every surface and every room into an "environment" of murals, painting, and sculptured piles of furniture and debris brought in from the street. A landlord, once observing that the entire pad had been turned into art, so to speak, would throw up his arms in alarm and head for eviction court or the local police precinct.

Accordingly, during that fall of American desolation, I decided to make a film about power, using the world of the A-heads as archetype, lugging along my Wollensak tape recorder into a previously prepared apartment, and filming and taping shoot-ups, fights, conversations. I also wanted to trace what I was certain these A-head artists would do to the apartment: adorn its walls.

My friend Szabo knew of an apartment at 28 Allen Street that was empty. I went to a dealer in A on the Lower East Side who charged $30 for four ounces of pure powdered amphetamine, a fantastic bargain. I told him about my idea to hold an A-head "Cabinet Meeting" and perhaps re-create a presidential press conference. He was excited: "Let me see the film when you get it done, please!"

I brought the A to the apartment in a brown paper bag and just left it on the kitchen table. I dispatched Szabo to wander around the set telling people about the apartment with free amphetamine down on Allen Street. All visitors had to do was let me film. The result gave insight into the finding of gold in Sutter's Creek. Within minutes the A-heads began to flock, and the sound of a trilling flute was heard in the hallway of 28 Allen Street, 'phet-freaks banging most urgently on the door.

I had brought with me about ten clip-on light fixtures and a bunch of three-hundred-watt photoflood lamps, which I clipped to the walls of the apartment so that any area could be lit up for filming. I then checked the illumination on the walls, feeling them to be most important for filming the construction of wall murals and collages. I surrounded the mattress with lights and attached one in the kitchen, too. I switched on the lights and filmed the clean, neatly arranged apartment.

I had been worried that when I first switched on the floodlights and began to film, people would get uptight. But nothing happened. The group just accepted the extra light and the camera as another tidbit of grooviness. That is, the babblers kept babbling, the painters kept painting, and the flautists kept fluting.

During the two days of filming several poetic luminaries showed up who had heard about it. Among them were poets Joel Oppenheimer and Gregory Corso, who brought with him his freshly married and pregnant wife from Shaker Heights, Ohio, Sally November Corso.

Meanwhile, I scurried from room to room, shutting lights on and off, shooting the shoots, changing the location of the microphone, changing tapes, changing film. For film changes I had sewn together two dark cloths into a large sack, inside which I could crouch in darkness to change film. I didn't want to take any chances with the "government-surplus" film with respect to accidental exposure of the photosensitive surfaces.

Among the participants was a young woman named Diane. She was around sixteen—sitting with the others on the mattress and floor of the bedroom, yakkety-yakking. Amphetamine had possessed her. She wore her long black tresses swept back into a vague tangled knot. Her eyes were huge and dark—capable of fixing a baleful glazed gaze on a partner of shoot-up, art, or grope. She wore a black short-sleeved scoop-neck body stocking. Her shoes and other clothes were in a brown bag on the window ledge between the rooms.

Diane drew eyelashes with ink and brush above her lips so that her mouth babbling torrentially had the look of a convulsing Cyclops. Next, her twitching Rapidograph pen began to work on her toe. She drew flower petals around the shoot-up sore. Then she ripped at the toe hole and peeled the stocking up to her thigh and spent the next hour drawing a maze of stick figures all over the leg. Soon she had cut a jagged circle out of the stomach of the body stocking with a razor blade. She studied her stomach, craning her head down, and then began to shave each pale stomach hair with the blade. Sometimes a meth minispasm would occur and the steel would nick the skin, leaving a thin red slice. Ouch. Then Diane sat back on the mattress and grabbed a notebook. "I'm going to jot some thoughts."

She wrote for several minutes, then picked up the single-edged razor blade again and started scraping her lips with it. I was busy at this time filming other people's shoot-ups. I glanced over at Diane and winced involuntarily, seeing her scraping her mouth. When little edges of lip skin were hooked up, she would pick the skin with pinching fingers and tear it off. Soon long blood-pink strips had been peeled from her lips. I found it hard to photograph the event, so unnerving was it to see and to hear the scritch-scratching of the razor.

Diane looked up at a fellow A-head and opened her stripped lips, "Hey, why don't *you* shoot me up? I could dig it." The guy was all too eager to accommodate her and leaped for the glass of needles. He filtered a solution of dope and filled to the brim an eyedropper with needle affixed. With a flourish he stuck the needle into a blue-gray vein on the underside of Diane's forearm. Jabbed would have been a better word. He slid the needle long inside the vein much farther than necessary. Then as he injected the dope, he shoved the needle to the hilt inside her and began to twist slightly so that the needle tip pushed up against the top of the vein from inside. The viewers could see the skin rise from the jabbing needle, like a mole burrowing across a putting green. It had to be painful.

I switched off the camera because I wasn't sure whether she was going into a "masochist riff" for the sake of the camera.

The pain didn't seem to bother her for long because she was soon writing in her notebooks. "I want to describe my first ice cream cone . . ." she began, jotting quickly.

I filmed a fight that would later comprise a vignette dubbed "The Glue-Bottle Violence Scene." It started calmly enough, with two A-heads working on art projects. The problem was that there was just one glue bottle and the bottle was just about empty. Surly waxed the two glue-needers as each tried to hook out some glue at the same time.

"Watch it, motherfucker!" one of them growled. At that he grabbed the glue bottle and smeared the entire contents on the portion of plywood on which he was laboring. This caused the freak scene immortalized in the film.

It could have gotten worse, but others intervened and a cut-up was averted.

Later in the year after being in an altercation and getting stabbed, key A-artist Jim Kolb was delivered, according to the tale, doa to the hospital. Just as he was being declared dead by the doctor in the emergency room and the sheet was about to be pulled over his face, a miracle occurred. His "body" suffered an amphetamine twitch-spasm, and he revived. When the doctor noticed the dope twitch, he rushed Kolb into surgery, and he was saved. This story was told and retold like some sort of religious parable.

I had great footage of arabesques and panels of micro-swirls, a woman standing on a chair drawing the minutiae of eternity on the wall. Someone removed a section of pipe leading to the radiator and drilled holes to make a flute.

I decided to sleep because I was very tired and had abstained from ingesting the white. I was the only one copping z's in the entire pad as the others raved and painted onward. As I drifted toward sleep, I overheard a conversation between Szabo and young Diane. Szabo wanted to borrow her blade so that he could cut a hatchway into her body stocking in order for them to make it. He apparently cut a successful passageway, for soon the groans and sighs were floating above the babble in the dark room. Others joined them, writhing in insatiable A-sex.

Poet Bill Szabo around the time of the filming of *Amphetamine Head*. Ink drawing by Ann Leggett.

In terms of power Jim K began to take over the pad. He ruled with the irrationality and violence of a textbook dictator. Then the amphetamine supply dipped toward zero, and people were getting grumpy and demanding more as they came down. I filmed. And filmed. And filmed. By the weekend, after a couple of days of filming, I had to go to work at the cigar store, so I abandoned the set on Allen Street. Several days later I returned to the Allen Street pad to take some shots of the pad's "final state." Its condition was that of bombed-out chaos. Then I carried my shot rolls of film back to the Secret Location on Avenue A.

Sound Track for *Amphetamine Head*

I sent the film off to be developed, thanks to Jonas Mekas. I also created a sound track for the opening credits. To get a hollow sound effect, I put my head under a pillow, holding the tape recorder microphone close, intoning, "Am Am Am Am Phet Phet Phet Phet ta ta ta ta mine mine mine Head Head Head Head!" (The tape is in my archive to this day.) My idea for the opening credits was to have hypodermic needles filled with colored inks squirting the letters onto canvas, *Amphetamine Head—A Study of Power in America.*

White House Cooperation with *Seven Days in May*

Meanwhile, the march toward assassination kept up its relentless step.

JFK himself urged director John Frankenheimer to make a movie of the political thriller *Seven Days in May*, "to the dismay of the Pentagon," as Arthur Schlesinger Jr. wrote in his book on Robert Kennedy. *Seven Days* told of a military takeover in 1974 against a young president who was making a disarmament treaty with the Soviets. The movie starred Burt Lancaster, Kirk Douglas, Ava Gardner, and Fredric March, with a script by Rod Serling, the author of the *Twilight Zone* TV series. Filming was completed in the days before Kennedy's trip to Dallas.

In mid-November *Look* magazine, with a circulation of more than 7 million, published an article recounting how the Pentagon had *grrred* "no" to requests by the director for a visit to the office of the Joint Chiefs of Staff while at the same time the president had allowed Frankenheimer and crew to tour the White House and to film the entranceways. They were also allowed to film a mock riot between pro-president and pro-coup partisans outside the White House July 27, ironically very near the day the Test Ban Treaty was inked in Moscow, pending Senate approval.

After Kennedy had read *Seven Days in May*, he commented to a friend that a military coup in the United States was possible under certain circumstances, "but it won't happen on my watch."

Bye Bye, Nam

In his book *Johnny, We Hardly Knew Ye*, key aide Kenneth O'Donnell said that the president had told Senator Mike Mansfield in the spring of '63 that he would order all troops out of Vietnam in 1965. "But I can't do it until 1965—after I'm reelected."

A Trip to Texas

There was considerable anger at JFK in the South because of administration enforcement of integration, plus, among some, because of his liberal image. In an attempt to "take his case to the people," he had chosen to go to Texas and to Florida to dazzle them with his *"Ich bin ein Berliner"* pizzazz.

Florida had gone for Richard Nixon, and apparently only having Lyndon Johnson on the ticket had won Kennedy Texas.

The president flew to Texas on November 21, first to Houston, where Camelot got huge ovations, then on to Ft. Worth for more palm thunder. Then on November 22, he landed at Love Field in Dallas with his wife, Jackie.

Waiting for JFK that morning was a welcoming ad in the *Dallas Morning News* with a sequence of rightist moans:

> WHY have you ordered or permitted your brother Bobby, the Attorney General, to go soft on Communists, fellow-travelers, and ultra-leftists in America, while permitting him to persecute loyal Americans who criticize you, your administration, and your leadership.

> WHY are you in favor of the U.S. continuing to give economic aid to Argentina, in spite of the fact that Argentina has just seized almost 400 Million Dollars of American private property?

"You know," the president joked to Jackie as he scanned the ad that morning in their hotel room, "we're heading into nut country today." In the speech he was on his way to make, JFK was going to chastise right-wing conservatives.

The Final Procession

Trapped in a hostile city where the lunchmeat necks had so recently spat on the UN ambassador, the man of Camelot wended to his doom. The Secret Service had allowed open windows in upper stories, for instance, the sixth floor of the Texas School Book Depository. And it did seem odd that immediately in front of JFK's limousine as the shots were being fired, a man raised his umbrella aloft as if to say, "Now!" (from frame Z-227 of the Zapruder film).

Then the Assassination

I was coming out of class at New York University just after noon. I tried to make a call. The phone was dead. People were crowded around taxis in the street, listening to the radio. Thus came word of the assassination. I was right in the midst of publishing a new issue of my magazine, buoyed by receiving a fresh and brilliant poem by my hero Allen Ginsberg.

How could I possibly have become involved with the peripheries of the Kennedy assassination? Here's how. I thought Lee Harvey Oswald at first glance was a horrid nut. Then came the rumors that Oswald had been in the Village, disrupting civil rights meetings, and my friend Al Fowler claimed that he had attended some of the same meetings.

Earlier in the fall of '63 Al Fowler had spent some time in his hometown, Albany, working on a manuscript of his poetry to give to Auerhahn Press, a project that never quite came to fruition. Then he returned to the Lower East Side, and I was allowing him to crash for a few days at the Secret Location in the back building on Avenue A.

I was still convinced he would become a top-rank American poet. I would read his notebooks and pull out poems to publish in *Fuck You*. After his visit home it wasn't clear whether he was shooting junk or not, but I still could not turn him away from the Secret Location. Now and then Al would don the priest's collar and a gnarly silver cross of the small Catholic sect of which he was an adherent. To me he was a poetic wonder.

Oswald in the Village?

The first issue of the *Village Voice* after the assassination came out on November 28. On the front page was an article headlined "Was Oswald in Village?":

The FBI was in Greenwich Village early this week in search of clues to Lee H. Oswald's past. Their investigation here is apparently based on information that the alleged assassin of President Kennedy had for a time associated with a youthful Mississippi-born rightist who disrupted a number of pro-integration meetings in the Village during 1961 and 1962. The information came from an East Villager who claims he knew both Oswald and the rightist slightly while all three were in the same Marine outfit. He says he saw the two men together on more than one occasion and claims that Oswald had taken photographs for the Southerner in the course of disrupting one meeting. The informant claims that the photographs were destined for a pro-fascist publication. There had been no information, prior to this disclosure,

that Oswald had been in New York for more than one night since his return
from Russia in 1962.

The informant identified himself as James Rizzuto. He also contacted
popular radio host Barry Gray. A five-page FBI memorandum dated November 25, 1963, stated, "Barry Gray, radio commentator, station WMCA,
NYC, advised one James F. Rizzuto had alleged he had info re one Yves Le-
andez, a close associate of Lee H. Oswald. Rizzuto furnished following info
to agents. Rizzuto states that he, Yves Leandes, Lee H. Oswald and possibly
one Earl Perry served together in U.S. Marine Corps in nineteen fifty-six at
Camp Le Jeune and Barstow, California." The FBI memo continued, "Rizzuto described Leandes as a close personal friend of Oswald and both were
professional agitators who attended meetings of the American Jewish Congress and other organizations and tried to disrupt meetings. Rizzuto stated
he thought both Oswald and Leandes belonged to an organization possibly
called 'States Rights Party.'" The memo recommended that the bureau contact Rizzuto in person to check these allegations out.

Two days later, November 27, another FBI memorandum, "Re Stephen
Yves L'Eandes AKA Frenchy," reported, "L'Eandes allegedly visited Russia
with Lee Oswald and one Earl Perry in 1960s. L'Eandes was seen active in
picketing the White House, heckling the American Jewish Congress, and
other mass meetings of the integration movement." The memo recommended that L'Eandes be identified posthaste and interviewed. The FBI interviewed Pat Padgett, wife of poet Ron Padgett, on November 25, at her
place of employment at 11 Waverly Place in the Village, where L'Eandes
once had lived.

Al Fowler himself had attended some of the meetings at which L'Eandes
had disrupted the events. He knew L'Eandes. "I liked him. He was amusing,"
Fowler later told me. He had witnessed L'Eandes create a disturbance at a
meeting of the Socialist Labor Party at the Militant Labor Forum on University Place, and he'd seen L'Eandes hanging out around the headquarters
of the General Strike for Peace in early '62, located at the Living Theater.

Fowler later recalled the last time he had met with L'Eandes:

The last conversation I had with L'Eandes prior to the big snuff took place in a
diner on Sheridan Square. He talked then about Fair Play for Cuba, etc. His

whole shuck was that he was a Cajun, and that his whole family, in the main, was around New Orleans. He even got into a dissertation on the French Quarter. He asked me how I felt about Cuba, and I told him just what you would expect I would tell anyone, and did. I told him Castro's noble struggles against the giant of the North were of no more consequence to me than any other replacement of any government by more government.

So in the heated horror of the postassassination turmoil, prodded by his close friend artist Ann Leggett, Al Fowler called the FBI, and he agreed to meet the FBI that evening at Stanley's Bar! He did not show for the meeting, so FBI agents stood outside Stanley's and queried those who entered the bar about Fowler and his whereabouts. I learned about this and became sorely alarmed!

What if someone told the FBI that Fowler was crashing at my Secret Location? What about all the film cans with my footage for *Amphetamine Head*? What about the footage from the Great March on DC? What about the torrid footage of Szabo and Ellen B? What about the stacks of *Fuck You/ A Magazine of the Arts*? What about my film equipment—camera, tripod, strips and cans of film everywhere, plus gaudy Jack Smith–esque hangings of colored cloths on the wall, with photofloods here and there attached to clip-ons? What would the FBI say about those if it raided the Secret Location?

I raced over to the Secret Location a block away and left a note for Al on the metal bathtub cover in the kitchen, next to my mimeograph machine. I was preparing a new issue of *Fuck You*, and all the poems submitted for the new issue were in the Secret Location, including Ginsberg's "The Change." To me it was a tableau foretelling jail time if the FBI should raid my place looking for someone who claimed to have seen Lee Harvey Oswald in the Village!

Here's the note I left: "My dear Al—as a result of the FBI scene, you are requested to REMOVE all your stuff from here—If it is not removed by Friday, I shall repadlock the door and bolt the windows, and you will procure your stuff at my discretion. Ed. S."

Al left a note in reply, written on the reverse of my note, when he returned to the Secret Location. He pleaded with me to let his belongings remain in the pad, while promising to stay away.

Then another note from poet Fowler: "Ed—as you can see, I've split. However—some of Ann's stuff is on trunk. She especially prizes the goblets therein, so be gentle.

"Thanks for all your help. Sympathy, & needed kick in the balls. Al"

Next to the note on the porcelainized tub cover was a blood splotch, likely from his shooting up.

A trio of historic documents that came about through the assassination of our president.

By November 29 the FBI office in New York City sent out a notice that the investigation was to cease. It had learned by then that Rizzuto, the original source to radio host Barry Gray, and L'Eandes and Landesberg were one and the same! Steve Landesberg later became a well-known television comedian, starring on the *Barney Miller* sitcom. Why he claimed that Oswald had disrupted political meetings in Greenwich Village remains a mystery. (Fowler

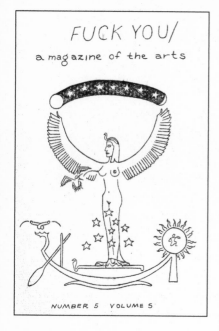

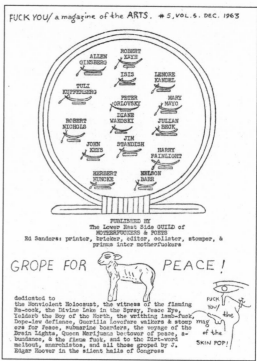

The issue I published just days after the assassination, with Allen Ginsberg's "The Change."

recalled seeing Landesberg some time later: "I ran into him a couple of years later. He had dropped the accent. He was wearing a nice suit. He came up to me on the street and offered me $600 to fly to Montreal and bring a box back with me, of unspecified contents." Fowler turned down the offer.)

Meanwhile, once the coast seemed clear after Fowler had moved out, I went back to work on the December 1963 issue (volume 5, number 5) of *Fuck You/ A Magazine of the Arts*. The Secret Location was safe. My mimeo was safe. Ditto for the footage for *Amphetamine Head—A Study of Power in America*. The studio was not to be raided by the police for another year and a half.

December '63 was one of those dazed, nightmare months all too common in America after an almost totally not understood calamity occurs, such as the assault on a slowed-down limousine convoy in Dallas.

The Arrival of 1964

The New Year came while the nation was still stunned by the assassination. Miriam was pregnant with our daughter, Deirdre. I rented an apartment on

East 204th Street off the Grand Concourse in the Bronx. There was a good hospital nearby, and the pad was very clean. We would live there until our daughter was born in September, then a few months later move back to Manhattan. I kept the Secret Location on Avenue A.

War, Always War—This One on Poverty

In Lyndon Johnson's first State of the Union Address on January 8 he announced that "this administration today, here and now declares unconditional War on Poverty. . . . We shall not rest until that war is won."

Of course, that was not the war at all. The war was the war when just weeks after JFK was in the ground much of the National Security Grouch Apparatus including the so-called liberals suffered hostile psyche squalls on the issue of Vietnam. (We had no idea at the time that Kennedy was set to pull all U.S. troops out of the Southeast Asia quagmire and no idea just then that Johnson was set to vastly increase U.S. involvement.)

Meanwhile, the rising tide of expectation from the Kennedy years was still in place, and so a "war on poverty" seemed just another aspect of that tide.

Belief in the Power of the Lower East Side and the Underground

In the Lower East Side, where I kept my Secret Location on Avenue A for my mimeo work and films, I still felt a gritty determination for a time of "total assault on the culture."

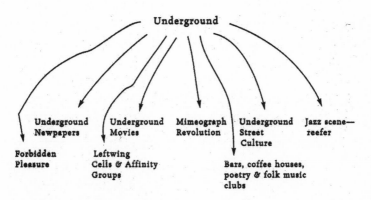

The structure of the underground.

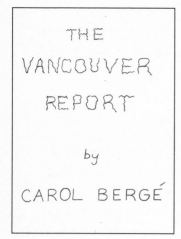

THE

VANCOUVER

REPORT

by

CAROL BERGÉ

"The Vancouver Report," with hand-drawn stencil cover and printed on rose-colored Granitex paper.

In February I published "The Vancouver Report" by Lower East Side poet Carol Bergé, which I had commissioned her to write. She had attended the Vancouver Poetry Conference the previous summer.

I thought it was a well-written sixteen pages on a famous literary conference, especially fair to Charles Olson, the "father" of the various movements on hand, and to Allen Ginsberg, fresh from his vision of a new direction. She was a tad harsh on Robert Duncan, I thought, but all in all an interesting account.

The Beatles in America

Even those of us on the Lower East Side without a television set had to notice that something called The Beatles had come to town. New York DJs helped drum-beat the throng of 25,000 who shrieked hello to the group at JFK airport when the Fab Four arrived for *The Ed Sullivan Show* on CBS and two shows at Carnegie Hall.

The Beatles were not about to be one-upped by the edgy New York press. At a press conference a reporter asked, "What do you do when you're cooped up in your rooms between shows?" George replied, "We ice-skate."

I read that the group's name had been inspired by Ginsberg, Kerouac, and crew. And that started me thinking about a blend of music and poetry. I couldn't help but notice how The Beatles' words were crystal clear! Intimately hearable! That would be my goal with The Fugs—that the words could at last star in the musical mix.

My Final Term at NYU

That spring I was completing my final term at NYU, taking a full course load. My favorite course was on Greek lyric poetry, taught by Dr. Bluma Trell, which opened the door for me to the great Sappho. Bluma Trell had a way of making Anacreon, Alcaeus, and, especially, Sappho and her complicated metrics come alive in my eager noggin! I was also translating Hesiod's long poem, *The Theogony*, that year, hoping to publish it on my mimeograph.

I was working weekends—Friday, Saturday, Sunday—on the 5:00 PM to 2:00 AM shift at the cigar store where I had toiled off and on, and learned a lot about the underground world of Times Square, since 1960. It was freaky. One evening a guy who worked at the 2-for-25¢ hamburger place next door came in for cigarettes. I asked him why he was barefoot. He replied, "I have a date with a Toe Queen, and my date likes dirty feet."

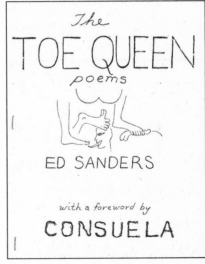

All that evening I wrote a series of poems depicting the life and times of "Tillie the Toe Queen" on white, elongated slats of thin cardboard from cigarette cartons. By the next weekend I had published *The Toe-Queen Poems*.

When I read them at Le Metro, the response, in applause and overwhelming laughter, was the first I had received for anything I'd ever read in public, and I think it was an impetus to form a satiric proto-folk-rock group called The Fugs a few months later. One of the first Fugs songs, never, unfortunately, put on an album, was a ditty called "Toe Queen Love."

Hanging Out with Allen Ginsberg!

One of the big events in early '64 was that I began to hang out with Ginsberg. When I was first exploring New York City in 1958 and 1959, I never thought in a cycle of centuries that I'd ever become friends with such a hero.

After the Vancouver Poetry Festival in the summer of '63, Allen returned to San Francisco for a number of weeks, then flew to New York, where he stayed with his brother, Eugene, in Long Island, then visited his father and stepmother in New Jersey. By early 1964 he was staying with Ted Wilentz in the apartment above the 8th Street Bookshop. There was a lot of literary cross-pollination at the Wilentz salon, as when Ginsberg met Bob Dylan there early in '64.

The author at a Fugs show flashing a mudra Ginsberg had taught him in 1964. Ed Sanders collection.

Then Allen and Peter Orlovsky located a three-room pad at 704 East Fifth Street, near Avenue C, on the sixth floor. It was just $35 a month—Hail to Thee, O Rent Control!

I met Allen for the first time outside Gem Spa on St. Mark's Place and Second Avenue, a fine Beatnik meeting place that sold great chocolate egg creams for 15¢. We went out drinking at Stanley's Bar one winter night, where the topic wended to visions, which he freely said he'd experienced.

"Are you having visions right now?" I asked.

"Yes," he nodded.

Ah Sunflower, weary of time, I thought. I was drunk. I went with him to his new apartment. He patted the pillow, urging me to stay, but I decided not to make it with him.

During those early months I went with him now and then to parties. There was one at photographer Robert Frank's house, where Allen introduced me to his generation, including people such as Norman Podhoretz; Frank's pretty wife, Mary, later a well-known painter; and poet John Hollander.

Ginsberg taught me a number of mantrams, singing them to me (and many others) to the *clack, clack, clink!* of finger cymbals. He also turned me on to the Hare Krishna chant (which The Fugs recorded with Ginsberg and Gregory Corso a few years later). Plus, he taught me a number of mudras—special positioning of the hands and fingers—based on what he had learned in India. I memorized three mudras and used them in public performances.

Roosevelt After Inauguration

Within days of my meeting the bard, we began the first of many capers together. This was a satiric little book by William Burroughs called *Roosevelt After Inauguration*, which I published in January '64 when the printer for the

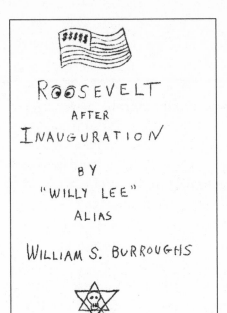

City Lights edition of *The Yage Letters* refused to publish it in late 1963. The book traces Burroughs's 1953 trip to the Amazon rain forest in search of ayahuasca, or yagé, a hallucinogenic plant averred to confer telepathic skills on its user. *The Yage Letters* also has letters by Ginsberg from 1960 describing his own experiences taking yagé. In succeeding decades the book became quite valuable. Here is Allen's cover, which I got him to hand-draw with a stylus directly on a stencil.

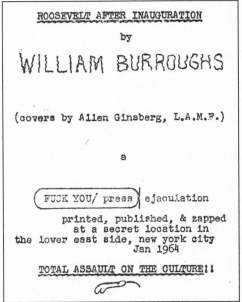

Roosevelt After Inauguration—my first caper with Ginsberg, January 1964.

Reading with Joel Oppenheimer at the Five Spot

I met Joel Oppenheimer on the Lower East Side poetry scene and in places such as Stanley's Bar on Avenue B and the Cedar Bar on University Place. He was a heavy drinker at the time, but almost always had a smile on his craggy face and a literary anecdote to share. He lived on the Lower East Side and had attended Black Mountain College in the 1950s. He was good friends with Robert Creeley, Ed Dorn, Fielding Dawson, and Gilbert Sorrentino. I started publishing his poetry in *Fuck You*, and we became pals. Then Oppenheimer invited me to read with him on February 17, 1964, at the Five Spot! The Five Spot was located at 2 St. Mark's Place, just off Third Avenue, and had featured geniuses such as Billy Holiday, Thelonius Monk, Charles Mingus, and Ornette Coleman. I was thrilled just to enter the front door!

Joel's and my reading were part of a series—on February 24, Robert Kelly and Fielding Dawson; on March 2, Barbara Guest and Charles Reznikoff; on March 9, Frank O'Hara and Arnold Weinstein; and, finally, on March 16, LeRoi Jones and Mack Thomas. I was nearly flabbergasted at the honor of reading alongside so many of the best minds of my generation.

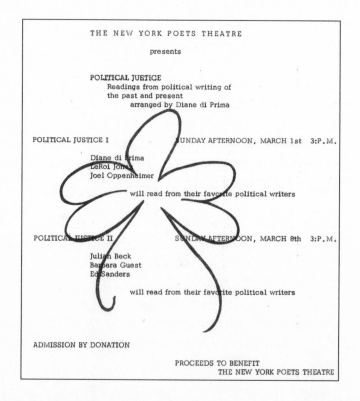

THE NEW YORK POETS THEATRE

presents

POLITICAL JUSTICE
Readings from political writing of
the past and present
arranged by Diane di Prima

POLITICAL JUSTICE I   SUNDAY AFTERNOON, MARCH 1st   3:P.M.

Diane di Prima
LeRoi Jones
Joel Oppenheimer

will read from their favorite political writers

POLITICAL JUSTICE II   SUNDAY AFTERNOON, MARCH 8th   3:P.M.

Julian Beck
Barbara Guest
Ed Sanders

will read from their favorite political writers

ADMISSION BY DONATION

PROCEEDS TO BENEFIT
THE NEW YORK POETS THEATRE

The afternoon of Sunday, March 8, 1964, I read at Diane di Prima's "New York Poets Theater" as a benefit for the theater, with Julian Beck and Barbara Guest. The reading theme was "POLITICAL JUSTICE, readings from political writing of the past and present." And wow! I was on the same bill as Julian Beck and Barbara Guest!

I kept on reaching out to famous poets, trying to get submissions to my magazine. For instance, I exchanged a few letters with Edward Dahlberg, to no avail. The same was true with Marianne Moore, to whom I had sent a recent issue and a letter asking for poetry. On March 9, 1964, she sent a note back, on her letterhead, 260 Cumberland Street, Brooklyn 5, New York:

> Thank you Mr. Sanders [which was typed, then the following handwritten:]
>
> Thank you. Magazine Something Coct You. [now typed] We writers can't make what we say, too plain, natural, and *simple* [handwritten] Reverent
>
> [typed] My trouble is too much to do, too many letters that wish answers, not strength enough or a long enough day. Two oclock bedtime several days in succession isn't good.
>
> *Courage*, we each must say?
>
> [signed] Marianne Moore

Harvey Brown and Peace Eye

I met a young man named Harvey Brown who hailed from Cleveland. He came from means—his grandfather had invented a crane for offloading river barges, and Harvey had inherited a large amount from his father's estate. By 1964 Harvey Brown was an avid supporter of another of my heroes, Charles Olson, and under Olson's tutelage was starting Frontier Press and cashing in some of his inheritance to pay for it. He was married and had young children. In early 1964 he offered to publish a book of my poems. I was overjoyed.

Olson had had almost as huge an impact on me—particularly *The Maximus Poems* and his manifesto "Projective Verse"—as Ginsberg, Dylan Thomas, Poe, Blake, and Eliot. Olson dedicated *The Maximus Poems* to "Robert Creeley, the Figure of Outward." I strived in my own modes to be "the Figure of Outward" to my own generation.

So much of the early months of 1964 was divided among my full-time studies at NYU in Greek and Latin, my underground film work at the Secret

Location, preparation of new issues of my magazine, and writing of an extended series of poems for the new book, which I decided to call *Peace Eye*. I was creating an extensive sho-sto-po (short story poem) called "The Gobble Gang Poems."

Crackdown on Coffeehouses and the Arts

Meanwhile in the harsh U.S. climate after the shooting of JFK, there was a crackdown on the arts in, of all places, New York City! The post–World War II creativity revolution, which had thrived in New York City during the late 1940s and through the 1950s, ran into censorship by the fistful in 1963 and 1964.

Back in '62 something called the New York Coffeehouse Law had been enacted. It stipulated that if a restaurant wanted to have live entertainment, it had to acquire a "coffeehouse license," which required submissions of blueprints, installation of sprinklers, more fire exits, kitchen flues. These installations were to be overseen by the corrupt New York City Building and Fire Code departments. The law allowed three stringed instruments and a piano, but not readers of verse.

I hung out at the coffeehouses that featured poetry readings as much as I could during those years. Many of us, including Allen G., myself, d. a. levy, Diane Wakoski, David Henderson, Ishmael Reed, and Marguerite Harris, read poetry in East Village coffeehouses, especially at the Café Le Metro on Second Avenue between Ninth and Tenth Streets.

The Department of Licenses, in particular, led the clampdown against poetry readings in coffeehouses, against the showing of certain avant-garde films (especially those that featured homosexual and erotic imagery), and against theaters such as Ellen Stewart's Cafe La Mama. Department officials would scan the *Village Voice* for listings of poetry readings and send out spores to issue summonses.

I attended meetings with Ellen Stewart of La Mama, Joe Cino of Cafe Cino, Jackson MacLow, and Allen Ginsberg to organize public opposition to the Department of Licenses. Particularly disturbing, reminding me of a faceless bureaucrat gone mad in a William Burroughs novel, was a Department of License official named Walter Kirschenbaum, who we heard was a Liberal Party appointee and was very obnoxious in the meetings. (Young firebrands Henry Stern, later to be head of the New York City Parks Department, and Ed Koch, later to be mayor, helped us.) We started a campaign that ultimately led to the city government pulling back and letting verse be heard without hindrance.

It has been speculated that the clampdown was inspired, at least in part, by the New York City establishment's desire to "clean up" the city in advance of the millions of visitors and their cash bonanza scheduled to arrive for the upcoming 1965 World's Fair. I doubt that. The clampdown may have been more an expression of right-wing meanness after the death of JFK and a slow buildup of war. It may take another fifty years or so to learn if the clampdown from the Department of Licenses really did have an element of right-wing repression and secret agencies.

Clamping Down on Jonas Mekas

Early in 1964 Jack Smith's *Flaming Creatures* had been shown three successive Mondays without any trouble at the Gramercy Art Theater. On February 15 the police issued a summons against the showing, and the Gramercy halted showings of underground films.

Jonas Mekas then began showing underground films at the New Bowery Theater, at 4 St. Mark's Place (later named the Bridge Theater, where The Fugs often played at midnight the following year). In February 1964 Mekas filmed the Living Theater production of Kenneth Brown's *The Brig.* (It won the docu award at the 1965 Venice Film Festival.) On March 3 *Flaming Creatures* was screened at the New Bowery Theater. After thirty of the film's forty-five minutes, police officers suddenly stood up and arrested all the people they could and seized the film and all the projectors they could get their hands on. Mekas was held in jail overnight.

A week later Mekas was again cuffed, this time at the Writers' Stage on East Fourth, for showing Jean Genet's *Un Chant d'Amour*, with its homosexual theme. Many intellectuals wrote in to complain, including Jean-Paul Sartre and Simone de Beauvoir. The case was tossed.

Jonas received a six-month suspended sentence for screening *Flaming Creatures*. He appealed the case all the way to the U.S. Supreme Court, which voted narrowly not to hear it. Abe Fortas was one of the justices who voted to hear the *Flaming Creatures* appeal. Later when he was up for the job of chief justice, right-wing nuts claimed that he was an aficionado of dirty flicks.

For the next few months the Park Avenue South home of the Film-Makers' Cooperative became the meeting place of underground filmmakers, sometimes to talk and argue with one another and sometimes to screen their films.

Barbara Rubin

In 1964 I met a young filmmaker named Barbara Rubin at Allen Ginsberg's new apartment at 704 East Fifth. She was brilliant and enigmatic. At the same time she was very carnal, yet she had a spiritual side that ultimately led her to Hasidism. She and Allen Ginsberg were lovers at one time. She was spunky and thought Big. In 1963 she completed a movie called *Christmas on Earth*, which had explicitly erotic sections, tracing in its twenty-nine minutes a group sex encounter in a New York City apartment.

By late 1963 Jonas Mekas had hired Barbara Rubin to work at the Film-Makers' Cooperative. In December of that year Barbara, Jonas, and a young man named P. Adams Sitney flew to an "experimental film competition" in Belgium. The three took films with them to screen at the festival, including Ron Rice's *Chumlum*, Stan Brakhage's *Dog Star Man* and *Window Water Baby*, Kenneth Anger's *Scorpio Rising*, and Jack Smith's *Flaming Creatures*.

The festival judges decided that *Flaming Creatures* was unfit to show. Jonas Mekas withdrew from the festival jury in protest. Jonas and friends gave a private screening of the film in their hotel. Meanwhile, on the last day of the festival in Belgium (at Knokke-le-Zoute) Jonas and Barbara shoved into the festival projection booth and began to screen *Flaming Creatures* to an unprepared audience.

Uh oh.

The festival honchos cut off the power. Reportedly the Belgium minister of justice appeared at the microphone to calm the audience. Meanwhile, the estimable Barbara Rubin found alternative power and began to project *Creatures* on his very face!

The Travails of Lenny Bruce

Everybody had heard about Lenny Bruce. The buzz on him was enormous. He was an authentic, if very frantic, comedic hero in the American underground. I knew that he and Allen Ginsberg were friends.

By early 1964 there were not many places the brilliant comic could play in the United States. Nevertheless he was able to do four Easter '64 gigs at the Village Theater on Second Ave. By then he had placed in his routines one of his most controversial pieces, which was inspired by strips from the twenty-second Zapruder film as published in the December 6, 1963, issue of *Time*. Bruce interpreted the film clips as depicting Mrs. Kennedy "hauling ass to save her ass" (though in fact Jackie had reached out to help pull a Secret Service agent aboard. Then she went back to cradle her husband).

After the concert gigs at the Village Theater (Bruce had lost his cabaret card and so could not perform where liquor was sold), Howie Solomon brought Lenny into his new Cafe Au Go Go on Bleecker Street, with skyscraper-voiced Tiny Tim as opening act.

On the third night of Bruce's run a guy in a dark suit named Herbert Ruhe from the NYC Department of Licenses (and formerly a CIA agent) plunked down $4.70 for a ticket and during the show took notes. The next day Ruhe visited Assistant District Attorney Richard Kuh, and then on April 1 two cops with a concealed Minofon wire recorder stealth-taped Bruce's gig.

Assistant DA Kuh brought the tape and transcription to a grand jury, which indicted Bruce, though the tape recording was somewhat garbled and crackly. On April 3 Bruce and Howie Solomon were arrested in Bruce's Go Go dressing room.

The Great Society

Almost five months to the day after John Kennedy was shot in Dallas, the words "Great Society" were first used by President Johnson at a Democratic fund-raiser in Chicago. "We have been called upon—are you listening?— to build a great society of the highest order, a society not just for today or tomorrow but for three or four generations to come."

It sounded good to me, except that he was surfacing as a warmonger. Nevertheless his Great Society showed the enlightened side of Johnson's viciously bifurcated personality.

In the early and mid-1960s there was plenty of evidence that things were going to change for the better. A whole generation came to believe that Good Permanent Change was going to happen right away. The integration and voting rights victories in the South gave the '60s such hope, and so did laws passed by a Congress and two presidents who still drew public inspiration from Franklin Roosevelt, the Great Depression, and New Deal legislation such as Social Security and child labor laws.

All in a great rush of months Johnson used his leadership to pass a bunch of Great Society laws. Among them were Medicare, Medicaid, the Freedom of Information Act, the Voting Rights Act, a law setting aside millions of acres of public land as permanent wilderness, and Johnson's executive order on affirmative action. It was his glory and the glory of a righteous Congress. At the same time, however, as if possessed by a demon of bellicosity, Johnson started up a ground and air war in Vietnam—with napalm, Agent Orange, fragmentation bombs, strategic hamlets, the Phoenix program, and secret bombings of Laos.

Wars eat social progress. Johnson's Great Society momentum was soon killed by the killing in Vietnam, Laos, and Cambodia and the ruination of Thailand with corruption. The outcry of resistance from millions of Americans, conducted in a creative and defiant mode, doomed his presidency, while guns spoiled the butter and napalm torched the bread and roses. In some ways he represented the worst aspects of American civilization—bellicose, too cozy with the secret, backslapping deal, too eager to send people toward certain harm.

FUCK YOU/
a magazine of the arts

number 5, volume 6

May 1964

I completed the tenth issue of *Fuck You/ A Magazine of the Arts* (volume 5, number 6) in May, just around the time I graduated from New York University.

As always, I took great joy in hand-lettering the cover glyph on the stencil. By then I owned an assortment of sharp-tipped, and rounded, styli. In lieu of a lightboard I used a flashlight to illuminate the drawing from behind, and beneath the somewhat flimsy stencil I positioned a fairly thick plastic sheet. It was important for the stylus not to overly gouge the stencil, and over the years I had learned the exact pressures required to cut the stencil's film without ripping.

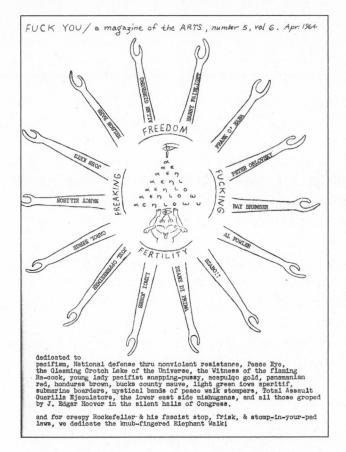

FUCK YOU/ a magazine of the ARTS , number 5, vol 6. Apr. 1964

FREEDOM

FREAKING

FUCKING

FERTILITY

ALLEN GINSBERG

HARRY FAINLIGHT

FRANK O'HARA

PETER ORLOVSKY

NELSON BARR

JOHN KEYS

NANCY ELLISON

RAY BREMSER

AL FOWLER

CAROL BERGE

JOEL OPPENHEIMER

SZABO!!

SONIA JONES

DIANE DI PRIMA

dedicated to
pacifism, National defense thru nonviolent resistance, Peace Eye,
the Gleaming Crotch Lake of the Universe, the Witness of the flaming
Ra-cook, young lady pacifist snapping-pussy, acapulqo gold, panamanian
red, honduras brown, bucks county mauve, light green iowa aperitif,
submarine boarders, mystical bands of peace walk stompers, Total Assault
Guerilla Ejaculators, the lower east side mishuganas, and all those groped
by J. Edgar Hoover in the silent halls of Congress.

and for creepy Rockefeller & his fascist stop, frisk, & stomp-in-your-pad
laws, we dedicate the knub-fingered Elephant Walk!

I had a bunch of beautiful poems in the issue that spring! Allen Ginsberg, Frank O'Hara, LeRoi Jones, Al Fowler, Bill Szabo, Carol Bergé, Diane di Prima, Joel Oppenheimer, Ray Bremser, Nancy Elison, John Keys, Peter Orlovsky, and Nelson Barr—all reflected in my glyphic table of contents page.

By the spring of '64 I had become active in the movement, just beginning, for the legalization, at least, of personal use of marijuana. To the shock of some of my friends, I mentioned in some of my "Notes on Contributors" that so-and-so was a grass dealer when he ACTUALLY WAS! In this issue I published a full-page editorial calling for legalization of what I called the Ra Herb, "A CALL TO ACTION—Stomp Out the Marijuana Laws Forever!"

My friends were fearful for me, but I didn't see any reason that I couldn't make such a call, under the Bill of Rights, and carouse in freedom for the rest of the 1960s! Little did I realize how many leaders of the counterculture—Tim Leary, Ken Kesey, d. a. levy, John Sinclair, and, in a way, John Lennon—would become Pot Martyrs in the backlash against the movement to legalize.

The editorial began:

OK, all you motherfuckers. We know that you're smoking more grass than a prairie fire. We're also hip that all you cocksuckers—1000's of you—are rehabilitating your lungs under conditions of agitation, metaphysical distress, fuzz-fear, & paranoia. Time is NOW for a Total Assault on the Marijuana Laws! It is CLEAR to us that the cockroach theory of grass smoking has to be abandoned. INTO THE OPEN! ALL THOSE WHO SUCK UP THE BENEVOLENT NARCOTIC MARIJUANA, TEEENSHUN! FORWARD, WITH MIND DIALS POINTED: *ASSAULT!*. We have the facts! Cannabis is a non-addictive gentle peace drug! The Marijuana legislations were pushed through in the 1930's by the agents and goonsquads of the jansenisto-manichaean fuckhaters' Conspiracy. Certainly, after 30 years of the blight, it is time to rise up for a bleep blop bleep assault on the social screen. *The fact IS* that 1000's of you exist all over the whole fucking U.S. scene, but we can't wait forever for your grass cadets to pull the takeover: grass-freak senators, labor leaders, presidents, etc.! The Goon Squads are few and we are many. We must spray our message into the million lobed American brain immediately! If there's public hysteria, we'll pull the classic Guerrilla Lovefare—enemy attack/we retreat enemy, retreat/we attack—scene!

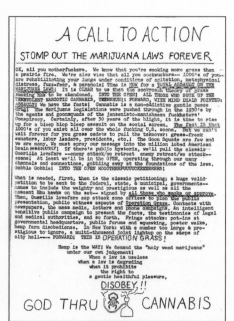

At least we'll be in the open, operating through our many channels and connections, gobbling away at the foundations of the laws, Gobble Gobble! INTO THE OPEN MOOOTHER-FUUUUUKKKERRRRS!

What is needed, first, then is the classic petitioning; a huge valid petition to be sent to the federal, state, & municipal governments—names to include the weighty and prestigious as well as all the nascent Bhu hawks on the set—signed by *all those who smoke or approve*. Then, Guerrilla Lovefare zap attack zone offices to plan the public presentation, public witness aspects of *Operation grass.* Contacts with newspapers, the mass media, letters and phone campaigns. An intelligent, sensitive public campaign to present the facts, the testimonies of legal and medical authorities, and so forth. Fringe attacks: pot-ins at governmental headquarters, public forums and squawking, poster walks, hemp farm disobedience. In New York, with a number too large and prestigious to ignore, a multi-thousand joint lightup on the steps of city hall— FORWARD! THIS IS OPERATION GRASS!

> Hemp is the WAY! We demand the "holy weed marijuana"
> under our own judgement!
> When a law is useless
> when a law is degrading
> when it prohibits
> the right to
> a gentle healthful pleasure
> DISOBEY!
> GOD THROUGH CANNABIS!

Some of my pals in Stanley's Bar thought for sure I would be rounded up by the fuzz. After all, it was early 1964. A few months later I would help organize the first Legalize Marijuana public demonstration, planned at my Peace Eye Bookstore. The cover glyph for that April issue featured many of my bacchic passions of '64: Egyptian glyphology; the hookah; D. H. Lawrence's Boat of Death in the form of outstretched scarab claws on top of which were my Speed-o-Print mimeo on the left and Bell and Howell battle camera on the right, plus two symbols of spurting—the Egyptian phallus to the right and a hypodermic needle with peace button balls on the left—while overhead there was a hovering and protective Egyptian Eye of Horus, with wings and an Ankh sign above.

These were the symbols I was certain would change the world. As for the squirting needle with peace signs adangle, while filming *Amphetamine Head*, I had witnessed amph-artists squirt arabesques of colored paint from hypos onto various surfaces.

The Glorification of the Needle

One thing I regret emphasizing in my publications was the defiance in shooting up. I had a bit of a cavalier attitude toward the use of the needle. In some apartments in the Lower East Side a hypodermic needle boiling on a gas ring was almost as prevalent as a folk guitar by the bed. Miriam noticed how, just as in later decades a person might ask, "Do you mind if I smoke a cigarette?" back in those days it was likely to be "Do you mind if I shoot up?"

Later when my friend Janis Joplin died from a hot shot, I started to regret all the drawings I published featuring images of the needle, such as in a pencil drawing that shows a needle in an Egyptian hieroglyph for "arm," which I drew in late 1963 for *Fuck You/ A Magazine of the Arts*, a sketch I decided not to use but trails on in my boxes of stuff.

The Sexual Revolution

I was fairly involved in those years with what was called the "sexual revolution" (for instance, I was on the board of directors of the League for Sexual Freedom). I was impressed with the way Ginsberg and Burroughs, through their court cases, had expanded utilization of the great American Bill of Rights. Ginsberg's sexuality—always open to the inspection of all— seemed a pathway, at least, to study closely. I've always thought that the great expansion of freedom in television, for instance (think *The Sopranos*), and in other art forms arose out of the work of Allen Ginsberg and William Burroughs. The Beats, through their public presences and their publications, pushed at the barricades of what could be said and done. But did they get the Presidential Medal of Freedom during their lifetimes? NO!

Like it or not, the birth control pill, which by the early 1960s had spread all over the counterculture and Beat scenes, gave young women a great freedom to ball anywhere and any time they chose. In this regard the issue of "fucking in the streets" bubbled up in my

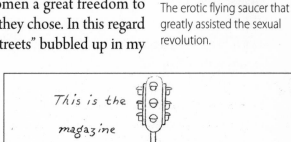

The erotic flying saucer that greatly assisted the sexual revolution.

sequences of hand-drawn stencils, and then, by the middle of 1964, Ted Berrigan had turned me on to a place that, without censorship, would burn stencils electronically from my drawings! Yay.

It was taken up by John Sinclair in his writings from Detroit and Ann Ar-

This is the magazine of street-fucking!

FUCK YOU/ a magazine of the arts

Drawing from a 1964 issue of *F.Y.*

bor, and he proposed it in the letterhead of his Trans-Love Energies.

FREE NEWSPAPER OF ROCK AND ROLL, DOPE, AND FUCKING IN THE STREETS

TRANS-LOVE ENERGIES
1510 HILL STREET
ANN ARBOR, 48104
(313) 769-2017

Dear Brothers & Sisters,

Later the Yippies (Youth International Party) issued a press release calling for a "festival of life" in Chicago during the Democratic National Convention of 1968. They announced that 500,000 people were going to make love in the parks and byways of the Windy City. It eventually dawned on me that balling in the streets was not an issue likely to prove important in the second half of the twentieth century. But it was an issue that burned brightly in my mind during the Bacchus days of 1963 and 1964.

A Long, Hot Summer of Drought

It was a hot summer, with a drought affecting the upstate water supplies for New York City. Miriam was very pregnant, and I was working weekends, as usual, at the cigar store. My intention was to enroll in graduate school at NYU and begin a journey toward a PhD, perhaps in Indo-European languages, or possibly prepare myself to become a professor of Greek. Things would intervene, such as my tardiness in actually applying for grad school and all the moil and mania of the New York underground during those groaning months.

I ran a series of readings that summer at Café Le Metro. I hand-drew stencils and printed flyers for the readings series on the Speed-o-Print on the bathtub cover at the Secret Location.

I had long forgiven Huncke for luring me into cashing those bad checks on his girlfriend's closed account the previous August. In fact, I taped his reading at Le Metro, the reel of which resides in my archive..

The author mc'd the summer reading series at Café Le Metro and also hand-drew the flyers on the Secret Location stencils

Lenny on Trial

On June 16 thirty-seven-year-old Lenny Bruce went on trial for obscenity at the courthouse at 100 Centre Street. His attorney was the well-known Ephraim London, assisted by Martin Garbus. Two days before the trial around one hundred demonstrators gathered to show Bruce support, but New York's mean, freedom-squelching side paid little attention.

Testifying for the prosecution were Herbert Ruhe from the Department of Licenses; John Fischer, editor of *Harper's*; Robert Sylvester of the *Daily News*; columnist Marya Mannes; right-wing professor Ernest Van den Haag; and several arresting officers. Testifying for the defense were Richard Gilman, drama critic for *Newsweek*; Dorothy Kilgallen, columnist and television panelist; Nat Hentoff, *Village Voice* columnist; Alan Morrison, editor of *Ebony*; Daniel Dodson, professor of comparative literature at Columbia; cartoonist Jules Feiffer; sociologist Herbert Gans; Forrest Johnson, a Presbyterian minister; and Jason Epstein, vice president of Random House.

On November 4 a three-judge panel, with Judge Creel dissenting, found Bruce and Howie Solomon (owner of the Cafe Au Go Go on Bleecker Street, where Bruce had performed) guilty. On December 21 repressionist ADA Richard Kuh got his way, and disgraced the Constitution in the process, when Judge Arthur Murtagh sentenced Lenny to four months in the workhouse.

Allen Ginsberg helped put together a big petition of intellectuals to help screen Bruce from the hounds, but to no avail.

Graduating from NYU

I had become friends with fellow Greek student Duncan McNaughton, who was soon to marry the secretary of the classics department, Eugenia Edelman, herself a graduate student in philosophy. McNaughton, the class whiz, was from Boston. After getting his degree in classics, McNaughton headed for graduate work in Oriental studies at Princeton and later received a PhD in English literature and poetics at SUNY Buffalo. In subsequent years McNaughton set up the Poetics Program at the New College of San Francisco and directed the program from its opening in 1965 until 1990. Eugenia became an environmental scientist working for the Environmental Protection Agency.

Around the final day of classes I turned McNaughton on to Olson's *Maximus Poems* and a few months later, not long after I had opened the Peace Eye Bookstore, gave him Pound's *Cantos*, even though I was harboring serious second thoughts about Pound. Nevertheless, Pound was a writer of an actual epic, and my studies in Homer, Hesiod, and Herodotus at NYU had fine-tuned my appreciation of epic—a passion that would blossom forth decades later in my own book-length verse projects, such as the nine-volume *America: A History in Verse*.

Meanwhile, I was trying to figure out how to make a living. My weekend gig at the cigar store on Times Square was not enough. Miriam was almost six months pregnant. We were still living in the Bronx apartment.

My Catalogs

In June I began putting out "rare book" catalogs. One day I went over to Allen Ginsberg's pad to scrounge some literary relics for my first catalog. (I'd heard of a signed Dylan Thomas dress shirt that'd shown up in someone's catalog.)

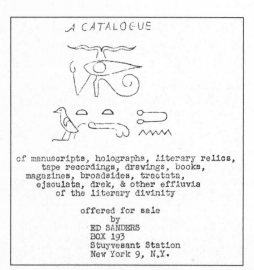

A CATALOGUE

of manuscripts, holographs, literary relics, tape recordings, drawings, books, magazines, broadsides, tractata, ejaculata, drek, & other effluvia of the literary divinity

offered for sale
by
ED SANDERS
BOX 193
Stuyvesant Station
New York 9, N.Y.

A. G. graciously donated his well-scooped cold cream jar by the bed and inscribed it as follows: "This is the jar of bona fide ass-wine or cock lubricant, into which I regularly plunged my hardened phallus to ease penetration of P. Orlovsky.... winter 1964," and signed it!

It became a famous literary relic, by word of literary mouth, but it was not the fastest-selling item in my catalog, most of whose items were snapped up by collectors and rare book libraries. I gave the jar later to photographer Richard Avedon during a Fugs photo shoot.

Allen also collected pubic hair from the famous and well placed, which I advertised in my catalog. Item numbers 42 and 43 sold briskly, helping thereby to relieve my summer of '64 impecuniosity. I put out a total of six catalogs during 1964 and 1965.

23. GINSBERG, ALLEN. Allen's Ponds Cold Cream jar with an inscription
in his hand which reads "This is the jar of bona fide ass-wine
or cock lubricant, into which I regularly plunged my hardened
phallos to ease penetration of the rosy A-hole of P. Orlovsky
and used vice-versa by P.O. on A.G. winter 1964 N.Y. (signed)
Allen Ginsberg." The inscription is on a strip of paper taped
around the jar. When we received this relic, there was still
A.G.'s cock-dent in the cream, but due to the πάντα ρεῖ scene,
it has fluxed out. What were thought to be arse flakes on
the rim have proven under microscopy to be tobacco hunks.
A literary document & relic never offered before in the
history of western civilisation........ $35.00

41. POUND, EZRA. A group of letters to a N.Y. poet. SEE ADDENDA
42. PUBIC, HAIR. "One conglomerate collection of pubic hair
contributed the night of Robert Duncan's reading in N.Y., N.Y.
cock hairs donated by - (signed) (with description) Allen
Ginsberg -extremely black curlies- Allen Katzman, Peter
Orlovsky, Paul Blackburn, Ronnie Zimardi, Kirby Doyle,
John Keys, Ted Berrigan, Harry Fainlight, & Ed Sanders."
Hair is contained in an envelope appended to the list and
descriptions....   15.00
43. PUBIC, HAIR. a packet of pubic hair gathered at a party
and described, verified, & listed for the lower east
side cock conspiracy by Allen Ginzap. Hair from Frank
Lima, Earl McGrath, Frank O'Hara, Joe Brainard, Joel
LeSeur, Aram Saroyan, Ron Padgett, Sandra Berrigan,
Arnold Weinstein, Edwin Denby, LeRoi Jones, Harry
Fainlight, G. Ungaretti (c'est Blanche, c'est Blanche)
Gerard Malanga, Robert LaVigne, Allen Ginsberg, Peter
Orlovsky, and others......... with descriptions....   15.00

Freedom Summer

Meanwhile, the newspapers were lit up with articles about Freedom Summer, which occurred from early June to late August. Love, persuasion, fortitude, and a thirst for justice came together when more than one thousand college students, most of them white and most from the North, went to Mississippi to work in forty-four local projects sponsored by the Student Non-Violent Coordinating Committee (SNCC). They lived in what were known as Freedom Houses or with local black families. Their main task was to register black voters and to work in what were known as Freedom Schools. It was exhilarating, thrilling, dangerous work that helped change a nation.

Friends from the Lower East Side went down during Freedom Summer. I was tempted but was graduating, working weekends at the Times Square cigar store, doing my films, and putting out numerous Mimeo Rev publications. Plus Miriam was six months pregnant.

Chaney, Goodman, Schwerner

On June 21 in Neshoba County, Mississippi, where klanmind ruled, a Freedom Summer volunteer named Andrew Goodman, twenty-one, went forth in a station wagon with James Chaney, twenty-one, and Michael Schwerner, twenty-four, to investigate the burning down of Mt. Zion Baptist Church near a town named Philadelphia. (The church had been arsoned by the Klan because it was to be a Freedom School.) They were arrested that afternoon on a traffic charge and held until nightfall and then released into the coils of klanmind. Their station wagon was found burned and charred near Bogue Chitto swamp the next day. Their bodies were found on August 4, buried in a fresh earthen dam six miles outside Philadelphia, Mississippi. Decades later I'm still overwhelmed by the image of the slender, nervous, newly wedded Rita Schwerner (shown in *Freedom Summer* by Doug McAdam) urging everyone to continue Freedom Summer even though the fate of her husband and his companions wouldn't be known for weeks.

Freedom Summer screamed in our minds in the Lower East Side. Crackers were arrested later in the year after the FBI offered a $30,000 reward, so two guys came forward to point out where the three had been buried. We followed the horror as best we could in the *New York Times* or the *New York Post* (then a liberal publication), but there were a lot of lacuna and dotted lines in our knowledge.

Confronting overt racist violence was difficult. Franklin Roosevelt couldn't get a federal antilynching law passed because of threats by Dixiecrats to kill New Deal legislation. I recalled how the Klan threatened to burn our church in Carthage, Tennessee, on the Nashville-DC peace march of '62. We were saved only by being hauled off to the safety of the local National Guard armory.

Despair, an Anthology

I was feeling down down down after the murders of the Freedom Summer workers, so I decided to publish an anthology called *Despair*, which came out in July 1964.

With despair as a theme, I had very little trouble attracting quality poems, especially from Ted Berrigan. Despair was in the air.

DESPAIR
poems to come down by

TED BERRIGAN

PAUL BLACKBURN

JOHN KEYS

AL FOWLER

HARRY FAINLIGHT

ED SANDERS

SZABO

DESPAIR
the magazine
of WAD-TECHNIQUE

a QUIVERING PARANOIA publication

Table of Contents, *Despair.*

THREE STAGES OF DESPAIR

1.

abcd efghi jk lmno

pq rstu vw xy z.

2.

ABCD EFGHI JK LMNO

PQ RSTU VW XY Z.

3.

Two purple shadows on the snow.

Ted Berrigan

Dear Ed

    went last night to visit X, who's mother
had come from Y to see him. Also his wife's mother
and his wife's luscious 17 year old sister. Evening
proved to be a horrible fiasco, as X's mother declared
"nothing is sacred around here" through weepings, and
me & baby & Sandra silently filed out. Since then I have
been reduced to abject despair, realizing that my just-
ification will not occur on this earth.

    The enclosed
poem(s), which oozed gently from my moist rancid brow
in cynical homage to my despair may be suitable for
your "Despair" number.

    Yours in pain,

    Ted.

PS: any mescalin?

The Civil Rights Act of 1964

Johnson signed the act on television on July 2, confiding to his aide Bill Moyers that the law had "delivered the South to the Republican Party during your life and mine." Racistcrats and conservatives had tried to begrunge the bill with over five hundred amendments and had filibustered, too, but with no success. The act set up the Equal Employment Opportunity Commission to help prevent discrimination in employment on the basis of race, religion, or sex. Many, if not most, restaurants and hotels complied right away. *It was a moment for Johnson and a moment for America.*

The War Starting
to Impinge

On July 11 Johnson lifted one of his pet beagles by the ears during a session with guests on the White House lawn. His action offended some of us at the time, and we started calling him Ear Grab. I satirized Mr. Ear Grab a few months later in an editorial in *F.Y.* In a well-known television commercial during those months a child called out to his mother, "More Park sausages, Ma!"

The Republican Convention

To the historic Cow Palace in San Francisco—built as a public works project by the New Deal—came the Party of Lincoln, now seized by right-wing railers like something concocted by Jonathan Swift. On Tuesday July 14, Dwight Eisenhower spoke to big applause, after which there was a ninety-minute reading of the platform. Then Governor Nelson Rockefeller of New York came to the mike (it was already pretty late) to propose some amendments to the platform. He was given five minutes to argue for a resolution against extremism (he had in mind the vicious nuttery of the John Birch Society) and another five for civil rights.

The convention had been almost totally seized by nuts, who shrieked their hatred at the centrist Republican. As if he'd read the futurist manifesto *The Pleasure of Being Booed,* the governor bucked the boos and threw them back. He seemed to be enjoying the rudeness. "This is still a free country, ladies and gentlemen," he said, but the wailing wing nuts wouldn't let him speak, forcing the governor's allotted five minutes to stretch to fifteen minutes of televised hiss.

GET YOUR PILES OUT OF VIETNAM !!

A FUCK YOU/ POSITION PAPER:
operation Fuck-in.

The Johnson   touch

" more dead gooks, ma "

IT makes us puke green monkey shit to contemplate Johnson's war in Vietnam. Lyndon Baines is squirting the best blood of America into a creep scene. Kids are "gook-bricking" in Asia without thought, without reason, without law. One has to reach in to the most pustular bugger lore to grope up sufficient scatologica with which to describe this cranky whale blubber fart-whiff. Surrounded by creeps, killers, & unknown butt-hooks whom history will puke upon, Johnson oozes onward. The citizens of the world are having the Great Fear zapped at them by a bunch of meshugahs.

THIS is addressed to the squack-hawk space cadet furburger grope multitudes who may freak upon this position paper. Time is now to call a FUCK-IN! Clearly a demonstration of peace by tender fornicating love-bodies will be a group screw zapped around the world, certainly the most interesting demonstration in the history of Western civilization. The fuzz might be able to stop the demonstration but there'd be many a tit hanging free, cocks thrust out of zippers, naked writhing bodies, & mouths in tender places, before they'd do so. On the next page you will find A DECLARATION OF CONSCIENCE CALLING FOR A FUCK-IN AGAINST WAR CREEPS. Please sign it. THE WEIGHT OF THE WORLD IS LOVE!!!! GROPE FOR PEACE !!

Anti–Vietnam War ad showing Mr. Grab.

Goldwater's Famous Speech

Barry Goldwater no doubt believed he was tying the casket of history with the threads of right-wing raillery in his July 16 acceptance speech, which he ended with words far-famed in their era: "I would remind you that extremism in the defense of liberty is no vice and let me remind you also that moderation in the pursuit of justice is no virtue!" This was true enough in certain limited circumstances, but not from the nuke-friendly lips of someone who'd voted against the Test Ban Treaty and the civil rights law and who wanted to resume cancer-spreading open-air nuclear bomb testing. Blinded by folly, the hissing right was sure the nation would vote a quick passage from New Frontier to Old Fortress. The hissers were wrong, for the moment.

Riots in Harlem

On July 16 a police lieutenant named Tom Gilligan shot a fifteen-year-old black kid named James Powell. The lieutenant later said that Powell had drawn a knife. Then on July 18 the Congress of Racial Equality (CORE) held a protest rally at 125th Street and Seventh Avenue. Afterward a group went to the local precinct and soon began hurling bottles and trash. When the Tactical Patrol Force was called in, a riot ensued, complete with what store owners hated very much: widespread looting.

We were thankful the riots didn't reach the Lower East Side.

Trouble in the Gulf of Tonkin

By the summer of 1964 Lyndon Johnson and his generals were looking for an excuse to spill more blood and drop more bombs. They had a resolution, already written months in advance, giving the president the power to expand the war at whim.

As *The Pentagon Papers* later revealed, the South Vietnamese that summer badly wanted to attack cross-border into North Vietnam and also bomb the North. The new U.S. ambassador to Vietnam, Maxwell Taylor, had been authorized to tell the Vietnamese that the United States was considering attacking North Vietnam. Such as attack "might begin, for example, if the pressure from dissident South Vietnamese factions became too great."

The chance to begin a full-scale war came in early August. The Defense Department reported on August 2 that North Vietnamese PT boats had fired torpedoes and shells at the destroyer *Maddox* while it was out "on a routine patrol" in the Gulf of Tonkin.

But the *Maddox* patrol was not routine. Rather, it was on an electronic spying caper and was in Vietnamese territorial waters—and no torpedoes were fired at it. It was not until Daniel Ellsberg released *The Pentagon Papers* in 1971 that the public learned the Gulf of Tonkin attack had been a fabrication of the military-industrial surrealists. Conferring with Allen Ginsberg, I had the presence of mind to write a letter on August 6, 1964, to President Johnson, mailing it to him at the White House:

Dear President Johnson,

Allen Ginsberg and I, poets and residents of the lower east side of New York City, were ardently pursuing a policy of persuading our fellow poets, artists, novelists, and musicians to register to vote in the coming election in order to enhance your chances of serving the country (and the world) for the next four years as president.

However, the rather insensitive methods with which you dealt with the problem of small boat attacks from North Vietnam cause us to ponder whether it is still morally demonstrable that you maintain a superior position over that of Barry Goldwater.

For instance, formal diplomatic protests were not made to the North Vietnam government as a warning against further harassment, before you decided to destroy those coastal marine positions. Perhaps the worst aspect of the entire situation is the tacit assumption that the American citizenry could not be supplied with more information before you ordered countermeasures. To inform your constituency that you are engaging in an act of war *just as* you are explaining to those to whom you are ultimately responsible, why you are doing it, is right in the line with the methods of an extremist.

No official reasons were given by the United States as to why the North Vietnamese were hitting against U.S. ships. Was it in reprisal against South Vietnamese naval intelligence raids into the North? Was it a paranoiac response on the part of the North Vietnamese against the presence of the Seventh Fleet?

Certainly we cannot ourselves mount a campaign to place you into office without some clarification of this entire situation. We can, perhaps, persuade some 1500–2000 voters of the necessity of voting for the Democratic candidate in 1964. These are *new* voters, those who have for one reason or another not voted in past elections. However, these voters are highly sensitive and articulate, those from whom you could expect an audible support in their dealings with the mass media.

We, as citizens and voters, must be informed in greater detail as to the complexities of our foreign policy. We hope that you may find time to issue statements in depth that spell out point by point the intricacies of the American positions with regard to Vietnam.

Please may we have some of your time in these regards? We, the artists, poets, writers of New York's lower east side await your reply.

Respectfully yours, Ed Sanders, Box 193, Stuyvesant Station, New York 9, New York.

I never received any kind of reply, and the day after I mailed the letter to Mr. Ear Grab, the Vietnam War, in effect, began.

The Gulf of Tonkin Resolution

On August 7 the U.S. Congress in joint session voted the Gulf of Tonkin Resolution, which gave Johnson full powers to stomp down North Vietnam on behalf of the Southeast Asia Treaty Organization (a rubber-stamp umbrella group). Thus the war in Vietnam expanded to North Vietnam based on a lie. Only Senators Wayne Morse of Oregon and Ernest Gruening of Alaska voted against it.

Letter to Olson

On the very day the joint session of Congress foisted the Gulf of Tonkin Resolution on an unsuspecting America, I wrote Charles Olson in Gloucester, Massachusetts, enclosing the manuscript for what would become my first "big" book of poetry, *Peace Eye*. I was still very insecure about it. "I'd like thee to take a look at these poems," I wrote to my mentor, "and give your thunder a roar or two to see if you still think there's a book there. . . . If it is possible to use glyphs, I enclose a full set of drawings corresponding to the ones in the poems. You are kind beyond shrieks to consider a book of poems."

At that time I had no idea that Olson himself would wind up writing an introduction to *Peace Eye*, which I was dedicating to my wife, Miriam. One idea was to have poet John Wieners write an introduction.

In the same letter I also offered to have the team of volunteer typists who typed for my projects help Olson type up, from handwritten versions, a new book of his Maximus poems. I noted that I'd heard from Harvey Brown that "there seems to be some problems in regard to the latest Maximus manuscript. We have here in the Lower East Side a team of typists more than willing to get to help prepare a Maximus manu! Let us know if there is ANYTHING we can do for you. Send the manu with instructions and we'll prepare sparkling copies for thee."

The Democratic Convention

I rode with Allen Ginsberg and Peter Orlovsky down to Atlantic City on August 24 to demonstrate on behalf of the Mississippi Freedom Democratic Party (MFDP) at the Democratic National Convention. The demonstration was a hint of the turbulence that would engulf the Democratic Party, trapped in the throes of the American military's thirst for war, four years later in Chicago.

Allen had one of his famous hand-painted posters, 24" x 36," with this message:

> DOWN WITH DEATH
> WAR IS *BLACK MAGIC*
> BELLY FLOWERS
> TO
> NORTH *AND* SOUTH VIETNAM

Adorning the poster were two flowers with faces and a hand-drawn sun and a moon.

The outside world was starting to impinge on our little Lower East Side Zone of Revolution.

The Mississippi Freedom Democratic Party

I was following, as best I could, the ups and downs of the MFDP, which led a heroic effort that year to become the actual delegates from Mississippi at the Democratic Convention in Atlantic City. It wasn't easy to discern, in the leaflets and articles I was reading, what was really going on.

SNCC had organized the party at a meeting in Jackson on April 26. The MFDP ran candidates in the June 2 Democratic primary for senator and for three House seats: Fannie Lou Hamer, Victoria Gray, John Houston, and the Reverend John Cameron.

They lost but then filed petitions to be on the November ballot as Independents. The Board of Elections laughed them away. Then the party decided to conduct a mock election process to challenge the Mississippi delegation at the upcoming Democratic National Convention.

They freedom-registered 80,000 voters; held mock precinct, county, and district caucuses; and, on August 6, held a state convention that sent to Atlantic City an MFDP delegation headed by Fannie Lou Hamer to try to unseat the racist Mississippi delegation. They were counting on LBJ.

LBJ wanted to sabotage the Mississippi Freedom Democratic Party's challenge of the all-white Mississippi delegation. There was to be a vote of the convention credentials committee. Martin King stood fully in support of the MFDP, while LBJ's forces assisted the all-whites in a move that smells to this day like rotting tofu.

Meanwhile, the FBI was wiretapping King's room at the Claridge Hotel in Atlantic City and feeding the transcripts on the nonce for Tonkin-hubris'd Johnson to read, helping him to shove his will as the Freedom Party was defeated.

It has been pointed out that many of the white Mississippians whose delegate seats Johnson preserved would support Goldwater in the fall. Also to be considered: Lyndon Johnson's thirst to micromanage an engulfing war, thinking he was FDR in the Map Room in 1943 studying the position of World War II troops and battlefronts on wall-sized maps.

It was the meanness of Guns in Dallas. The meanness of four children bombed in Birmingham. The meanness of right-wing nuts. A Mean Streak that smeared itself across the skies.

Getting Invited to Literary Soirées

I began to get invited to literary parties, such as those thrown by Ted Wilentz in his apartment above the 8th Street Bookshop. I met writers such as Norman Mailer, Gunter Grass, Norman Podhoretz, and Gil Sorrentino at these literary soirées. An example is a note from Gil, who sent poems that I published in *F.Y.*: "Dear Ed, OK. Here are three poems from *The Perfect Fiction*, the works that we talked about @ the Wilentz's the other night. I hope you like them—if you don't, don't bother to return them please. My best to you—Gil."

Note from Gil Sorrentino.

Parties at the Dakota

I also started getting invited to Panna Grady's parties at the Dakota, a landmark New York City building, constructed circa 1881–1884 and located at 1 West Seventy-second Street just off Central Park. Its brick and sandstone walls are adorned with balconies, corner pavilions, and terra-cotta panels and moldings. It has a steeply pitched slate and copper roof featuring ornate railings, stepped dormers, finials, and pediments.

Panna was a wealthy supporter of writers, and at a gathering in the late summer/early fall of 1964 for novelist Gunter Grass I was chatting with her and suggested she expand her considerable help from novelists to poets. I mentioned Charles Olson as a great American genius worthy of her support. My suggestion bore fruit a year and a half later.

That was the party where I met Norman Mailer. Holding his hands up, jutting from his body in a kind of sparring position, he addressed me as if he were boxing. "You're the guy that puts out *Fuck You*. I have a poem you can publish." He sent it a few days later, a poem titled "Executioner's Song," and I published it in the "God" issue.

The God Issue

All through August and some of September I produced the God issue of *Fuck You/ A Magazine of the Arts*, volume 5, number 7, with a beautiful cover by Robert LaVigne.

I gathered some brilliant works by Charles Olson, John Wieners, Allen G., Robert Duncan, William Burroughs, Robert Kelly, Carl Solomon, Gregory Corso, Philip Whalen, Michael McClure, Judith Malina, Paul Blackburn, Al Fowler, Philip Lamantia, Norman Mailer, and others. I was proud of the issue.

The back-page image featured glyphs of my current passions: freedom to use

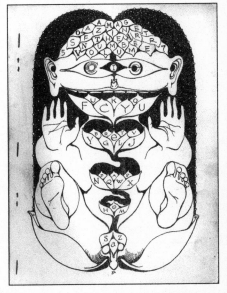

The God issue.

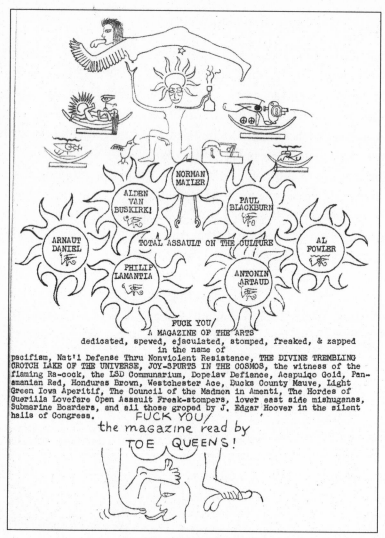

"God" issue Table of Contents.

magic mushrooms, hookahs, the Egyptian scarab, pot, the Lawrencian Boat of Death, the peace sign, spurting dongs, hypodermic needles, and Peace Eye and its Wayward Tongue. A little too much of the needles, of course, but it was a parcel of what was actually going on in the Lower East Side in the underground.

One feature of the issue was a "position paper" that made proposals regarding the crackdown by various New York City bureaucracies on underground movies, poetry readings in coffeehouses, and public performances. The Department of Licenses, in particular, had raised its cudgels to censor the avant-garde.

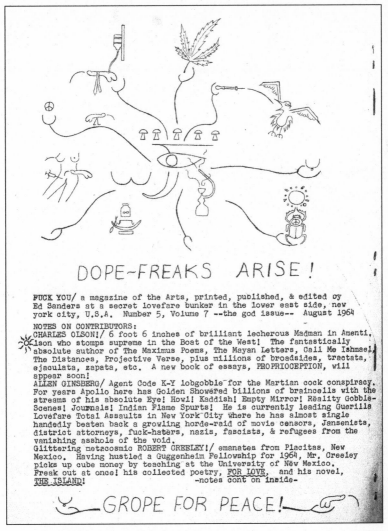

DOPE-FREAKS ARISE!

FUCK YOU/ a magazine of the Arts, printed, published, & edited by
Ed Sanders at a secret lovefare bunker in the lower east side, new
york city, U.S.A. Number 5, Volume 7 --the god issue-- August 1964

NOTES ON CONTRIBUTORS:
CHARLES OLSON!/ 6 foot 6 inches of brilliant lecherous Madman in Amenti,
Olson who stomps supreme in the Boat of the West! The fantastically
absolute author of The Maximus Poems, The Mayan Letters, Call Me Ishmael,
The Distances, Projective Verse, plus millions of broadsides, tractata,
ejaculata, zapata, etc. A new book of essays, PROPRIOCEPTION, will
appear soon!
ALLEN GINSBERG/ Agent Code K-Y lobgobble for the Martian cock conspiracy.
For years Apollo here has Golden Showered billions of braincells with the
streams of his absolute Eye! Howl! Kaddish! Empty Mirror! Reality Gobble-
Scenes! Journals! Indian Flame Spurts! He is currently leading Guerilla
Lovefare Total Assaults in New York City where he has almost single
handedly beaten back a growling horde-raid of movie censors, Jansenists,
district attorneys, fuck-haters, nazis, fascists, & refugees from the
vanishing asshole of the void.
Glittering metacosmic ROBERT CREELEY!/ emanates from Placitas, New
Mexico. Having hustled a Guggenheim Fellowship for 1964, Mr. Creeley
picks up cube money by teaching at the University of New Mexico.
Freak out at once! his collected poetry, FOR LOVE, and his novel,
THE ISLAND! -notes cont on inside-

GROPE FOR PEACE!

"God" issue back-page image.

I was beginning to hone and polish my philosophy of the scholar-activist, utilizing my emphatic Fuck You Press writing style. I wanted my position paper to be heeded. I interviewed Ginsberg and placed portions of the interview in the position paper.

It began:

Shriek! Shriek! The Goon Squads are loose! We are motherfucking tired of the brickout of books, movies, theatre groups, dope freaks, Times Square gobble scenes, poetry readings, night club acts, etc. in New York. The Department of Licenses, the freaks in the various prosecutors' offices, the nazis, the

fascists, et al., have joined psychoses for a Goon Stomp. Poets have been bricked out of their readings—Lenny Bruce puked from MacDougal street—Theatres raided—Actors freaked—Grove Press zapped by creeps! Coffee houses harassed—film makers censored—dreamy eyed loiterers & hustlers seized & humiliated—& even the Times Square dance hall scenes have been stomped! Their motives, particularly those of the prosecutors and the lawyers of the Dept of Licenses, seem to be a) self-aggrandizement, focusing the yes of the press on themselves in order to groove up politically, b) the whenever-I-hear-the-word-culture-I-want-to-reach-for-my-gun syndrome, & c) the low budget, low payoff scene. We don't give a frozen rat dick how brilliant Police Commissioner Murphy is or how effective the Supreme Court is, or even how liberal Mayor Wagner is, when all over N.Y. we are getting slimed off the set! If a city or state official lacks a very liberal sensitivity toward sex, cocksucking, dope & welfare, then the fuckhate should be zapped off the set. It's hard not to be bitter against these ... "vice crusaders farhting through silk" waving their penny whistle censor's flags. The lowliest shoe shine hustler creep mishugana on times square is worth more to a society than all the Calvinist lawyers in Department of Licenses, all state film censors, all the gelded or armored-over fugitives from the vanishing asshole of the void!

I was very revved up.
"Resistance to the Goon Squads," I complained,

has been sporadic & sometimes effective, but more often the poets & artists have adopted the Cockroach Retreat. . . . However, Allen Ginsberg, with his golden gift tongue of Thoth, in high level behind-the-scenes conferences, by infinite phone calls, manipulations, freaks, fucks & gropes, has managed to cool the scene for poetry readings in restaurants & coffee houses & has rallied support in the city council and (Democratic) Reform movement toward rewriting New York's oppressive coffee house law. His Lenny Bruce petition, signed by everyone from Lower East Side dope moguls to the Richard Burtons, is a fantastic collage of a new commitment to artistic freedom.

The language in the position paper was a bit overblown, but there WAS a climate of oppression from around 1964, in the administration of Mayor Robert Wagner, up into the early years of Mayor John Lindsay, who took office in 1966. It was the liberal and culturally attuned John Lindsay, in my opinion, who played a big role in the ebbing of the censorship and oppression in the Great City. But not in 1964, when the campaign against culture was in full ax.

I went on in the position paper of '64 to present some advice from Ginsberg on "Guerrilla Lovefare" tactics. Most of all Allen Ginsberg warned against emanating hostility. ("If you charge the Soft-Machine directly, the Machine will be directly charged by your hate," Burroughs had written.)

When asked about tactics in street demonstrations where the Goon Squads have blown their cool, Ginsberg replied:

> If you don't emanate hostility, the chances of being noted by Goon Squads is lowered considerably but not entirely.
>
> Carry movie cameras & tape machines to protect yourself from official undeserved Goon Squad violence. If you're occupied taking pictures of the cop hitting you it's self-evident court proof that the cop should be bounced from his job.
>
> I still think *Gentle Mass Movements* on Times Square could end the Vietnam War. (Violence gives them an excuse to ban demonstrations.)
>
> Every time I go out on a march, the adrenaline runs through my body making me afraid. I can handle it if all I've got to face is the hostility of the cops, but the hostility rising out of the middle of the mob I'm in completely confuses me so that I just want to run away.

True words then, true words now.
Then I asked him about a "Ginsbergian Blueprint for Resistance."

He replied, "Register & vote":

Come on to your representatives like a self-righteous citizen, it seems to pack weight. If you're abused, write a clear self-righteous citizen's letter to the newspapers, send a copy to the local authorities & to the mayor. Either get a personal lawyer or get connections with some specific legal aid body or get the number of a lawyer & cover your activities in advance by knowing the laws & their legal implications. If you smoke pot, suck cock, shoot junk, march in the street, or talk dirty, know what the legal ground rules are, & protect yourself in advance.

All the energy that goes into injustice collecting, vague cultural complaints, putdown sneery conversations, & bad poetry could, without psychic loss, be switched over to lucid concrete self-protective or mutual-protective action. 5 minutes spent looking at the technicalities of the Stop & Frisk law are as charming as an hour's romantic griping about it in paranoiac bathrooms.

I was beginning to learn organizing principles that would help me for the rest of my existence on Gaia.

My friend novelist Doc Humes recommended what I called the "25 x 25" plan.

"You start," I wrote,

with a list of 25 city officials, 25 people each calling a few a day on an issue— makes the appearance of a phone flood of 625 irate citizens! If it's the FBI that's bugging you, set up an FBI newsletter & tell all, or a Dept of Licenses newsletter, etc.—document your story. Get ALL the facts. Get a press list & hand out press releases. Join hands with sympathetic reporters & news outlets—figure out *exact* program! Onward ATTACKED BY CREEPS! On the offensive.... We defy all censors, fuzz, goon squads! We're going to eat at their foundations, weaken them, lessen them, most of all we're going to stir their armored-over repressed psyches with the hot breath of our love.

My position paper ended with my usual call for freedom to ball in the street "or anywhere under the Rays of Ra" and for legalization of pot, plus I took a stand on magic mushrooms: "And what's all this ... about 'clinical investigations and calibrated study' of the hallucinogens! Turn the flip-mixtures loose! Why should a bunch of psychologists hog all the highs? FREEDOM FOR HALLUCINOGENS!!"

The paper also called, sensibly enough, for a "ten year timetable for fucking & sucking in the movies." And then this futuristic exhortation: "When THE FEELIES arrive we MUST have the social conditions set up for audience film-fucking."

I closed with a shout toward the Repressionists:

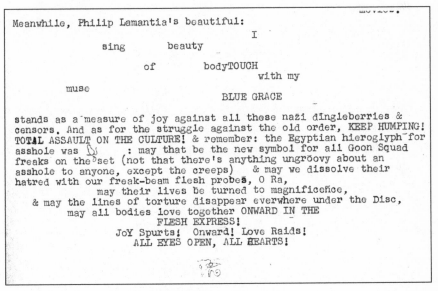

```
Meanwhile, Philip Lamantia's beautiful:
                                 I
         sing        beauty
              of         bodyTOUCH
                                 with my
      muse
                         BLUE GRACE

stands as a measure of joy against all these naži dingleberries &
censors. And as for the struggle against the old order, KEEP HUMPING!
TOTAL ASSAULT ON THE CULTURE! & remember: the Egyptian hieroglyph for
asshole was       : may that be the new symbol for all Goon Squad
freaks on the set (not that there's anything ungroovy about an
asshole to anyone, except the creeps)   & may we dissolve their
hatred with our freak-beam flesh probes, O Ra,
              may their lives be turned to magnificence,
    & may the lines of torture disappear everwhere under the Disc,
         may all bodies love together ONWARD IN THE
                    FLESH EXPRESS!
         JoY Spurts!  Onward!  Love Raids!
            ALL EYES OPEN, ALL HEARTS!
```

The finale of the position paper.

It was the only time in the history of Western civilization that the actual Egyptian hieroglyph for asshole was used in an editorial essay.

Applying to Grad School a Bit Too Late

That summer of '64 I applied to grad school, but my application, I was informed, was received too late for the fall academic year. I liked the faculty at NYU, including Bluma Trell. And I also dug the erudite Professor Frank Peters. Plus I'd taken a graduate level course in Mycenaean (Linear B) under Professor J. Alexander Kerns. In addition, the classics department had allowed me access to its papyrus laboratory, which had a number of excellent books on gnostic amulets, Greco-Egyptian issues, and the like.

My screwup in registering for grad school too late made a huge change in my life's course. If I'd applied a few weeks earlier, I could have safely been on a voyage to becoming a classics professor.

Nevertheless, even though I was not a matriculated student, I took part in a production of Euripides' *Trojan Women*, put on by the NYU Classics Club and directed by Professor Bluma Trell. I was Menelaus, husband of Helen, the launcher of many ships. Also in the cast was Carly Simon, soon to be a recording star.

A Cigar to Phil Whalen

Meanwhile, I came home from work at the cigar store after my shift was over just in time to call the taxi service we had listed on the wall by the phone. Miriam was just about to give birth to Deirdre, at Bronx Lebanon Hospital. It was early in the morning on September 4, 1964.

A few days later I sent a pink-wrapped cigar to poet Phil Whalen in San Francisco! Whalen had gone to Reed College with Gary Snyder and Lew Welch and now was a key person on the San Francisco literary scene. His poems in Don Allen's epoch-making anthology, *The New American Poetry*, astounded my generation. One thing I miss from those years is a friendship by mail with Phil, who replied to my letter with the cigar celebrating Deirdre's birth.

Phil enclosed various literary relics for my catalog, including some drawings and a poster for a poetry reading by Whalen, Snyder, and Welch. Phil also wanted me to run an announcement in *Fuck You/ A Magazine of the Arts* for a patron to send him an electric organ and the Schirmer complete Bach organ works, which I did.

"Please specify," Whalen further wrote, "that the organ have 2

123 Beaver St. San Francisco 94114

Dear Ed,

Many congratulations & love & welcome Miss Dierdre in 90 times 9! Enclosed are relics, fourure de con &c.

I hope the great Godfuck will arrive soon, before I'm holed off to Amida's Great western Lylypond.

Be sure that you send notice to

Mr. ROGER E. STODDARD
CURATOR, HARRIS COLLECTION
BROWN UNIVERSITY LIBRARY
BROWN UNIVERSITY
PROVIDENCE, R.I. 02912

because he might possibly be interested in glomming the enclosed posters & announcements dealing with OUR RENAISSANCE { creak. creak.} He's already bought copies of our broadsides.

Please specify that the ORGAN have 2 manuals & a 32° note pedal keyboard. The manuals and a 32-note pedal keyboard. Manufacturers preferred are Conn, Baldwin, or Allen. Gulbransen is no good, an unreliable transistor system not yet perfected—and they run a non-union shop. Wurlitzer is unacceptable; their machine is shoddily built and don't tune right."

```
adv ★ Bach scene for Phil Whalen ★ adv-
From a letter to the fuck you/ Editor-
ial Board:"...As I told Alvin Ginsberg
& Jonathan Williams & all the others
who have inquired,: Find me a patron
to send me an electric organ & the 8
volume set of the Complete Organ Works
of J.S. Bach (G. Schirmer & Co., N.Y.C.
). I think it's much easier to get
THINGS than money in USA... & I like
to make music, & I'm too old to run
up & down North Beach any more, I stay
home all the time." Support genius!
      Freak out an organ!
adv ★ Phil ★ Organ ★ Whalen ★ Bach ★ adv ★
```

Charles Olson's Introduction to My Book

To my lasting gratitude Charles Olson wrote an introduction to my book *Peace Eye.*

Ed Sanders' language
   Advances
     in a direction of production
     which probably isn't even guessed
     at; and which symbols & allegories
     are more evidences of than the more
     usual, and recent, and principally existent
     since the use of a new metric by Sappho &
     Alcaeus only. Prior production—from 550 BC
      back—conceivably more interesting now
as aid and abetment to help recognition of
forms & inventions "weak" only because
the size of the substance needed
for them is like, say, the
      earth. That is, it takes the earth
      to make a feather fall.
      Charles Olson—
      Wednesday, October 7th, 1964

The Folklore Center

Israel Young, who ran the Folklore Center, a cultural center frequented by many folksingers and musicians, became a friend. I used his mimeograph to print an issue of *Fuck You*. I knew him as a great supporter of the avant-garde, and of course there was his connection to fast-rising Bob Dylan. Izzy had been in the group picketing Columbia Records when it censored Dylan's "Talking John Birch Society Blues" in 1963.

The Folklore Center was at 110 MacDougal Street, on the block between West Third and Bleecker that contained the Gaslight, the Kettle of Fish, the San Remo Bar (dear to the Beats and the *Partisan Review* crowd), Rienzi's coffee shop, the Fat Black Pussy Cat, Minetta's Tavern, the Player's Theater, the Night Owl, and Manny Roth's Café Wha (where Jimi Hendrix would be discovered).

Johnson's Victory

In general, there was Great Exhilaration that Lyndon Johnson won the race for the presidency. We had no idea of the torture that the flawed LBJ was to inflict on the soul of a great nation.

Meanwhile, Kerouac Folding the Flag on Park Avenue

Much of the '60s had to do with what to do about the American flag.

Ken Kesey had purchased a six-acre farm near La Honda, California, from the money he'd made from *One Flew over the Cuckoo's Nest*. It was the time that Kesey and his pals, called the Merry Pranksters, began holding Acid Tests. The Pranksters arrived in New York City in the wildly painted bus named Further, driven by none other than Neal Cassady. It meant something that *On the Road*'s Dean Moriarty—Neal Cassady—was Further's driver.

Allen Ginsberg quickly went to see Neal. Then Neal and Allen drove in the psychedelic bus to pick up Jack Kerouac at his house in Northport, Long Island, and the bus, sporting the banner "A Vote for Goldwater Is a Vote for Fun," brought him back to meet Kesey at a Park Avenue apartment. The Pranksters had put an American flag on the back of the living room couch in Jack's honor. However, Kerouac, spotting the flag in the hectic apartment full of Merry Pranksters, some making home movies, was disconcerted, and he carefully folded the American flag and set it aside.

The Pranksters had placed the flag on the couch deliberately, in a reference to Kerouac's character Sal in *On The Road*, who as part of his duties working as a guard in a military barracks accidentally puts an American flag upside down on a sixty-foot pole. "Do you know you can go to jail for putting the American flag upside down on a government pole?" a fellow guard warned him. Sal replied, "'Upside down?' I was horrified; of course I hadn't realized it."

What to do about the flag?—an archetypal '60s question.

Locating Peace Eye

Right around the time that Kerouac was folding the American flag in a swank Park Avenue apartment, I was busy looking for a storefront to rent in the Lower East Side. I wanted to open the Peace Eye Bookstore. I was a new father, had family obligations, and needed to have a source of income beyond weekends at the Times Square cigar store, plus whatever my rare book catalogs engendered. Selling books and literary relics was remunerative enough that I decided to open a bookstore and "scrounge lounge." I could put my mimeograph machine there and create a cultural facility as well.

I found a perfect store at 383 East Tenth Street, between Avenues B and C, just a few hundred feet away from my favorite bars, the Annex and Stanley's. It had been a Kosher meat market. I signed a two-year lease for Peace Eye on November 10, 1964. The first year the rent was $50 a month, which went to $60 for the second year. The owner was something called "The Sixth Street Investing Corporation." I went to its offices at 405 Lexington Avenue to sign the lease. I must say, the owner rarely intervened, however controversial the Peace Eye Bookstore became during its two years on East Tenth.

Tuli Kupferberg, Beat hero, lived next door, above the Lifschutz Wholesale Egg Store, with his longtime mate (later wife), Sylvia Topp.

Tuli Kupferberg

I met Tuli Kupferberg outside the Charles Theater on Avenue B back in 1962. He was selling his magazine *Birth* to those who were attending the screening. He offered to let me publish a poem. I'd seen his picture in a number of books. I learned a little bit later that he was the guy who'd "jumped off the Brooklyn Bridge," as described in *Howl*. (It was actually the Manhattan Bridge.) I later asked him why. He replied, "I wasn't being loving enough."

He didn't like to talk about the jump. Later he commented in the book called the *Annotated Howl*:

> In the Spring of 1945 at the age of 21, full of youthful angst, depression over the war and other insanities and at the end of a disastrous love affair, I went over the side of the Manhattan Bridge.
>
> I was picked up tenderly by the crew of a passing tug and taken to Gouveneur Hospital. My injuries were relatively slight (fracture of a transverse spinal process) but enough to put me in a body cast.
>
> In the hospital wards I met other suicide attempters less fortunate than me: one who wd walk on crutches and one who wd never walk again.
>
> Throughout the years I have been annoyed many times by "O did you really jump off the Brooklyn Bridge?" as if that was a great accomplishment. Remember I was a *failure* at the attempt.
>
> "Had I succeeded there wd have been 3 less wonderful beings (my children) in the world, no Fugs, and a few missing good poems & songs, & some people (including some lovely women, *hey!*) who might have missed my company.

We were very glad he failed at the jump. The world would have missed such poetic classics as "Nothing," "The Ten Commandments," "Morning Morning," "CIA Man," "Einstein Never Wore Socks," and "When the Mode of the Music Changes."

Bard Ted Berrigan wrote something profound about Tuli for a reading Tuli gave at Israel Young's Folklore Center:

An Appreciation
Despite the fact that he is very wise, and in
spite of his sweet and Saintly nature, Tuli
Kupferberg is a truly marvelous poet. He is
probably the first and last of a disappearing
breed of Wandering Hebrew minstrels, a street

singer who shambles sadly through the slums of
the world dispensing love, joy and jokes
indiscriminately. That's what I call true
poetry.

Tuli was born on September 28, 1923, on Cannon Street, in the far-down-there Lower East Side (a street mostly torn down later to make room for one of those big housing projects). Tuli recounted his heritage:

Both of my parents came from Galicia, which was a province in northeastern Ostertreich-Hungary—Austria-Hungary before World War I. They were both Galicianas. My mother came from the Ukrainian section and he came from the Polish section. They met here. They are all Hasidim. So the Hasidic movement was all over Poland and Russia and Hungary. So, they were brought up in Hasidic households, but both of them broke, eventually, once they came to America. They met here. One must have come in 1905 and one in 1909, I'm not sure.

His father ran a sequence of luggage shops in New York City, and Yiddish was spoken at home. "My father wanted, like a lot of his other relatives, wanted to open a store or a little factory. One of my uncles had a luggage factory. So my father opened luggage stores in three places during the Depression, and failed three times."

Later in life Tuli's dad, as Tuli recalled,

became a clothing machine operator, in men's clothing. The union eventually became the Amalgamated Clothing Workers of America. And he was involved in the early strikes; something that he didn't even know I would be interested in, but I found out later—the bosses were Jews, and the workers were Jews, and it was sweatshop. The way American clothing is now produced all over the world, that was done here, you worked under terrible (conditions). And the bosses also hired thugs to break up union meetings, and so on. My father got arrested and beaten up a few times.

As a child Tuli liked the music he heard at his parents' social club:

They had klezmer music at these things. I would go as a little kid, that high maybe [motions with his hand]. Five years old, I remember. I remember the music, and I would stand watching the musicians, that was the best part of the wedding. There would be, like, one every week. The music really fascinated me. They were mostly dance melodies. There was a huge—there was Yiddish radio that I listened to up until my early 20s, which came on every Sunday, which had a wide variety; like the *Jewish Daily Forward* had these Jewish intellectuals analyzing—they had an intellectual program, they would analyze the news, then there were advertisements, and then [laughs] there was a clothing store—I remember some of the advertisements on it. I'll sing one of them for you.

He sang:

Joe and Paul Estora Bargain Niggen
Joe and Pal Minkenna Bargain kriegen
A Suit A Coat A Gabardine
Bringt deine kleinen zing

Then there was one that went:

Marshak's Malted Milk, it's good for kleine kinder
Planters peanut oil it good for backen cake.

He claimed to have received his sense of fun and joy from his mother. "I realize that my father was a very isolated, stern person; not a happy camper; he was one of 16 children. But my mother was a very lively woman; had a lot of humor, and she loved country things, and she loved society. And I realize this is a kind of Russian-Ukrainian characteristic, so whatever I have of conviviality, I think, came from her."

He graduated from New Utrecht High School in Brooklyn and got a degree from Brooklyn College. At Brooklyn College "I belonged to the jazz club, and I saw Charlie Christian play with a battery operated guitar, at some black bar near Brownsville." He wrote poems and short stories and later moved to Greenwich Village, where, in the 1950s, he met Sylvia Topp.

I originally knew of Tuli from his appearance in Beat Generation anthologies, such as *The Beats*, and from his poetry published in the *Village Voice*. During the last few years we had become friends.

The Physicality of Peace Eye

Peace Eye had three rooms, a courtyard in the back, and a basement that featured huge waterbugs on the posts. The walls were white, and the metal ceiling I painted red. Peace Eye's back room, with a door leading to the rear courtyard, had a bathroom and sink, plus a gas-fueled burning device next to the sink. I think the device was used to singe chicken feathers because there was a convex mound of something on the floor that was hardened to the point that I had just covered it over with black floor paint when I first rented the store. I thought it might be congealed chicken grease. I had put a couch back there for the occasional guest.

My friend artist Bill Beckman made a sign made out of the glass door of a library bookcase, which I hung on the inside of the front window. It had the words "Peace Eye Bookstore." On each side of the words was an Eye of Horus 𓂀. The outer window already had the words "Strictly" and the Hebrew letters for "Kosher." I decided to leave both in place. I moved my mimeograph from the Secret Location in the back building on Avenue A to the freshly painted Peace Eye Bookstore.

Bugger—An Anthology

As the first publication in the new store, I gathered together an anthology titled *Bugger—An Anthology* in November, with poems by myself, Bill Szabo, Allen Ginsberg ("This Form of Life Needs Sex"), Ted Berrigan, John Harriman, Ron Padgett, Al Fowler, John Keys, and Harry Fainlight. Some of the Howlean "Best Minds" of 1964.

Meanwhile, after the poetry readings at Café Le Metro poets began to congregate at Stanley Tolkin's dance bar, called the Dom, located in the basement of the Polish National Home building on St. Mark's Place between Second and Third Avenues.

I thought of a line dance called "The Bugger" right around the time of the anthology and tried to create a B Line at the Dom. Stanley came rushing out to stop the line just as it had successfully formed on a jukebox blast of "I Wanna Hold Your Hand."

This was the year of "Oh, Pretty Woman" by Roy Orbison; the Drifters' "Under the Boardwalk"; "Leader of the Pack" by the Shangri-las; and the Animals' "House of the Rising Sun." "I Wanna Hold Your Hand" had spent seven weeks at the number one position on the charts.

When I was in high school, I followed rock-and-roll and country and western tunes as if they were sacred chants, but by '64 I was more attuned to civil rights songs and jazz. Inspired by poets dancing at the Dom, I began paying attention to jukeboxes for the first time since the mid-1950s and wondering about fusing poetry and this new generation of pop tunes. I was getting the urge to form a band.

Also in November '64 I published, for Lawrence Ferlinghetti of City Lights, a limited edition of Claude Pelieu's *Automatic Pilot*, translated by Mary Beach.

The cover of *Bugger—An Anthology*, a book that Gary Snyder dubbed "A Child's Garden of PerVerse."

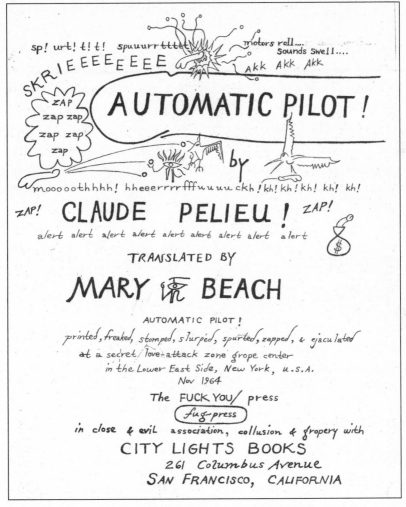

Ed Sanders's hand-drawn cover for *Automatic Pilot*, November '64.

The Founding of The Fugs

During those years we all sang together a lot. There was often a guitar in apartments in the Lower East Side, along with a water pipe and collections of folk music and jazz LPs in milk crate storage boxes. Singing together was one of the glories of my youth. One of my favorite lines on civil rights marches was "I've got a home in Glory Land / that outshines the sun!" We sang "Down by the Riverside" when members of the Klan surrounded our church in Tennessee and began pelting it with rocks during the Nashville-Washington Walk for Peace back in the spring of 1962.

One night after a poetry reading at Café Le Metro, Tuli Kupferberg and I visited the Dom, where we watched poets such as Robert Creeley and Amiri Baraka (then still known as LeRoi Jones) dancing to the jukebox. Then Tuli and I retired to another bar on St. Mark's, where I suggested we form a musical group. "We'll set poetry to music," I proclaimed. Tuli was all in favor of it.

We drew inspiration for The Fugs from a long and varied tradition going all the way back to the dances of Dionysus in the ancient Greek plays and the "Theory of the Spectacle" in Aristotle's *Poetics* and moving forward to the famous premiere performance of Alfred Jarry's *Ubu Roi* in 1896, to the *poèmes simultanés* of the Dadaists in Zurich's Cabaret Voltaire in 1916, to the jazz-poetry of the Beats, to Charlie Parker's seething sax, to the silence of John Cage, to the calm pushiness of the Happening movement, to the songs of the civil rights movement, and to our belief that there were oodles of freedoms guaranteed by the Constitution that were not being used.

At first we didn't have a name. An early one I came up with was "The Yodeling Socialists." Tuli was too anarcho for that, and even though I am the only Beatnik who can yodel, he wasn't into the Great Yod. Another early name for The Fugs was "The Freaks." Tuli and I immediately began writing a bunch of songs. In a notebook in late 1964, I jotted:

> Songs for the Freaks:
>   1. Banana
>   2. Little Mary Bell (Blake's poem)
>   3. I Love to Tell the Story (Christian hymn from my youth)
>   4. How Sweet I Roamed from Field to Field (Blake)
>   5. Take Me Away to That Land of Peace

On the next page of the notebook were some possible lyrics to number 5:

> Take me
>   take   take
>   away
>   way   way
>   to that land
>   of peace

come o come   with me
to that land of peace

where   we   meet
    all rainy
        under the
            ashen tree
peace o peace
come stomp me on!

Wish I had finished it and put it on the first Fugs album.

Tuli and I decided to invite a young man named Ken Weaver to join us in our new rock-and-roll/poetry adventure. (The term "folk rock" had not yet been invented.) Weaver had been a drummer with the El Campo, Texas, Rice Birds marching band when in high school, and he owned a large buffalo hide drum. He had been tossed out of the air force for smoking pot, and he proudly displayed his discharge papers on the wall of his pad. He had been a volunteer typist for various Fuck You Press projects and, with his drumming skill, was soon an eager participant in the unnamed group with the very tentative title "The Freaks."

I told the Folklore Center's Israel Young about my plans to form a band. His advice was "Don't do it."

The Founding of LeMar

I talked it over with Allen Ginsberg, and we decided to form the Committee to Legalize Marijuana (LeMar). Joining us was a guy named Randy Wicker, a gay activist who not long after ran one of the first Protest Button stores on the East Side. We soon organized probably the first demonstrations to legalize grass in American history.

This history-making two-hour stroll around Tompkins Square Park advocated three main points, valid right up to the early years of the twenty-first century:

1. Legalize the use of Marihuana
2. Legalize the sale & transport of pot
3. Free all prisoners.

MARIHUANA MARCH

27 DECEMBER   *   Sunday Afternoon   *   from Noon to 2 P.M.

AROUND TOMPKINS SQUARE (Assemble at 8th & B, stroll clockwise)

PICKET AND WALK FOR LEGALIZATION OF MARIHUANA.

REPEAL MARIHUANA PROHIBITION!!! Like liquor prohibition, pot prohibition violates personal liberty, promotes racketeering & invites mass evasion of the law. But while alcohol is demonstrably productive of hangover, cirrhosis of the liver, violence & Dylan Thomas scenes, Marihuana on the other hand is in ALL respects gentle, benevolent and absolutely non-addictive. We defy anyone to produse one shred of evidence that Marihuana is in any way addictive! Or that it produces at any time any adverse, depressive or other toxic effects!

What grounds except invincible ignorance, conscienceless stupidity, or sheer cussedness & perversity could cause legislators to punish this harmless pursuit of happiness?

Given the facts, who except the powerful liquor, pep-pill, nicotine, & medical lobbies would dare raise a voice against Marihuana?

Hundreds of thousands of responsible New Yorkers smoke pot all the time. Why should these citizens be harassed, arrested, ill-treated & black-mailed? Why, except to impose totalitarian conformity, should governments invade the privacy of our homes?

LEMAR (Legalize Marijuana) advocates: 1. Legalize the use of Marihuana

2. Legalize the sale & transport of pot.

3. Free all prisoners.

JOIN US! Come to Tompkins Square Sunday, December 27th at 12: Noon to 2:00 P.M.

LEMAR
c/o Peace Eye Center
383 East 10   NYC 10009

First legalize grass demonstration in U.S. history (I think), Tompkins Square, December 27, 1964. Flier printed at the newly opened Peace Eye Bookstore.

The Free Speech Movement

The Free Speech Movement at the University of California was total music to the mind when it arrived in late '64, at the close of a year of clampdown in New York City. The Ping-Pong ball bounced from the West: the Free Speech Movement! Yay!

Freedom Summer had energized the colleges. A student at UC Berkeley named Mario Savio had been down in Mississippi that summer working with SNCC, and he returned to UC Berkeley to witness and help lead the resistance to administration attempts to stop civil rights activism among Berkeley's students, especially by SNCC and CORE.

I followed the Free Speech Movement as best I could from articles in the *Village Voice* and sometimes the *New York Times.* Savio had been a patient of Miriam's father, a doctor with a practice in Glen Oaks, Queens, on Union Turnpike.

On October 19 a young man named Jack Weinberg was arrested at a CORE fund-raising table on campus and hundreds of students sat down around a police car when officers tried to take him away. After a thirty-six-hour sit-down Weinberg was released and the Free Speech Movement began. It practiced the civil rights tactics of sit-ins, nonviolent confrontations, and use of the media.

Within days there was a big student strike whose banners were seen around the world. According to the movement's analysis, colleges were slave units for training dutiful drudges for corporations. Protesters demanded student participation in how universities were run.

On December 5 there was a large rally and occupation of Sproul Hall in protest against the suspension of Savio and other students. The frostocrats called in the police and National Guard to arrest those sitting in, which resulted in a student strike and a walkout of faculty.

On December 7 Mario Savio was dragged from the mike before an audience of 13,000 at the Berkeley campus. In the end, however, the university acceded to the demands of the Free Speech Movement for campus political freedom.

It was welcome and inspirational news in the Lower East Side and the Village, as the words "Free Speech" made their mark. Thus 1964 came to a close in the rapid ointment of Time.

A few weeks later in the *Village Voice* I spotted an ad for a "Free Speech Hoot," featuring the Danny Kalb Quartet, John Hammond, and Judy Roderick at a hotel up on Sixty-third Street. Kalb would go on to found the Blues Project.

Free Speech, part of the Great Bill of Rights—use it or lose it.

1965

I was tasting a tad of renown. My magazine was very sought after; I was publishing many of my literary heroes. And articles were now being written about me. Since 1960 (when junkies kept breaking into my mail box at 266 East Fourth), I'd had Box 193 at Stuyvesant Station. The employees at Stuy were themselves pretty far out and tolerant, even when letters started coming into "Ed Sanders, Fuck You, Stuyvesant Station, New York" or "Fuck You, Peace Eye Books Store." I never had a single complaint from them during those years. It made me proud of being in a free country and having a tolerant post office branch.

A supporter named Everett Gellert, who was a magazine publisher, bought me a groovy A. B. Dick electric mimeograph machine, which I almost immediately put to use as soon as it was installed in the second room of Peace Eye. I kept my original beautiful little Speed-o-Print mimeo in the Secret Location on Avenue A but soon donated it to a poet named John Keyes, who took it with him when he moved to England. I used the new A. B. Dick to print *Fuck You/ A Magazine of the Arts*, volume 8, number 5, which came off the press in February.

Writing Songs

As for the band Tuli and I had agreed to found, our first duty was to create some songs. I already had four Blake poems, inspired by Allen Ginsberg, set to music. Two, "How Sweet I Roamed from Field to Field" and "Ah, Sun-Flower, Weary of Time," would appear on our first album. I had a Wollensak tape recorder already, by our bed in Miriam's and my new pad on East Twenty-seventh, and on it I composed a bunch of tunes, "Comin' Down," for instance, and other ditties such as the falsetto "Toe Queen Love," which, alas, never was recorded anywhere but in my mind.

Tuli created "Jack Off Blues," "Hallucination Horrors," "That's Not My Department," and "Ten Commandments." I dashed off "Coca Cola Douche," "Swinburne Stomp," "The Gobble," and "The I Saw the Best Minds of My Generation Rock."

One of Tuli's most popular and lasting songs was "Nothing," written to the melody of a Yiddish folksong. It may have had part of its origins in Louis Aragon's Dada manifesto: "No more painters, no more writers, no more musicians, no more sculptors, no more religions, no more republicans, no more royalists, no more imperialists, no more anarchists, no more socialists, no more Bolsheviks, no more politicians, no more proletarians, no more democrats, no more armies, no more police, no more nations, enough of these idiocies, no more, no more, NOTHING, NOTHING, NOTHING."

Some of Tuli's songs were "out there," such as "Caca Rocka" and "Hallucination Horrors," but a good number would become "classics," such as "The Ten Commandments," "Kill for Peace," "Morning Morning," "CIA Man," and "Supergirl."

Once Tuli told me how he got the idea for "Kill for Peace." He had spotted the sentence "Pray for Peace" on a letter and then, in his noggin, sprouted the idea for a modification, leading to a Fugs classic tune. We heard over the years that soldiers in Vietnam were known to sing it.

One night in Peace Eye Ken Weaver began jotting some lines for his "I Couldn't Get High" in a notebook. We got excited, and I took over to continue putting some of his lines into a notebook.

As for the name, my main ideas, "The Freaks" or "The Yodeling Socialists," were set aside when Tuli Kupferberg came up with "The Fugs," named after Norman Mailer's euphemism for "Fuck," which he utilized in his World War II novel, *The Naked and the Dead.*

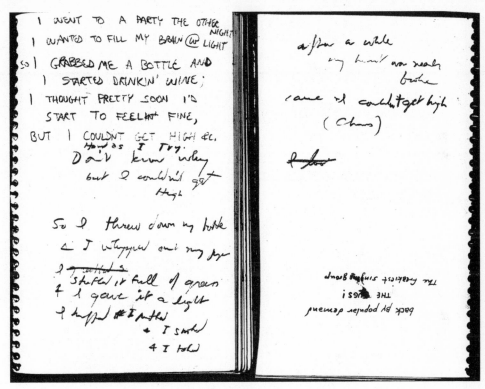

Original note page for "I Couldn't Get High," composed at Peace Eye all in one swoosh.

Marijuana Newsletters

One project for the Committee to Legalize Marijuana was the *Marijuana Newsletter,* which I published at Peace Eye. I hand-drew on stencils and typed the two issues of the *Marijuana Newsletter,* one in January and another in March.

As in my magazine I ran humorous "ads" in the *Marijuana Newsletter.*

The *Marijuana Newsletter* created quite a stir and set in motion various currents in the nation for change. It showed that you could publish such a newsletter, and get away with it. It led to people such as d. a. levy in Cleveland and John Sinclair in Detroit publishing their own calls for legalization.

I ran a "Pot Market" report, and we had a "Best Stash" contest (which was won by the brilliant Ron Padgett). LeMar was supposed to pay the bard a $5 prize. Did we?

While writing this memoir, I finally mailed Padgett his long overdue fiver, forty-four years late.

The MARIJUANA NEWSLETTER!

published by New York City LEMAR as a public service, to disseminate information toward the legalization of Marijuana. The MARIJUANA NEWSLETTER will print position papers, medical testimonies, & general information about the campaign to legalize marijuana. We shall agitate! We shall print the data. We have the facts about marijuana, the gentle benevolent herb.

ISSUE # 1. JANUARY 30, 1965. ABOLISH PROHIBITION! LEMAR! 25 CENTS

Edited by Randolfe Wicker, Ed Sanders, Peter Orlovsky, C.T. Smith.

Lemar

New York City Lem ar is a voluntary association formed to educate the pub lic concerning Mar ijuana & the urgent need to legalize it. Like liquor pro hibition, pot pro- hibition violates personal liberty, promotes racketeer- ing, & invites mass evasion of the law. But, while alcohol is demonstrably productive of hang- over, cirrhosis of the liver, violence & Dylan Thomas scenes, Marijuana on the other hand is in ALL respects gentle, benevolent, & absolutely NON- addictive. We defy anyone to produce one shred of evi- dence that Mariju ana is in any way addictive! or that it produces at any time any adverse, depressive or other toxic effects.

LEMAR continued on page 4

The Wicker Report

by Randolfe Wicker

THE NEW YORK TIMES

Versus

THE TRUTH

It should come as no surprise that the same New York Times which finds teenage drinking alarming whether it be legal (New York-Connecticut border towns) or illegal (Darien, Connecticut) views the spread of the world's se- cond most popular intoxi- cant -- marijuana-- with a special horror and Puritan ism.

The Times, stout aging mother of American journal ism, has unfortunately allowed its own biases to both color and distort most

continued page 3

WILLIAM Burroughs SPEAKS!

It is unfortunate and illogical that Cannabis, known colloquially as 'reefers' 'marijuana' 'charge' etcetera is the only drug of this group singled out for specific and definitive legal sanctions. The reasons given for these sanctions are demonstrably spurious. The La Guardia Report plus a mass of medical and pharmacological test imony have shown that Cannabis is neither harmful nor habit forming There is no evidence to show that crimes are committed under under the influence of this drug and alcohol remains the crime producing drug. How many crimes are committed every day by citizens who would not have committed the crim inal act if they had not been drunk? It is fre- quently maintained that Cannabis leads directly to the use of heroin.

BURROUGHS cont page 3

Trouble with Jim Bishop

Randy Wicker, C. T. Smith, and Peter Orlovsky were arrested February 6 for selling the *Marijuana Newsletter* on the streets of the West Village. The ACLU agreed to handle the case.

After the first issue of the *Marijuana Newsletter* was published, an estab- lishment columnist, Jim Bishop, wrote a hostile column about it, which was nationally syndicated. A sample paragraph trumpeted, "Its use produces

We have the facts about the miracle herb marijuana ~7~

Open letter to Jim Bishop
continued from page 1

juana since he was thirteen years old. He is now in his fifties, retired, and is neither mentally dull nor is he in any stretch of the imagination insane.

Dr. Robert S. deRopp, a prominent biochemist, narcotics expert and author of Drugs and the Mind, states in his book that "...the problem it (marijuana) has brought results more from the types of people indulging in the drug than from the effects of the drug itself." Furthermore, in the Mayor's Committee on Marijuana of New York City, Mayor LaGuardia stated in the foreward of a report on marijuana that, "I am glad that the sociological, psychological, and medical ills attributed to marijuana have been found to be exaggerated..."

You further stated in your article that, "Pot is the first step on the narcotics ladder," and that those who smoke marijuana, "...can soon be moved up to heroin." Again you seem to disagree with Dr. deRopp who states in Drugs and the Mind that "The practice of marijuana smoking was not observed to lead to addiction..." Also the findings of Mayor LaGuardia's committee that, "The instances are extremely rare where the habit of marijuana smoking is associated with addiction.."

—continued next column—

BUCKS COUNTY
MAUVE

the pinnacle of pennsylvania pot

"You can be sure
if it's B.C. Mauve"

an excellent grade of grass
ideal for pot blending

LEMAR is purchasing and collecting books for its MARIJUANA LIBRARY. We want every book or article ever written about marijuana. Please send to LEMAR BOX 133 NEW YORK, N.Y. 10009. We will have the most complete pot library in the history of western civilization!

You have also states in your article that, "...the use of marijuana leads to crime..." Again I refer you to Dr. deRopp who states that, "No direct relationship could be demonstrated between marijuana smoking and crime..." and also that, "The antisocial aggressive, and sadistic elements of the personality uncovered by the drug are responsible for the crime, rather than any specific crime producing properties of marijuana... It is probable that alcohol is more responsible as an agent in crime than marijuana." Also, I refer you to the LaGuardia report, "In most instances, the behavior of the (marijuana) smoker is of a friendly sociable character. Aggressiveness and belligerency are not commonly seen, and those showing such traits are not allowed to remain..." And again from the pen of Dr. deRopp, writing about a marijuana gathering "A boisterous, rowdy atmosphere did not prevail and on the rare occasions where there appeared signs of belligerency in one of the smokers he was either ejected or forced to become quieter."

The committee appointed by Mayor LaGuardia of New York City also discovered that marijuana is less habit-forming than either alcohol or tobacco. Marijuana was found not to lead to the use of stronger drugs nor was it found to cause insanity or violence.

—continued page 9

prolonged sensation, thirst, hunger for sweets, delusions of grandeur, delusions of persecution, hilarity and delirium. The chronic use of marijuana induces mental dullness and insanity. . . . Pot is the first step on the narcotics ladder."

Uh oh. The heat was on. "It is time for those of *us* who believe in law and order to tell our police departments that we stand beside them in their struggle."

page 2

POT IS FUN! *The* MARIJUANA NEWSLETTER

C.T. SMITH Reviews
LaGuardia
REPORT

LaGuardia Report
republished in hard-cover
by Oliver Layton Press $4.95
340 Riverside Drive, N.Y.C.
or telephone orders to
Mr. Robert Bashlow Un 4-7027

The Marijuana Newsletter wishes to
congratulate the Oliver Layton
Press on its courage and determina
tion to republish the classic report
of the LaGuardia Committee on Marihuana, originally published in 1944.
This report was made by unimpeach-
able experts and has the value that
it was limited in scope to the City
of New York, which means that the
"problem" was treated comprehensive-
ly, and the additional value that
it is entirely free of the hysterical bias which has characterized
other published materials. Yet the
force of that bias has in fact been
exerted upon the LaGuardia Report,
which has been made largely inacces
sible to the public, by virtue of
the fact that copies cannot be found
on the shelves of the public library nor bought from book-dealers.
We are therefore proud to carry
public notice of its republication.

"On Sept. 13, 1938 the N.Y.
Academy of Medicine was informed
of Mayor LaGuardia's concern about
the Marihuana (SIC) problem and of
his desire 'that some impartial
body such as the N.Y. Academy of
Medicine make a survey ... to determine the pertinent facts ....' "
Such was the far-sighted and aca-
demically respectable circumstances
under which this report was made at
a cost of $22,500, and in view of
subsequent abusive statements, it
is worth noting that at the time it
was accepted by both the city and
--continued on page 4

CASSIDY'S CLOSINGS
The latest pot market report

Latest reports show a rise
in heat decreasing in direct
proportion to distance from the
corner of MacDougal & Bleeker
Street. The market is just
emerging from a severe recession
resulting from a sudden and
severe police crackdown in which
several wholesale sources were
eliminated. Despite continued
heat new sources have appeared
and several varieties are now
on the market. Latest closings
show:

mexican green:	$15-30/oz.
	$100-160/lb.
cuban green:	$15-30/oz.
	$100-160/lb.
acapulqo gold:	$25-35/oz.
	$140-200/lb.
black gunji:	$30-40/oz.
	$150-225/lb.

(the latest Pot Statistics
compiled through the services
of the Hippie Dope Exchange,
will be printed in each issue
of the Marijuana Newsletter.)

ANNOUNCING
THE BEST STASH
contest

We will award $500 to
the person submitting
the best essay on the
THEORY OF THE STASH.
Entries should be profusely
illustrated with examples
from grass-head lore.
We will print the
winning entry.

I published an "Open Letter to Jim Bishop" by William Burroughs in the March 15 issue. Burroughs wrote:

Dear Mr. Bishop, I have been a fan of yours for about five or six years. Your column has always held my interest on the many occasions I've had to read it. On March 2, 1965, the *Seattle Post Intelligencer,* Seattle's Hearst outlet, printed your article entitled: "Marijuana Newsletter—a Shocking Revelation."

As I read your column I was indeed shocked at what you wrote about marijuana. In your article you wrote that "The chronic use of marijuana induces mental dullness and insanity."

This may surprise you, but I know a man who has smoked marijuana since he was thirteen years. He is now in his fifties, retired, and is neither mentally dull nor is he in any stretch of the imagination insane....

You further stated in your article that, "Pot is the first step on the narcotics ladder," and that those who smoke marijuana, "...can soon be moved to heroin." Again you seem to disagree with Dr. deRopp who states in *Drugs and the Mind* that "the practice of marijuana smoking was not observed to lead to addiction." Also the findings of Mayor LaGuardia's committee that, "The instances are extremely rare where the habit of marijuana smoking is associated with addiction."

Burroughs went on to challenge, because of the badly written quality of Bishop's column, whether he had actually written the column himself.

In the same issue we also printed Bishop's actual column from the *New York Journal-American*, a paper that would not survive the television age. I drew a couple of "ads" on stencils for the Bishop rebuttal issue.

From all this hirdum-dirdum over a mimeographed newsletter printed at the Peace Eye Bookstore came Pot Trouble to others, such as poets d. a. levy in Cleveland and John Sinclair in Detroit, who took up the LeMar call to set up chapters in other cities.

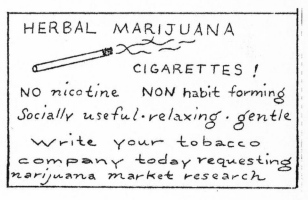

HERBAL MARIJUANA CIGARETTES !
NO nicotine   NON habit forming
Socially useful·relaxing·gentle
write your tobacco
company today requesting
marijuana market research

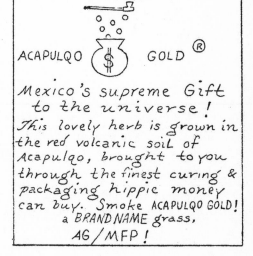

ACAPULQO ($) GOLD ®
Mexico's supreme Gift
to the universe!
This lovely herb is grown in
the red volcanic soil of
Acapulqo, brought to you
through the finest curing &
packaging hippie money
can buy. Smoke ACAPULQO GOLD!
a BRAND NAME grass.
AG/MFP !

Orlovsky and a Break-In

On February 21, just three days before the opening celebration of Peace Eye, someone broke in to the store and stole Fugs equipment, including Ken Weaver's groovy wide buffalo hide drum. To show what a good-souled person Peter Orlovsky was, he was passing Peace Eye that night at midnight and noticed that someone had broken in. He went inside, nailed the door shut, and left a note apologizing for not staying the night to ward off further robbery attempts: "12 AM. Seemed you were on verge of getting robbed—window glass broken—door closed but unlocked—desk chair overturned—& I don't have yr home phone no. to call & tell you—Have nailed the door, and will leave by side entrance—you might be at work (at the cigar store on Times Square) will call you there—I hope I don't regret not having spent the night here in case other robbers try to enter again. Love, Peter." (This was written on the back of an issue of the *Marijuana Newsletter*.)

Throughout the 1960s and beyond owl-eyed Peter O. was always a cheerful helper. Once in Washington Square Park he showed up after having escaped from a ward at Bellevue Hospital. (He periodically went bonkers.) He sold me right off his back a pajama top sporting the logo of the hospital, for $4. I used to wear the top at early Fugs concerts. It's true that Peter could get a bit freaky under the influence of amphetamine. Miriam recalls him once showing up at our apartment and proceeding to help clean in an A-amplified rush, swabbing with a toothbrush the coils on the back of our refrigerator.

He was a remarkable poet. His poem in Don Allen's *New American Poetry*, "Second Poem," written in Paris in 1957, was one that astounded my generation.

The First Fugs Concert

A Brillo box first appeared in a Warhol exhibit at the Stable Gallery in New York City in '64. The ones I saw were made of plywood, with silkscreened Brillo images on the sides. They made an impact in the noggins of the Fuck You Generation.

When I founded The Fugs, I had an idea of using one of Warhol's Brillo boxes as a drum. Ted and Sandy Berrigan had one in their apartment on

East Ninth. Oh, I lusted for that Brillo box! I should have gone to Andy himself; I bet he would have given me a supply of Fugs Brillo box drums! Another opportunity for a Date with History slipped from our frantic grasp!

Ken Weaver certainly could have used a Warhol Brillo box as a drum for the first Fugs concert, held at the grand opening of the new location of Israel Young's Folklore Center, on Sixth Avenue at West Third Street. Instead, when the junkies stole his buffalo hide drum from Peace Eye, he was forced to perform on a drum made from a Krasdale peach box!

Possible Fugs Brillo box drum. We could have attached a guitar pickup on Warhol's Brillo and made world musical instrument history!!

Silkscreened Warhol Flowers

By 1964 Warhol had begun making startling and controversial movies. Meanwhile, his bold adventures in painting continued. He had completed work on the first Electric Chair paintings and on twenty images of a young woman spread on the dented roof of an auto, who had leaped off the Empire State Building, a work called "White." In January the two-panel "Blue Electric Chair," for instance, was exhibited in France to great acclaim.

While the Factory, Warhol's studio, was being covered in aluminum foil, from January to April '64, he started working on the painted wood Brillo boxes, an act of creativity razor-sharp in its controversy. The New York World's Fair opened in the summer of 1964. Andy had been commissioned to do a mural for the American pavilion, so he prepared a 20' x 20' work in black and white called "The Thirteen Most Wanted Men," which featured the police mug shots of criminals. It was installed, along with works by Robert Rauschenberg, Roy Lichtenstein, and others. The governor of New York, Nelson Rockefeller, was displeased with the work and ordered it removed. Rockefeller already was well known for such things—he had ordered a famous Diego Rivera mural in Rockefeller Center painted over during the 1930s, and during World War II Rockefeller had censored a government-sponsored movie by Orson Welles.

Ginsberg reading a magazine at Peace Eye, with Warhol flower on the wall in the background, 1965. Ed Sanders collection.

Warhol was instructed to remove or replace "Wanted Men" within twenty-four hours. When World's Fair officials would not accept his idea for a substitution (a painting with panels of a public official named Robert Moses), Andy went out to the World's Fair pavilion and had the work painted over in silver.

Andy's friend Henry Geldzahler came along with him to the fair. Geldzahler suggested that Andy give up the "death and disaster" series he had been painting for a number of months. To show what he meant, Geldzahler pointed to some flowers in a magazine. The result was a great series of poppy flowers, truly glyphs of joy, based on a photo from *Modern Photography* magazine. The flowers were wildly successful and predicted the American flower power movement three years ahead of its time.

I asked Andy if he'd do some banners for the opening of Peace Eye. He said sure and suggested I go down to Orchard Street and get some colored cloths, which I brought up to his studio. Shortly thereafter he silkscreened three banners—red, yellow, and blue—of his poppies. I placed them on the walls of Peace Eye.

The Grand Opening of Peace Eye Bookstore

The Fugs began to rehearse at the Peace Eye Bookstore, and they became popular events as scads of friends began to show up to hang out during run-throughs. We hooked up with The Holy Modal Rounders, a duo consisting of Steve Weber and Peter Stampfel, who agreed to perform with us at the Grand Opening of the Peace Eye Bookstore on February 24. Also performing, in addition to me, Tuli, and Ken Weaver, was poet Bill Szabo, on "amphetamine flute."

Official invitation to the Grand Opening of the Peace Eye Bookstore, the celebration of the third anniversary issue of *Fuck You/ A Magazine of the Arts*, and the world premiere performance of The Fugs.

The store was totally packed for the Opening. I affixed the three Andy Warhol silkscreened flower images to the walls of Peace Eye. *Time* magazine sent a team of reporters. A limousine arrived, depositing author James Michener in evening attire. He told me that Andy Warhol had urged him to attend.

I asked the crowd to stand back, and The Fugs set up. I made sure the performance was taped. We did about twenty minutes, with ditties such as "Nothing," a tune called "Bull-Tongue Clit," also "The Ten Commandments" and the "Swinburne Stomp," featuring a few stanzas from A. C. Swinburne's play *Atalanta in Calydon*. One of my professors from NYU, Frank Peters, was there. His favorite tune from The Fugs set that night, he told me, was "Swinburne Stomp." William Burroughs asked me, "Which one is from

Fuck You, volume 5, number 8, February 1965, Table of Contents.

Time?" I pointed out the reporter with the first name Chris. He stared at the guy and replied, "I thought so." Burroughs disliked *Time* intensely. I think it had to do with *Time*'s coverage of Burroughs shooting his wife, Joan Vollmer, to death in September 1951.

I had boxes of *Fuck You*/s on hand. I waited until the place was filled up and then, with Peter Orlovsky's help, started distributing the free copies to the crowd.

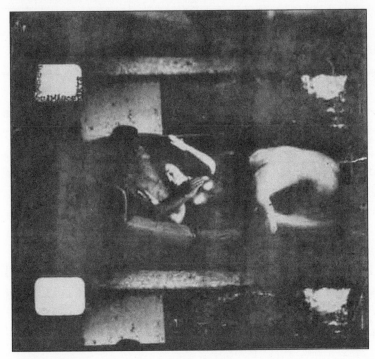

Andy Warhol cover, *Fuck You.*

One point of controversy was my publishing W. H. Auden's great erotic poem, "The Platonic Blow," in the third anniversary issue. As a fan of *The Age of Anxiety*, I was convinced it was Auden's poem. It is a masterful work, worthy of Auden in rhyme, sound, and metric. Jason Epstein, a big-time editor at Random House, was on hand and skeptical. I had collected two copies of Auden's poem, one originating from a person at the Morgan Library, which supplied the text I printed. Andy Warhol also prepared the cover for the third anniversary issue, a frame from his Couch movie.

The schedule was relentless. Three days later we performed at the Gallery 111:

The Fugs will perform at the Gallery 111
at 111 St. Marks Place, Saturday
February 27, 1965, 4 p.m.

The performances kept coming, from now until the final concerts of the 1960s, in February '69 with the Grateful Dead and the Velvet Underground in Pittsburgh, then at Rice University in Houston, and concluding at the Vulcan Gas Works in Austin.

The Hideous Rolling Thunder

The schedule for Lyndon Johnson also was relentless, as the United States began a hideous bombing campaign named "Rolling Thunder" less than a week after the Grand Opening of Peace Eye. Its targets were chosen at first for their psychological/political significance rather than for their military worth.

On an average day eight hundred tons of bombs were dropped. Think of it—eight hundred tons! Rolling Thunder was supposed to be an eight-week quickie, but the Fates wove else and the Thunder stretched timeward in a skein of grief and evil for three dread years.

The Viet Cong stood firm, against which then there was "graduated pressure"—that is, more slaughter from America. But as U.S. protesters sometimes chanted, "The people! united! can never be defeated!" And so ten years of American explosions floated past the looms of murder.

The First Selma March

There were 29,500 humans in Selma, Alabama, west of Montgomery, 15,100 of whom were black—that's over 50 percent—yet only 1 percent of voters were black. For seven weeks that year the great Martin Luther King led hundreds of Selma's citizens seeking to register.

Sheriff Jim Clark led his troops with billy-club bashes and the jolts of cattle prods as 2,000 were arrested. A black youth named Jimmie Lee Jackson was shot in the stomach and died.

Martin King and 770 were arrested picketing the county courthouse in Selma. Sheriff Clark and his crack clutter of crackers continued with cattle prods and smashing clubs as they marched 165 children to a "makeshift" jail.

After the whites killed Jimmie Lee Jackson, Martin King inspired a march on March 6 from Selma to the state capitol at Montgomery, fifty miles away. The purpose of the March 6 action was to get the vote for blacks. Attorney General of the United States Nicholas Katzenbach advised Martin King not to actually take part in the walk. Southern Christian Leadership Conference deputy Hosea Williams walked in King's place.

Protesters marched out of the city of Selma, two abreast, toward the Edmund Pettus Bridge over the Alabama River. As they crossed the span, two hundred state police with whips, tear gas, and clubs assaulted them and knocked most to the ground.

It had the leathery look of something un-American. The grainy footage was like a lurching underground movie but told a grainy groan of despicability on televisions around the world. It was an early example of footage-forged social change. The next day in Selma, James Reeb, a Unitarian minister from Boston, was beaten to death by crackers—a murder case still open.

Selma Two

MLK led another march, two days later, with 1,500 on hand, but the marchers turned back because Dr. King sensed that the local power structure was ready to spring a violent trap on the marchers just beyond the bridge leading from Selma.

Selma Three

On March 21 Martin Luther King began march number 3—fifty-four miles in five days—joined by luminaries such as Joan Baez, Harry Belafonte, Ralph Bunche Jr., Sammy Davis Jr., and Leonard Bernstein. Johnson sent federal marshals, 1,000 military police, and a slew (1,900) of "federalized" Alabama National Guardsmen to protect the legal march. "Segregation's got to fall. . . . You never can jail us all," the marchers chanted. Twenty-five thousand gathered in Montgomery on March 25 for the closing rally.

We followed Selma in the Lower East Side. It seemed like something Great was happening.

The Fugs at the American Theater for Poets

On March 8 The Fugs, "the freakiest singing group in the history of Western civilization," performed at the East End Theatre, located at 85 East Fourth Street, run by poets Diane di Prima and Alan Marlowe. The Fugs for this concert were Sanders, Kupferberg, Weber, Stampfel, Fowler, and Weaver.

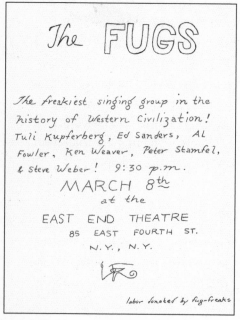

The FUGS

The freakiest singing group in the history of Western Civilization! Tuli Kupferberg, Ed Sanders, Al Fowler, Ken Weaver, Peter Stamfel, & Steve Weber! 9:30 p.m. MARCH 8th at the EAST END THEATRE 85 EAST FOURTH ST. N.Y., N.Y.

labor donated by fug-freaks

Hot off the Peace Eye mimeo, complete with forty-five-year-old masking tape to pin to Peace Eye wall.

Al Fowler and Bill Szabo were early members of The Fugs. Both were hooked on heroin, which made it difficult for them to come to rehearsals or keep to an exact, nonsweaty schedule. So they soon went their ways.

I'd met Diane di Prima and her husband, Alan Marlowe, at the Phoenix Bookshop on Cornelia Street. All of us had seen her famous photo sitting up on the piano at the Gaslight Café on MacDougal Street—a Beat Generation image for the Ages.

Diane typed a flier called "Special Events" for the American Theatre for Poets for the week of March 3–9. March 3 saw Brion Gysin's "Permutations and Permutated Portraits," plus Robert Filliou, "Street Fighting/Whispered Art History." Then March 4, at midnight, Dick Higgins performed "Requiem for Wagner the Criminal Mayor." On Monday, March 8 were The Fugs, "Tuli Kupferberg, Ed Sanders, Kenneth Weaver in a new rock-and-roll program." The next day, March 9, Allan Kaprow gave a talk called "The Techniques and New Goals of Happenings." Tickets were $2; students, 99¢.

A Three-Day Fug Festival

On March 29–30 and April 5 there was the same lineup, but without Al Fowler. We couldn't really have a junkie in a band that didn't make a lot of money. He couldn't take time to rehearse, for instance. "Admission: $2, students and grass-cadets 99¢."

I had learned from Allen Ginsberg to have a press list. For the rest of his life he kept feeding me lists of press contacts. During his later years his press list was at least twenty pages long! And I quickly learned techniques of hyperbole, as in "They're here!! Back by popular demand, The Fugs, the most unbelievable singing group in the history of Western civilization!"

THEY'RE HERE !!

BACK BY POPULAR DEMAND

The FUGS!

THE MOST UNBELIEVABLE SINGING GROUP

IN THE HISTORY OF WESTERN CIVILIZATION !!

HOURS AND HOURS OF INCREDIBLE LISTENING PLEASURE!!!

Tuli Kupferberg, Ed Sanders, Ken Weaver, Peter Stampfel,
& Steve Weber: The FUGS! Rock & Roll, Folk Spews, Amphetamine
Operas, spontaneous Freak-beams, Dope Incantations;
including all the legendary FUG HITS!! COCA COLA DOUCHE,
JACK OFF BLUES, HALLUCINATION HORRORS, THE I SAW THE BEST
MINDS OF MY GENERATION ROCK, THE SWINBURNE STOMP, TEN
COMMANDMENTS, TOE QUEEN LOVE, & 100's MORE. PLUS the FIRST
public presentation of the new East Side dance rage:
The GOBBLE!

YES YES YES

A THREE DAY FUG- *festival*

MARCH 29～ MARCH 30 ～ APRIL 5
9:00 *pm*

THE EAST END THEATRE
85 EAST FOURTH ST.

phone reservations. OR3-3377

Admission: 2oo, *students & grass~cadets:* 99¢

Leaflet for the three-day Fug festival.

The three-day Fug festival featured the world premiere of what we actually hoped might become an underground dance sensation: "The Gobble." Unfortunately, it was about forty years ahead of its time.

A Fugs Show Cost Me $250,000

I sometimes wore the cloth flower banners Andy Warhol had made for the opening of Peace Eye as a kind of shawl, especially at Fugs shows. At the three-day festival Tuli wanted to sing a ditty he'd just written. It was not my favorite tune, so I had him sing it bent over, with his head near the floor.

During his bent-over crooning, I draped the yellow Warhol Flower silkscreen over him. He crooned a cappella to the melody of the James Bond movie theme *Goldfinger,* his tune with the title "Pussy Galore."

It began:

They call her Pussy Galore
She's a girl from the Eastern Shore
And she flew out to fame
And her name it is Pussy Galore
A fink named Goldfinger
Tried to play some stinkfinger
With our Pussy but she wouldn't give in
to a coldfinger...
et al.

Later in the concert, during the freakout we always provided at the end of "Nothing," when we rolled on the floor and broke things—I was always smashing up tambourines—that very night, perhaps in a pique of self-abnegation, I tore up the beautiful Warhol banner, the very one I had used to drape the bent-over Tuli during "Pussy Galore," at the conclusion of "Nothing." It was a very expensive tear-up.

Another of the Warhol colored silk-screened flowers, the green one, I used as a rain cape and accidentally left in a deli near the Peace Eye Bookstore.

The single red Warhol banner I managed to keep. Decades later Miriam and I sold it. It's now called "The Peace Eye Diptych." Not long ago I saw it in a Sotheby's auction listing, where it sold for $250,000. That's why I say a Fugs show in which I tore up a Warhol banner cost me $250,000, and if I count the time I left the Warhol flower screen in the deli, that places my loss at $500k!!

APO-33 for Burroughs

I was hanging out with William Burroughs quite a bit in the first half of 1965. He gave me a manuscript to publish! I was excited and designed it according to my usual up-Beat, bacchic-American, use-the-Bill-of-Rights design methods.

The Peace Eye Diptych," lately auctioned for $250,000.

I decided to have a volunteer retype the manuscript onto mimeograph stencils, which turned out to be a mistake because then I had to photostat the numerous images in the text, cut each image out, and glue it into its appropriate position. I published the book, gluing the images onto the mimeographed text, then gave a few copies to Burroughs. I was willing to hand-glue the images into as many copies as could be sold. I felt proud and happy.

Burroughs sent his buddy Brion Gysin up to see me during my shift at the cigar store. He told me that Bill didn't like the edition. I had forgotten to tell the typist, my friend Elaine Solow, to keep the columns exactly as Burroughs had composed them so that the text would be absolutely accurate. The columns had gotten changed in the typing.

I disagreed with Burroughs; I thought the edition was beautiful! My feelings were hurt, but I kept a tab on my lips. Burroughs was Burroughs, one of the Founding Beat Quartet (K, G, B, and Corso).

Maybe only fifteen to twenty copies escaped out into the world. The rest I threw away. I bet that Burroughs collectors, and there are plenty, go nuts trying to buy the Fuck You Press edition of *Health Bulletin: APO-33, a metabolic regulator.*

Spring Arts Festival in Buffalo

I flew to Buffalo in early April to take part in the Spring Arts Festival, which included visiting Charles Olson's classes and giving a poetry reading with Olson and John Wieners at the Student Union.

HEALTH BULLETIN:APO~33
WILLIAM BURROUGHS

APO-33 title page, with the usual F.Y./ Press glyphs, including a spurting Bell and Howell camera.

CHLORHYDRATE
D'APOMORPHINE

FACTEUR DE RÉGULATION ÉMOTIONELLE

INDICATIONS– ANGOISSE––
––ANXIÉTÉ –– ÉMOTIVITÉ––
––INSOMNIES–– FUCKED UP––
INTOXICATIONS–– TOXICOMANIES––

published by the FUCK YOU/press:

Prof. Elaine Solow, Textual & Sexual Consultant;
Chairman of the Headcopping and
Manuscript Preparation Division.
Dr.'s Ken Weaver & Peter Orlovsky, Collating Consultants.

Ed Sanders, Scat.D., Imperial Lotus Freak, Designing &
Printing Departments

TOTAL ASSAULT ON THE CULTURE !

fug-press

BURROUGHS MONOGRAPH 1

HEALTH BULLETIN:

APO-33

a metabolic regulator

WILLIAM S. BURROUGHS !

William S Burroughs

A Report on the
synthesis of the
APOMORPHINE FORMULA

Olson had invited Wieners, his student at Black Mountain College in the 1950s, to join him at the University of Buffalo, where Olson had an endowed chair. Wieners, born in Boston, had a degree from Boston University, and his book, *The Hotel Wentley Poems*, had made a big impression on the poets of my generation. His poetry was featured in Don Allen's *New American Poetry*. I met him in 1962 when he worked at the 8th Street Bookshop, and I published him several times in *Fuck You A Magazine of the Arts*.

At a bar we all frequented in Buffalo, Gregory Corso, who was on the University of Buffalo guest faculty, smoked pot openly. Charles Olson lit up some "Asthmador" brand cigarettes, containing stramonium and belladonna to relieve the effects of asthma, to mask Corso's pot. Olson said it was to "keep Corso from blowing us out of Buffalo."

Like other faculty Corso was required to sign the so-called Feinberg certificate:

Education and Cultural

Enthusiasm Greets Poets Olson, Weiners, Sanders

A large, enthusiastic audience crowded the Haas Lounge last Tuesday evening, April 6, to hear a 'Dialogue" by Charles Olson, John Weiners, and Ed Sanders.

Poems" and "The Ace of Pentacles", his most recent book, including one entitled "To Ed Sanders and David Posner."

Ed Sanders, using a variety of

ED SANDERS

The program, which appeared as more a recital than a dialogue, was part of the Spring Arts Festival.

John Weiners, a graduate of Boston College and founder of the

JOHN WIENERS

vocal effects, read a portion of "Poem From Jail" and selection from ————**You,** a literary magazine, and **Peace Eye,** a collection of poems published in Buffalo this year. Sanders is presently editor of a controversial magazine, **Marijuana Newsletter.**

Charles Olson read a sequence from **New Maximus** and his well-known poem "The Librarian". Upon request of John Weiners, Olson read an untitled poem written the past week.

The entire program, if not completely understood, was well-received. When talking with several students afterwards, Ed Sanders said he felt the audience to be very intelligent and sophisticated. He noted that the Buffalo area appears to be having a growth of interest in culture and art that is not merely an imitation of New York. He commented on the "genuine concern in arts" that is being shown in Buffalo and on the university campus.

CHARLES OLSON

magazine **Measure,** read seven selections from "The Hotel Wentley

Worlds of Crisis, Malraux, Camus

By JOEY ELM

"We are in an age of crises and have always been in one," stated Andre Peyre, Chairman of the Department of Modern Languages at Yale University, in a lecture given here last Thursday on "The Crises of Modern Man as envisioned by Malraux and Camus."

Dr. L. Silber, Chairman of the Department of Modern Languages here at Buffalo, introduced Professor Peyre to a capacity crowd assembled in Butler Auditorium. Professor Peyre was invited to Buffalo by the Senate Convocation Committee. Dr. Silber, in his preliminary remarks stated, "Professor Peyre is regarded as a Prometheous in the field of French literature."

In Dr. Peyre's estimation Malraux is a genius. Malraux, believes Peyre, considers man to have a sense of the past. Man knows how to profit by the examples of history. We have to imagine that which we know in order to meet the crisis of the future. Malraux believes that men of the arts such as he, have a constructive awareness of the future. Many of the ideas advanced by Malraux are based on the philosophy of Kier Kegaard . . . "We live forward but understand backward." Both Malraux and Camus are imbued with a sense of history. They apply ideas to find a remedy for evils of present crisis — so people may avoid pitfalls. These men measured what they have said. They do not unnecessarily use words. Suprisingly, Professor Peyre noted that neither Camus nor Malraux are clear thinkers but rather men who have lived their thought. Ideas which are not put into action are useless and not profitable. According to Malraux, man must search for his own salvation in fear and trembling. Malraux was born of an upper middle class Parisian family. He decided to lead a life of adventure and abstained from identifying himself with Western Europe. His aim was to see Europe from a distance. Therefore he voyaged to the continent of Asia to discover what Europe would look (Cont'd on P. 15)

Freshman Today, A

Freshman Weekend, w gins today, lists events t est all students. Sponso the Freshman Class Coun Allenhurst House Coun Goodyear South House and the Goodyear East Council, the weekend inc mixer, a basketball ga hootenany, a semi-formal and a free game day in Union.

Tonight, from 8:30 p.m. night, a mixer featuring th X's Band, will be held i year cafeteria. Refreshme be served, and the admis free for Freshmen and 5 for all others.

Tomorrow afternoon p.m. a basketball game is between the Freshmen gi

Sparer to

Mr. Edward Sparer, Dire the Legal Services Unit bilization for Youth (MF gvie a lecture today at 2:

MYF Training

in the Conference Theate lecture will include a introduction to the work done by MFY as well as co the topic "Special Needs People for Legal Aid."

MFY, similar to Hary Harlem, has been doing welfare work among the neighborhoods of lower M tan. It offers vocational tion to the unemployed a employable of New York Nursery school or free b

WEEKLY CALENDAR . . . APRIL 9-1

From beat-up University of Buffalo student newspaper, April 9, 1965.

Anyone who is a member of the Communist Party or of any organization that advocates the violent overthrow of the Government of the United States or of the State of New York or any political subdivision thereof cannot be employed by the State University. Anyone who was previously a member of the Communist Party or of any organization that advocates the violent overthrow of the Government of the United States or of the State of New York or any political subdivision thereof is directed to confer with the President before signing this certificate.... This is to certify that I have read the publication of the University of the State of New York, 1959, entitled Regents Rules on Subversive Activities together with the instructions set forth above and understand that these rules and regulations as well as the laws cited therein are part of the terms of my employment. I further certify that I am not now a member of the Communist Party and that if I have ever been a member of the Communist Party I have communicated that fact to the President of the State University of New York.

Less than a month later Corso was fired because he refused to sign the loyalty oath. There was a picket organized by the Faculty-Student Committee for Academic Freedom, as reported in the University of Buffalo student newspaper.

Peace Eye

Peace Eye, poems, with the introduction by Charles Olson, was published in the spring of 1965.

The First Fugs Session

Since I'd met Harry Smith at Stanley's Bar in the fall of '62, I'd run into him at film screenings and at Stanley's. I had no idea at first of his prominence as the compiler of the *Anthology of American Folk Music*. I knew him as an avant-garde filmmaker, artist, and occultist. I had visited his apartment up on West Sixty-five and marveled at the works on the wall, which included a mirror whose frame was adorned with lightning bolts and Smith-made designs. Harry came to a number of early Fugs performances. I usually called out to him from the stage. He liked it when I introduced, say, Tuli's song "Nothing," "In the key of Metaphysical Distress—Nothing!!"

Then he told me he could arrange for a recording session for Folkways Records. I went to the Folkways office at 165 West Forty-sixth Street, where I met Moe Asch, the owner. He okayed Harry supervising a Fugs recording session. Harry had gotten a loan from Moe using as collateral some or perhaps all of the mythological string figures that Harry had glued onto boards. He had in mind a publication of them.

Gregory Corso Firing Protested; Picket Staged at Crosby Hall

Monday evening from about 8:00 until 9:30 p.m. the Faculty-Student Committee for Academic Freedom staged a picket in which over 70 people participated, to protest the firing of Gregory Corso for his refusal to sign the played a sign which stated the following: "Private, autonomous, independent picket in behalf of Gregory Corso, poet and educator, offered in protest **not by any means** to champion the right of a Communist to teach at UB, but

Student-Faculty Committee Picket Outside Crosby Hall

Feinberg disclaimer certificate. The committee, after meeting for a half hour in Norton, proceeded to Crosby Hall where Mr. Corso's class was scheduled to meet.

The marchers, under the leadership of Kim Darrow, Henry Simon and Jeremy Taylor, student members of the executive committee, carried signs calling for the abolition of the Feinberg Certificate and condemning Corso's dismissal. The group sang such songs as "My Country 'Tis of Thee" and 'Oh Freedom" and raised such chants as "Feinberg must go."

For a time, a small group, not participating in the picket, dis-

by virtue of the inherent and universal apoliticality of the poet."

The pickets increased in number throughout the demonstration. To climax the picket the demonstrators marched around Hayes Hall, past Diefendorf Hall to Norton Union, chanting loudly most of the way. A letter of protest was sent to Dr. Robert F. Berner, Dean of Millard Fillmore College.

A spokesman for the group expressed satisfaction with the picket and indicated that there would be an accelerated program of action against the Feinberg law and certificate.

He would come to Peace Eye and give me demonstrations of complex string games, which he would weave with his fingers, holding his hands apart while telling various stories associated with the particular string configuration just then stretched from fingers to fingers.

Harry examined a list of tunes I had lying on the Peace Eye desk. He chuckled at a proposed Fugs tune (never recorded) "Whenever I'm in an Airplane Crash, I Reach for My Fly."

For that first afternoon Folkways session in April 1965 at Cue Recording on West Forty-sixth Street, The Fugs consisted of me, Tuli, Ken Weaver (on conga drum), Steve Weber (on guitar), and Peter Stampfel (on fiddle). I had prepared a sequence of twenty-two songs, in a certain order, and we recorded them in one long flow, then recorded them a second time. Steve and Peter also recorded some of their Holy Modal Rounder tunes during the session.

At first we set up our positions—but seemed uncertain on how to proceed. "Just get going," Harry Smith commanded from the control booth, and so we did just that. We arrayed ourselves in front of microphones and began recording the sequence of twenty-two.

In the middle of the session a guy from Folkways showed up with a contract and modest cash for each player. The contract was for "The Fugs Jug Band." I scratched out the words "Jug Band" on the contract.

Harry, as far as I know, received no financial reward for the recording. He asked for a bottle of rum, which I bought. During the session, I think perhaps to spur us to greater motivity and energy, he came in from the recording booth to the room where we were singing and smashed the bottle of rum against the wall.

We took no breaks (except to sign the contracts), and Harry instructed the recording engineer just to let the tape keep running to catch the patter between takes. Little did I know that the tunes from this initial quick, maybe three-hour session would stay in print through the rest of the century and beyond.

On April 21, 1965, this picture was taken of me holding a "Pot Is Fun" sign at the Peace Eye Bookstore. In an interview that day I declared;

Pot should be made legal the way alcohol is. The government should get the benefit of taxes on marijuana. The tobacco companies should be doing market research. Since more and more people are using it daily, and since it can't really be put down—at least, not without spending more money than the space program is costing us—we think pot should be taken out of the hands of criminals. It should be controlled. And the only way to control it is to make it legal.

Tape box for first Fugs recording session,
Cue Recording, 117 West Forty-sixth Street;
containing takes for "Defeated," "Home Made Yodel,"
"Nothing," "Saran Wrap," "Supergirl," "Swinburne
Stomp," and "Kill for Peace"

Ed Sanders inside Peace Eye.
Ed Sanders archive.

Another aim of Lemar is to get the people who use marijuana to stand up and agitate for its legalization. There are at least a quarter of a million potheads in New York City alone. Most of these aren't what you'd call beatniks at all. They're lawyers and newspapermen, writers, doctors, business executives—respectable professional people. If these people would break their silence and come out for the legalization of pot, our campaign would begin to make some headway.

Such was the hope in the spring of 1965.

War War War

That same spring saw the rise of militancy on the part of both the military-industrial complex and the left. We'd already seen back in March the hideous Rolling Thunder attack by the U.S. military against Vietnam. A series of antiwar teach-ins had begun to raise people's awareness of what was actually going on. Such information couldn't be gotten from the New York dailies, only from the leaflets and brochures of the ever-increasing antiwar movement.

In May 1965 Johnson sent troops to Santo Domingo, in a further disavowal of Franklin Roosevelt's "Good Neighbor" policy, which was already mostly in shreds because the CIA had been messing around in various Central American countries to get at Fidel Castro and overthrow him.

When the military-industrial complex wants to put something over on a populace, it moves as quickly as a three-card monte player on a cardboard box in Washington Square Park, and as mysteriously. But rising up against the military-industrial surrealists was lonely. A Gallup Poll that summer showed 61 percent of the population backing the U.S. war in Vietnam and 24 percent saying no.

I couldn't figure it out! It was difficult roaming around the Lower East Side, standing in Stanley's Bar, or riding the subway scanning the *New York Times* or *I. F. Stone's Weekly* to get any kind of clarity about why a great nation was invading a small island democracy. The only answer I could think of is that Johnson was behaving evilly. We were all like overwhelmed animals spinning in cages. One answer would have been to do what Phil Ochs did: write songs that would raise the issues of the war and Santo Domingo as long as people listened to finely crafted melodies.

Phil created a fine song in response to the hemic hands: "The Marines Have Landed on the Shores of Santo Domingo." Here's a verse from it. Notice how elegantly and tightly he put together his lines:

> The fishermen sweat, they're pausing at their nets, the day's a-burning
> As the warships sway and thunder in the bay, loud in the morning.
> But the boy on the shore's throwing pebbles no more, he runs a-warning
> That the Marines have landed on the shores of Santo Domingo.

It raises what Johnson did to a height no reading of microfilm in later dusty years can match.

The Mansfield Film at Cordier & Ekstrom

I was invited by filmmaker Willard Maas to do some filming, with others, on March 18 at an opening of Charles Henri Ford's "Poem Posters" at the Cordier & Ekstrom Gallery, located on Madison Avenue at Seventy-sixth. I'd met Ford, who had an apartment at the Dakota. I knew about his banned gay novel, *Young & Evil*, coauthored with his friend Parker Tyler in the 1930s. Maas would supply the film. I agreed and lugged my Bell and Howell to the opening, where I shot a couple of rolls of film as I followed actress Jayne Mansfield around.

She was very beautiful, and very pregnant, and said yes when I asked if I could shoot her. In one memorable scene she was holding a small lap-dog up to her full lips and they were licking each other. Others were also shooting film that night. The subsequent twenty-four-minute film, *Poem Posters*, has been described as "an invaluable historical document that shows Factory stars Edie Sedgwick and Gerard Malanga cavorting with Beat legend William Burroughs, musician Ned Rorem, film critic Parker Tyler, literary enfants terribles Frank O'Hara and Ted Berrigan, pop artists Jim Rosenquist and Andy Warhol, and many fabulous unknowns. Jayne Mansfield makes a show-stopping appearance—this is probably one of her last images."

The Jayne Mansfield sequence was just about the only footage I shot during the 1960s that would survive.

Filming at the Dakota

Panna Grady continued to invite me and other Fugs to parties at her apartment at the Dakota, and we became friends. At one of her soirees she said that Tim Leary, at a dinner party, had suggested to her that he was the Second Coming.

I asked Panna if I could do some filming at her apartment, and she agreed. A day or so later I showed up at the Dakota. I had made a big cloth banner with the words "Mongolian Cluster Fuck" on it, which I unfurled in her sumptuous living room. I invited Piero Heliczer and several damosels willing to take off their clothes to the filming. Soon everybody was naked in front of the "Mongolian Cluster Fuck" banner.

Panna saw what was going to happen and quickly sent her maid home for the day.

It was actually pretty innocent footage. I brought along a large ball of papier-mâché, which I had painted gold, and filmed a sequence, "The Dance of the Bugger Ball," with Heliczer holding the golden ball and parading around the room with the naked duo.

Harry Smith's Freakout at Peace Eye

Ken Weaver and I were hanging out in Peace Eye the night of June 8 when Harry Smith popped by for a visit. He wanted to borrow some money, just a couple of dollars, which I did not have. He freaked out and tore up three highly scholarly publications he was carrying—*Cheyenne and Arapaho Music* by Frances Densmore, *North American Indian Musical Styles* by Bruno Nettl, and *Place Names of the Kruger National Park*, from the Department of Bantu Administration, Republic of South Africa. And he tossed them onto the floor.

He also tore from the wall, and ripped into two pieces, an original *Tree of Life* print he had given me, published in a limited edition of five hundred in 1954 when Harry was working for Inkweed Arts, a company owned by his friend Lionel Ziprin. I reattached the torn *Tree of Life* and placed it back on the Peace Eye wall. It was an archetypal instance of the artist's famous antsiness. Here, for the history of it, are the three torn-up publications and the reattached *Tree of Life*, saved all these years in my archive.

Meanwhile, I was preparing another issue of *Fuck You/ A Magazine of the Arts* (volume 5, number 9), which I whirred off my electric mimeo in July.

The torn-up *Tree of Life*.

The three torn-up periodicals.

Cover of volume 9, number 5.

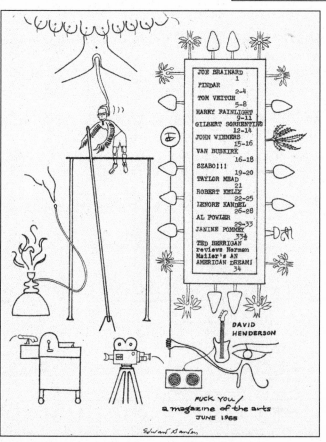

Table of Contents.

The magazine was swinging more from the personal to the political. As I was drawing the cover, I wanted to use an image of a racing motorcycle, so I went over to William Burroughs's apartment to borrow one. The weather was quite warm, but William was working in a suit and tie, designing some collages. I asked if he had some pictures of motorcycle racers, and right away he walked over to a filing cabinet, pulled open a drawer, and quickly found an image of a racing 'cycle, which I was able to utilize on the cover! Many thanks, Bill.

I also drew a page titled "A Declaration of Conscience Against War-Creeps," which called for a fuck-in against the war.

A Declaration of Conscience
AGAINST WAR-CREEPS.

we are lovers & gropers, with enormous phalloi full of tender-ness, with sweet snatches of joy, with apertures & appendages ready to poke, freak, fuck, & wiggle for our communal bene-volence, to create with our bodies an area of peace. To offset the negative karma of the war in Vietnam, we agree to meet at a romantic screwable pub-lic location to hold a FUCK-IN. We call upon the cocksmen, snapping pussy & lovers of the world to join with us to

FUCK FOR PEACE !

name & address

☐ I will Fuck-in. _____

☐ Preferring to eat dick, I will suck-in. _____

after you sign
please send this declaration
to Ed Sanders
Peace Eye Bookstore
383 E. 10th St. New York City

A call from the summer of 1965.

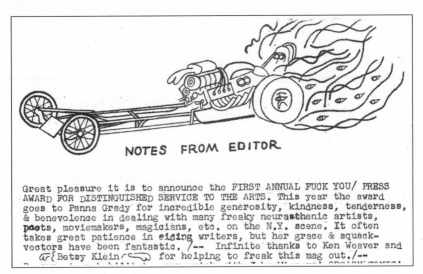

Great pleasure it is to announce the FIRST ANNUAL FUCK YOU/ PRESS
AWARD FOR DISTINGUISHED SERVICE TO THE ARTS. This year the award
goes to Panna Grady for incredible generosity, kindness, tenderness,
& benevolence in dealing with many freaky neurasthenic artists,
poets, moviemakers, magicians, etc. on the N.Y. scene. It often
takes great patience in aiding writers, but her grace & squawk-
vectors have been fantastic. /-- Infinite thanks to Ken Weaver and
Gr{Betsy Klein for helping to freak this mag out./--

F.Y. Award to Panna Grady "FOR DISTINGUISHED SERVICE TO THE ARTS."

Filming at the Secret Location

John Wilcock published an interview with me in the *Village Voice* in the June
17, 1965, issue. Around that time I invited Wilcock to the Secret Location to
view a film session for *Mongolian Cluster Fuck* with Gerard Malanga and a
young woman named Diane H. Ken Weaver and a young woman named
Terry T. were balling on the shiny mattress of the Secret Location when the
Mongolian Cluster Fuck crew arrived.

Ken Weaver was temporarily staying at the Secret Location. He and I
had freshly painted the bedroom, and then I had rehung the bright cloth
drapes from Orchard Street on the surrounding walls. Then I had attached
clip-on lights with photofloods around the upper edges of the walls.

Diane was hesitant to make out with Gerard in front of the camera, although she was willing to blow him, so I took Wilcock out for a snack down
the street. When I came back, Gerry and Diane were fucking away, although he had a tendency to V-frick, that is, to pull himself up into a fuller
view of the lens for the sake of the camera. Anyway Diane screamed for him
not to spurt in her. So at the last few seconds he pulled and crouched over
her smooth breast-tips and came on them with viscid white strands.

I brought the camera close to the breast-tips. Malanga noted how the
camera was purring onward. He then lowered his head to the wet semen and
started slarfing it up, long spurt-strands dangling from his lips to the breasts.

The Background of the Bridge Theater

Meanwhile, The Fugs began to play sold-out shows at midnight on Saturdays during June and July at the Bridge Theater. The theater was located at 4 St. Mark's Place, very near Bowery/Third Avenue, and it was a key location in the battle those years against censorship by the New York City Department of Licenses.

The Fugs sweatshirt.

It was a time of ferment, anguish, and revolution in Lower East Side arts. It may be a hundred years before our descendants learn what level of involvement there was, by the police and intelligence agencies say, in the crackdown against the arts in the city.

A Yale student named John Anderson started performing with us. He was an excellent bass player and could sing excellent harmonies. He was also an artist and designed the red, white, and blue Fugs logo, which we spray-painted on sweatshirts, using a stencil John created.

We also sold black Fugs panties, with a gold "Fugs" on each and an arrow leading downward to the mons veneris.

I designed and printed *The Fugs Songbook* on the Peace Eye mimeograph, which we sold at performances and in the Peace Eye book catalogs.

Revolutionary Egyptology

I somehow found time that summer to teach a course in Revolutionary Egyptology at the Free University, located in a storefront at 20 East Fourteenth near University Place. The course's title piqued the attention of the secret police. (Them commies, you know, will even use hieroglyphics to spread the rev.)

The Criminal and Subversives Section of the New York State Police kept files mainly on leftists and "subversive elements." A study of the state police a few years later revealed that among the thousands of cards listing data on potential slime-commies, "One card noted that XXXXXXX was teaching a course in 'Revolutionary Egyptology.'"

The Fugs Songbook, summer of '65,
hot off the mimeo, 50¢.

Table of Contents!

Note: unless otherwise zapped, the words & the music are by
the same Fug composer.

Here is a list of the FUGS, several of whom, for various
reasons, play with the fugs only occasionally. An asterisk
marks the FUGS who recorded the Folkways FUG ALBUM.

Tuli Kupferberg * - baritone, harmonica, fartophone.
Ed Sanders * - saloon tenor, dick chimes, percussions
Ken Weaver * - "high"tenor, drums
Steve Weber* - Amphetamine soprano, electric guitar
Peter Stampfel*- fiddle, electric guitar, harmonica
Vinny Leary-- electric guitar, harmonica
Moe Mahoney- electric guitar

The FUG SONG BOOK
prepared by Ed Sanders, Ken Weaver, &
Betsy Klein at the evil
PEACE EYE BOOKSTORE
383 East 10th Street
New York, N.Y. 10009

notes on Fugs by Ed Sanders

The Berkeley Poetry Conference

It was one of those events whose power seemed to move beyond itself through invisible Platonic currents—such was the Berkeley Poetry Conference that summer, where important poets gave readings and talks, with parties afterward and the chance to hang out by the hundred-hours bard with bard.

Gary Snyder, Charles Olson, Robert Creeley, Joanne Kyger, LeRoi Jones, Lew Welch, Jack Spicer, Robert Duncan, John Sinclair, Lenore Kandel, Ted Berrigan, Ed Dorn, Allen Ginsberg, and others (including the author of *America: A History in Verse*) were there. To me it was a life-changing event. Grove Press paid for half of my airplane ticket.

It was Charles Olson's bacchic/bardic reading on July 23, 1965, at UC Berkeley's Wheeler Hall that stirred the greatest legend. For over three hours he spontaneously read his verse and talked on poetics. It had an impact on the level of his famous 1950 manifesto, "Projective Verse," which works its subtle enforcement in matters of American poetics up to this day.

I had no inkling of it, but Olson had become infatuated with a young woman attending the conference named Suzanne. I walked with him and Suzanne across the Berkeley campus toward Wheeler Hall to his lecture. Olson pointed out the on-campus house of one of his heroes, Carl O. Sauer, the author of *Northern Mists*, an epochal research into early sea migrations from Europe to North America. Then Olson entered the hall and began his talk.

I sat in the auditorium and was enjoying my hero's enlightening talk when, to my shock, Suzanne handed me a disturbing note:

> How can those people dig FEAR like his? And I mean that *is* where it's at. Like he said "All *my boys* have gotten ahead of me" last night. etc etc & he has no new poems to offer, and no huge group here as compared with say, Ginsberg or even Creeley who really brought them in. And he was so scared, and feeling good, as though he would (maybe) *do* good, that I couldn't tell him this morning that I couldn't marry him. And he's renting a house and car, and phoned the marriage bureau etc etc. And I'm going crazy. I mean I love him, but I love you too, and Dave, and Creeley, and oh, the young boys with their casual *bodies*.

I wondered what to do. Then I replied, jotting next to her message, "Don't leave. We'll make sure we all stick together as a group. I'll get Creeley to stick with the O. The O will understand without any direct NO. Just that we'll all stick together."

Suzanne replied, in handwriting, "Ed I feel like a ghoul staying here watching this. I mean it. I can't stand it. He said he has never asked anyone to marry him before and he really wants to."

I replied, "Really, you'll freak him out if you leave. Look, you'll not be alone. Sit tight, face it. Creeley, Ginsberg, Dorn, Wieners, dig it. I repeat. a. It's obvious you can't leave. b. The O can take anything (any news). c. You'll just have to give him the news, at the

Ed Sanders at the Berkeley Poetry Conference, July '65. Ed Sanders collection.

proper time. d. After the reading, I'll alert the poets that we have to scoop him up and engulf him, until such time that you can have opportunity to tell him."

To which she replied, "Dear Ed: I really do love you. Love, Suzanne."

(All this was written on the front and back of a pink flier announcing a lecture on "A Political Solution in Asia" by Professor Alex Garber, July 22, sponsored by the Young People's Socialist League, in Berkeley, which the researcher can find among the author's archive files at the Dodd Center at the University of Connecticut.)

During the conference Robert Duncan wrote his fine antiwar poem called "Uprising," which ended:

> and the very glint of Satan's eyes from the pit of the hell of
> America's unacknowledged, unrepented crimes that I saw in
> Goldwater's eyes
> now shines from the eyes of the President
> in the swollen head of the nation.

July 25

Bob Dylan was "booed off the stage" at the Newport Folk Festival for utilizing electric instruments. It did seem to measure his switch to the good-time-yet-anguished rock-and-roll center-right—less protest, more electricity. (And he never would come out against the Vietnam War, though this was the year he gave Allen Ginsberg some money to buy an Uher tape recorder on which the poet composed his excellent poem "Wichita Vortex Sutra.") Maybe it was too quick a transition from Woody to Fender for the fans of folk clinging to the image of artisans in cabins building banjos out of turtle shells. I could never figure out what the booing was about.

July 28

Johnson sent 50,000 more troops to Vietnam, increasing the total to 125,000. Monthly Drafts to the army would climb from 17,000 to 35,000. It was just about now that the mantram "Hey, hey, LBJ, how many kids did you kill today?" which he could sometimes hear in the White House from demonstrations on the street, began to wreck his presidency.

Night of Napalm

The Fugs performed a benefit entitled the "Night of Napalm" at midnight, August 7, at the Bridge Theater. We had learned about the use of napalm and defoliants in Vietnam, and it seemed almost too horrible to chant about.

Tuli prepared a tape of patriotic songs, which we played. We performed our regular set, with songs such as "Kill for Peace," "Nothing," and my "Strafe Them Creeps in the Rice Paddy, Daddy." (I later used it as part of the "War Song" suite on our album *Tenderness Junction*.) The band also worked up my "No Redemption" chant, which I had intended to utilize in *Amphetamine Head—A Study of Power in America*:

No Redemption No Redemption
No Redemption from Evil and Sin
No Redemption from the Hate and the Horror
No Redemption No Redemption
The River is full of Corpses

The River is full of the Boats of Death
No Redemption No Redemption...
and on and on

Then we enacted what we called "The Fugs Spaghetti Death." We had boiled pot after pot of spaghetti at Betsy Klein's apartment that afternoon until we had almost an entire wastebasket full of spaghetti. We threw globs of the spaghetti at one another and at the audience. It was all over the stage, and we began to slip, slide, and fall.

I spotted Andy Warhol in the front row. It appeared that he was wearing a leather tie—then *blap!* I got him full face with a glop of spaghetti.

> The **FUGS!** present a
> # NIGHT OF NAPALM
> IN SUPPORT OF THE
> ASSEMBLY OF UNREPRESENTED
> PEOPLE.
> Songs against the war.
> Rock & roll bomb-shrieks.
> Terror thru the wall!
> Heavy metal orgasms!
> Watch all the fugs die in a
> napalm raid! See whole
> intellects disgorged in the new
> fug spaghetti death!
> one night only, the
> NIGHT OF NAPALM!
> _MIDNIGHT SATURDAY AUGUST 7_
> The BRIDGE   4 St. Marks Pl.
> Admission: $1.50   Reservations: OR 3-460

Another surreal night at the Bridge Theater. And a huge job the next afternoon, scraping strings of dried spaghetti off a barren stage.

The Attempted Setup of Allen Ginsberg for Pot Arrest

I returned from the Berkeley Poetry Conference freshened and full of projects. Among other things, I needed to do the final work—the text for the booklet and the sequencing of the tunes—for The Fugs first album. The Fugs were performing at standing-room-only midnight concerts at the Bridge Theater.

But all of a sudden I learned that the federal Bureau of Narcotics and Dangerous Drugs (BNDD, a forerunner of the Drug Enforcement Agency) was trying to set up Allen Ginsberg for a drug bust. Everybody who learned about it, at least in the Lower East Side, was angry and disgusted. At the time Allen was camping with Gary Snyder for a month in the Cascades, Crater Lake National Park, and Mount Rainier, reading Milarepa's poems aloud in the morning.

Allen responded to the attempted setup with his own decades-long investigation into the involvement of U.S. government agencies in dealing and drug smuggling. What happened was this: A couple of young men, Jack Martin and Dale Wilbourne, had been arrested for alleged possession of

lemar
THE NEW YORK COMMITTEE TO LEGALIZE MARIJUANA
Box 133 Stuyvesant Station   New York, New York 10009

Steering Committee: Allen Ginsberg, Peter Orlovsky, Ed Sanders, C.T. Smith, Randolfe Wicker

PRESS RELEASE
--- for immediate release AUGUST 10, 1965

FEDERAL NARCOTICS AGENTS ATTEMPT TO FORCE DEFENDANT
TO SET UP ENTRAPMENT OF INTERNATIONALLY FAMOUS
POET ALLEN GINSBERG

Four Federal Narcotics Agents, including the supervisor of the
New York Bureau of Narcotics, met with federal defendant,
Jack Martin in closed session in order to set up an entrapment of
internationally famous poet Allen Ginsberg, who has voiced protest
against the marijuana legislations on television· and in the newspapers. Agent Bruce Jensen acted as spokesman for the four agents.
Agent Jensen told Mr. Martin, under arrest for alleged possession
of marijuana, that his bail would be raised from $5,000 to
$100,000 (onehundred throusand dollars) and additional charges
would be added to his indictment unless Martin would help federal
agents set up Mr. Ginsberg for a marijuana arrest.
"We want Ginsberg," Agent Jensen stated.

In a recent article, The New York Times wrote that
"second to John F. Kennedy, Ginsberg would seem to be the most
widely aclaimed American cultural ambassador." Mr. Ginsberg is
vacationing in California and was unable to be reached for comment
about the attempted entrapment.

LEMAR (The New York Committee to Legalize Marijuana) was
also cited by Agent Jensen as a target for government marijuana
implantation.

Sworn affidavits and taped interviews concerning this affair
are in the hands of lawyers. Information may be obtained by
contacting Ed Sanders, a member of the steering committee of
New York Lemar, at THE PEACE EYE BOOKSTORE
383 East 10th Street
New York, New York 10009

LeMar press release on the attempted setup of Allen Ginsberg, August 10, 1965.

marijuana. Four BNDD agents met with Martin and threatened additional charges, plus a bail bump-up from $5,000 to $100,000, unless he set up Ginsberg for a pot arrest. (Ginsberg had been very outspoken for legalization. The photo of him at a LeMar march with the "Pot Is Fun" sign had been published around the world.)

"We want Ginsberg," one of the agents had said.

Once I learned about the incident, I wrote and printed a press release under the aegis of LeMar. I sent the release out on August 10. It raised quite a stir.

A Raid on the Secret Location

Three days later, around midnight on August 13, plainclothes police—I never knew whether they were New York police or maybe the feds—raided my Secret Location on the Lower East Side, where I had my film equipment set up and ready to go. I also had stored there stacks of issues of my various publications. I learned about the raid from a downstairs neighbor.

It was never clear whether they knew of the Secret Location on the second floor or not. At the time, because the officers initially were looking for pot, I heard from another resident of the building that when the raid occurred, the guy on the ground floor suggested that they raid my studio if they wanted pot.

In any case they knocked on my door. I wasn't there, of course; I was home at 224 East Twenty-seventh (Miriam and I had recently moved there with our daughter, Deirdre, from the Bronx). They went down to the court-yard of the back building, pulled down the fire escape ladder, went up the ladder, and got into the Secret Location. They pretty much ransacked the place, and according to the downstairs neighbor who had suggested they check out my pad, the officers took away a quantity of my publications.

Several days later, again at night, plainclothes officers returned, went up the ladder again, broke the window onto the fire escape, went in, and then proceeded to remove EVERY SINGLE REEL OF FILM! There must have been at least 10,000 feet of footage. My entire underground film career, Gone!

I called up the Ninth Precinct and demanded to speak to a detective. He suggested that I "sue for them."

Was this action connected with the feds attempting to set up the bard of "Howl"? Was it part of the general clampdown in New York City, beginning in '64, on people such as Lenny Bruce and Jonas Mekas? I didn't know for sure because the annals tracing these things are usually more hidden than the inner workings of the Crypteia (the secret police of ancient Sparta), the Okrana (the czarist secret police), and the KGB/CIA complex.

What was clear was that my underground film career was, for now, over. Gone were the footage of the Great March on Washington, all the thousands of feet of *Amphetamine Head*, the footage of Szabo and Ellen balling in glory, the footage at the Dakota, the footage from The Fugs Cross-Country Caravan (such as kneeling on the porch of Burroughs's boyhood home in St. Louis at dawn), the footage of Malanga and the wet breasts, and even the footage of my brother's wedding in Missouri. I used to fantasize that the wedding would show up spliced to the Dance of the Bugger Ball in some Times Square porn house.

I complained about the raid to the *East Village Other*, which wrote a brief piece in which I claimed that as soon as things loosened up a bit on the personal freedom front, I'd be in the neighborhood theaters with my epic *Mongolian Cluster Fuck*. Except that the fuzz now had all the footage of that, too.

There was no doubt that things were heating up. That same month, August, I received a letter from a guy in Sydney, Australia, who wrote, "I have been advised by the Customs Dept. that (Ed Sanders') Catalogue No. 5 has been seized by them. . . . They are holding same pending whether these may be a prohibited import or not."

Demonstrations Against Federal Narcotics Agents

The Fugs and others held a benefit at the Broadway Central Hotel for defendants Jack Martin and Dale Wilbourne. Federal agents showed up outside the gig and harassed people! I'll never forget the image of filmmaker Jack Smith, his face bloodied from a confrontation with the police outside the Broadway Central. He and others (but not The Fugs) were arrested at the benefit. So there had to be ANOTHER benefit, this one at Art D'Lugoff's Village Gate, on the afternoon of August 22, at which The Fugs again performed. "A benefit for Jack Smith, Jack Martin, Dale Wilbourne, Irene Noland, and Piero Heliczer—all crudely, illegally and violently treated by FEDERAL NARCOTICS agents. . . . Sunday! at the Village Gate, 3–7 p.m."

Neal Cassady at Peace Eye

One afternoon early in September 1965 Neal Cassady pulled up on East Tenth Street outside Peace Eye ☉ ⌘ in a beat-up old '55 Studebaker station wagon that had only second gear! He wanted a joint, which as the world headquarters of the Committee to Legalize Marijuana, I was able to supply on the nonce. He also wanted some amphetamine. He proposed trading the Stude for an ounce. I walked him two and a half blocks over to Nelson Barr's pad across the street from Stanley's Bar and arranged for the swap.

PROTEST AGAINST The *rudeness, brusqueness, crudeness & violence* of NARCOTICS AGENTS!!

A BENEFIT for JACK SMITH, JACK MARTIN, DALE WILBOURN, IRENE NOLAND, & PIERO HELICZER *all crudely, illegally & violently treated by* FEDERAL NARCOTIC AGENTS -- money is needed for court & perhaps appeal expenses

Therefore a benefit at the VILLAGE GATE — _underground movies_! WARHOL, VEHR, LINDER, HELICZER, ANGER SMITH, VANDERBEEK. FRANK, LESLIE, & others Plus The **FUGS**!

plus! THE CINEOLA TRANSCENDENTAL ORCHESTRA! and John Vaccaro, Beverly Grant, Baby Jane Holzer! & Mario Montez! SUNDAY! at the VILLAGE GATE Thompson & Bleeker St. 3-7 p.m. AUG 22 Admission 3:00 reserv. 677-6777

The Fugs at the August 22, 1965, protest. Flier I printed at Peace Eye.

Studebaker, similar to the one Neal Cassady was driving.

Neal's letters from those months indicate he was always trading in jalopies while On the Road. An auto junkyard was a roaming Beatnik's best friend. A couple of months later Cassady drove me and Peter Orlovsky in a careening path down the Pacific Coast Highway in The Fugs' VW van from San Francisco to Ken Kesey's commune at La Honda.

The Thought of Going to California

There were big demonstrations scheduled in October at the Oakland Army Terminal, where soldiers were being shipped to Vietnam. The sponsoring group was called the Vietnam Day Committee (VDC), which had put on very successful antiwar demonstrations earlier in 1965. The VDC planned a nationwide protest known as the International Days of Protest Against American Military Intervention, which was scheduled to take place on October 15 and October 16. I had the idea to lead The Fugs across country, doing antiwar concerts and demonstrations along the way, culminating in an appearance at the Oakland demonstrations. I began planning for the first Fugs Cross-Country Tour.

A Moment of Antiwar Glory at Carnegie Hall

There was a Sing-In for Peace on September 22 at Carnegie Hall to a capacity crowd of 2,800. Fanny Lou Hamer, cofounder of the Mississippi Freedom Democratic Party, brought the house down. Joan Baez sang, among others, and so did The Fugs! We sang "Kill for Peace," with just Weaver on conga and John Anderson on bass because Steve Weber, our guitarist, missed the gig.

Some in the audience booed the act before we were announced. *Uh oh*, I thought, as we stood at the mikes, but the crowd loved us! Some were even dancing in the aisles. In the next issue of the *Village Voice* Jack Newfield wrote a piece about the "Sing-In for Peace" in which he noted, "The politicos in the crowd laughed at and booed the Seven Sons, a long-haired electronic rock 'n' roll quartet, but when The Fugs—the underground Rolling Stones—performed 'Kill for Peace,' several couples began to frug in the aisles of the cultural temple Isaac Stern saved from demolition."

After we left to thunderous applause, Ken Weaver was backstage when he realized that he'd left his conga on the stage, so he went to retrieve it.

Blocking his path was eminent folksinger Theodore Bikel. Twice Weaver tried to retrieve his drum; twice Bikel stopped him, threatening to call security. Weaver called him a fucking Nazi. Perhaps there was a bit of cross-class scrounge-analysis against our East-Side-elegant drummer on the part of the elegant Bikel.

Pete Seeger and Phil Ochs were wildly received, and the concert ended with the Chambers Brothers leading the packed throng in "Down by the Riverside."

But the war went on for another nine and a half years.

Recording Some Tunes to Entice Verve/Folkways

We wanted to entice Jerry Schoenbaum, who was running a label called "Verve/Folkways," into signing us. Verve/Folkways was the Blues Projects' label. We prepared a sequence of songs and went uptown to a place called Sanders Sound studio for the second Fugs recording session, which occurred on September 22. Moe Asch paid for the session, but the masters were to be owned by me. He said all he wanted was to be paid back for the session if Verve/Folkways decided to put out the album.

Among The Fugs tunes we recorded at this session were Steve Weber's new "Boobs-a-Lot," plus another Weber tune, "An Empty Heart." We also recorded my reworking of parts of Ginsberg's "Howl " into "The I Saw the Best Minds of My Generation Rock" and an antiwar chant I wrote, "I Command the House of the Devil." Weaver sang his "I Couldn't Get High," and we recorded his "Slum Goddess of the Lower East Side." To entice Verve/Folkways, we slurred the word "fuck" in the opening line of Tuli's "Supergirl": "I want a girl that can [slur] like an angel."

Players for the Verve/Folkways session were Sanders, Weaver, Kupferberg, Anderson (on bass), Weber (on guitar), and Vinny Leary (on guitar).

Yes! Getting on Verve Folkways! I sent the new demo to Schoenbaum, but to our shock he decided not to sign The Fugs!

Preparing The Fugs First Album

To our lasting gratitude Moe Asch, after the Verve/Folkways turndown, agreed to put out The Fugs album on Folkways' Broadside label. I figured out a sequence of tunes, listening to the original Cue Recording session and the Verve/Folkways session over and over on my aluminum-bodied Wollensak at our apartment on East Twenty-seventh.

I went up to Folkways with Harry Smith and edited The Fugs first album. Harry was all business as we sequenced the takes onto a reel. He would rock the reel back and forth across the playback head, getting a kind of growling sound, until he located the exact spot to cut for a perfect sequencing. He was very skilled at cutting the tape on a grooved metal block, then affixing a small length of splicing tape connecting the end of a tune to some leader tape, then cutting the leader tape (to have several seconds between songs), then finding, through the growling tape method, the exact location of the beginning of the next tune, and so forth.

I wrote some liner notes, which Moe Asch printed into a booklet, plus the song lyrics. Here are the songs in that album:

1.	Slum Goddess	Weaver
2.	Ah, Sunflower	Sanders, Blake
3.	Supergirl	Kupferberg
4.	Swinburne Stomp	Sanders, Swinburne
5.	I Couldn't Get High	Weaver
6.	How Sweet I Roamed from Field to Field	Sanders, Blake
7.	Carpe Diem	Kupferberg
8.	My Baby Done Left Me	Sanders
9.	Boobs-a-Lot	Weber
10.	Nothing	Kupferberg

I had no idea that we were making "history" and that the album would stay in print for the next flow of decades and beyond. All I felt was that that sequence of songs and performances represented the very best that The Fugs could do at that time. I was determined to take the music forward, onward, and upward. I wanted to do some albums that would Stay New for the ages. My youthful energy and bacchic defiance obscured the difficulties of that desire.

With The Fugs' first album under way, I stepped up the sequence of gigs to try to raise money for the Protest Tour.

September 24

"Fugs leaving for the Cross Country Vietnam Protest Concert Tour—Two Big Shows," East End Theater, 8 and 10 P.M. $1.50

September 26

"Fugathon. . . . benefit for the Fugs' Cross Country Vietnam Protest Caravan" at the Bowery Poets Coop, 2 E. 2nd.

The Fugs outside the Peace Eye Bookstore, summer of '65. Standing: Weber, Kupferberg, Stampfel; seated: Sanders, Weaver. Ed Sanders collection.

A Police Informant Trying Out for The Fugs

Meanwhile, I ran an ad in the *Village Voice* looking for a guitarist or a bass player to accompany us on the cross-country tour. I interviewed four. The first was Larry Coryell, not yet famous, with a very expensive guitar; we couldn't afford him. The second was underage, so I turned him down.

The third turned out to be a police informant! I know this because George Plimpton called me at Peace Eye and told me that a famous crime reporter had brought to a party a police informant who had just tried out for The Fugs! Good thing I hadn't been that impressed with the way he played the guitar.

SUNDAY
The FUGS !!
in a
FUGATHON!
dancing · freaking · singing ·
· group~gropes ! ·
LIVE & DISCOTHEQUE ! · THRILLS!
a benefit for the
FUGS' CROSS COUNTRY
VIETNAM PROTEST CARAVAN
at the
BOWERY POETS COOP
2 E 2nd St (2nd floor)
Sept 26th Sunday
3 p.m.
refreshments served
99¢ (viet cong ½ price) 99¢

The fourth one, whom I hired, was named Jon Sheldon, who later became a doctor.

In my notebook of preparations for the cross-country tour was the following notation: "Work on Three Part Harmony." Always one of my chief concerns throughout the 1960s.

I published a two-page press release on the Peace Eye mimeo: "Announcing the Fugs Cross Country Vietnam Protest Caravan, October 8–28th."

I also mentioned a midnight concert in the middle of the Great Salt Desert, in celebration of "Group Gropes

Announcing the

FUGS' CROSS COUNTRY

VIETNAM PROTEST CARAVAN !

OCTOBER   Dear Friend: 8th to 28th

The FUGS, Folkways Recording Stars, New York's most fantastic protest rock 'n' roll peace-sex-grass-psychedelic singing group, direct from a 4 month standing room only run at the Bridge Theatre in New York's Lower East Side, will be in the Berkeley San Francisco area October 15-23 and will be available for concerts, interviews, demonstrations, & dancing.
    The FUGS write all their own material, utilizing the literary and artistic heritage of the Lower East Side combined with the energy of the civil rights and peace movements. THE FUGS have written music for many literary sources, William Blake for instance (Ah Sunflower, Weary of Time), Swinburne (The Swinburne Stomp), Ginsberg (The I Saw the Best Minds of My Generation Rock), et cetera. Some of the Fugs' songs deal extremely frankly with sexual themes (Coca Cola Douche, Slum Goddess, Group Grope) or with the problems of peace & war (CIA man; Kill For Peace, Mutant Stomp; Strafe them Creeps in the Rice Paddy Daddy) or, in many cases, with general tender ballads, satires, chants & body rock. There are 70 songs in the Fug repertoire.

    THE FUGS will leave New York on October 8th. They will proceed to California via auto caravan, giving concerts & holding demonstrations along the way. Concerts are scheduled at the Universities of Missouri & Kansas, Ohio State U., Antioch College, Dickinson College, Indiana U., and wherever spontaneous concerts may be held. 1000's of leaflets protesting against the situation in South Vietnam will be distributed along the route. On October 13, there will be a midnight concert in the middle of the Great Salt Desert in support of Group Gropes & the American West.

    In addition, there will be a series of 10 minute silences observed by the FUGS at the following historic locations:
    a) the grave of James Dean in Indiana.
    b) the KINSEY INSTITUTE FOR SEXUAL STUDIES at Bloomington, Indiana
    c) the beginning of the Oregon Trail, Independence, Mo.
    d) William Burroughs' birthplace in St. Louis
    e) Maryville, Kansas where Michael McClure was born
    f) the cottage in Berkeley where HOWL was written.

and the American West." We also intended to hold a graveside Fugs concert at James Dean's stone.

Lee Crabtree, a friend of Ted Berrigan's, volunteered to drive. We located a Volkswagen bus, which we rented by paying the past-due parking bill for the bus at writer Bill Brammer's apartment on the Upper East Side. Brammer was a well-known writer from Texas, part of a group who called themselves the Mad Dogs and included my friend Bud Shrake, Dan Jenkins, and Larry L. King. Brammer had written a novel, *The Gay Place*, in 1961 and was a pal of Bill Beckman's.

I turned over the key to Peace Eye to my comrade, poet Ted Berrigan, and left him in charge. Just before The Fugs departed on their cross-country tour, Ted sent a telegram to me at Peace Eye wishing us success on the voyage. He signed it "Bob Dylan."

We took off in our packed microbus on October 8—five Fugs, Miriam, Deirdre (then just over a year old), plus a portable sound system, a guitar amp, some drums, and a few hundred copies of *The Fugs Songbook*.

Uh, oh, right away we discovered there was something wrong with the engine. It barely pulled us up the ramp to get on the New Jersey Turnpike. We limped onward, about thirty miles per hour, and there went my carefully calibrated set of events. We missed a gig at Muhlenberg College in Pennsylvania.

Finally, we stopped a few days in Bloomington, Indiana, where we had a new engine put in the VW van. Tuli paid for it.

A Visit of Support for the Kinsey Institute

The Fugs had announced plans to hold a picket of support for the Kinsey Institute in Bloomington. When we showed up, we were invited to visit the Institute, where we met the staff, who volunteered to show us some of their pornographic art. They asked what country and time I was interested in. My mind flashed with ideas. Victorian erotomania? Should I request some eighteenth-century Norwegian teabag fetish art?

We performed a concert at the house of a guy named Frank Hoffman, who was affiliated at the time with the institute. Frank and I at night went to the Kinsey Institute to pick up some pornographic films to show at his house after our performance, which was taped, I guess, for the institute's archives.

We had planned to do an outdoor concert at James Dean's grave, and I had a call from CBS-TV, Channel 8 Indianapolis, which wanted to film it. But we were running so late, we barreled across the Midwest toward our appointments in the "Western Night."

We surged onward, pausing at dawn at William Burroughs's birthplace at 4664 Pershing, in St. Louis, where we trooped up on the porch to hold, on October 18, 1965, a silent vigil for a minute or two in honor of our mentor. I left a note on the porch:

Thank you,
The Fugs
on
October 18, 1965
at 6:00 a.m.
held a silent
vigil
in honor of William
Burroughs' birthplace
at 4664
Pershing,
St. Louis

The actual sign we knelt next to on William Burroughs's St. Louis porch.

I filmed the dawn kowtow on the Burroughs porch, and then we sped onward.

The packed Fugs VW bus, with a sign on the side, "FUGS FOR PEACE," pulled into the driveway of Terrence Williams; his wife, Nancy; and their three young sons, on Missouri Street in Lawrence, Kansas. Williams was a rare book librarian at Kansas University (KU) who had been given a grant by the university to purchase publications from the Mimeograph Revolution. He was a regular customer of the Peace Eye rare books catalogs.

I had set up the visit from the Peace Eye Bookstore. Terrence Williams recalled it: "One day Ed called me to say that the band was traveling to California in a VW bus to attend an anti–Vietnam War rally. They were driving first to the University of Indiana. He asked if we could put them up in Lawrence for a few days as they traveled west. Without asking my wife, I said, 'Sure. When will you be here?'"

Williams further reported:

Ed Sanders, Tuli Kupferberg, Steve Weber and Ken Weaver brought the Lower East Side to our house. And these larger-than-life people from the foreign nation of New York did literally fill our house. My wife Nancy had lived for a time in Greenwich Village, and she was a welcoming and open-minded person. Like me, she held a firm anti-war position, but neither of us had taken our beliefs much past signing petitions and attending rallies. Her only concern about our houseful of musical war protesters was drugs.

Borrowing from James Brown, I had banned all pot from the cross-country tour. We were controversial enough, with copies of *Fuck You* and *The Fugs Songbook* aboard the bus. The only possible indication of "drugs," as Terrence Williams noted, was when he spotted Steve Weber tardily and lengthily staring at the round window of the clothes dryer as it tumbled and tumbled a load of wash.

The Fugs performed a set at the home of KU English professor Ed Grier. (A few weeks later Grier would suggest I approach the ACLU for help after the police raid on Peace Eye Bookstore.) Lawrence had a well-developed underground scene. We met a young poet named George Kimball, who, out one night in town, ran into a man walking in William Blake nakedness. Kimball, later a well-known sports reporter, was arrested while picketing the Lawrence Draft Board with a sign "Fuck the Draft" and was soon off to New York City, where in early '66 he drove Panna Grady and me up to Gloucester, Massachusetts, to visit bard Charles Olson.

During our two-day stay in Lawrence our bass player, Jon Sheldon, had had enough of the cramped VW van and he split. We were grateful for the additional floor space in the van. Steve Weber on guitar and Ken Weaver on conga were more than adequate music underneath our lyrics.

Then we sped across the prairies and mountains to the West Coast. In San Francisco all The Fugs stayed for the first few days of our visit at a two-story apartment owned by Judith Wehlau, a friend of Tuli's, on Downey Street, just down the hill from Michael and Joanna McClure's pad.

I was eager to scare up some paying gigs. We auditioned at the Matrix, a folk/jazz club at 3238 Fillmore, which was somehow associated with a new group I had heard about, the Jefferson Airplane. During our audition I noticed how wonderfully our quiet driver, Lee Crabtree, played the electric piano set up on stage! We didn't get the gig, but Crabtree was soon a member of The Fugs.

We had money problems. I reached out to Panna Grady in New York, who graciously sent a check. Don Allen helped sell a full run of *Fuck You/ A Magazine of the Arts*, which covered more of our expenses.

I managed to get us a multiday gig at a coffeehouse at 1339 Upper Grant Avenue, in North Beach, called Coffee and Confusion, but after one set the owner fired us! A songwriter named Ivan Ulz ran the open mike at Coffee and Confusion and was upset at our firing. He organized a revolt by coffeehouse employees, who demanded that the owner bring us back, with the result that The Fugs, with our risqué, antiwar repertoire, finished the brief run. We made just a few dollars, but it paid for gas for the VW bus.

October 22

A gig with The Fugs, Lawrence Ferlinghetti, Paul Krassner, and Allen Ginsberg at the Berkeley Community Theater, a benefit for the Vietnam Day Committee.

October 29

The Fugs at the Orb Theater, 1470 Washington, San Francisco. With a 50¢ "suggested donation" at the Orb, the influx of moolah was scant.

October 30

The League for Sexual Freedom held a "Legalize Cunnilingus" demonstration at Union Square in San Francisco. A few Fugs took part.

Down and Out

While we were in San Francisco, poet Charles Plymell sent me a note about a gallery a friend of his was opening on Halloween. It was called the "Raped & Strangled Art Gallery." It was located at 883 Golden Gate Avenue. I gulped and allowed us to play.

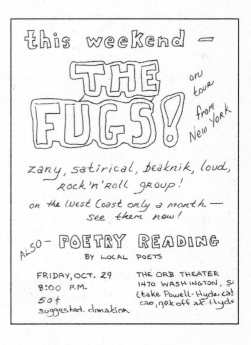

this weekend —
THE FUGS!
on tour from New York

zany, satirical, beaknik, loud, Rock 'n' Roll group!
on the West Coast only a month — see them now!

ALSO — POETRY READING
BY LOCAL POETS

FRIDAY, OCT. 29
8:00 P.M.
50¢
suggested donation

THE ORB THEATER
1470 WASHINGTON, S.
(take Powell-Hyde cable car, get off at Hyde

PICKET
TO
LEGALIZE
CUNNILINGUS
(oral contact with female genitals)
Saturday — Oct. 30 — NOON
at Union Square

Sexual Freedom League
Box 14007, San Francisco

It was a Halloween costume affair, but The Fugs were already in Fugs costume, so we came as we were: On the Edge, Out There, a Bit Famished, but bearing with us a tender child, Deirdre, then almost fourteen months old.

It was a wild night. The Fugs, Miriam, and young Deirdre slept on the gallery floor. Crashing on the floor of something called the Raped and Strangled Art Gallery made it certain, if certainty needed further

As far as I know, Western civilization's first legalize cunnilingus demo.

certainty, that we were "down and out." I remember as a kid in the dorm at Missouri University reading George Orwell's *Down and Out in Paris and London*. Now I was there, Down and Out in San Francisco in an overloaded VW bus with hungry and very talkative Fugs, wife, daughter, sound equipment, *Fugs Songbook*, on the edge of panic. Miriam somehow lost one of her tennis shoes. And for a while we didn't have the cash to get a new pair.

Fugs Gig with Country Joe and the Fish and Allen Ginsberg

Ed Denson, manager of a band just then forming called Country Joe and the Fish, contacted me about performing with Allen Ginsberg on the campus of the University of California, Berkeley on November 5. I agreed, and they put out a flier around Berkeley for the gig, held in a chemistry lecture room, whose central table, down in the front of the room, we used as a stage.

We had a large crowd, given the scantiness of the prepublicity. First Country Joe and the Fish performed (it was their first performance ever!), then Ginsberg, sitting lotus position in the middle of the chemistry table stage. The Fugs closed the show, a highlight of which occurred when Steve Weber fell back off the stage, landing on his back while keeping the beat perfectly and not missing a note. I collected the money, dividing it exactly among all the performers, $20 each, which caused Allen to grumble a bit because his renown obviously (his image was featured prominently on the poster) had led to the crowd paying the $1 admission.

1 Slum Goddess
2 Kill For Peace
3 COCA COLA DOUCHE
4 DIRTY OLD MAN
5 AH SUNFLOWER.
6 SUPER GIRL
7 STRAFE THEM CREEPS
8 GROUP GROPE
9 I command the house
10 Wet Dream over You
11 I saw the Best Minds
12 I Feel like home made
13 How sweet I roamed from Field
14 Nothing

Fugs set list, San Francisco, fall of '65.

Benefit for the San Francisco Mime Troupe

The night after the gig with Country Joe and Allen Ginsberg, The Fugs performed at a benefit for the San Francisco Mime Troupe. A young man named Bill Graham managed R. G. Davis's troupe. Its commedia dell'arte production of *Il Candelaio* was declared too smutty by the San Francisco Parks and Recreation Commission, but the Mime Troupe performed it nevertheless and was busted.

Bill staged a benefit for the group's legal defense fund. The Family Dog, a leading psychedelic-era concert promoter, offered its help, and Bill, who had been concentrating on his mime troupe duties and was not aware of the dance craze, listed The Family Dog as performers on the "Appeal" party poster, thinking they were a dog act.

The November 6 fund-raiser was an eye-opener for Bill Graham. His goal had been to raise money for the troupe and to headline the censorship, but he was amazed by the highly energetic and artistically adorned throngs of youth who came to the Howard Street Loft, drawn there by the allure of the Jefferson Airplane, The Fugs, Sandy Bull, the John Handy Quintet, and the Mothers of Invention. Thousands arrived, inspiring Bill Graham, who put together two more "Appeal" parties in December and January.

It was Bill Graham's first concert production.

S.F. mime Troupe

WILL HOLD AN

'APPEAL' PARTY

924 HOWARD STREET (BETWEEN 5ᵗʰ & 6ᵗʰ STS.)

SAT. NIGHT — NOVEMBER 6

FROM 8 P.M. TILL DAWN

Entertainment, Music, Refreshments!　・・・ DONATION: AT LEAST $1ᵒᵒ ・・・ Engagement, Commitment & Fresh Air!

R. G. Davis, director of the San Francisco Mime Troupe, was found guilty on November 1 of performing in the public parks without a permit. The four-day trial was pointless because the court did not allow the only relevant issue, freedom of speech and assembly, to be considered.

The trial settled nothing. The Mime Troupe is determined to fight until the parks are returned to their only "owners," the people of San Francisco.

For this is what it is all about: Who owns the parks? Chairman Walter Haas and his fellow members of the Recreation and Parks Commission? They apparently think so, for they revoked the troupe's permit on the grounds the Mime Troupe's commedia dell'arte production of "Il Candelaio" was not in "good taste" or "suitable" for "their" parks. The troupe defied the ban to test a constitutional issue: the commission's power to interfere with free expression. Then Municipal Judge FitzGerald Ames ruled that the commission's revocation power was "a matter of law" and not for the jury to decide. Thus the commission's powers were not allowed to be contested, and Davis was found guilty.

The only legitimate purpose for issuing permits is to schedule events properly - preventing time or place conflicts. The contents of performances is not a matter for the commissioners to judge. And Walter A. Haas's idea of good taste is NOT a "matter of law"!

There are adequate laws to handle any crime committed in the parks. Was the Mime Troupe accused of being disorderly? No. Of creating a public nuisance? No. Of obscenity? No. It was banned because it did not conform to the commissioners' standard of "good taste" (whatever that may be). If the commissioners believe the troupe violated any law, then let them charge the troupe with a violation of that law.

WHO OWNS THE PARKS? The people of San Francisco. The parks are very large and there is room for us all -- room for any expression of any idea. Freedom of speech and freedom of assembly do not stop where Mr. Haas's good taste begins.

What is the effect of the commission's action and the court's failure to confront the issue? Our freedoms are lessened, for when one means of expression is cut off, who knows what will be next? The 20,000 persons who enjoyed the troupe's free park performances in the past four years will no longer have that opportunity, thanks to the "good taste" of six commissioners.

THE CREATIVE LIFE OF SAN FRANCISCO IS NOW DIMINISHED AND THE PARKS ARE CONSIDERABLY LESS JOYFUL.

The following artists will appear at the APPEAL PARTY on behalf of the San Francisco Mime Troupe:

JEANNE BRECHAN	THE FAMILY DOG	JOHN HANDY QUINTET	JIM SMITH
SANDY BULL	LAWRENCE FERLINGHETTI	JEFFERSON AIRPLANE	ULLETT & HENDRA
THE COMMITTEE	THE FUGS	SAM HANKS	& OTHERS WHO CARE

FOR FURTHER INFORMATION, CALL GA: 1-1984

Neal Cassady Driving Us to La Honda

In early November Neal Cassady drove me and Peter Orlovsky from San Francisco to Ken Kesey's place in La Honda. Neal drove our Volkswagen van very fast on the twisting Pacific Coast Highway, sometimes straying into the other lane on the curves, while talking nonstop. One curve Neal was rapidly negotiating while he was praising race driver Stirling Moss. "Moss," he said, "can go into a power slide on a curve while adjusting his goggles at the same time." Neal mimicked adjusting his goggles as we careened around the curve.

The Fates were not ready to snip, so we reached La Honda safely.

A day or so later The Fugs began to wend the packed VW bus back across the Great States. First to Los Angeles, where we stayed with the Mothers of Invention keyboard man, Don Preston.

The Fugs in Placitas

Next we traveled onward across the desert and visited Robert and Bobbie Creeley in Placitas, New Mexico, a small town north of Albuquerque, in November 1965. Bobbie and Bob graciously put us up for several days. Right after we arrived, Bob Creeley drove down to the store and purchased cigarettes for those who smoked in an act of instant analysis of the band's impecuniosity.

Bobby shot some footage of us as we came out of our VW van, including Miriam Sanders and our fifteen-month-old daughter, Deirdre.

Miriam and I wandered out in the open fields. She was looking for cacti near their house and found antique Native pottery shards.

Ed cleaning his Bell and Howell, Steve, Bob Creeley, by The Fugs' VW van, Placitas. Photo from footage shot by Bobbie Louise Hawkins.

(*Left*) Steve, Lee Crabtree, Ken, Placitas. (*Right*) Tuli and Steve.

Deirdre, Miriam, in shadows, Placitas. Photos from footage shot by Bobby Louise Hawkins. (*Right*) Some 1965 shards found near the Creeley house in Placitas.

Two Letters to Charles Olson

I wrote my mentor on the return trip to New York City. The first note was dated November 9, 1965, when we stopped at Los Angeles:

Dear Charles—
Well, the Fugs have been on a coast to coast concert tour—stayed in the Berkeley-S.F. area for three weeks. Ginzap was on a couple of concerts with us—the Zap is now billed as Folk Rock Mantra-ist. We are on the way to the Creeley conspiracy in Placitas. Traveling w/ wife, daughter Deirdre, and the 4 other Fugs. It's been a great month touring, although I sometimes feel like I'm traveling with Albanian hillsmen storming Byzantine nunneries.

Ginsberg, with the Orlovsky brothers, in the microbus soon to travel around the states. Michael McClure writing Rock Message Units for the local S.F. singing groups. He and Ginzap & Bruce Conner practicing daily on rhythm mantras. Some of it pretty good. Why don't you write a song for the Fugs: Olson message to the young & humm the tune into a tape recorder—send tape and text. We've done a lot of Blake: Ah Sunflower Weary of Time; How Sweet I Roamed from Field to Field; Oh Rose Thou Art Sick; Swinburne Stomp (a chorus from *Atalanta in Calydon* "Before the Beginning of Years.), Ginzap, etc.

Next I proposed that Olson hook up with Panna Grady:

2 days later—

Now at Creeleys'. Extremely hospitable, kind, generous. 6 fug maniacs on the Placitas set. Now to the real reason of letter.

A very elegant lady on the N.Y. literary scene with a large opulently furnished apartment at the Dakota on 72nd and C. Park West, living alone, I believe an Esterhazy countess with Rockefeller money, has on several occasions mentioned interest in having you stay with her for a while—to meet you, etc. She has a maid or two—incredible apartment. (I filmed part of mongolian cluster fuck there) very large with lots of phones & whole sections I'm sure you could be alone in.

She's an excellent cook the type who'll spend 8 hours making Hungarian horse radish with income from scads of stocks—she entertains on the highest social levels & throws the most interesting of the N.Y. literary in-bashes. Why don't you bop in to N.Y. and spend some time there. I'd be glad to like handle any details, arrange the date, or help in whatever way. In any case, you now have a N.Y. base on the most comfortable level, with $, lots of those Kennedy/Shriver/ freaks all around.

Send me some poetry for an issue? How about any prose you may have written, a message from the big O to the young Turks, for the prose issue of F.Y./?

Terrence Williams [KU rare books curator] mentioned with joy and delight that you might freak in to K.U. for a two week scene. The Cree is not too far away—he could come & be someone to talk to, maybe. Let me know if anything I can do in N.Y. for you.

Instant publication of course, of any project you have in mind.

Love,

Ed

Onward to New York City

After visiting and replenishing our vim in Placitas, there followed a long, nonstop surge across the prairies. We arrived back in New York City broke, beat, metaphysically distressed, yet full of grit and determination. The lights had been turned off at Peace Eye, and we needed to pay rent on the store and on our pad on Twenty-seventh.

One good mote of news: Our record was out! *The Village Fugs Sing Ballads of Contemporary Protest, Point of Views, and General Dissatisfaction* (later known as *The Fugs First Album*), on the Broadside label. The cover featured a Dave Gahr photograph taken in an empty lot down the street from the Peace Eye Bookstore. At least we weren't listed as The Fugs Jug Band.

The impact was almost instantaneous. The sequence I chose, from those two early sessions, with the help of Harry Smith, which we edited on a tape machine at Folkways Records before leaving for the cross-country tour, was to catch on and become, some say, a classic American folk recording.

The Founding of the *East Village Other*

While The Fugs were on the cross-country road trip that fall, an underground newspaper called the *East Village Other,* and more often just referred to as *EVO,* founded in the summer, was beginning to flourish. It set up shop in a storefront at 147 Avenue A, between Ninth and Tenth, across from Tompkins Square Park. It was in a perfect spot to monitor that part of the Lower East Side.

I had followed *EVO* since its planning stage. In fact I was offered an ownership position by Walt Bowart if I'd get involved. I knew Bowart as an artist and a bartender at Stanley's. In later decades he became an important scholar in the field of robowash and hypnotic/narcotic behavior modifications and wire-ups of programmed agents.

I meditated seriously about jumping into the *EVO* project. In the end I turned it down because of all my obligations—filmmaking, publishing, Peace Eye, The Fugs, my family, and poetry.

Early *East Village Other* contributors included Ishmael Reed, Allan Katzman, John Wilcock, and Bill Beckman, with his Captain High cartoon panels. Beckman would soon design The Fugs' stage set at the Astor Place Playhouse.

How much did *EVO* cost back then? Twenty-five cents a copy. A feature of each *EVO* issue was a Slum Goddess pictorial, inspired by The Fugs tune.

Around the nation were web presses, sturdy printing machines with large rolls of newsprint attached, which normally were used to print used car brochures, college newspapers, and the like. There was always a slot in the production schedules for these web presses to print almost anything anybody wanted, including the burgeoning underground press.

Other underground newspapers began to flourish as well, including the *Los Angeles Free Press, Chicago Seed, San Francisco Oracle, Milwaukee Kaleidoscope,* Detroit's *Fifth Estate, Berkeley Barb, Georgia Straight,* and *Great Speckled Bird.* They were part of the glory of the '60s brought to us by the unused portions of the Great Bill of Rights.

These newspapers were in good part paid for by ads from the zones of psychedelic commerce (plus movies, concerts, head shops, record companies, and "personals"), which the National Security Grouch Apparatus disliked intensely to the point of breaking them up. Red Squads were ever busy scheming to stomp the undergrounds to death, and the CIA itself chomped its tweedy fangs into the underground press movement later in '67.

Another Letter to Charles Olson

Olson sent text for the upcoming prose issue of *Fuck You* and had replied in the positive regarding meeting Panna Grady, so I immediately wrote back on December 2:

> Dear Charles, Joy to get all your letters. Called Panna G. today—she's planning elegant dinner parties for you—you can stay I hope for a while? Just let me know a few days in advance so I can set things up. Ok. Thanks for the wonderful piece for F.Y. Hard to transcribe on the typewriter. I'll send thee a dummy copy for your proofreading.
> Love,
> Ed.

I was determined to fulfill a role as a bardic matchmaker.

Peaceful Life on East Twenty-Seventh

No matter how weird and freaky it was out there on the streets of New York City, we tried to keep it fairly normal at home. We decided to wall off the weirdness, believing that children should be protected from creepiness, dirt, and maelstromism. In December Miriam and I were visited at our new pad by distinguished Italian writer Fernanda Pivano, translator of Hemingway and the Beats. She wrote of it in her book *C'era una volta un beat*: "*Un'immagine della pacifica casa di Ed Sanders, dove il turbolento poeta viveve con la moglie Miriam e la bambina. Si era fatto dei classificatori con grosse scatole di cartone e tutta l'organizzazione della casa era molto improvvisata e a sfondo nomadico. Ogni tanto doveva traslocare in fretta per evitare che la moglie venisse coinvolta negli arresti.*"

The
FUGS
are back from their cross-country TOUR !
dope-grope rock'n'roll, meat-shrieks & rice paddy frenzy
MIDNIGHT SATURDAYS
The Bridge Theatre
4 St Marks Pl.
reservations: OR3-4600 $1.50
"YOU ARE ALL A FUG GENERATION!"

After returning from the cross-country tour, we started playing again at the Bridge Theater at midnight and at the Cafe Au Go Go on Bleecker Street, where Lenny Bruce had been arrested!

I printed a flier at Peace Eye when we were held over at the Au Go Go: "The Fugs held over, Cafe Au Go Go, 152 Bleecker through Dec. 26."

Playing the Au Go Go was real eye-opening; we were performing at the same venue as the Blues Project, Jesse Collins Young and the Youngbloods, the Jim Kweskin Jug Band, Paul Butterfield, Howlin' Wolf, Richie Havens bent down close to his guitar and doing Dylan as well or better than Dylan, and others. I learned many things hanging out at the Go Go. It exposed me to a level of musicianship that made me realize I was going to have to bump up The Fugs to a much more elevated mode in order to survive in this zone of the Music Game.

For me the weeks The Fugs played the Cafe Au Go Go were a time of wonderment. We met Dylan's and Haven's manager, Albert Grossman, there. He checked out our act but decided not to manage us. I'd seen Josh

The Fugs and Richie Havens, Cafe Au Go Go, December 10, 1965. Ed Sanders collection.

The **FUGS!**
~ held over ~
CAFE
AU GO GO
152 Bleeker

~ through Dec. 26th ~

reservations: SP 7-4530

" YOU ARE ALL
A FUG GENERATION "

Singing "Slum Goddess," December '65, at the Cafe Au Go Go. Ed Sanders collection.

Also performing at the Cafe Au Go Go, the Jim Kweskin Jug Band!
Photo courtesy of Bill Keith.

White at Grossman's Gate of Horn in Chicago the spring vacation of 1958, when I was at Missouri University.

Rastignac at the End of Balzac's *Pere Goriot*

I was determined to survive and thrive. I felt Jean-Paul Sartre's apothegm "We are alone, with no excuses," through every fiber of my youthful identity. In the slight rise of ground between Avenues C and B, in front of the Peace Eye Bookstore, I felt like the character Rastignac at the close of Balzac's *Old Goriot*, who, faced with defeat, calamity, metaphysical distress, poverty, the smashing of dreams, and an obstinate caste-based system of haves and have-nots, took a vow at the hilltop of Père Lachaise cemetery: "Rastignac walked a few steps to the highest part of the cemetery, and saw Paris spread out below on both banks of the winding Seine. Lights were beginning to twinkle here and there. His gaze fixed almost vividly upon the space that lay between the column of the Place Vendome and the dome of the Invalides; there lay the splendid world that he had wished to gain. He eyed that humming hive … and said with defiance, 'It's war between us now!'"

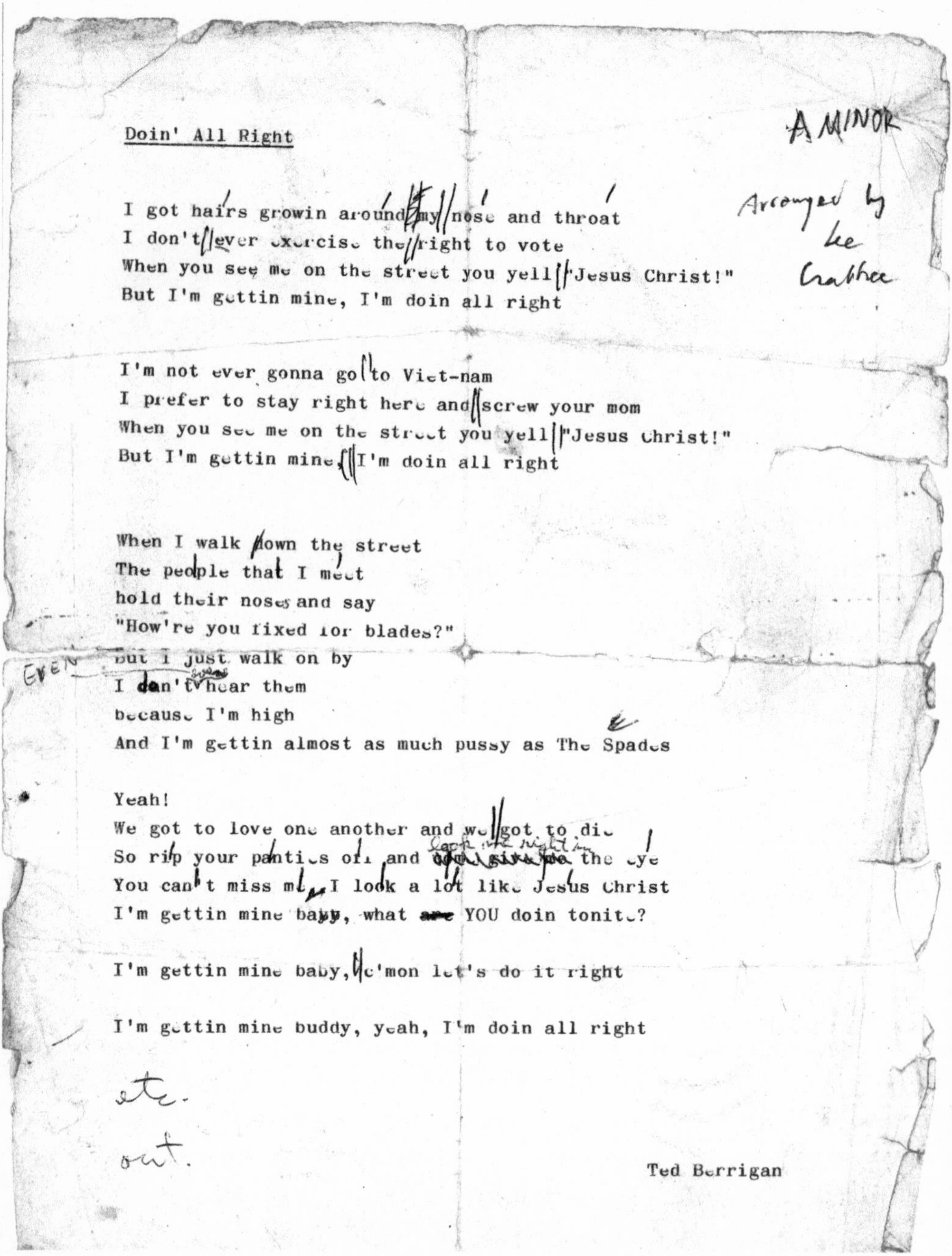

Doin' All Right

A MINOR

Arranged by Lee Crabtree

I got hairs growin around my nose and throat
I don't ever exercise the right to vote
When you see me on the street you yell "Jesus Christ!"
But I'm gettin mine, I'm doin all right

I'm not ever gonna go to Viet-nam
I prefer to stay right here and screw your mom
When you see me on the street you yell "Jesus Christ!"
But I'm gettin mine, I'm doin all right

When I walk down the street
The people that I meet
hold their noses and say
"How're you fixed for blades?"
But I just walk on by
I don't even hear them
because I'm high
And I'm gettin almost as much pussy as The Spades

Yeah!
We got to love one another and we got to die
So rip your panties off and look me right in the eye
You can't miss me, I look a lot like Jesus Christ
I'm gettin mine baby, what are YOU doin tonite?

I'm gettin mine baby, c'mon let's do it right

I'm gettin mine buddy, yeah, I'm doin all right

etc.

out.

Ted Berrigan

The original draft of Ted Berrigan's tune.

I felt the same way. I was determined to make a living from my art. There was no turning back. No graduate school. No quietude of scholarship. No Quaker and Catholic Worker–inspired peace work. It was Fugs. Fugs and Counterculture, LeMar and the Mimeo Rev! And getting our brains on tape! I was determined to improve The Fugs' music, making it better and thus more impactful, while at the same time not changing our lyrics, our level of satire, our bite and humor.

Meanwhile, Pot Martyrdom continued: Tim Leary was arrested on December 23 in Laredo for grass. (He went on trial on March 9, 1966, and was given thirty years in the slams!)

It was a harsh time for the arts because the arts were assaulting some of the Power Zones of the right-wing culture and demanding the freedoms of the U.S. Constitution. I'd already had a taste of this time a few months earlier when police undertook a warrantless search of my Secret Location.

I was extremely determined to put The Fugs on a firm financial footing. I sensed that there was an audience willing to plunk down cash to view our Spectacle and hear our music. I always thought that The Fugs WERE their tapes. The best investment, I felt, was to try to record The Fugs as much as possible and to keep the tapes. Under the adage "Tapes don't lie." The Fugs, to me, were the tapes of their musical pieces.

December 20

I read poetry at Israel Young's Folklore Center with Ted Berrigan. (It had already moved from 110 MacDougal to 321 Sixth Avenue, on the second floor next to the Waverly Theater, west side of the avenue.)

In late '65 Ted wrote a song for The Fugs, "Doin' All Right," which went on our second album.

As leader of The Fugs, I found myself in the unenviable position of hiring and firing. Steve Weber was becoming a problem. He had missed our triumphal performance at Carnegie Hall back in September, so we were forced to perform before a sold-out crowd with just a bass and Weaver on the conga. Weber was loath to practice. I was determined to morph and mutate our music into the level of the bands I had been watching intently at the Cafe Au Go Go.

In one of our recent gigs we were in the midst of performing "Slum Goddess" and suddenly the uptempo feel of the guitar utterly vanished. I looked over at Weber, and he was seated in a chair with his head resting on the set list on his guitar. He was asleep! He was a bit difficult to travel with. We replaced him with Lee Crabtree on piano.

We did New Year's Gig, January 1, at midnight, going into January 2, at the Bridge Theater. It was Saturday night. We were getting stronger! Slowly, through practice practice practice (what my hero William Blake urged artists to do), we were turning our untuned rawness into a kind of Raw Beauty.

1966

The Raid on Peace Eye

The Fugs gave a midnight concert at the Bridge Theater, Saturday into Sunday, January 1–2, after which I went home to our apartment on East Twenty-seventh Street and hit the hay. Then *Zzzont Zzzzzunh! Zzzuht! Zzzuh!* There was an insistent buzzing of the downstairs door around 4:30 AM. It was Tuli Kupferberg. He said there were policemen inside Peace Eye. We took a cab back down to 383 East Tenth.

The lights were on inside the store, and a window was broken. There were police cars outside, and there were a couple of police officers in the store. A few were also in the middle room where I kept the Fuck You Press mimeograph machine and piles of uncollated publications, such as *The Toe-Queen Poems*, the *Marijuana Newsletter*, *The Fugs Songbook*, *Bugger (an Anthology of*

The Peace Eye Bookstore front window, 1966. Ed Sanders collection.

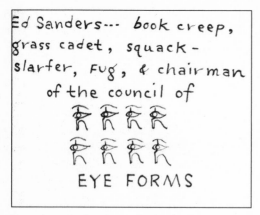

Ed Sanders--- book creep, grass cadet, squack-slarfer, Fug, & chairman of the council of

EYE FORMS

From the author's archives, this fragile sign on the lower right side of the Peace Eye front window, 1966.

Buttockry), Auden's "Platonic Blow," and various issues of *Fuck You/ A Magazine of the Arts*. The officers were examining some pages.

I was wondering what it all meant as I grabbed a hammer and some wood and started boarding up the broken window and fixing the front door. A cop was stationed outside on the street. As I was hammering, he said, "I don't care personally, but the sergeant is upset."

In recent months I'd begun to get the attention of law enforcement. For one thing, an undercover police informant had auditioned for the band. So I couldn't help but wonder, had the police deliberately smashed their way in?

It was not long before I became aware of Sergeant Charles Fetta, who was then assigned to the Ninth Precinct. Fetta did seem upset and appeared to have a case of phallophobia, commingled, I thought, with a splash of phallophilia because he seemed miffed about instances of exposed male genitalia in some of my publications. Maybe a bit too miffed.

He asked, "Are all these publications yours?"

I thought I should show some confusion and not really answer. My generation knew Lenny Bruce's dictum—"deny deny deny"—to the walls of our being, so I thought maybe if I appeared vague, I could avoid legal trouble.

Next, the sergeant's hand seemed to tremble as he thrust an issue of *Fuck You/ A Magazine of the Arts* close to my face. "What about that?" he asked, as he pointed to the cover.

He was clutching the cover to volume 5, number 4, which showed a boy I had copied from a Danish tobacco package at the cigar store where I worked on Times Square. Next to the lad was an Egyptian deity with a peace sign on his head and a spurting phallus.

He wanted to know what the cover meant. Was the bird threatening the boy? What's that bird going to do with that boy? The sergeant was so upset over the cover that I was later surprised when it did not show up as one of the exhibits in my trial the following year.

I was placed under arrest and the police carted away some valuable boxes of my publications. Tens of thousands of dollars worth, as measured in eBay wealth, say forty years ahead. I asked for a receipt (which they promised to supply but never did).

The Ninth Precinct headquarters was at 321 East Fifth. The Ninth covers all the Alphabet Part of the Lower East Side, Houston to Fourteenth, and Broadway east to the East River. We arrived at the polished wood-paneled front doors, which to me had a kind of medieval feel to them. We pushed through and inside. The officers within the precinct house seemed eager for my arrival.

The FY cover that so upset the sergeant.

Indeed, there was a marked contrast of facial expressions between the grumpy arresting officer and the policemen at the station house. For being such a serious matter—that is, the booking of a likely criminal, me—there certainly was a lot of mirth in the Ninth Precinct. "Hey, you're Peace Eye!" one officer boomed. I nodded.

"Hello, Peace Eye!" another exclaimed. I nodded.

"Let me take a look!" another commented and smiled, and laughing officers passed magazines hand to hand.

In my press release issues several days later I described being driven to the precinct house: "I was taken to the 9th precinct where they spent several hours rolling on the floor screaming with glee as they contemplated the copies of *Fuck You/ A Magazine of the Arts, Bugger, The Platonic Blow, The Marijuana Newsletter* and other goodies they had scarfed from Peace Eye. During this time, however, several officers were carefully examining the New York State Penal Code to find a felony to place upon me. I steadily informed them that it was a misdemeanor. It was."

All they could come up with to validate the sergeant's trembles and shakes was a misdemeanor charge of possession of obscene literature with intent to sell.

I was asked to sit at a desk, where an officer asked me questions and typed on a nonelectric typewriter, *peck peck peck.*

Name, address, phone, age, height, weight, then he asked if I had any tattoos, to which I replied, "No." Meanwhile, various officers kept on chuckling
and chortling, reading through issues of *Fuck You*.

About a half hour later, my arresting office, Sergeant Fetta, along with another officer, came into the room where I was being questioned. Fetta said,
"Okay, Sanders, get into that room and take off your clothes."

"What's up?" I replied. Then I noticed he was holding the very issue
whose cover had so upset him back at Peace Eye.

"I thought you said you didn't have any tattoos." He was pointing to the
"Notes on Contributors" page, where I often placed humorous and specula-
tive comments about the poets in the issue.

In this particular issue I stated that Ed Sanders had "the Ankh symbol
tattooed on his penis" and "the first 53 hieroglyphs of Akh-en-Aten's Hymn
to the Sun Disk on his nuts."

I was escorted to the bathroom, where I was asked to lower my trousers.
Then the two of them bent down fairly closely—I thought a bit **too**
closely—to scope my pants-down groin area in a vain search for Akh-en-
Aten's "Hymn to the Sun Disk." I was grateful they did not lean down so
closely that I could feel the huffs of their agitated nostrils upon my privies.

In the press release I sent out upon my bust, I noted the historic aspect of
the nut-gaze: "I am the only person in the history of American obscenity
cases who has had his penis examined during station house questioning." At
least they didn't try to touch it or otherwise look underneath, say, for hidden
evidence of ancient Egyptian hieroglyphs. When they were satisfied I didn't
have Akh-en-Aten's famous hymn written down there on the thrill farm, I
was driven to the New York Criminal Court Building at 100 Centre Street,
also known as the Tombs.

As we passed through the bowels of the Tombs, wending toward the
courtroom, we paused along a rail. I said to Sergeant Fetta, "You know, I'm

ED SANDERS/ the editor of FUCK YOU/ a magazine of the Arts. A pacifist dopethrill
psychopath & Guerilla Lovefare spaceout. In addition to having the Ankh symbol tattooed on his penis, you will find the first 53 hieroglyphs of Akh-en-Aten's HYMN
TO THE SUN DISC, on his nuts. Puke out 35¢ for his Poem From Jail (CITY LIGHTS BKS)!
NELSON BARR/ well well well! Still nothing has occurred as a result of this motherfucker burning his draft card in front of a NBC camera. A poet & actionist. Divides
his time between dope, peace, scatophilia, & balling all that good snapping-pussy at
Evil Stanley's Bar.

The Note on Contributor that so upset the arresting officer.

going to win this. I'll fight it all the way to the Supreme Court. And when I win, I'm going to throw a big party, and invite you to come to it."

Even so, I was not feeling spiritually uplifted. I was feeling the morning terror that the unjustly accused feel—sliding in through the robotic front doors of the Tombs/Criminal Court Building. It reminded me of some dirty electric shoebox.

Then I went before the judge.

On the one hand I felt upbeat and defiant; on the other I felt like a plate of lemur urine. It lifted my heart a bit to see friends in the courtroom. My bail was a mere $500. My sister and her husband came down from Westchester County and put up a savings passbook to vouch that I would show up in court hearings.

Word spread quickly in the counterculture. Allen Ginsberg did a benefit poetry reading in LA at midnight on January 21 at the Cinema Theater. Friends and supporters sent donations for my defense, among them Norman Holmes Pearson, Frank O'Hara, George Plimpton, and John Ashbery. Artist Joe Brainard sent six ink drawings for me to sell to help pay legal expenses.

I tried to get information on the arresting officer. I heard he was a go-getter, looking to become lieutenant or captain. I worked to get him moved out of the 9th Precinct. I asked friends to write to our liberal New York City mayor, John Lindsay, and complain about Fetta. These efforts seemed to

Ed Sanders, mug shot after Peace Eye bust.

ED SANDERS looks at the shambles of his **Peace Eye Book Store** after release from jail.

Cover photo from the *East Village Other*. With the Warhol banner in the background, I'm trying to sort out the police chaos of my desk after getting out on bail.

bear results, though it was difficult to measure precisely. For whatever reason, by the time of my trial next year he had been reassigned to the 111th Precinct out in Bayside, Queens.

The United States was at a true crossroads on the issue of freedom to publish. Right at the moment that Sergeant Fetta was insisting on gazing at my private parts to determine whether some of Akh-en-Aten's "Hymn to the Sun Disk" was tattooed thereupon, the Grove Press *Naked Lunch* case was before the Massachusetts Supreme Judicial Court, the state's highest court. A lower federal court had already ruled that Burroughs's masterwork was obscene, and the Supreme Judicial Court's decision declaring Burroughs's novel not obscene would not be announced until July 7. Allen Ginsberg's lengthy testimony in the Massachusetts *Naked Lunch* case back in 1965 was key in setting the trial record upon which *Naked Lunch* was freed. I was lucky to have Ginsberg on my side. Even so the issue of freedom to publish was very hot, very alive, and very much up in the air.

More than one friend suggested I get in touch with the ACLU, so one morning I brought a full run of all thirteen issues of *Fuck You* to the New York ACLU chapter, located at 156 Fifth Avenue, and had a chat. To my enormous gratitude, the lawyers agreed to take the case! Yay! And put a notice about the decision in the March '66 ACLU newsletter.

Meanwhile, I kept trying to bring Charles Olson and Panna Grady together, as in this note to him on January 24, 1966:

Dear O,

I suppose by now you have heard of my arrest on a F.Y./ porn charge. A.C.L.U. handling the case/ should have very little trouble on appeal, although It'll be tied up in the courts for years.

Now: (a) what's the scene re: Panna? I think John Wieners is freaking in there around this week & then will disappear after the semester break. Anytime

---

POETRY READING BY ALLEN GINSBERG

BENEFIT FOR ED SANDERS

Funds raised at this benefit will be used to meet legal expenses of Ed Sanders, owner of the PEACE EYE BOOKSTORE (383 E. 10th St., N.Y. N.Y. 10009) & publisher of a mimeographed poetry magazine which has printed the works of Allen Ginsberg, Norman Mailer, Charles Olson, Robert Creeley, Robert Duncan, Gary Snyder, Michael McClure, Lawrence Ferlinghetti, Gregory Corso, & other leaders in the literary world. Sander's publication can be found in some of the most important libraries in the world, including the Museum of Modern Art, the New York Public Library, the Library of Congress, Oxford University, Brown U., the University of California, etc., etc. At 5 am January 2nd, Ed Sanders was arrested on the charge of possessing obscene publications.

Says Sanders, "If the authorities succeed in stomping out my poetry magazine, it will be one more creepy encroachment on our right to enjoy satirical, freaky, and politically sensitive writing of the types I have been publishing......So, if you can contribute toward legal expenses, I will be totally grateful. Otherwise, I stand to be freaked off the scene......"

CINEMA THEATRE
1122 North Western Ave.
Hollywood, California 90029

✦ HO 7-5787 ✦

MIDNIGHT FRIDAY, JAN. 21

you want to bop down, is fine with her. There'll be a huge freak scene for Norman Mailer's new book of essays on the 13th there, so you may or may not want to stomp in for that action. Her # TR 4–7481. 1 W. 72nd Street.

Wanting Supporters to Come to My Trial

I wanted to get as many supporters as possible to come to the trial. The problem was that it kept getting postponed! It seemed as if the trial would occur on March 26, so I sent out a press release

> You are cordially invited to
>
>   the trial of
>
>   Ed Sanders
>
>   for obscenity charges dating
> from January 2, 1966
>
>   MONDAY , March 20th, 1967
>   New York City Criminal Courts Bldg.
>   100 Centre Street
>   Part 2B   4th Floor   10 Am- all day
>
> The prosecution has found the following publications
> objectionable and will base its case on them:
>
> 1) Fuck You/ a magazine of the Arts, #5,vol 7 and
>   #5, vol 8.
>
> 2) The Platonic Blow, by W.H. Auden
>
> 3) BUGGER
>
> 4) Blacklist #1 (a poetry magazine)
>
> 5) Farewell the Floating Cunt, by D.A. Levy
>
> 6) Peace Eye , poems by Ed Sanders
>
> 7) King Lord/ Queen Freak, poems by Ed Sanders
>
> 8) The Beautiful Book, by Jack Smith
>
> 9) 3 pages from Fuck You/ a magazine of the Arts,
>   #5, volume 9: a) the cover B) a picture by Joe
>   Brainard of Superman whose penis is saying Hi Foll:
>   c) a petition calling for an international Fuck-in
>   against the war in Vietnam
>
> The trial will take place before a three judge panel,
> and may last one or two days.

Publisher Picked Up In Pornography Raid

Ed Sanders—editor and publisher of *Fuck You, A Magazine of the Arts*—will be represented by the Union in his defense against the charge of possession of obscene literature with intent to sell. Sanders will plead April 5.

NYCLU Cooperating Attorney Martin M. Berger will argue the publication is not "obscene" because it does not appeal to prurient interests. And, according to the Union, the magazine does have "redeeming social significance." The mimeographed magazine of verse includes the work of several well-known poets, among them Allen Ginsberg and Norman Mailer. Sanders distributes it free.

The case emanated from a *Village Voice* interview of Sanders and an irate reader's letter to Police Commissioner Vincent Broderick. Sanders was visited by police officers twice in December. Then, early one January morning, police entered his East 10th St. bookstore.

When Sanders arrived at the scene, he found that the window and door were broken, his private back room was ransacked, and copies of several publications were missing. Police said they were investigating a possible burglary. Finding no burglar, they arrested Sanders.

and mailing to friends and supporters. I listed what some of the "evidence" of smut against me might be. To my chagrin, after my expert witnesses (such as John Ashbery and Kenneth Koch) and a bunch of friends showed up, the trial was postponed.

Meanwhile, 1966 was a big year for me. *The Fugs First Album* was getting praised, and we recorded our second album. We

Invitation to a trial.

began to perform at several Off-Broadway theaters: the Astor Place Playhouse on Lafayette Street and the Players Theatre on MacDougal Street. All during the early triumph of The Fugs, the impending trial for the Peace Eye Bookstore raid loomed in dread in my mind. During the coming year I would spot my arresting officer here and there around the Lower East Side, even in bohemian bars such as the Annex.

My next hearing was April 6, but I decided not to try to pack the court. Instead, I opted not to upset the Success Cart, so I deemphasized my court travails, no longer trying to attract a crowd of people to court hearings. Instead it became my secret burden. For the ensuing almost year and a half I suffered through a series of court appearances every few weeks without calling on friends and supporters to show up. All in all it was about ten court dates. I was on a rock-and-roll time schedule and didn't go to bed until around 4 AM. So I had to scrape myself up draggingly early, cab down to 100 Centre Street around 9:00 or 10:00, confer with my attorney, and then wait to see what happened.

I'd sent a press release about my possible trial to Cleveland poet and publisher d. a. levy, one of the marvels of the 1960s. He responded with a plea at a poetry reading at the Gate in Cleveland, then sent the cash to me with a note.

the enclosed to help yr court costs etc — collected at a reading at the GATE — cleveland ohio 3/25/66

d. a. levy

The Gate was the coffeehouse in the basement of Trinity Cathedral where d. a. was arrested for promoting smut. He granted an interview to the *Cleveland Plain Dealer* in January 1966, which was published on page one under the headline "BEATNIK LEADER WANTS MARIJUANA LEGALIZED IN AMERICA."

Inspired by LeMar, d. a. had started publishing the *Marrahwanna Quarterly*. To say the least, it caused a stir in Cleveland. "I felt that someone had to come out in the open and challenge the hysterical arguments and myths spread by the police, the press and the government," he told an interviewer at the time.

This was the year that the police put him on their list. Cops with body wires monitored the poetry readings levy attended. A few months after he had collected money for my defense at the Gate, police attended another reading there, looking for pot (and finding none) but secretly taped the reading, and voila! a poem was read with the word "cocksucker" in it. Shortly thereafter a grand jury indicted levy for obscenity.

(On December 1, 1966, narcotics officers raided Cleveland's Asphodel Bookstore and seized nine crates of d. a.'s publications on the grounds that they advocated the legalization of hemp. Jim Lowell, the Asphodel's owner, was arrested. Also seized, as if it were the era of Dostoevsky, was a mimeograph machine! When levy's grand jury indictment was unsealed, the establishment *Cleveland Press* sported a headline: "Grand Jury Named Beatnik Poet in Secret Indictment on Filth.")

Soon after my arrest Harvey Brown wrote from Cleveland with an offer of help. He was ready to publish a second edition of *Peace Eye* and inquired about publishing my translation of Hesiod's *Theogony.* He was willing to help underwrite my court costs.

His Frontier Press was sailing along. Charles Olson had asked him to tell me he was sending in an essay for the upcoming prose issue of *Fuck You/ A Magazine of the Arts.*

An Offer from a Record Company

At the end of 1965 Steve Weber had left The Fugs. We ran ads in the *East Village Other* and *Village Voice* for a replacement and found Pete Kearney, a guitarist who worked at the NYU bookstore. Pete Kearney had a gravelly, high-tenor harmony, which can be heard on "Coming Down" on *The Fugs Second Album.* He looked good on stage. We sometimes called him "Bomb Eyes" because they had a haunting combination of wastedness and wildness.

I met a human being named Bernard Stollman who owned a record company called ESP Disk, which his parents were bankrolling for him. We lunched at a vegetarian restaurant by Union Square and worked out a tentative deal to record for his company. The Fugs very badly wanted an Off-Broadway theater where we could set up scenery and lights to work our tunes and routines. ESP agreed to acquire us a theater. I was not very impressed with Stollman, but ESP did rent us a theater. However, all costs for it, and more, were slurped out of our pitiful royalty rate for the second album. It was only after I had learned more about music contracts that I realized what a hideous deal Stollman offered the acts he enticed to work for him. The oi is still oi-ing in the Oi over the ESP contract terms.

So again without any outside help, such as a lawyer or an agent, we signed a strange, shackling contract. We had signed a strange piece of paper with Folkways, and the deal with ESP was stranger. For example, the ESP royalty rate was 25¢ per album, regardless of the retail price, which in 1966 was $5 per unit. The 25¢ included both publishing and recording royalties, so our royalty rate was less than 3 percent, one of the lower percentages in the history of Western civilization.

Opening at Astor Place Playhouse

While we were recording *The Fugs Second Album*, we began a run at the Astor Place Playhouse on Lafayette Street across from what is now the Papp Theater. Our opening night was January 21, and we performed at the Astor Place Playhouse for three months.

Artist Bill Beckman, on the staff of the *East Village Other* and author of a successful cartoon series, "Captain High," designed The Fugs museum in the lobby of the Astor Place Playhouse. He also made the sign for the Peace Eye Bookstore. He lived with his wife, Deborah, on East Ninth, east of Tompkins Park. Deborah and my wife, Miriam, were close friends during the 1960s.

Using the Strobe Light

I rented a strobe light, with a dial to set the speed of the strobe. We pointed it at the audience at the end of "Nothing," whereupon I switched it on during the musical freakout that we always entered during the end of the tune. I had read that about fifty-eight strobes per minute tended to give visual hallucinations. That was the setting on the strobe dial.

Bill Beckman, in Fugs sweatshirt, 1966.
Photo courtesy of Deborah Beckman.

Deborah Beckman, Miriam Sanders, Tompkins Square Park, 1966. Photo courtesy of Deborah Beckman.

Recording *The Fugs Second Album*

One good thing happened as a result of The Fugs relationship with ESP—we met engineer/producer Richard Alderson, who owned (with Harry Belafonte) RLA/Impact Sound Studios at 225 West Sixty-fifth Street, a building later torn down when Lincoln Center was constructed. Alderson had built his own studio to experiment with electronic music.

The Fugs on stage at Astor Place Playhouse, 1966, Bill Beckman's stage design in the background; left to right: Pete Kearney, Vinny Leary, Ken Weaver, Ed Sanders, Tuli Kupferberg, Lee Crabtree. Ed Sanders collection.

Alderson came to New York City in the early 1960s from Ohio. Alderson had fixed up an old Ampex reel-to-reel tape recorder acquired from Frank Sinatra's music publisher in the Brill Building. The Ampex had been injured in a fire, but Alderson used it to record Nina Simone live at Carnegie Hall. He also recorded a Charlie Parker Memorial, featuring Bud Powell, at Carnegie. In '62 or '63 Alderson recorded Bob Dylan at the Gaslight Café on MacDougal with a Nagra tape recorder.

By 1965–early 1966 Alderson was doing live sound for a living. His first big live gig had been going on the road with Harry Belafonte to do the sound. He did live sound for Albert Grossman's act, Peter, Paul, and Mary. Grossman wanted him to build a sound system for Dylan's world tour in '65–'66, which Alderson did. He went out on the tour, which ended in early '66, to record gigs and run the sound system. Alderson was barely off the Dylan world tour when Belafonte wanted to go on the road immediately. Alderson didn't want to do it. Instead he stayed behind, thank goodness, to do *The Fugs Second Album*.

Alderson originally had an investor in his recording studio named Tamara Safford, who put in around $7,000 or $8,000. Belafonte then invested a considerable amount of money in RLA, around $80,000, and its name was changed to Impact Sound. The studio, awaiting being torn down for the Lincoln Center Parking Garage, had egg carton sound baffling on the ceiling, with Alderson himself exposing a raw brick wall and putting in a partition so that he could live in the back. Chip Monck, then the lighting designer for the Village Gate, had offices upstairs in the same building. Even though condemned, the building lasted for around seven years.

RLA Studios/Impact Sound had a four-track Ampex recorder and a two-track, which was state of the art for 1966; even The Beatles recorded four-track. So *The Second Fugs Album* involved many four-track to two-track to four-track bounces to free up tracks for overdubs. Richard Alderson wasn't one of those "don't touch the console" technobots, so we were able to learn the art of recording while we cut the tunes. He had good ears and good ideas, and he brought precision to our recording.

The First Fugs Album had taken two approximately three-hour sessions; for the second album we spent about four weeks in Alderson's studio. We wanted to do some good electronic rock and roll. We sensed the truth of the adage "Tapes don't lie," and we wanted to get beyond tribal primitive in our recording techniques, believing that if we could "get our brains on tape," we'd arrive as recording artists.

For the second album the musicians consisted of me, Kupferberg, Weaver, brilliant keyboardist Lee Crabtree, Vinny Leary on guitar, Pete Kearney on guitar, and Jon Anderson on bass. We quickly formed a fairly tight recording unit.

With our newfound renown we acquired some equipment. Ampeg gave us some amplifiers in exchange for our "endorsement," and Ken Weaver advanced from congas to a full set of rock-and-roll drums. John Anderson stenciled his red, white, and blue Fugs logo on the bass drum head.

I had an idea for an extended piece that would involve spontaneous music, dialogue, poetry. I sketched it out for the band. Lee Crabtree thought of the name for it, "Virgin Forest." We felt like we were entering new ground. Alderson dubbed in exciting frog sounds. Vinny Leary made his guitar into an electronic music instrument of greatness.

We stitched together "Virgin Forest"—picking the best sections of takes, mixing together fragments. "Out of the foam" (for which there were five takes), for instance, we spliced the beginning out of take four and the rest out of take five. For "Me Want Woman," we did the same thing, using, out of four takes, the beginning from take three and the "Me Want Woman" section from take one.

I've heard that "Virgin Forest" impressed The Beatles when they heard it, and it seems to have helped give them some ideas to create extended pieces, such as "A Day in the Life" on *Sgt. Pepper's Lonely Hearts Club Band.*

Betsy Klein, an early Fugs supporter (we cooked the spaghetti for the "Fugs Spaghetti Death" at her apartment), sang harmony on "Morning Morning" and sang a duet with Ken Weaver on "Virgin Forest." We'd heard that Peter, Paul, and Mary had taken over one hundred takes to get a basic track for one of their tunes, so we weren't worried about something like seventy-one takes for "Morning Morning."

Our harmonies still lacked the polish of the Beach Boys, but just as we did in our first sessions back in '65, we stood in front of Alderson's microphones and gave forth all the totally attentive energy and genius the Fates and our genetic codes would allow us to summon. Some of the songs on our second album are not what is currently known as PC, or politically correct, and we might not now write them in quite the same way, but they were true to the testosterone-crazed era in which they were created.

In addition to genius Ted Berrigan, other poets and songwriters submitted songs to The Fugs. One was a young man, born in the Bronx, named Lionel Goldbart, who used to hang out at the Peace Eye Bookstore. He submitted a few tunes, two of which we recorded. The first was a satire called "Dirty Old Man," which wound up on our new album; the second was "River of Shit," which we recorded the following year for our Reprise album, *It Crawled into My Hand, Honest*. In another submission poets Jack Micheline and Al Fowler approached me all excited on Avenue B, near Stanley's Bar at Twelfth Street. They were laughing as they thrust into my hands some notes for a song called "Sugar Shit." SS is heroin cut with sugar. It was a tune The Fugs never recorded. There were additional "out-there" submissions from various lyricists over the years.

Life becomes a frenzy when you're on the edge of "stardom," writing songs, drinking too much, nursing hashovers at the crack of noon, dealing with fans hanging outside your apartment, signing autographs on Avenue A, listening to gossip-mongers churning and writhing, running a bookstore and press, worrying about the Fuck You/ bust, recording, doing concerts, both striving for and cringing from fame.

Everything is a writing surface in the mania of Sudden Fame. While I was waiting for a bus on Second Avenue, some lines from Charles Olson's great poem "Maximus from Dogtown—I" came to mind:

> We drink
> or break open
> our veins solely
> to know...

I began to sing it, and within a few minutes, on the bus, I wrote "I Want to Know," which we immediately recorded for the second album.

We suffered a mild greed spasm. Ted Berrigan told us an anecdote about short story writer Damon Runyon, who reportedly had a sign above his desk, "Get the Money." Inspired by that, we formed a company called G.T.M. Enterprises to market T-shirts, Fugs underwear, and buttons.

For the first few months of 1966 my old friend Nelson Barr served as manager of The Fugs. At the same time we hired a publicist named Tim

Fugs at auto dealership, early 1966, arranged by Fugs publicist Tim Boxer; left to right: Ed, Lee, John, Pete, Vinny, Ken. Ed Sanders collection.

Release party for *The Fugs Second Album*, March 31, 1966.

The Fugs Second Album cover.

Boxer, who brought in gluts of ink for us. One of the publicity events Tim lined up for The Fugs was at a car dealership.

Catered macrobiotic food was served at the official opening of The Fugs Museum, designed by artist Bill Beckman, and the release of *The Fugs Second Album*. Tim Leary showed up, and a fun time was had by all.

Here's the lineup of songs for the album:

1. Frenzy	2:04	Ed Sanders
2. I Want to Know	2:00	Ed Sanders, Charles Olson
3. Skin Flowers	2:20	Ed Sanders, Pete Kearney
4. Group Grope	3:40	Ed Sanders
5. Coming Down	3:46	Ed Sanders
6. Dirty Old Man	2:49	Lionel Goldbart
7. Kill for Peace	2:07	Tuli Kupferberg
8. Morning Morning	2:07	Tuli Kupferberg
9. Doin' All Right	2:37	Ted Berrigan, Lee Crabtree, Vinny Leary
10. Virgin Forest	11:17	Ed Sanders, Richard Alderson, Lee Crabtree

Allen Ginsberg wrote liner notes for the album.

It's war on all fronts. "Breakthrough in the Grey Room" says Burroughs - he meant the Brain."Total Assault on the Culture" says Ed Sanders. The United States is split down the middle. On one side are everybody who make love with their eyes open, maybe smoke pot & maybe take LSD & look inside their heads to find the Self-God Walt Whitman prophesied for America. "Fool said the Muse, look in your heart and write." Dylan goes beyond: "Catch me disappearing in the smoke rings of my mind." I say, I'm confused, I'm frightened, I don't know. Who's on the other side? People who think we are **bad**. Other side? No, let's not make it a war, we'll all be destroyed, we'll go on suffering til we die if we take the War Door. Yogis and Beatles say there is no other side - "We can get along." Can't we? I say we can get along. People in there think sex body loves are bad - I say make love to them. They need it most. We all have to be funny saints to survive. Birchites are lacklove, Republicans and Democrats too are lacklove, Communists lack love, Narco fuzz and White South Governors lack love. "Turn on the love freak beam vectors - zap zap total assault" says Sanders. NOW sings Sanders and the Fugs come camping and screaming along, out in the open where every ear can hear the soul politics ecstasy message - They've put it in Front.It was behind Rock all along, from the beginning in Nigeria where Spades danced to the vibration in the belly made by drums worshiping Yourba God Chango the Penis our Creator. The message moved with the slaves up the Mississippi, like, Jazz was always an underground ecstatic religion just like it used to be in Africa. It crossed the Atlantic from Harlem to Liverpool and in the Cavern & Sink the teenage sexfiend children of Mersey dance in circles in a community like darkest Africa and worship

Chango George and all the rest of the beautiful Changos. It made England shake it's ass, and that also is the first lesson in Indian Yoga - wakening the Muladhara Chakra, the center of self between anus and pee machine. It saved England, which now has long hair and worships the "Naked Human Form Divine" - Blake prophesied that centuries ago, it's all coming true. America rocks, but the message was still unclear, the humane Self-joy physical vibration didn't find the right words till Dylan began to sing his mysteries.
The Fugs came to tell the truth that was only dreamy till they opened their mouths for Whitmanic orgy yawp! Group Grope, Dirty Old Man, Skin Flowers and Frenzy! Teenagers rise up and understand!! When they scream "Kill For Peace" they're announcing publicly the madness of our white haired crazy governments. They're telling the whole nasty Military Secret out loud, where every ear shall hear, like it says in the beautiful Bible. Dirty Old Man? Who said he was dirty, some **other** dirty old man masturbating in the bathroom with one hand and hypnotizing you with the Network official News thru a microphone in the other hand? Coming Down! A moment of honesty, sure we all suffer because of the mass of hate broadcast in this country. It's worse than any other synthetic drug! It's all been secret till now, the mess our Country's soul is in, now the Fugs expose the whole bring down with their blast of Joy - Doing All Right says the Bearded one! The Bible says that when Christ comes back, "every eye shall see." Now every ear can hear, and when the Fugs break thru the monopoly blockade and their Image is broadcast on National Television, every kid in America and most white haired old suffering men will turn then on with Relief at last and every eye shall see.   *-Allen Ginsberg*

Allen Ginsberg's liner notes, *The Fugs Second Album*.

The Fugs shared the Astor Place Playhouse with other ESP acts, such as Albert Ayler, and every Wednesday night featured Jeanne Lee, 1964 Downbeat Poll winner, and pianist Ran Blake, at 8:30 (admission just $1.50).

Jan Kerouac

I first heard of Jan, the daughter of Jack and Joan Kerouac, when I was attending the University of Missouri in 1957–1958 and drank at a place called the Italian Village near the campus. Joan Kerouac and her very young daughter were living nearby, in Columbia, with an artist who used to drink at the Italian Village. He would show us letters from Jack Kerouac to Joan.

Back then I did not know about "The Big Scroll" of April 1951. For three weeks that April Jack Kerouac hardly left his pad on West Twentieth Street for a moment: He was typing out a 120-foot scroll that rolled on the floor. It was the basic manuscript for *On the Road*.

Joan was pregnant at the time and made the scroll flow possible through the grace of her servitude. "I was growing in my mother's stomach while she brought him plates of food," Jan Kerouac later wrote.

The fourteen-year-old daughter of Jack Kerouac began to hang out in The Fugs milieu. She looked older than her years and drank heavily in bars such as the Annex, just around the corner from Peace Eye.

She was very sexually active. One friend who made it with her described how she pulled on her nipples while they were balling. The manager of the Astor Place Playhouse late at night encountered Jan and a Fugs guitarist making out atop the drum riser on stage in the gloom.

She was everywhere around the Lower East Side during 1966. Years later she showed herself a fine writer, publishing her first novel, *Baby Driver*, in 1981 and a second one, *Train Song*, in 1988.

Trouble Trouble Trouble

One evening just as we were getting ready to perform at the Astor Place Playhouse, I learned that an assistant district attorney was in the audience. I vowed not to alter the show a whit, and we didn't. Soon thereafter the district attorney's office filtered the word to us that it had decided against pressing charges.

On another evening a man who identified himself as the vice president of the Coca Cola Company attended a show and was offended by our ditty "Coca Cola Douche." He came up to me backstage and threatened to sue.

"Go ahead and sue us!" I begged. "Please, please, sue us!" I was thinking of the enormous publicity that would accrue in such a case.

Burning a Flag of the Lower East Side

Our shows were very controversial for their day, though they were nothing when measured against what would be allowed, on television for instance, in the year 2011. Lenny Bruce had been prosecuted not long before by an overzealous hater of personal freedom. And so naturally we were nervous when more representatives of the New York District Attorney's Office attended a show at the Astor Place Playhouse. We decided not to confront them and did not alter a single wiggle, erotic expletive, or complaint about the Vietnam War in our show. Only years later, after we got our FBI files, did we realize that there was a full-fledged investigation by the government of The Fugs.

At the Bridge Theater, however, an antiwar group had burned an American flag, which is always controversial in America. As a result there were front-page news stories and police and fire inspectors at all the East Village theaters.

We decided to burn a flag representing something we held very, very dear to make the point that it's just a flag and you could still love a book even if you burned its cover. So we painted a flag that said "Lower East Side," and on stage at the Astor Place Playhouse we torched it. Well-known columnist Sidney Zion misreported in an article read by New York City officials that The Fugs had burned an AMERICAN flag during a concert. (I had told him we had burned a "flag of the Lower East Side.") The NYC establishment assumed it had been a U.S. flag, so the theater was right away visited by fire inspectors and building inspectors, and soon The Fugs had to leave the Astor Place Playhouse, after a run of almost four months.

Here's some of the April 19, 1966, article by Sid Zion that got The Fugs snuffed out of the Astor Place Playhouse:

An artists and writers committee, led by Allen Ginsberg, the poet, charged yesterday that "petty officials" in the Lindsay administration were conducting a campaign of harassment to drive avant garde artistic endeavors out of the city.

Fugs concert, Astor Place Playhouse, just minutes before we burned the Lower East Side flag, 1966. Ed Sanders collection.

"The current drive against the avant garde arts, against the consciousness-expanding drugs, the clean-up of Greenwich Village and 42d Street, and many, many other cases can be explained only as a desperate gathering of evil or sick forces to delay the development of man," Jonas Mekas, film critic and filmmaker said in a statement adopted by the committee yesterday at a press conference in the Bridge Theater at 2 St. Mark's Place.

The group charged that The Fugs, a politically oriented rock 'n' roll singing group, was being harassed by the License Department. According to the committee, personnel of the License Department had warned the owner of the Astor Place Playhouse, where The Fugs have been performing, that unless the group "toned down" its show, the license for the theater would be revoked. As a result, the committee said, the owner, Mrs. Muriel Morse, has shut off the box office telephone. Mrs. Morse could not be reached for comment, but the telephone is "temporarily disconnected."

Assistant License Commissioner Walter Kirshenbaum "categorically" denied the charges yesterday. And Ed Sanders, leader of The Fugs, said he believed "the pressure is off." In fact, Mr. Sanders said that his group burned an American flag at a performance last Saturday night and that nothing had happened as a result.

Section of *Chappaqua* Filmed at Astor Place Playhouse

Before we were tossed out of the Astor Place Playhouse, we had time to appear in Conrad Rooks's film *Chappaqua*, for which we performed some songs. Robert Frank was the cinematographer. I recall groveling on the stage of Astor Place while Paula Prentice in long leather boots stomped on mock LSD-suffused sugar cubes.

The War the War the War

Ken Weaver, Ed Sanders on a march down Fifth Avenue, 1966. Ed Sanders collection.

A headline in *Le Monde* for April 13:

Les B-52 américains bombardent pour la première fois le Vietnam du Nord

For the rest of the decade and beyond it loomed above our lives like the ancient curse of Agamemnon—those B-52s above the North.

The New York City Department of Licenses

In the April 28 *Village Voice* Stephanie Harrington wrote an investigative piece titled "City's Censorship Role Is Being Questioned." The New York City Department of Licenses, "because of its zealousness," she wrote, "may be in the process of putting itself out of business as the . . . censor of the avant garde." Artists and theaters and coffee shops had raised their voices against these overzealous censors.

The Department of Licenses had issued summonses to the 41st Street Theater, where the Film-Makers' Cinematheque had shown films, because the films displayed "sexual immorality, lewdness, perversity, and homosexuality." The license creeps had issued summonses to the Bridge Theater with respect to a program in which an American flag had been burned to protest Johnson's unexpected increase in troops and in bombing of the north in the war in Vietnam.

The license officials had issued summonses to a member of the Artists and Writers Protest Committee for putatively operating a dance hall and selling liquor without a license at an anti–Vietnam War party. Artist Leon Golub was one of the organizers of the committee. The Department of Licenses raided the party.

The New York chapter of the American Civil Liberties Union, which had agreed already to handle my Peace Eye raid case, was considering suing in court over the License Department's authority to ooze into a theater, sit in seats, look at the films, performances, plays, etc., being shown, then on its own decide to revoke the theater's license or refuse to renew the license. (It will be recalled that an ex-CIA agent, working for the Department of Licenses, had testified against Lenny Bruce in the Cafe Au Go Go case back in 1964.)

As Stephanie Harrington accurately reported, "Private parties at which liquor is served with the hope that the guests will make donations are a common method of fund-raising among church groups and political candidates." I recall a LeRoi Jones rent party I had once attended that had plenty of booze, wild dancing, pot, and gluts of Fun.

Mayor Lindsay requested the department's commissioner, Joel Tyler, to meet on May 4 with members of the New York Eternal Committee for Conservation of Freedom in the Arts, whose steering group included Allen Ginsberg and Jonas Mekas. It took a fresh young mayor ultimately to call off the hounds of the License Department.

The Ghastly Attention of the FBI and the Justice Department

Meanwhile, the popularity of The Fugs brought us the attention of federal law enforcement. A few weeks after *The Fugs Second Album* was released, there was an investigation of The Fugs by the FBI and the U.S. Department of Justice, which I learned about years later when I obtained part of my files under the Freedom of Information Act.

Someone at a radio or television station wrote an indignant letter to the New York City district attorney. The letter contended that *The Fugs Second Album* was pornographic. The letter of complaint was forwarded to the U.S. attorney, who, in turn, sent it on to the FBI. Of course, in those years the FBI was known to write letters to itself, or set up such letters, to justify investigations of American activists.

In the early summer a DOJ memorandum stated that a postal inspector had finished an investigation: "He advised The Fugs is a group of musicians who perform in NYC. They are considered to be beatniks and free thinkers, i.e., free love, free use of narcotics, etc. . . . It is recommended that this case be placed in a closed status since the recording is not considered to be obscene."

I felt a surge of patriotism when I read this memo years later among the documents turned over as a result of a Freedom of Information request. Plus this! If we'd only known about this letter, we could have put a sticky label on the record: "Ruled NOT obscene by the United States Government and the Postal Service!"

DOJ memo declaring Fugs Album not obscene.

A Trip to Gloucester to See Charles Olson

In late spring, in a rickety old green Ford station wagon, writer George Kimball drove me, Panna Grady, and English poet George MacBeth to Gloucester, Massachusetts, to hang out with Charles Olson. I'm pretty sure it was the first meeting between Olson and Grady, and it rekindled my cunning scheme, hatched the previous year, for her to help the genius of Gloucester, whose financial status was always on the edge, especially since he had left his professorship at Buffalo.

I brought a gift to Olson of a French edition of Hesiod's *Theogony*, with the original Greek helped by a French crib. It was the edition into which I had handwritten the "Out of the Foam, O Aphrodite" section of "Virgin Forest" on the second album.

Olson was glad to see us, recounting a recent visit by Tim Leary (who had given him a vial of pure LSD). We had dinner at the best place in town, called the Tavern, followed by a long walk on the beach by the harbor.

I'm not totally certain this initial meeting between Panna Grady and Charles Olson had anything to do with it, but Grady rented a fancy stone house in Gloucester, where she spent the summer and early fall with her daughter. She had an affair with poet John Wieners that year but broke it off, and she and Charles Olson would travel to England together in the late fall.

June 12 at Town Hall

A young fan named Henry Abramson put up money for The Fugs to "move uptown" to a concert at Town Hall! The Town Hall gig came along at a miracle moment for us. We were without a theater, having been tossed from the Astor Place Playhouse. I used the $1,500 concert fee from Town Hall to rent the Players Theatre on MacDougal Street, and we soon began a long, long run.

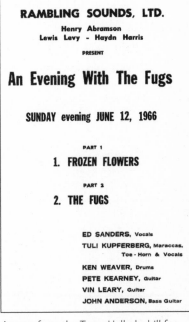

RAMBLING SOUNDS, LTD.

Henry Abramson
Lewis Levy - Haydn Harris

PRESENT

An Evening With The Fugs

SUNDAY evening JUNE 12, 1966

PART 1

1. FROZEN FLOWERS

PART 2

2. THE FUGS

ED SANDERS, Vocals
TULI KUPFERBERG, Maraccas,
      Toe - Horn & Vocals
KEN WEAVER, Drums
PETE KEARNEY, Guitar
VIN LEARY, Guitar
JOHN ANDERSON, Bass Guitar

A page from the Town Hall playbill for the gig.

Robert Shelton reviewed the Town Hall concert in the *New York Times*. To my enormous relief, given his stature among writers on current music, Shelton liked the show! Among his comments:

> The Fugs might be considered the musical children of Lenny Bruce, the angry satirist. Their music, while growing in capability, is secondary to their lyrics, patter and antics. Complete personal freedom, whether in sex or in drug experiences, seems to be one of the Fugs' ensigns. Two songs, including "Turn On, Tune In and Drop Out," were dedicated to Dr. Timothy Leary, the researcher in use of psychedelic drugs. "Kill for Peace" lambasted the United States policy in Vietnam.
>
> While obviously far out by most accepted standards of popular music, the Fugs are clever, biting and effective satirists. In settings of poems by William Blake and Charles Olson, they showed a gentler nature. While not for every taste, the group can be commended for its originality, courage and wit.

The Players Theatre

Located at 115 MacDougal, the Players Theatre was owned by a gentleman named Donald Goldman, who did not seem to mind our rough language and wild stage antics. His theater manager, on the other hand, was an ex-army guy named Howard Dwyer, who didn't like the word "fuck." In fact his face went red at it, and although all other words were okay, he seethed at the use of fuck in our routines. Thank goodness theater owner Goldman was more worldly and didn't care about our language. *Whew.*

The Café Wha was located in the basement, and there were oodles of Greenwich Village sidewalk traffic, so our shows started selling out when we

Ed Sanders collection.

opened in July. Our run there during 1966 and 1967 lasted over seven hundred performances. During the summer and fall we did three shows a night on the weekends—8:00, 10:00, and midnight. The theater was filled, and the shows were fluid, well done, and hot. It was the peak time for The Fugs.

A Patriotic Flavor

We always struck a theme of patriotism. Examples are our red, white, and blue logo and our ad in the *Village Voice* for our run at the Players Theatre.

Pete Kearney left the band, and during that first summer at the Players Theatre Jon Kalb, brother of Dan Kalb of the Blues Project, was our excellent lead guitarist. And so the summer of '66 Fugs included Sanders, Kupferberg, Ken Weaver, Jon Kalb, Vincent Leary, and Lee Crabtree. We were joined at various points in our run at the Players Theatre by Jake Jacobs, a fine arranger and singer. For a while we hired a vocal coach, Bruce Langhorne, reputed to be the inspiration for Dylan's "Mr. Tambourine Man."

With our second album on the charts and our shows sold out, we were treated to the eerie sensation of sudden fame. Though I lived in an apartment in a slum building, fans located it and hovered outside near the incredibly dingy ash cans and their squashed lids connected by chains to the cans.

Famous people began to watch our shows at the Players Theatre, and we were thrilled to shake the hands of stars such as Richard Burton, Peter O'Toole, Tennessee Williams, and Leonard Bernstein in quick backstage visits. To Kim Novak we gave a Fugs T-shirt, hoping she might pop it on.

Patriotic ad and red, white, and blue Fugs ticket.

The Fugs' Renown Among the Literati

In addition to renowned guests such as Kim Novak, "New York Intellectuals," including those associated with the *New York Review of Books*, began to appear at Fugs shows at the Players Theatre that summer. Elizabeth Hardwick actually wrote a good review of the show, which we cherished. Novelist Philip Roth also came to a show on an evening that Tuli sang "Jack Off Blues," which always brought an explosive round of applause from the audience.

Tuli singing "Jack Off Blues," Players Theatre, MacDougal Street. Ed Sanders collection.

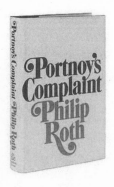

It was around then that Roth began *Portnoy's Complaint*, which was published in 1969. A lingering question is this: Was *Portnoy's Complaint* inspired by the "Jack Off Blues" lyrics?

Could there have been royalties for Tuli? Probably not. Shakespeare did not have to give credit, and certainly no bread, for plundering histories of Denmark when writing *Hamlet.*

Copyright © *1965*
Tuli Kupferberg

(*Right*) Tuli's "Jack Off Blues" from our 1965 performance book.

Jack Off Blues

Woke up this morning with my sweetheart in my hand
My head was empty and my heart was full of sand
I got them jack off blues

My baby left me for another man
I guess I'll have to do the best I can
I got them jack off blues

I feel so lonely when I come alone
Just like a hobo without no home
I got them jack off blues *Instrumental!*

I need a full-fleshed women, I need her bad
Without a woman life's too sad
·I got them jack off blues

A woman is a woman, a man is a man
A finger's but a finger but I got other plans
Good bye good bye jack off blues
Good bye bug off jack off blues

(*Below*) Fugs playbill, Players Theatre, MacDougal Street. Royalties, Mr. Roth?

SHOWCARD

AN EVENING WITH
the FUGS

Elizabeth Hardwick, I'm afraid, captured my Entity of 1966 in an essay published in the December 15 *New York Review of Books*. "What we might have hoped for," she wrote,

was the mad anarchistic pantomime of The Fugs, of Tuli Kupferberg in "Kill for Peace." Looking like some obscene Yeshiva student, he has a catatonic relaxation that does more in one pornographic slump than all the agit-prop frenzy of *Viet Rock*. The Fugs are neither art nor theater, but noise ("total assault") and Free Speech. Still they make all sorts of popular entertainment obsolete. After "Coca Cola Douche" it is not the easiest thing in the world to sit through the first act of *The Apple Tree* and watch Barbara Harris and Alan Arkin in the garden of Eden, trying to "evolve" a word for love. The Fugs are soft, liberal exhorters to "Group Grope." There is a schizophrenic sweetness and dirtiness about them and the leader of the group, Ed Sanders, is a dismayingly archetypal American. If he weren't "groping for peace," he would have been in the Twenties an atheist, in the Thirties a Trotskyite. But he is an actor, possessed of a subversive energy that does not come forth on records and certainly not in his books of verses, or whatever you might call these "lyrics." In person he is a new, indefinable image. (Kupferberg is a more accomplished actor, but he is not the prime spirit of this group, a group whose purpose is far from evident.) Ed Sanders in dirty black cotton pants, a horrible white plastic vest, dirty red scarf, matted hair, holding a mike with a cord, is some sort of parody of all the MC's of history. He looks like James Jones, or a foul Bob Hope. Neither he nor his "slum goddess of the lower east side" is aphrodisiac, but they are wildly funny because he and his songs have trapped the infantilism of smutty little boys. To be clean and well-dressed and concerned about homosexuality or four-letter words: that is the real madness. It is not free sex, but free speech they celebrate: dirty words, dirty feet, laughter. The Fugs are idealogues of some kind, not orgiasts; their ideas are few and simple, and all of them are pacific. The young couples in the audience, soiled, long-haired, were strangely soft and domesticated also, as if they had some parody nest, with a few pans, a few drugs, and then, all smudged and sweaty, tucked themselves into a passive sleep. Still there is something final about The Fugs. It is hard to see how Alan Jay Lerner can carry on after "My Baby Done Left Me and I Feel Like Homemade Shit."

Subletting a Pad in the Summer

Miriam and I and Deirdre sublet a furnished apartment on East Thirteenth that summer. We rented it from Tom McNamara, a columnist for the *East Village Other*. It was a very hot summer. I purchased a new reel-to-reel tape recorder and spent lots of hot hours working on new tunes.

Chart-Anguia

On July 9 the Troggs' "Wild Thing" was number seven on the singles list and "Paperback Writer" was number two. And wow! there on the album charts! The Fugs! at eighty-nine, just above Martha and the Vandellas' *Greatest Hits*! It spawned the peculiar hunger that I call "chart-anguia," a thirst to get on the charts again, difficult to do with tunes like "Kill for Peace" and "I Feel Like Homemade Shit." Even so, for a few years I compulsively looked at the Billboard or Cashbox charts, even though none of my projects got very far up in the lists!

TOP 100 Albums

JULY 9, 1966

Pos.	Title / Artist (Label)	Last Week
26	SOUTH OF THE BORDER — Herb Alpert & Tijuana Brass (A & M LP/SP 108)	30
27	LONELY BULL — Herb Alpert & Tijuana Brass (A & M LP/SP 101)	28
28	TIME WON'T LET ME — Outsiders (Capitol T/ST 2501)	22
29	SPANISH EYES — Al Martino (Capitol T/ST 2435)	18
30	WHY IS THERE AIR? — Bill Cosby (Warner Bros. W/WS 1606)	34
31	GLORIA — The Shadows Of The Knight (Dunwich 666)	38
32	JUST LIKE US — Paul Revere & The Raiders (Columbia CL 2451/CS 9251)	27
33	BOOTS — Nancy Sinatra (Reprise R/RS 6202)	33
34	THE SONNY SIDE OF CHER (Imperial LP 9301/LP 12301)	39
35	MRS. MILLER'S GREATEST HITS (Capitol T/ST 2494)	21
36	GARY LEWIS HITS AGAIN (Liberty LRP 3452/LST 7452)	42
37	THE MOVIE SONG ALBUM — Tony Bennett (Columbia CL 2472/CS 9272)	26
38	THE BEST OF RONNIE DOVE (Diamond D/S 5005)	31
●	TRY TOO HARD — Dave Clark Five (Epic LN 24198/BN 26198)	49
40	HOW DOES THAT GRAB YOU? — Nancy Sinatra (Reprise R/RS 6207)	40
41	THE BEST OF HERMAN'S HERMITS (MGM E/SE 4315)	45
●	A NEW SONG FOR YOUNG LOVE — Lettermen (Capitol T/ST 2496)	52
51	SOUNDS OF SILENCE — Simon & Garfunkel (Columbia CL 2469/CS 9269)	43
52	LOVE (Elektra EKL 4001/EKS 74001)	58
53	TRINI — Trini Lopez (Reprise R/RS 6196)	41
54	CRYING TIME — Ray Charles (ABC Paramount ABC/ABCS 544)	46
55	BALLAD OF THE GREEN BERETS — S/Sgt. Barry Sadler (RCA Victor LPM/LSP 3547)	48
56	FIDDLER ON THE ROOF — Original Cast (RCA Victor LCO/LSO 1093)	57
57	BILL COSBY IS A VERY FUNNY FELLOW, RIGHT! (Warner Bros. W/WS 1518)	63
58	I WANT TO GO WITH YOU — Eddy Arnold (RCA Victor LPM/LSP 3507)	47
59	WHEN A MAN LOVES A WOMAN — Percy Sledge (Atlantic 8125/SD 8125)	65
60	HOLD ON — Herman's Hermits (MGM E/SE 4342)	51
61	DIONNE WARWICK IN PARIS (Scepter M/S 534)	66
62	MOONLIGHT SINATRA — Frank Sinatra (Reprise F/FS 1018)	44
63	DIRTY WATER — Standells (Tower 5027)	69
64	ONE STORMY NIGHT — Mystic Moods (Philips PHM 200-205/PHS 600-205)	71
65	RUBBER SOUL — Beatles (Capitol T/ST 2442)	50
●	THE MORE I SEE YOU/CALL ME — Chris Montez (A & M 115)	79
67	I HEAR A SYMPHONY — Supremes (Motown M/S 643)	60
76	WAYNE NEWTON, NOW! (Capitol T/ST 2445)	59
77	EVERYBODY LOVES A NUT — Johnny Cash (Columbia CL 2492/CS 9292)	74
78	I STARTED OUT AS A CHILD — Bill Cosby (Warner Bros. W/WS 1567)	85
●	GETTIN' READY — Temptations (Gordy 918/S 918)	—
80	I'M SO LONESOME I COULD CRY — B. J. Thomas (Scepter 535/S 535)	68
81	UPTIGHT — Stevie Wonder (Tamla M/S 268)	88
82	MOODS OF MARVIN GAYE (Tamla 266/S 266)	91
83	THINK I'LL GO SOMEWHERE AND CRY MYSELF TO SLEEP — Al Martino (Capitol T/ST 2528)	89
84	ANDY WILLIAMS' NEWEST HITS (Columbia CL 2383/CS 9183)	61
85	MY WORLD — Eddy Arnold (RCA Victor LPM/LSP 3466)	87
86	SOUL MESSAGE — Richard "Groove" Holmes (Prestige PR/PRS 7435)	84
87	LIGHTLY LATIN — Perry Como (RCA LPM/LSP 3552)	97
88	TIJUANA BRASS VOL. II — Herb Alpert & The Tijuana Brass (A & M LP/SP 103)	95
89	THE FUGS (ESP 1029)	99
90	MARTHA & VANDELLAS GREATEST HITS (Gordy 917/S 917)	94
91	CALIFORNIA DREAMIN' — Bud Shank (World Pacific WP 1845/WPS 21845)	96
92	MUSIC: A BIT MORE OF ME — David McCallum (Capitol T/ST 2408)	75

There we were! on the Cashbox list, up there with Martha and the Vandellas!

The Revolution at Fillmore and Geary

Meanwhile out in San Francisco, rock shows, augmented by poetry, were going full blast at the Fillmore Ballroom. As Ralph Gleason, esteemed jazz writer and chronicler of the psychedelic music revolution, described it, "It's an old joint, built in the year One, and used for decades as a dancehall. It's an upstairs loft at Fillmore and Geary with several small balconies and a café or lounge. There's no booze, only soft drinks, near beer and food. And it has become, in recent months, the general headquarters for the artistic revolution that is taking place here."

Friday and Saturday, July 15 and 16, the Jefferson Airplane and Grateful Dead were on the same bill, filling the Fillmore. Attendees were treated on Saturday to a half hour version of Wilson Pickett's "Midnight Hour" performed by the Dead and the Airplane all together, with Marty Balin, Pig Pen, Joan Baez, and Mimi Farina sharing the vocal. Wish you'd been there? Me, too.

The next night there was a sold-out benefit for the Artists Liberation Front, a masked Mardi Gras–themed ball, with the Mime Troupe, Garry Goodrow, the Sopwith Camel, and others. Robert Creeley read, and Allen Ginsberg, too, wearing an Uncle Sam top hat and performing sections of his just completed and remarkable poem "Wichita Vortex Sutra." Allen received a standing ovation at the Fillmore that summer night. Wish you'd been there? Me, too.

The Mystery of Frank O'Hara

The summer saw the death of brilliant poet Frank O'Hara, struck down by a dune taxi on Fire Island July 24. Charles Olson wrote in a letter, "Oh Lord I hate the fact that he will not continue to be a master." Allen Ginsberg wrote one of his finest poems for O'Hara, "City Midnight Junk Strains."

Frank had sent $50 to help defray my legal expenses and had agreed to be an expert witness at my upcoming Peace Eye raid trial.

This was the year that I was filmed at Peace Eye for a National Educational Television series *USA: Poetry*. I shared a segment of the series with O'Hara. (It was broadcast September 1, 1966. It was Frank's final reading.)

The day after O'Hara's tragic death on Fire Island, Bob Dylan had his motorcycle accident in Bearsville. He suffered an injured neck and other bruisings. Allen later told me that several weeks later he visited Dylan in Woodstock, bringing him some books, including Rimbaud, Blake, Dickinson, and Shelley.

I flew out for a quick trip to Kansas City for a Family Reunion. I was attired in striped pants and rock-and-roll finery. The success of The Fugs at the Players Theatre enabled me to flash a thick wad of cash. I was a bit overwhelmed by the sudden glut of money (as temporary as it turned out to be) and even explored purchasing my childhood home on Cemetery Hill in Blue Springs. A few years later Janis Joplin joked with me about purchasing HER hometown! It was part of the phenomenon of Sudden Rock-and-Roll Cash.

A Call from Jack Kerouac

Kerouac called me at the Peace Eye Bookstore one night in the late summer. He wanted me to jot down a poem, so I did. He said it was about "Mother

Kali, Hindu goddess who gives birth and eats back her children." Then he dictated:

> The Secret
> of Kali
> The basket
> is a casket
> Signed,
> Jack Kerouac

He sometimes walked past Peace Eye on the way to Allen's up the street. Orlovsky stopped by the store after one of Jack's visits. He'd blown the author of *Subterraneans* and complained just a bit about it, he confided to me, in the same conversation, that he had not fully dug the taste of John Wieners's duck-buttery lingam.

Performing with Little Anthony and the Imperials

One interesting gig for The Fugs the summer of '66 was at the El Patio Beach Club, billed as a "College Mixer" with Little Anthony and the Imperials. "Girls not permitted in slacks," the ticket read. It was exciting to share the bill with the creators of top-ten classics such as the doo-wop "Tears on My Pillow" of '58 and 1960's "Shimmy, Shimmy, Ko Ko Bop."

Lenny Bruce Memorial

On August 3 Lenny Bruce was found face down on the bathroom floor, a needle sticking from his right arm and a blue bathrobe sash around his elbow, in his house in Los Angeles.

The Fugs sang "Carpe Diem" at the packed Lenny Bruce Memorial held at the Judson Memorial Church on the edge of Washington Square Park on August 12, with Bob Fass producing the recording of it for WBAI. The Fugs performing at the Bruce Memorial can be found on The Fugs boxed set *Don't Stop! Don't Stop.*

A Bomb Scare in the Musette Bag

We were very excited about our free outdoor concert in Tompkins Square Park, scheduled for the evening of August 16. The audience filled up the park from the new bandshell all the way to Tenth Street at the park's northernmost point and spilled out onto the sidewalks of Avenues A and B. There must have been over 10,000 on hand.

Walt Bowart, editor of the *East Village Other*, spotted my nemesis in the crowd, Sergeant Fetta, who had led the raid on Peace Eye, and asked him, "What do you think of the concert?"

Fetta: "You call this a concert?"
Bowart: "Do you have any comments you'd like to make about this concert?"
[loud music]
Fetta: "About what?"
Bowart: "About this music? About the lyrics."
Fetta: "Why don't you go about the audience asking them? With this crowd here tonight, it doesn't seem to matter what I think."

We were asked by the cops to turn down the amplifiers because our tunes, such as "Slum Goddess of the Lower East Side" and "Group Grope," could be heard all the way to Fourteenth Street. We got through our first set, and we were backstage hanging out.

Suddenly there were police officers on the stage. And who should come back behind the scrim to see us but my nemesis, Sergeant Charles Fetta!?

"We've had a telephone call that there's a bomb planted in the park."

A guy from the Lower East Side Civic Improvement Association came to the microphone and intoned, "The police have informed us that there is a bomb in the park. It's probably just a hoax, but will the audience please move back from the pavement and benches onto the grass?"

A totally packed Tompkins Square Park for the free Fugs concert, August 16, 1966. Ed Sanders collection.

There were a few boos and hisses.

I then went to the mike and told the crowd that we were cooperating with the bomb search. Meanwhile backstage, Fetta was looking for bombs in people's musette bags, you know, joint-sized receptacles.

Finally we went back on stage and resumed our concert with "Ah Sunflower, Weary of Time," "Supergirl," "Turn On/Tune In/Drop Out," and, of course, the epoch-shaking Kupferberg masterwork, "Monday nothing, Tuesday nothing."

To me the police action smacked of fascism. And I pulled as many strings as I could to get Sergeant Fetta transferred out of the Lower East Side.

September 13

Panna Grady sent me a postcard from P.O.B. 14 Riverdale, Gloucester, Mass.

Dear Ed,

Charles (Olson) said—two nights ago—why don't we send you a telegram—haven't seen him since to do it so this is instead to tell you we both would like to make the visit we'd planned earlier with your wife and child. I'll be here till mid-Oct., so anytime.

Love!

Panna Grady.

Airmail, 8¢, postcard, to Mr. Ed Sanders

Box 193

Stuyvesant Station, NY, NY from Gloucester

Poseidon's Mane

I decided to take up Panna and Charles's kind invitation to visit. Ken Weaver and I flew from New York to Boston on the Eastern Shuttle, then took a cab to Gloucester to see the O in midafternoon, his morning. Olson had to clear away books from the stove to make us tea.

We had dinner. Then we were sitting in the kitchen at Fort Square. We were to stay in the house rented by Panna Grady near Dogtown Commons. (She was not there that night.) Olson had a bottle of orange-red psilocybin pills, plus a bottle, literally, of acid he'd gotten from Tim Leary. He went into a back room and returned with the bottles of LSD and 'cybin.

"Want a swig?" he said, thrusting the liquid acid in my direction, as if it were a shot of rum in a bar by Half Moon Bay. "A swig!!" I exclaimed, knowing full well that 500 micrograms was more than enough—why should we risk some 500,000 mcg gulps? So we settled on the psilocybin. Olson had apparently tried some in December of 1960 and in February of 1961, and there was the remainder in a bottle, almost six years later.

Olson shook out a handful of red orange pills. I took about eight; Weaver, as I recall, had twelve; and Olson, at six foot seven, had an initial twelve or so, then a few more. We sat talking in the kitchen as the magic mushrooms began to bring us the Galactic Mush.

Olson drove us over near the part of Gloucester called Dogtown where we were to sleep. He drove slowly, so slowly that when I looked back a line of cars was close pressed behind us. He pulled over, as I recall, to let some of them roll by; then we proceeded. I felt a great surge of confidence that my mentor, the O, was driving and would get us there safely. Then I glanced to the front seat, and Olson had turned into the Greek god Poseidon! literally! the Horse from the Sea! with kelp in his mane matted and wet.

So onward drove Poseidon—the seat cushions washed in the froth of his greeny mane, which seemed ornamented with sea wrack, bone bits, shells, and oceanic oddments! I thought, well even if I am bonkers, the driver, my hero, my guru, my bard, was Safety Assured! Until we passed a clump of what appeared to be boulders, in the gloom to the left.

"Woooo, look at the elephants!" Poseidon shouted.

At last we arrived at the stone house, rented by Panna, with stone-arched doorway and sat in the living room to talk. Meanwhile, the psilocybin was having a profound effect on me. It seemed as if the house had become the Chapel Perilous, and I began to walk outdoors, spend a few minutes in the dark, then return back to the Chapel. I did this a few times and seemed to live through life cycles as I left the house, walked through the woods, then returned.

In one life cycle I spoke Akkadian, building a mud brick hut by the River Euphrates. In another cycle I was a Hasidic store owner on Hester Street in the Lower East Side.

Weaver later kidded me about calling out to the trees when I wandered out of the stone house and onto the lawn. Olson, meanwhile, talked onward. Weaver pointed toward O: "Look at those sparks coming out of his forehead." I looked. The top of his head seemed enormous and was showering with blue arcs!

On a table was a jade and silver cross that Dean Stockwell had given John Wieners. I asked Olson, "What is there to hold on to?" He handed me the cross. I tasted it and felt it melt in my mouth.

When I went outdoors, Charles warned me about the "quarry." I recall he was speaking about sachems and Algonkian longhouses. Finally in one of the life cycles I got lost in the woods, crashing among trees—leaves in long hair. I must point out that I was in my full rock-and-roll attire—all in red: red boots, red sweater, red pants, and a red scarf. Finally I thrashed down into a street. I thought maybe there had been an accident and I was dead and in fact might have been in Sheol, or purgatory, or some kind of William Burroughs Gray Zone.

I walked through deserted Gloucester streets and was just getting ready to go into a house for shelter. Good thing I didn't. A police car came along, and I hailed it. He was at first suspicious of a young man dressed all in red, with leaves affixed up and down the redness.

I recalled poet Gerrit Lansing's address on Main Street in Gloucester and called him from the police station. Gerrit's friend Derek picked me up and drove me back to Dogtown, where Olson and Weaver were still talking! It seemed they had not moved an inch during my adventure!

I called Miriam at our pad on Avenue A, and once again she helped me to land from another trip into the universal mosaic. She always talked me down from On the Road Orbit during those years. During the psilo' trip I was thinking I should give up The Fugs and return totally to poetry. I told Miriam that over the phone from Gloucester. But I was trapped in Fugland.

The polka-dotted jacket I wore for the dinner with Jerry Wexler of Atlantic Records. Ed Sanders collection.

A Hunger to Record Again

It would have been difficult to break up The Fugs right at that moment. Jerry Wexler of Atlantic Records had expressed interest in signing us. I had gone out to dinner with him at an uptown Chinese restaurant and had visited his office to pitch having The Fugs on his label. At that time it was the label of The Rolling Stones. He'd also put out an album of Allen Ginsberg reading his great poem *Kaddish.*

The Loss of John Anderson and Jon Kalb

The summer of 1966 was a time of Glory for The Fugs. We were playing sold-out shows at the Players Theatre, and we had an album on the charts. It seemed as if this Glory would last forever! Then a kind of calamity occurred—first our hot lead guitarist, Jon Kalb, decided he wanted to return to college! And second, our hot bass player, John Anderson, received his Draft Notice, now that he had dropped out of Yale.

I hatched a scheme for The Fugs to accompany John to his Draft Board naked, but alas, it was not to be, and after his father showed up, John allowed the Draft to go forward. Soon he was "Pfc John Anderson, 206th Sig. Co. at Fort Bragg, North Carolina." After serving in Vietnam, he returned to Yale, graduated, then got a law degree from Harvard. His legacy: The Fugs first and second albums and our red, white, and blue logo.

Limo-Anguia and a New Pad

There is a condition called "limo-anguia," in which young people in rock bands have a hunger to be taken around in limousines. I actually rented a limousine to look for an apartment to rent amid the slums of the Lower East Side.

Miriam, I, and Deirdre, now two years old, moved from East Thirteenth Street at the end of the summer. For a while we stayed at the Chelsea Hotel, then we moved into an apartment at 196 Avenue A at Twelfth Street.

I signed the lease on October 15. It was a floor-through, with a marble fireplace; it had once, I was told, been a dental office. There was a buzzer system, and the apartment was on the second floor. There was a door off the kitchen that led to a flat-roofed area that we could possibly use in the summertime, put tables and chairs out there and maybe plants.

It was another calm pad where we tried to wall off the weirdness. We allowed no one except close friends to visit. We were to live there until early 1970, when I flew off to Los Angeles to write about the Manson "family."

During the first few weeks in the new apartment on Avenue A, we allowed our friend Al Fowler, and his mate, poet Mimi Jacobsen, to store their belongings, including some furniture. But it became difficult to allow Fowler access to our pad because, as Miriam recalls, he would arrive, she would let him in, and he would proceed to grab items that he could sell to fuel his habit, so we had to ban him. Al and Mimi moved soon to Minnesota, where she had been raised and had attended the University of Minnesota. They began to raise salukis commercially and were together until 1971.

Fowler continued writing, though he grew to hate junk with a passion. In 1971 he was struck on the head from behind by a guy wielding a pipe, which left him an epileptic, prone to severe seizures. He served several jail terms in the North Country. Al remained in Minnesota until after his final jail sentence. He returned to New York City in 1979 and lived with his mother, Bertha, until his death.

On January 23, 1980, Al Fowler either fell or was shoved into the path of an oncoming subway train in Manhattan. He showed up at the ticket booth, gave his name, then collapsed into unconsciousness. He lingered for nine days, never recovering consciousness, then passed away. It was two weeks after his fortieth birthday.

Meanwhile, in the fall of 1966 times were more or less flush for us in our new pad on Twelfth and A. The Fugs were selling out most of our shows at the Players Theatre, and I was in the midst of negotiating with a major label, Atlantic Records!

Trouble Inside The Fugs

We were still playing at the Players Theatre during the fall of 1966. The loss of Anderson and Kalb dented us badly. With these personnel changes, we decided to define The Fugs as Ed Sanders, Tuli Kupferberg, and Ken Weaver.

The Fugs' relationship with ESP records was, to state it mildly, turbulent. We were told, for instance, that Organized Crime was illegally manufacturing Fugs records and selling them. We can be forgiven for not really believing that the Genovese crime family would bother with The Fugs when there were The Beatles, The Stones, Mantovani, and Petula Clark to rip off.

The owner of ESP had insisted on ducking some of the lyrics of Ted Berrigan's song, "Doin' All Right," when we mixed it. "I ain't never going to go to Vietnam / I'd rather stay right here and screw your mom." "Screw," after the level duck, became like a "humm."

Things didn't add up. A close relative of the label's owner told me the family viewed the owner as unstable and helped bankroll in lieu of therapy or confinement.

I was determined to put together a brilliant band. For a while we had a fine guitarist named Stefan Grossman, who replaced Jon Kalb.

Reading at the 92nd Street Y

Monday, October 24, in the evening, Robert Creeley and John Wieners read together at the 92nd Street Y. I was asked to introduce them. Wieners was very happy at reading, for the first time, at such a prestigious place, where T. S. Eliot, W. H. Auden, e. e. cummings, and other emeralds of poesy had plied their bardery in the past.

There was a party at the Chelsea Hotel afterward. Charles Olson called Bob Creeley at the Chelsea party and insisted that Bob hand the phone to John Wieners. Then he informed Wieners that he and Panna Grady were traveling to London together. It must have been a blow to John and did not reflect well on Olson, who must have known the joy Wieners was experiencing that night, reading with Creeley at the prestigious 92nd Street Y. (Wieners and Grady had had an affair that summer, but she had broken it off.)

the poetry center

THE 92ND STREET YM-YWHA   92ND STREET AND LEXINGTON AVENUE. NEW YORK, NEW YORK 10028   FI 8-1500

ROBERT CREELEY   and   JOHN WIENERS

Monday evening, October 24   Poetry Center Members: Free*
1966   8:30 o'clock   Others: $1.50

ROBERT CREELEY was born in Arlington, Massachusetts and attended Harvard University, Black Mountain College and the University of New Mexico (from which he received his M.A.). He has taught at Black Mountain College, where he edited the Black Mountain Review, and at the University of New Mexico; he is presently teaching at the State University of New York in Buffalo. He is the recipient of a Rockefeller Foundation Grant, a Guggenheim Fellowship, the D.H. Lawrence Fellowship from the University of New Mexico and the Levinson Prize for poetry. Mr. Creeley's works include a book of poetry, For Love (Scribner's, 1962), a novel, The Island (Scribner's, 1963) and a book of short stories, The Gold Diggers (Scribner's, 1965).

JOHN WIENERS, born in Boston in 1934, graduated from Boston College. He also attended Black Mountain College, where he studied under Robert Duncan and Charles Olson. He became associated with the Poets' Theatre in Cambridge and his two one-act plays were produced by the New York Poets' Theatre and the Judson Poets' Theatre in New York. In 1957 he founded the magazine, Measure, and his first book of poems was published by Auerhahn Press in San Francisco. He received an award from the Poets' Foundation in 1962, and continues to write in Boston. Mr. Wieners is the author of Ace of Pentacles (James F. Carr & Robert A. Wilson, 1964). This is his first appearance at The Poetry Center.

ED SANDERS will introduce the poets.

Coffee will be served in the Art Gallery during intermission.

The invitation to the Creeley-Wieners reading, a bit tattered from being in my archive for over forty years.

The Fugs to California in Late 1966

We played the Earl Warren Fairgrounds in Santa Barbara with Eric Burdon and the Animals. It was the first time I'd had my shirt torn off by fans. It wasn't pleasant, youthful fingers grabbing the skin of my arms and back.

I met a hot singer named Janis Joplin at the California Ballroom in San Francisco, where she was performing with Big Brother and the Holding Company. She asked me about ESP Records, which was trying to get Big Brother to sign a recording contract. I urged extreme caution in dealing with ESP.

While The Fugs were in California, we appeared on the Les Crane television show. Phil Ochs was in the audience, and we became friends, with many capers together over the years.

Jimi Hendrix at the Wha

I was grateful to get to know a great young guitarist, Jimi Hendrix, who was performing at the Café Wha in the basement next to the Players Theatre. Jimi came to some Fugs shows, where I was wearing a wide-brimmed cowboy hat, which seemed to turn him on to the idea, and he began himself to sport a cowboy. I attended some Hendrix shows at the Wha, where he was performing as Jimi James and the Blue Flames. I remember him turning around to glare a couple of times at his players as they fell out of musical focus.

One evening as we chatted, Jimi Hendrix told me he didn't like his voice. I told him his voice was beautiful.

It was right around the time the wah wah pedal was invented, and Dan Green, who was working for The Fugs at the time as equipment manager, turned Jimi on to the wah wah, and soon afterward he began utilizing it in his songs. Then Hendrix was discovered and taken to England, where he soared all the way to the Monterey Pop Festival of the following spring.

The Frank O'Hara Award

On December 30 I received a letter from attorney Edward Ennis announcing that the Trustees of the Poets Foundation had selected me for a $500 award "in recognition of your contribution to poetry." The award was given "in honor of the memory of Frank O'Hara." I was very grateful.

1967: The Year of Love
and the Great Be-In

Gary Snyder began the Human Be-In on January 14 in the Golden Gate Park polo field with a riff on a conch shell. The formal name for the event was "Gathering of the Tribes for a Human Be-In."

The name, of course, came from the sit-ins in the South to integrate lunch counters, say, at Woolworth's and later the popular teach-ins against the war in Vietnam. Now it was be-in, and this one event set the cultural tone of the year, along with the rhymed doublet: flower power.

There were 20,000 there to surge in primary-color splendor with the fine Pacific psyche light at last outshining the puritanical searchlight from Plymouth Rock as the Grateful Dead, the Jefferson Airplane, Quicksilver Messenger Service, Jerry Rubin, Gary Snyder, Tim Leary, Lenore Kandel, Allen Ginsberg, and others made words and music. All across America that spring there were be-ins, smoke-ins, love-ins, tipi-ins, and in-ins. These set the tone of 1967, even in the counterculture haunts of the Lower East Side.

Angry Arts Festival in New York City

Meanwhile in New York City, there was a big cooperation among artists, musicians, writers, and moviemakers to scream out against the war in Vietnam. It was called the Week of the Angry Arts.

About sixty filmmakers contributed short anti–Vietnam War films to the Week of the Angry Arts. These were first screened in New York on January 30 at NYU's Loeb Student Center on West Broadway. Among the film artists were Stan Brakhage, Shirley Clarke, Robert Frank, Hillary Harris, Jonas Mekas, Ken Jacobs, Storm de Hirsch, John Hawkins, Stan Vanderbeek, Robert Breer, Dick Preston, and the group known as USCO. (A version of this Week of the Angry Arts films can be rented from the Film-Makers' Cooperative.)

There were a wide variety of public performances in dissent against the war. From January 29 to February 5 hundreds participated on themes such as "Folk Rock Dissents" and "Avant Garde Musicians Dissent," with compositions by Phil Corner, Morton Feldman, Earle Browne, Malcolm Goldstein, and others, at the Community Church; "Dancers Dissent"; a "Napalm Poetry Reading" at the Community Church, with Muriel Rukeyser, Denise Levertov, Robert Creeley, John Logan, and Robert Bly; "Photographers Dissent"; and many other events, all now evaporated into the mists of the past. The Fugs took part in the "Folk Rock Dissents."

Then immediately after the Week of the Angry Arts there was further repression of artistic freedom. Charlotte Moorman was arrested for performing a bare-breasted cello piece at the Filmmaker's Cinematheque on February 9. She was scheduled to perform Nam June Paik's *Opera Sextronique*, plus Max Matthews's *Lullaby*, the latter played topless, with Moorman donning various masks and wearing a black skirt. She bowed the cello with items such as a bouquet of flowers. It was during *Lullaby* that plainclothes policemen interrupted the performance, tossed everybody out of the theater, and took her to jail, where she spent the night.

What she did next is a sterling example of what an artist should do under attack. To show the judge in her trial what the *Opera Sextronique* was really about, Moorman re-created the first two movements, right after her arrest, in a studio as filmmaker Jud Yalkut filmed the performance. The judge ultimately refused to allow the restaged *Opera Sextronique* to be screened in court, but the Opera remains to this day a historical re-creation of a moment of New York City repression, 1967 style.

Meanwhile, on January 25 The Fugs went up to Atlantic Records and signed a multialbum contract.

Fugs signing with Atlantic Records, January 25, 1967: Tuli, Ed, Ken, Ahmet Ertegun, Jerry Wexler.

We did a demo recording at the Atlantic Studios. Jerry Wexler then suggested we record at Bob Gallo's Talent Master Studio on Forty-second Street and Broadway. It was a block away from the cigar store where I had worked the night shift off and on from 1960 until 1965 when I opened the Peace Eye Bookstore.

It was a well-known studio. Bob Gallo was instrumental in the production of a good number of hit singles, such as James Brown's "It's a Man's World," "96 Tears" by Question Mark and the Mysterians, and, soon, "Groovin'" by the Young Rascals. He would write for and produce such acts as Otis Redding, Patti LaBelle, Aretha Franklin, The Drifters, and Bo Diddley. Atlantic Records' Jerry Wexler had arranged to buy into Bob Gallo's Talent Master recording studios.

Recording at Talent Masters

Beginning in early February the lineup was Ed Sanders, Ken Weaver, Tuli Kupferberg, Jake Jacobs, Lee Crabtree, and some great studio players—Eric Gale on guitar, Chuck Rainey on bass, Robert Banks on piano and organ, and Bernard Purdie on drums.

Chris Huston was our engineer. Huston was a young Englishman who had been the guitarist for a group called The Undertakers, which had recorded an album at Gallo's studio. Huston went on to engineer and produce sessions for such groups as Led Zepplin, The Who, War, the Rascals, Todd Rundgren, Van Morrison, Blood, Sweat and Tears, Mitch Ryder and the Detroit Wheels, Ben E. King, The Drifters, Patti La Belle and the Bluebelles, Solomon Burke, Mary Wells, Wilson Pickett, John Hammond Jr., James Brown, not to mention Question Mark and the Mysterians.

When recording at Talent Masters, we noticed that there were all these unused sixteen-track Otis Redding instrumental tapes in the tape storage room. We listened to some of them. They were great!! What a temptation! They featured guys like the great studio drummer Bernard Purdie. All we would have had to do was stick on our own wild Fugs lyrics and vocals and we'd have had a bunch of quick tunes!

It gave us the idea to cut some songs with some of the hot Atlantic session players. So we booked some legendary Atlantic players—Bernard Purdie, Eric Gale, Chuck Rainey—to cut some basic tracks. This ensemble recorded the track, for instance, to "River of Shit," Lionel Goldbart's tune.

I was struggling mightily, through plenty of rehearsals, and shifting and adding musicians in the studio, to make an album that was both revolutionary and commercially appealing.

Jake Jacobs performed on guitar, vocals, bells, sitar, and vibes, and Lee Crabtree, on organ, piano, and flute. Jacobs had been in a band called The Magicians, which had taken over the gig of house band at the Night Owl on West Third from the Lovin' Spoonful, when the latter had surged to fame. Jake had a beautiful voice and was an excellent arranger.

We recorded "Nameless Voices Crying for Kindness," based on a line from an interview Allen Ginsberg gave that I had spotted in the underground newspaper the *Los Angeles Free Press*. We recorded "Hare Krishna" that winter, with Allen Ginsberg singing lead, Gregory Corso on harmonium, Maretta Greer and Peter Orlovsky singing along, and Jake

Jacobs on sitar. Allen came to me and suggested he might copyright the melody. I replied, "It's a 5,000-year-old tune!" And so that plan was scrapped. I was busy making lists of possible titles for the Atlantic album: *Weirdness Pie* was one, *Ablution in the Abyss* was another, *Aphrodite Mass* was yet another, plus *The Fugs Eat It.*

Still Playing at the Players Theatre

While The Fugs recorded at Talent Masters, we played weekends at the Players Theatre.

On the *David Susskind Show*

The Fugs appeared on the prestigious *David Susskind Show* in early 1967. Susskind was a leading television producer and winner of numerous Emmy awards. In my archives is a reel of tape containing the interview, which in the interest of completeness I listened to while writing this book.

The tape commences with Susskind introducing us:

Some of the most rebellious people I know, and some of the most way-out people—they are The Fugs, and I'd like to present them individually: Ed Sanders, he founded The Fugs in '65, a poet, he's also the editor of the *Marijuana Newsletter*, a graduate of New York University, Ed Sanders was born in Kansas City, Missouri; next Ken Weaver, also a poet, he's been with The Fugs since the group was formed; and Tuli Kupferberg, who in addition to his Fugs activities also teaches a course on the Sexual Revolution at the Free University of New York, and he is the editor of the Birth Press. Now The Fugs make record albums—they're musicians, and they have extraordinary tunes and songs—"Kill for Peace," "Slum Goddess," "We Love Grass," "Group Grope," "What Are You Gonna Do After the Orgy?" "Hallucination Horrors," and "Bed Is Getting Crowded" [rise of laughter]. Now, WHY do you compose such songs, and where can you sing and perform them, Ed?

Ed: All over the United States. We perform at colleges, campuses, coffeehouses, and theaters. Why do we write songs like that? Because it feels good [another round of laughter]. No, because it's a manifestation of certain concerns we have about changes in sexual mores in this country, and it has to do with our opinions on a number of psychosocial, and philosophical, and religious and spiritual things.

Susskind: Yeah, but these songs are pretty dirty.

Ed: Because we have seventy songs, man, you just went through our song-book, and copied out—you left out some songs I bet you couldn't say here.

Susskind: Yes, I have left those songs out [more laughter]. But the language is so guttural.

Tuli: Like guttural, like in the gutter.

Susskind: Yes.

Tuli: I thought you meant guttural, like in the German language.

Susskind: Are you sort of doing what those people do who write dirty stuff on walls? Doesn't it amount to the same thing?

Tuli: Some of that's good poetry [big laugh].

Ed: "The words of the prophets are written on the subway walls." You miss the point. The point is that we're taking highly charged language, we're taking poetry, some of which is highly charged with sexual connotations, and we're dropping it into modern music, into pop music, into rock and roll, into chants and religious statements, and social statements. Some of it involves using the Blip words, the four-letter words, the seven-letter words, and the sixteen-letter words that are banned on the airwaves, but which we can say in the context of theater, and we actually say them on albums.

Tuli: These words are implied in all the other music; it's just that they are euphemistic. But I think that most young people who sing those songs know what they're singing about.

Ed: Hey, man, the American automobile has revolutionized sex. The backseat has revolutionized. . . . You can't go out to Freakville, Arkansas, without having everybody knowing what's on page thirty-seven of the *Kama Sutra*. They know all about pot and music and the "backseat boogie."

Susskind: Why do you look this way? Ken, why no haircut ever?

Ken: Actually, I'm emulating Uncle Sam. He has long hair and a beard [laughter and applause].

Tuli: Not only Uncle Sam, but Abraham Lincoln, Alexander Hamilton, George, Ben Franklin, Andrew Jackson.

Susskind: Is the whole thing adding up to total rebellion—appearance? . . .

Ed: Not at all. The point is there's no reason for a man to restrict himself to repressive clothing [pointing to Susskind]. Your suit has embellishments; you've got some sort of modified Beatle boots on [lots of laughter]. The point is, there's a way of expressing yourself through clothes; there's a way of going around expressing yourself colorfully, with artistry; it's esthetic. If more people tried to make their lives more esthetic, and more complexly and richly colorful, then you'd have a more interesting and fruitful voyage as a human being.

Susskind: Doesn't it add up to slobness?

Ed: Up against the Wall! We dress very carefully. We're not slobs.

Tuli: Aren't you bored by black jackets?

Susskind: No, not particularly.

Susskind: What is it about the sexual mores of the country that give you a pain?

Ed: The repression of sex by people who are growing old and are afraid they're going to die is often manifested in war hysteria.

Susskind: What's wrong with the sexual conventions of America today. What is it that you're so angry about?

Tuli: The fact that people can be punished by indulging in any kind of sexual practice they want that does not hurt anyone.

Susskind: You're for total promiscuity?

Ed: No, people want a full spectrum of sexual activity. . . .

Susskind: Let's not get too clinical.

Ed: If a man and woman discover that they want to live together in a monogamous situation without any adultery, then that's fine. Although there are some in the United States that want to engage in group marriages, or situations where they have matrilinear descent for children, you have situations where three or four people want to live together, you have where people don't want to marry at all; you have a right to be a homosexual. The point is, man, you've got to examine the sexual possibilities, and in all the sexual possibilities where there is no violence and no one hurt, then they should be allowed by the law.

Tuli: These are crimes without victims.

Susskind: How about drugs. Do you advocate complete permissiveness, Ken?

Ken: How do I feel about drugs? I really like them [big surge of laughter]. I don't foist what I like on other people. I never tell people to take LSD.

Susskind: Do you take LSD?

Weaver: I have taken it, yeah.

Susskind: Do you find it productive?

Weaver: Unutterably beautiful.

Susskind: Can you describe what it does for you that makes it unutterably beautiful?

Weaver: Nope [burst of laughter from audience].

Susskind: Is marijuana part of your lives?

Ed: The Fugs take no formal positions about any of these things. It's not like we're running some sort of Freak Cell here, that's giving out manifestos, but some of us, I particularly, happen to believe in the legalization of marijuana. I think marijuana is a gentle, benevolent herb falsely prosecuted by alcoholics and creeps [laughter].

Susskind: You think it does no harm?

Ed: I think it does infinite good to the human psyche, and I think it should be sold in vending machines just like cigarettes and combs in Howard Johnsons.

And on it went, this tape from early 1967, giving a slice of Fugs Thought before a large national television audience. This was at a moment of fairly great fame for The Fugs.

On the Cover of *Life* Magazine

In late January and early February I was interviewed a number of times by Barry Farrell, who was writing a piece on the New York underground for *Life* magazine. A photographer came to 196 Avenue A and took some pictures. I had no idea I would be on the cover.

Sudden Fame

I learned I was on the cover of *Life* magazine for the February 17 issue when the Johnny Carson television show called to have me on as a guest. Before I would appear, I insisted on Carson allowing The Fugs to sing "Kill for Peace" as a protest against the Vietnam War, which was refused. In retro-

Ed Sanders, a leader of New York's other culture.

spect I should have taken up the offer. Maybe I could have started to appear regularly, like Truman Capote, in front of late-night millions. For a while I basked in the Glory of being on the cover. I remembered my bet with Lanny Kenfield that The Fugs would some day be on the cover of *Time* magazine. For now *Life* would do.

On February 12, for instance, we flew to a large celebration in Toronto called "Perception '67," with Marshall McLuhan, The Fugs, Richard Alpert, Allen Ginsberg, Tim Leary (who was not allowed into Canada), and Paul Krassner. My issue of *Life* was on the newsstand at the Toronto airport, where it was minus five degrees outside! No one told us that fame did not automatically mean getting a glut of money. It was sometimes not so easy to pay the rents for our apartment on Avenue A and the Peace Eye Bookstore. Nevertheless, it's a place of masks, this fame, so when my father visited New

York City from Kansas City not long after I was on the cover of *Life*, I went out in a limousine to pick him up at the airport. He stayed at the 1 Fifth Avenue Hotel and enjoyed himself immensely.

I remember there was a party for Jimi Hendrix at a club in Sheridan Square in the West Village, where brilliant photographer Margaret Bourke-White was on hand. She mentioned me being a *Life* cover, and she pulled down her blouse to show me a tattoo above one of her breasts.

"The Fugs Turned Them On"

This was the headline of a front-page article in the *Toronto Daily Star* for February 13 tracing The Fugs' performance at the Perception '67 weekend. The article reported:

> At 11:15 last night, the whole psychedelic weekend at the University of Toronto fused into a blinding white light. Everybody who was a psychedelic anybody blew his mind. It happened as a New York group called the Fugs held a "concert" in hallowed Convocation Hall. Dr. Richard Alpert, who says you don't need drugs to blow your mind if you're turned on, pulled a fur coat he was holding over his nose, sprawled on a stage raiser, and tapped his foot to an anti–Viet Nam song titled "Kill for Peace." Crazy-clothes fashion designer Tiger Morse nodded madly, her oversize sunglasses bobbing with the beat. Michael Hayden, the 24-year-old behind the 10-room mind excursion of popcorn, strobe lights and total experience, grinned happily at Fug Tuli Kupferberg. Cynic Paul Krassner tried to look bored, then laughed and bounced up and down; poet Allen Ginsberg giggled and bobbed his beard in time to "Knock! Knock! Knock!" Suddenly the whole audience of 2,000 heard the Fugs screaming words that are only an echo today—and probably won't be heard again.
>
> What everybody had been talking about for two days finally happened; the whole place just sort of turned on.

Some Hostility

It wasn't always so friendly to be suddenly famous. Someone mailed a package to me at my post office box in the East Village. I opened it up in the lobby of the post office. It was a brand-new copy, with a bright red dust

jacket, of the Modern Library edition of Dostoevsky's *The Idiot*. As I
held it, the cover popped open and
I heard a kind of mousetraplike
whacking sound. I saw that the inside had been very neatly cut away
to make a square compartment into
which were arrayed a battery, a
spring-driven on/off switch, and
some wires attached to some small
cylinders. I walked over to the
counter and told the clerk, "I think

The card from Postal Inspector J. R. Stephens, who
took the fake bomb from me.

someone has sent me a bomb." Wow, did the postal employees scatter!

It was very handsomely designed but turned out to be a fake bomb. The
"explosive" cylinders, wired into place to look dangerous, were actually
CO_2 cartridges of the sort that were used to power model rockets. Whoever sent it had glued a card to the inside of the cover:

Big Boy has the Contract
Red is the Finger
You are the Mark

Not long thereafter an anonymous phone call came to our apartment
on Avenue A, with our two-year-old daughter asleep in her room. The caller
announced that he was first going to bomb my house, then the home of
Frank Zappa. As a result for the next ten years we had to have an unlisted
telephone number.

Craziness

By early 1967, around the time I was on the cover of *Life*, sometimes there
were fans hanging out on the street at Avenue A and Twelfth, beneath our
second-floor apartment. To get things done, I had to detach myself from the
craziness. One time a guy named Joe Forn, a friend of Tuli's, somehow got
in through the buzzer and came to our door. When I answered his knock,
he had a wild look to his eyes, he handed me a lightbulb, paused, then said,
"Please give this to Tim Leary. I know you know him." Then he trundled
back down the flight of steps to the street.

A few days later he was back, knocking at the door. I opened it. He said to forget about giving the lightbulb to Tim. His arms were bare, and he twisted the left arm and the right so that I could see the not-yet-quite-healed slash marks where he had cut his wrists.

"Give this to Tim Leary" stayed in my mind throughout the rest of the '60s.

Plimpton

There was another, more pleasant phone call, this one from George Plimpton. He wanted to go on the road with The Fugs, perform with the band, and write about it. Things got pretty wild on the road, and I didn't want George Plimpton snoozling around. Plus, I was still puzzled over the police informant that George had called me about, who had posed as a guitarist and tried out for The Fugs (from an ad I'd run in the *Village Voice!*) in the fall of '65, so I turned down his request.

Awareness of the Diggers

It was right around this time, amid the craziness of being on the cover of *Life*, getting the hostile phone call, hearing the crazy guy with the lightbulb saying, "Give this to Tim," that I became aware of the San Francisco Diggers.

They proposed to transform the economics of the Now through the Creativity of Sharing. One of their lasting concepts was the concept of the Free Store, in which items were given away free. The essay "Trip Without a Ticket," in *The Digger Papers*, a free newsprint anthology published in 1967, reported:

> Diggers assume free stores to liberate human nature. First free the space, goods and services. Let theories of economics follow social facts. Once a free store is assumed, human wanting and giving, needing and taking become wide open to improvisation.
>
> Someone asked how much a book cost. How much did he think it was worth? 75 cents. The money was taken and held out for anyone. "Who wants 75 cents?" A girl who had just walked in came over and took it.
>
> A basket labeled *Free Money.* No owner, no Manager, no employees and no cash-register. A salesman in a free store is a life-actor. Anyone who will assume an answer to a question or accept a problem as a turn-on.

By early 1967 the Diggers had established a Free Store in the middle of the Haight-Ashbury district, with a sign outside, the "Free Frame of Reference." Inside were piles of old clothes and other free items. Each day at 4 PM the Diggers gave out free food on the Panhandle of Golden Gate Park.

They acquired their name from the "Christian communist group in early Cromwellian England that took over the fields, tilled them, and then gave away the surplus food," as an article in the February 16 *Village Voice* succinctly described it. The Diggers made a big impression in the Lower East Side, especially in the minds of activists such as Abbie Hoffman and me.

Jade Companions of the Flowered Dance

Inspired by the example of the Diggers, in late February I joined with other psychedelic communards, including Peter Stafford, Linn House, and several others, to form a corporation to establish a group called "Jade Companions of the Flowered Dance." It was an umbrella group in whose name I was about to turn over operation of the Peace Eye Bookstore to the community.

The Jade Companions had membership cards. A fine example of 1967 Visit-the-Universe florescence on the front and what appear to be Mayan hieroglyphs on the back. By the way, this card belonged to Barry Rosenberg. Barry, I have your card.

Thus I followed, in my own way, the San Francisco Diggers' concept of the Free Store.

University of Buffalo Spring Arts Festival

The Fugs played two completely packed concerts at the University of Buffalo gymnasium on March 9. We were told that the school lost $5 million in endowments after Fugs lyrics were published in the student newspaper.

LeMar had been successfully brought to the university by Michael Aldrich and even received funding as an official university-sanctioned organization, with famous writer Leslie Fiedler as its faculty advisor. (This was in distinction to what happened to two other attempts to start LeMar chapters—the first by poet d. a. levy in Cleveland and the second by John Sinclair in Detroit, both of which resulted in harassment by local authorities.)

A Possible Album Cover

Jerry Wexler sent The Fugs to Joel Brodsky's studio for a photo shoot. I had an idea for a cover image: a young model attired in a bikini, posed with her legs jutting upward and widely spread, with the three Fugs standing just behind the legs, holding knives and forks. The title would then be *The Fugs Eat It.*

The prospective cover photo for the first Fugs Atlantic release, *The Fugs Eat It.*

I decided to allow the *Village Voice* to run in its March 23 issue this picture from the Joel Brodsky shoot and a story on how The Fugs had completed their new album on Atlantic. It was probably a dumb thing to do. I typed a list of credits before turning the mixed tapes over to Atlantic Records.

I worked with composer Gary Elton on a long work called "Aphrodite Mass." A feature of the "Mass" was my setting, in Greek, of a section of Sappho's "Hymn to Aphrodite," plus the only instance in music of the Latin words *necesse in via struprare,* or, "It's necessary to ball in the streets," occurring in the history of Western music. I went to a lecture by Timothy Leary,

```
                credits for

             The Fugs album:


Ed Sanders-- vocals

Ken Weaver-- vocals, drums

Tuli Kupferberg-- vocals, erectorine

with Allen Jacobs-- guitar, vocals, bells, sitar, vibes

and   Lee Crabtree-- organ, piano, & flute.

Hare Krishna sung by Allen Ginsberg, Maretta Greer & the
              FUG chorale, with Gregory Corso on harmonium
                             & Allen Jacobs on sitar.
additional musical assistance:  Eric Gale, guitar
                                Chuck Rainey, bass
                                Robert Banks, piano organ
                                Robert Banks, organ, piano
                                Bernard Purdie, drums

consultant for vocal arrangements: Allen Jacobs

Heavy Metal Music-- BMI


engineer &          coordinator of squack: Chris Huston
Recorded at Talentmaster Studios, N.Y.C.

production supervision: Ed Sanders


SIDE A 1 Turn On/ Tune In/ Drop Out    Sanders- Leary
       2 Knock Knock,                   Sanders-Crabtree
       3 Wide Wide River                Goldbart -Weaver
       4 Nameless Voices                Sanders
       5 Wet Dream                      Sanders

Side B 1 Seize the Day                  Kupferberg
       2 CCD                            Sanders
       3 Hare Krishna                   Ginsberg-Zeus
       4 Dover Beach                    Kupferberg-Arnold-Moses
       5 Aphrodite Mass                 Sanders--Elton
```

Typed list of credits for Atlantic album.

and thus his exhortation "Turn On, Tune In, Drop Out" became the hook line of the opening song on the Atlantic album. The album was completed by early April, and the future looked bright indeed for The Fugs.

On April 20 I sent a letter to Jerry Wexler at Atlantic. I was feeling good! On top of it! Sailing upward! Triumph for The Fugs was just a few weeks ahead! An album out maybe as soon as the summer solstice of 1967, to join the great albums of the Summer of Love. Wow!

"Dear Jerry," my letter began.

This is to acquaint you with the Fugs album which we have been working on for the last few weeks. We have created what we feel to be a balanced package of messages of satire, protest, tenderness and love. The album contains songs in all four categories. We have drawn strength for the album from rock, Indian, electronic and even gospel music, making sure all the while that the album has a literary and measured artistic flavor....

We are headed today for Santa Monica and Berkeley and you can be sure I am going to advertise the album at our press conference and at the concerts.

I concluded the letter by asking for a meeting in the near future "concerning a Fugs single. Maybe," I continued, "you'd be interested in producing it."

A Jerry Wexler Fugs single! Just the thought of it was a thrill because of his history of hits such as suggesting "The Tennessee Waltz" to Patti Page in the late 1940s! The Drifters brilliant "Money Honey" in '53, Ray Charles's '54 "I've Got a Woman," and Wilson Pickett's recent smashes, "In the Midnight Hour" and "Mustang Sally." The fifty-year-old Wexler, I thought, could have helped morph The Fugs, through a single, into a nationally powerful act in spite of the eros, the antiwar fervor, and our natural tendencies to offend.

Off to San Francisco

Our concert at Santa Monica Civic the night of April 21 was nearly sold out. We were told that there were some right-wing nurses picketing the show outside. Eileen Kaufman, the supportive wife of Out There Beat poet Bob Kaufman, threw a party for us in LA after the gig, but we had a late night flight to San Francisco and had to miss it. Dang!

We stayed in San Francisco for a few days, after performing at the Berkeley Community Theater on April 22.

The Haight-Ashbury, just noodling toward the Summer of Love, was an eye-opener. We did a free concert with Country Joe and the Fish at the Panhandle Park for the Diggers. I've often wondered if Charles Manson, just out of jail and living in the area, was there.

I went to see the Grateful Dead and, for the first time, a Full Light Show. I've wondered if

The Fugs poster for the Berkeley Community Theater, April 22, 1967.

this particular Grateful Dead show was the one in which Manson, tripping on LSD, experienced the Stations of the Cross.

I stopped by Janis Joplin's house. She was excited about a packet of flower seeds Richard Brautigan had given her, with a poem glued to the side.

Editor Don Allen drove me out to the bohemian community of Bolinas, veering quite wildly along the Pacific Coast Highway. We were discussing a collection of my poetry for Grove Press.

"Good Production Job, Ed"

After returning from the West Coast concerts, I went to Atlantic Records for a meeting with the owners. I played the album for them as they sat around a long table in a conference room. At the end one of them said, "Good production job, Ed."

A couple of days after the meeting Jerry Wexler called me at home on Avenue A and said Atlantic was not going to release the album. Not only that, we were being tossed off the label. It was a brief, stunning call. It looked for several months as if our career among major labels as over. I heard that one of the Ertegun brothers' spouses had not really dug our beautiful rendition of "Coca Cola Douche," the idea for which I came up with after reading an article in *Newsweek*.

Nevertheless, getting unfairly tossed off Atlantic after we were encouraged to make whatever album we wanted left us without an album to greet the Summer of Love. It prevented The Fugs from putting out an album in the Glory year of 1967 to join *Sgt. Pepper, Big Brother and the Holding Company, Alice's Restaurant, Procol Harum,* Jimi Hendrix's *Are You Experienced,* and "All You Need Is Love." In fact, The Fugs were prevented from putting out a studio album for a whole crucial year.

All my plans for living on Art, creating a thriving band that toured and sold records, seemed to crash into the dirty sidewalk outside Peace Eye. In any case my heart in its polka-dotted jacket was all brok'd up.

CIA Scandal

Just two weeks after the Great Human Be-In in Golden Gate Park came very bad news from *Ramparts* magazine about the CIA and very soon after that further accusations by District Attorney Jim Garrison of New Orleans, a brave and patriotic American, about the CIA and the shooting of President Kennedy. The center-left magazine *Ramparts* was just about the most influential American magazine of its era in its vehement and ethical advocacy. *Ramparts* ran large ads in the *Washington Post* and *New York Times* on February 14 to announce an article in its March issue: "The CIA has infiltrated and subverted the country's student leadership. It has used students to spy. It has used students to pressure international student organizations into Cold War positions, and it has interfered in a most shocking manner in the internal workings of the nation's oldest and largest student organization."

The CIA went tweedily bonkers. It naturally wanted to know how much *Ramparts* had learned of the inner workings of the agency. It flipped together some detailed files on *Ramparts* backers and sicced the IRS on as many as possible. For instance, on February 15, after a CIA request, the IRS forked over copies of *Ramparts*'s tax returns to Richard Ober, the CIA counterintelligence officer looking to harm *Ramparts*. Not long after a right-wing break-in man (hired as well by right-wing California grape-growers to steal César Chávez's supporter list in an attempt to break the national grape boycott) stole the *Ramparts* CIA files in California. They were brought to DC, where two CIA officers took a look at them.

Meanwhile March 1, at the Abbey Road studio in London, The Beatles recorded John Lennon's era-stirring tune "Lucy in the Sky with Diamonds" for *Sgt. Pepper's Lonely Hearts Club Band*. My friend Barry Miles, a confidant of The Beatles, would send me letters now and then on the recording of this great album, including word about a marvelous tune about a "yellow submarine."

The very day of "Lucy in the Sky" was the day that District Attorney Jim Garrison announced the arrest of fifty-four-year-old Clay Shaw, formerly the head of the big International Trade Mart in the Crescent City, on charges of having conspired to kill John Kennedy. On March 17 a three-judge panel ordered Shaw to stand trial. (Shaw would be acquitted in early '69, though books such as *Deadly Secrets* by Warren Hinckle [one of the founders of *Ramparts*] and his coauthor William Turner would pretty much successfully argue that Shaw had connections with Lee Harvey Oswald. It was later revealed that at the time of Shaw's trial, CIA director Richard Helms had ordered his top assistants to "do all we can to help

Shaw." Jim Garrison's 1970 book, *A Heritage of Stone*, offered a taste of historic truth. Perhaps Garrison will one day receive his proper due for helping
to lay out the assassination for what it was: a coup d'état.)

At the time I followed Garrison's investigations in underground presses
such as the *Los Angeles Free Press*. Garrison's work, which aroused the ire of
the military-industrial-surrealist complex, and Mark Lane's 1966 book,
Rush to Judgement, made us wonder who was really running the so-called
American democracy.

The Peace Eye Bookstore in the Hands of the Community

I had turned Peace Eye over to the "community." I decided to let it reform itself according to the needs of the Be-In Generation. When I came back to
the Lower East Side from touring, I noted that there were lots of books in
the garbage cans out front. I was told they needed the wall space for psychedelic designs.

There were mattresses in all three rooms, and the place was packed at night
with young people, and a few not-so-young people, sleeping in what I called the
Mattress Meadow. What the community needed was space to crash.

The Young Man Named Groovy

His name throughout the Lower East Side was "Groovy." When I turned the
Peace Eye Bookstore over to the community, Groovy was in charge of the
Mattress Meadow. Once I counted sixteen mattresses in the three rooms of
the store. Groovy oversaw the operation of the Mattress Meadow, and I
came to admire him.

Groovy spent some of his time finding safe crashes for the swarms of
kids arriving on the Lower East Side. He was a legend in those streets, even
though he'd been there for only a few months. Few knew his real name, but
everybody within flashback distance of Tompkins Park had a Groovy anecdote to tell.

Groovy preached the message that a person could both serve AND stay
high and party while trying to do good. Groovy would spend countless
hours listening to the cracked home lives of runaways or soothing them out
of bad trips. He was lanky, calm, cool, tall, and stubborn, and he wore a

harmonica on a wire holder around his neck. He had a moody face, jutting jawbones, slender shoulders, and a tattoo, "Bourbon Street," on his left forearm. He was a genuine hero to the Hippies who set up their primary color zone in the Lower East Side that summer.

Groovy helped put the Spirit of Goof back into the picture of a better world. Groovy dealt a little grass now and then and acted as a kind of Better Business Bureau to instill honesty in the trade. He tried to intervene against drug burners. Among grass and acid dealers he was a fearless ethics officer and had numerous sharp-voiced confrontations with burners and short counters.

And Then Touring

In my life as a poet I returned to the University at Buffalo on May 3.

The poster for the reading listed me as an "Egyptologist." While I was in Buffalo, I went to a café with Robert Creeley, and we talked about the sometimes-cruel exigencies of existence. He wrote out a recent poem on a paper napkin and handed it to me.

Good advice from the bard.

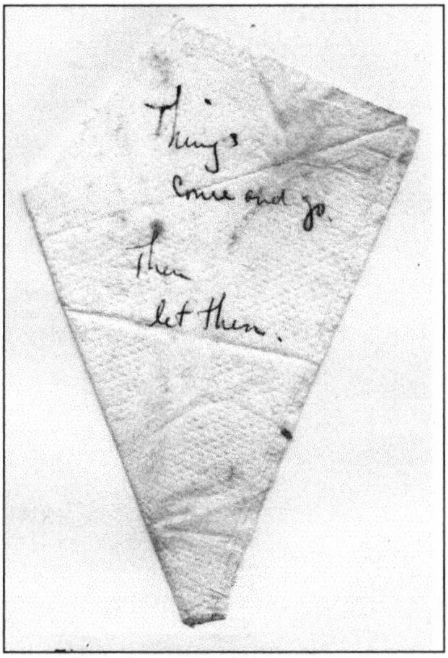

Meanwhile, The Fugs were doing some more touring. It cost $6 on May 12 to take a cab from the Lower East Side to JFK airport for a flight to Madison, Wisconsin, for a gig with Allen Ginsberg. The Fugs at that moment consisted of Sanders, Weaver, Kupferberg, Jake Jacobs on guitar, and Geoff Outlaw on bass.

That evening with Allen Ginsberg we performed at the University of Wisconsin Stock Pavilion to 1,700 attendees, almost a full house. "Judging from the wild applause," wrote a reporter for the *Capital Times*,

> uproarious laughter and spellbound stares, the audience was an appreciative one. Much to the horror of anyone who expected a big Haight-Ashbury pot party, the audience was not entirely made up of hippies. There was a fair sprinkling of respectable academics, well-coifed sorority girls, and middle-aged housewives. The Fugs, probably the only act in the world who could follow Allen Ginsberg, make the Rolling Stones look like Little Lord Fauntleroys. As the Lower East Side of New York's gift to folk culture, the six sang such "golden gassers" as "I Am, Therefore You Aren't" [a number from our fifteenth album with words by St. Thomas Aquinas], "Slum Goddess of the Lower East Side," and "Kill for Peace." The last number is a savage satire on our military efforts in Vietnam, and is evidence, if all their other songs were to be forgotten, of the "redeeming social importance" of the Fugs—which elevates them from the level of the raucously obscene.

We took part in a be-in, with flowers and burning wands of incense, in Madison before flying onward to Cleveland the next day.

While The Fugs were in Madison, I received a call from the Peace Eye Bookstore landlord. He was very disturbed over my turning over the running of the bookstore to the community. There was a guy, he told me, who was giving karate instructions in the back courtyard; plus someone had strung a tightrope in the courtyard, apparently between the buildings, and was conducting a wirewalking workshop! All this had to stop, or I'd have to close Peace Eye.

So one chore when I got back off the road was to take the bookstore back from the community. I was especially sad to be forced to toss out Groovy, who was the maître'd of the Peace Eye crash pad and Mattress Meadow. Groovy went forth to a shaky future during the upcoming Summer of Love, where he continued to try helping runaways find crash pads.

Benefit for d. a. levy

On May 13 The Fugs and Allen Ginsberg flew to Cleveland from Madison, where we did a benefit reading for d. a. levy and book dealer James Lowell at Strosacker Hall on Case Western Reserve's campus. levy had become one of the nation's first Pot Martyrs, a Martyr of the Mimeograph Revolution, and a Martyr for the Right to Read Erotic Verse.

It all began with the *Marijuana Newsletter*. I sent a copy to d. a. On April 19, 1965, he sent a post card to LeMar: "Please put me on your mailing list & I will sign petitions . . . wd distribute the Marijuana Report if I could afford." d. a. jumped to the cause with the same tenacity that had glued him to the letterpress. He thought he'd bring the legalization campaign to Cleveland, and he started the *Marrahwanna Newsletter* (later the *Marrahwanna Quarterly*), after which he became one of the first of the 1960s Pot Martyrs—joining Ken Kesey, Tim Leary, John Sinclair, and many others. The police put him on its list. The first issue of *Marrahwanna Newsletter* from Cleveland came out in early '66, price 10¢. The second issue came out in the summer, with part five of d. a.'s *North American Book of the Dead*.

The publication d. a. continued as the *Marrahwanna Quarterly*, with an emphasis on poetry and d. a.'s comments on the Cleveland police and psyche-delic scene (acid had just been made a federal crime). It was the eerie drone of the police state that began to unnerve him. Cops with body wires monitored the poetry readings levy attended. They hated the *Marrahwanna Quarterly*.

Not long after a reading at the Gate, on November 16, 1966, which po-lice taped and which included an obscenity in a poem (not one of levy's), d. a. was indicted for obscenity. On December 1 narcotics officers raided the

Asphodel Bookstore, seizing nine crates of d. a.'s publications on the grounds that they advocated the legalization of hemp and a mimeograph machine. Jim Lowell, the Asphodel's owner, was arrested. On January 9, 1967, the establishment *Cleveland Press* blurted a headline, "Grand Jury Names Beatnik Poet in Secret Indictment on Filth." The *Press* wrote that levy "is a widely known figure around University Circle beatnik haunts." (The squares had no idea that in just a few weeks the word "Hippie" would blow the word "Beatnik" away as a pejorative in the pejoracracy.)

d. a. went into hiding but on January 16 turned himself over and was released on bail. Then on March 28 d. a. was rearrested and charged on five counts of contributing to the delinquency of minors because at the Gate, he had read obscenity to a fifteen-year-old girl and a seventeen-year-old boy. The lad's parents had discovered a poster in his room and complained to the police. "Specifically," the *Plain Dealer* reported, "Levy is charged with accepting immoral and indecent poetry from the boy and publishing it, as well as reading and distributing it at the coffee house."

Levy pleaded not guilty. The judge insulted levy by asking how much he earned a day. levy answered, "I sell poetry for 89 cents a day." The judge set bail at $2,500 while cracking, "Maybe you should charge more than 89 cents."

Case Western Reserve law professors and students held a picket line, some holding "Legalize levy" protest signs, outside the Criminal Court Building. All this led to The Fugs and Allen Ginsberg coming to Cleveland on May 13 to do a benefit to help pay for levy's many expenses.

When The Fugs and Ginsberg landed in Cleveland on the day of the concert, straight from our success at the stock pavilion in Madison, I went with Allen Ginsberg, d. a. levy, and about fifty supporters to the basement of Trinity Cathedral. The police were on hand, and we were told that we would be arrested if we read poetry, so we decided to sing. We lifted forth the anthem "We Shall Overcome" and, at Ginsberg's suggestion, a few rounds of "Hare Krishna," which we had recorded for the new Fugs album that had just been nixed by Atlantic Records.

"Who's in charge here?" Allen Ginsberg asked of the police in the cathedral's basement.

"Nobody's in charge" was the response.

As I recall, the concert raised about $1,500 for levy's costs. levy continued to publish the *Marrahwannah Quarterly* and began an underground newspaper, the *Buddhist Third Class Junkmail Oracle.* Decades later when a friend of mine interviewed levy's prosecutor, he couldn't even remember the case.

On May 14 we flew back to New York, where it was time to face my own court case.

The Fugs Performing with Andrei Voznesensky at the Village Theater

Before my trial began, I met brilliant Russian poet Andrei Voznesensky during his visit to the States for some readings. Andrei was staying at the Chelsea Hotel on West Twenty-third Street.

One evening Voznesensky came to Allen Ginsberg and Peter Orlovsky's apartment on East Tenth, between Avenues C and D. I stopped by that night, and we were watching a critical documentary on the FBI, on television. "You mean," exclaimed Voznesensky, his eyes widening with surprise, "you can criticize the Secret Police on television!?"

"Sure," I replied. "Fuck them."

On May 18 Voznesensky took part in an anti–Vietnam War reading at the Village Theater (later the Fillmore East) located on Second Avenue at Sixth Street. I recall how strongly he performed his poetry, standing with his legs apart and reciting from memory. It was a brave thing for him to do, to take a stance against a U.S. war. Others reading that night included Ted Berrigan, John Ashbery, Gil Sorrentino, Sam Abrams, Jerry Rothenberg, Gregory Corso, Paul Blackburn, Joel Oppenheimer, Robert Creeley, Jackson MacLow, and Clayton Eshleman. The Fugs performed at the close of both sets of the performance.

Not many days later Voznesensky was seized from the streets. The way I heard it at the time was that filmmaker Barbara Rubin was showing Voznesensky a synagogue in the Lower East Side when, all of a sudden, he was whisked away by Soviet security types and flown back to Moscow.

In June 1967, just a couple of weeks after the whisk-away, Voznesensky was scheduled to read at a poetry festival at Lincoln Center, but the Moscow Writers Union kept him from appearing. According to a *New York*

Times account, the reason was "the open friendship that he showed to American society and American writers during his tour of the United States last May."

A Mood of Personal Defiance Following Court Hearing

Meanwhile, my own seemingly incessant court appearances for the Peace Eye/F.Y. bust, now going on for almost a year and a half, was dragging onward. As the months surged past, I was feeling more and more defiant. I was suffering court appearance after court appearance. I was required to show up at every one, lest I have my bail revoked and risk being jailed. For one of my hearings I arrived dressed all in white—white shirt, white tie, white boots, white suit (with Eyes of Horus painted on the lapels). This sartorial statement in white went by okay with the rather stern and death-aura'd judge named William Ringel.

But then for the next hearing I showed up attired entirely in red: new red satin Tom Jones shirt, red jacket, red corduroy pants, red Corfam shoes, and red socks. It was the outfit I had worn during my psilocybin adventure with Weaver and Olson in Gloucester.

The judge, again the grouchy guy named Ringel, was not pleased with my spiffy, all-rubicund attire. "Young man!" he practically screamed, "this is not a ski lodge! The next time you come to court wearing a proper suit and tie!"

"Yes, sir," I replied, while mentally telling him to take a walk down Vomit Alley waving a sponge!

During the hearings there were several ACLU attorneys who worked on my case. My attorney as we went to trial was Ernst Rosenberger. I was very impressed with him. Ernst, I learned, was very active in the civil rights movement. He'd been a volunteer attorney defending Freedom Riders arrested in Jackson, Mississippi, in 1961, and he was taking part in voting rights cases in the South throughout much of the decade. Later he became a State Supreme Court justice and then an associate justice of the New York Supreme Court Appellate Division.

Just a few days after the benefit for d. a. levy and the big antiwar reading at the Village Theater, my trial from the Peace Eye Raid of almost seventeen months previous was about to begin.

The Fuck You Trial

One of our plans was to wait for a correct trio of judges. And so as we went into the hearing at 100 Centre Street on May 22, Rosenberger analyzed the judges and decided we were ready for trial. My judges were William Ringel, Mitchell Sherwin, and Daniel Hoffman.

I was not so certain. I was particularly worried about the baleful Ringel, who, at a previous hearing, had ruled against a motion by Rosenberger to suppress the evidence in the case as having been gathered in violation of the Fourth Amendment, that is, with improper search and seizure.

I called my expert witnesses from the lobby of the court building. They were two eminent poets, Kenneth Koch and John Ashbery. I located Koch at his tennis court and so he showed up in court with a tennis racket. Both waited in the courtroom during the trial. The prosecutor was Assistant District Attorney John J. Moyna. One indication that we might sail through this nightmare occurred when I heard Moyna, while reading the indictment, pronounce "lascivious" as "láhshivous," with accent on the first syllable. Another thing that looked good: None of my judges had been on the trio (John Murtagh, Kenneth Phipps, and James Randall Creel) who had convicted Lenny Bruce back in 1964.

And so it began.

The assistant district attorney had a unique prosecution strategy. He decided that my announcements about certain of my underground films and some satiric advertising I typed and drew into the magazine provided proof I had violated the law regarding obscenity. Satire and reality sometimes reside in the same part of the brain, at least in my prosecutor's.

The only prosecution witness was Sergeant Charles Fetta, who by trial time had been transferred to the 111th Precinct in Bayside, Queens. Moyna elicited from the sergeant the time line of the arrest. Fetta was not asked about looking for Akh-en-Aten's "Hymn to the Sun Disk" on my testicles.

Prosecutor Offended by Lady Dickhead Advertising Company

The prosecution entered only five exhibits to show my malicious and evil intent to expose the literati of America to smutty advertisements and editorial comments. ADA Moyna began, "Now, if the Court please, I would invite the Court's inspection to certain parts of People's Exhibit #1, #2, #3, #4, respectively. The position of the People is that not the entire magazine is pornographic. We concede that, but that there are certain advertisements herein which advertise hard-core pornography and I would invite . . . the Court to inspect the exhibits right now."

Rosenberger then commented, "Do I understand from your statement, Mr. Moyna, that what you are offering in evidence is not the entire magazine but only those sections to which you now draw the Court's attention?"

Judge Ringel then interjected, "No, that's not what he's saying. As we understand Mr. Moyna, certain parts or portions of these exhibits are pornographic and the People do not contend that all of it is pornographic."

ADA Moyna agreed. He was contending that satiric advertisements in a mimeographed underground magazine were the core of the smut case: "Specifically, the advertisements, Your Honor, they violate Section 1141."

(Section 1141 of the New York State Penal Code reads, "A person who sells, lends, gives away, distributes or shows, or offers to sell, lend, give away, distribute, or show, or has in his possession with intent to sell, lend, distribute or give away, or to show, or advertises in any manner, or who otherwise offers for loan, gift, sale or distribution, any obscene, lewd, lascivious, filthy, indecent or disgusting book, magazine, pamphlet, newspaper, story paper, writing, paper, picture, drawing, photograph, figure or image, or any written or printed matter of an indecent character . . . is guilty of a misdemeanor.")

The prosecution was counting on the word "advertises" to nail me into the slams! I couldn't believe it! I was having a bit of difficulty following the line of reasoning, but as the prosecutor read into the record my so-called advertising, I had a hard time keeping from guffawing out loud.

Ringel then asked Moyna to "specify just what you are claiming is pornography." It was time for the Lady Dickhead Advertising Company to appear for the first time in the court cases of Western civilization.

The assistant district attorney then read the following, as interpreted by the court reporter: "People's Exhibit #1 is purple-colored 8 ½ x 11 sheet which reads 'Fuck You Magazine of the Arts, Promoting Pornography through its subsidiary Ladies Dick-Head Advertising Company.'"

I recalled it as among the pages the tremble-handed sergeant had thrust toward my face in the dawn of Peace Eye when I was trying to nail shut the broken window and door.

It seemed to me, watching it all from the defense table, that the prosecution was not presenting its strongest case. W. H. Auden's "Platonic Blow,"

The innocent-looking cover of the W. H. Auden–F.Y./ Press torrid "Platonic Blow"

which I published in the issue with the Warhol cover, was much more erotic than, say, the Lady Dickhead ad, any day. I'd also published it as a Fuck You Press pamphlet, and I had watched with regret as the police hauled away from the Peace Eye raid thousands of future dollars worth of copies.

Moyna continued: "People's Exhibit #2 is a yellow 8 ½ x 11 sheet and I quote the part that we contend is pornography or at least the advertisement that is pornography. This is approximately half-way down the page: 'For the next issue of Fuck You Magazine of the Arts, we would like to have a sister fold photograph of a Fuck-Maid of the Century. What we want is a large photo of a couple fucking, done in color, preferably, in order to show the tit-free magazine. . . . So all photographers who have some fuck photos, please have them sent to Ed Sanders.'"

Compare this transcript with the actual "ad":

may order, at trade discount, from Peace Eye...
N.Y., N.Y. 10009. /-- For the next issue of Fuck You/ a magazine of
the arts, we would like to have a centerfold photograph of the
FUCKMATE OF THE CENTURY. What we want is a large photo of a couple
fucking, done in color preferably, in order to show the tit-freak
mags the direction for their foldouts. So, all photographers who
have some fuck photos, please zap them to Ed Sanders./-- The first
Fuck You Editorial Board movie, MONGOLIAN CLUSTER FUCK, is nearing
completion. If anyone has a stuffed ram to loan us, that is the only
thing holding up finishing the movie. /-- Ed Sanders new book of poetry
with a foreword by Charles Olson, is out. New Yorkers may have trouble
getting it, since Ted Wilentz has banned it from THE EIGHTH STREET
BOOKSHOP. You can slurp it up at the PEACE EYE BOOKSTORE & Scroungo
Lounge at 383 E 10th N.Y. City. $1.50/-- If you're pissed off at
the war-creeps or if the draft is trying to stomp you, freak it up
with CNVA 325 Lafayette St. N.Y., N.Y. specializing in peace walks,
petitions, defense establishment peace-invasions, submarine boardings,
etc.; or dial in Dave McReynolds of WAR RESISTER's LEAGUE 5 Beekman
N.Y., N.Y. McReynolds is a brilliant architect of any new humane
politics./--

FUCK YOU/ the magazine of GRASS-SMUGGLING !!

Ad from the district attorney's case (the number 2 at the lower left denotes this page as being Exhibit #2).

Moyna did not mention the sentence "FUCK YOU/ the magazine of GRASS-SMUGGLING."

Then Moyna read onward: "People's Exhibit #3, specifically we invite the Court's attention to the eighth page entitled, 'Advertisements,' and the first in the top left-hand corner, the column beginning in the top left-hand corner part of

Ad from volume 5, number 7, the "God" issue, with cover by noted Beat-era artist Robert LaVigne.

the page it reads as follows: 'One orgie asks for the movie—now being shot on the location on the Lower East Side. Scenes being filled require large numbers of rope specialists and especially young ladies snapping pussy for snook freegin.'"

FUCK YOU

THE TALK OF THE TOWN

Notes and Comment

We shall freak onward in the Rays of Ra . This is our THIRD ANNIVERSARY ISSUE & Fuck You/ a magazine of the Arts will continue forever. The Fuck You/ Editorial Board cluster fucks onward, trailing blazing hookahs of glory, empty Amyl-nitrite vials, di-methyl-tript parsley, & orange LSD basketballs by the 1000's. TOTAL ASSAULT! Onward in the FLESH EXPRESS. The next issue of Fuck You/ a magazine of the Arts will be a gigantic PROSE ISSUE containing millions of pages of ultimate prose spews. Please zap us w/ your manuscripts. /--- ABOUT THE COVER: by ANDY WARHOL from his banned COUCH MOVIE. It was kindly Thermofaxed & glued by William Linich. The superstars are, left to right, Rufus Collins, Kate Heliczer & the fellow leaning down to muff Kate, is, of course, Gerard Malanga /---- SHRIEK! SHRIEK! announcing THE FUGS!!!! an unbelievable group of singers featuring Tuli Kupferberg on farto-phone, Brillo Box, finger cymbals, & various percussion instruments; Ed Sanders on organ, sex organ, & Harmonica; Srabo on Amphetamine Flute & recorder ; Ken Weaver on snares & big stomp Buffalo hide drum; & guest stars. Dances, dirty folk spews, rock & roll, poetry, Amphetamine operas, & other freak-beams from their collective existence. These creeps barf from an unbelievable bag. There has never been any thing like the FUGS in the history of western civilization!! For bookings, we are for sale, please contact Ed Sanders at the PEACE EYE BOOK STORE.

help wanted   help wanted   help Fug-press editorial assistants, typists, young lady head-copping specialists, & hordes of snapping pussy needed for the following projects: a) completion of the new Fuck You/ press publication by William Burroughs called BURROUGHS MONOGRAPH #1: Apo-33 A Metabolic Regulator. b) preparing the fug-press publication "BANANA, an anthology of Strap Verse, Dike Shrieks, harness poems, & worshipful emanations from the Shrine of The Bull Tongue Clit" c) answering the many Fuck You/ editorial board Cock Spurt Alerts. d) assistance in preparing the huge upcoming prose issue of FUCK YOU (#5, vol 9)/---
MOVIES!! 1) Will all the stars & super stars of Ed Sanders under ground epic (two years in the making) please report back for certain retakes. The director has been plagued by stars disappearing into Hillside Hospital & Central Islip, & the hip chick star tendency to vanish somewhere in New Jersey. Even though you may have married that dentist, please bring you snatch back for a few more reels of Amphetamine Glory. The WORLD PREMIERE of AMPHETAMINE HEAD will occur in spring, 1965! 2) The Editorial Board of Fuck You/ a magazine of the arts announces its first moviemaking venture::

MONGOLIAN CLUSTER FUCK
a short but searing non-socially redeeming porn flick featuring 100's of the lower east side's finest, with musical background by Algernon Charles Swinburne & THE FUGS!!

TOE QUEENS, ARISE!
--continued next page--

Then came time for People's Exhibit #4, as Moyna interpreted it, gazing at a page of the magazine: "The fifth page entitled the 'Talk of the Town,' reading as follows, at the lower right-hand corner of the page, the paragraph which begins with the numeral 2, 'The editorial board of Fuck You Magazine of the Arts announces its first movie making venture, the Mongolian Cluster Fuck, a short but searing, nonsocial redeeming pornographic featuring a hundred of the lowest east side finest musical ballroom, Charles Swingbeard and Fuck, etc."

Charles Swingbeard! I bet the ghost of A. C. Swinburne was chuckling above his grave! And the world was not quite ready, probably still isn't, for a rock band called Fuck.

MONGOLIAN CLUSTER FUCK
a short but searing non-socially redeeming porn flick featuring 100's of the lower east side's finest, with musical background by Algernon Charles Swinburne & THE FUGS!!

There was not a single question regarding the exhortation "TOE QUEENS, ARISE!" Then Moyna announced, "That constitutes the People's case."

Judge Ringel pointed out that there were five exhibits and only four had been described for the record.

Moyna then brought forth People's Exhibit #5, Jack Smith's *The Beautiful Book*, which consisted of a series of photos from *Flaming Creatures* pasted onto a sequence of pages. "We argue," he said, "that each picture herein is pornographic."

Ringel: Each picture is pornographic, that's your contention?
Moyna: That's our contention.

Cover of Jack Smith's *The Beautiful Book*, silkscreened and designed by Marian Zazeela (note court stamp in upper right: "Defs-Peo Exh. #5").

The oi was oi-ing in the Oi.

Opposite are a couple of sample pages from *The Beautiful Book*.

About half of the pictures in *The Beautiful Book* are of cover designer Marian Zazeela. The judges seemed of the opinion that at least one snap was smutiferous. I couldn't figure out the one to which they were alluding.

I had a few copies of *The Beautiful Book* at Peace Eye. Somehow they all disappeared, a sad situation because the publication featured nineteen hand-tipped black-and-white contact prints of photos taken in Smith's Lower East

Side apartment, mostly from the winter of 1962, not long before Smith filmed *Flaming Creatures*. The book also included a famous snap of Smith beneath the Brooklyn Bridge taken by Ken Jacobs. Piero Heliczer, who had starred in the "Dance of the Bugger Ball" sequence I shot for *Mongolian Cluster Fuck* at the Dakota, had published *The Beautiful Book*, which sold for $4 in 1966. Now it's worth about $10,000—one reason I wish the fuzz had not carted my copies away to the Ninth Precinct!

Meanwhile, there was more fliffle. And more floffle relating to this and that. Then the prosecution rested, and it was time for my defense. Kenneth Koch and John Ashbery were in the courtroom, ready to testify.

My able attorney, Ernst Rosenberger, began my defense. The first thing he did was to make a motion to dismiss the charges. He attempted to present arguments to back up the motion, but the irascible Judge Ringel kept breaking in.

Rosenberger: Your honor, at the conclusion of the People's case, the defendant respectfully moves to dismiss on the grounds that the People have failed to make out a prima facie case as against him. This is on several grounds, your honor, and which I would like to go into. . . .

Ringel: Tell your client to sit down.

Rosenberger: which I would like to go into, serially.

Ringel: Go ahead.

Rosenberger: First, Your Honor, as to no piece of evidence before the Court is there more than one item. There are only five items offered and they are five separate items. However, in the absence of any sale, specifically, the statute requires possession of six identical items.

Rosenberger had them! They did not have six copies in evidence of "The Lady Dickhead Advertising Company" or any proof of actual sale of anything.

Ringel said, "Let me see (Section) 1141, please."

Next there was a discussion of Jack Smith's *The Beautiful Book*. Moyna had claimed that all the pictures in Smith's book were illegal smut.

Rosenberger asserted, "It's our contention, Your Honor, that that booklet (*Beautiful Book*) constitutes one book. And that you cannot take each page of a book as a separate item but where a book is offered that book must be viewed as a book. It must be viewed as a book in considering it as a whole and as the Supreme Court has laid down guidelines for cases involving free speech, any work must be viewed as a whole. You cannot view one page of this and one page of that as being separate items."

Rosenberger read from the *Eros* magazine case (*Eros* was published by Ralph Ginzburg, who was indicted by the feds, and the case went to the Supreme Court) in which the U.S. Supreme Court took note of the considerable testimony on pandering. But in the Peace Eye/Fuck You case there was no pandering.

"The Supreme Court," pointed out Rosenberger, "in case after case has held that the work must be utterly without redeeming social value and the only exception which the court has permitted to that is a case in which the evidence proves beyond a reasonable doubt a pattern of pandering. . . . Your Honor this record [The Peace Eye trial] is silent on any of those considerations. . . . There is no evidence of pandering. These works must be judged on their own as to a prima facie case whether the isolated portions which are submitted and the People have conceded that the entire works are not without redeeming social value, are not totally obscene. Your Honor, based on that, we submit that the People have failed in establishing a prima facie case."

ADA Moyna replied, "The People's case . . . rests exclusively on that section of Section 1141, which proscribes the advertisement of hard-core pornography. It's our contention that those parts of these magazines that were submitted to Your Honor's consideration, constitute such advertisement, and in that light we conceded, only for the purpose of this prosecution, that we stand mute, actually, on the remaining portions of the magazine."

Judge Ringel then denied the motion to dismiss.

Next, Ernst Rosenberger approached me for a private conference. He had a suggestion. He felt that the ADA and the testimony of Fetta had not really presented much of a case. Rosenberger's proposed that we rest our case without testimony. I thought about it for a few moments, then agreed.

It was a gamble. Rosenberger then addressed the Panel of Three Dour Gents: "If Your Honor pleases, at the conclusion of the People's case, the People having rested, the defendant rests Your honor, and the defendant moves for a judgement of acquittal on the ground that the People have failed to establish his guilt beyond a reasonable doubt."

Then Ringel, for the panel of three, granted the motion to dismiss!

Ringel asserted, "The motion to dismiss is granted, the Court has a doubt with respect to the proof required under 1141, particularly, Subdivision 1 and in connection with Subdivision 4 with respect to the presumption. This is not to be interpreted as the Court's condoning or approving the language, and, at least, one of the photographs that appears in the (Jack Smith) exhibit here, they're a little sophomoric to put it mildly and certainly one of them is—may well be considered pornographic. However, on the question of law, of the violations of the statute as to the distribution and as to ownership of the alleged People's Exhibit #1 and #2 which are the advertising material, that has not been established. Under all of the circumstances, the motion is granted."

Ringel wasn't so kind to Andy Warhol's *Blue Movie* two years later, ruling it obscene. But I had had the historic ACLU behind me, with all its strength and genius, plus a prosecution that pronounced lascivious "láshivous" and relied too heavily on the salacious power of the Lady Dickhead Advertising Company.

The dismissal was so sudden that instead of twirling and jumping for joy, I just stood there, drained from nineteen months of secret dread and plodding tired into a robotic courtroom so many times. I looked around for Fetta to invite him to the victory party at the Peace Eye Bookstore, but he was already gone.

There was a bit more colloquy from the judges, and then I went my way.

It was time to party. I painted the Peace Eye floors and cleaned up the mess remaining from when I had turned it over to the community and it had thrown away many of the books. I prepared an art show featuring all issues of my magazine and the artwork of friends, including Spain Rodriguez and even Gregory Corso. I sent the invitation to Sergeant Charles Fetta.

It was a packed party on a hot summer night, including Allen Ginsberg and many friends. Ernst Rosenberger brought an assistant district attorney (not Moyna) to the celebration. During the celebration some neighborhood kids began to toss firecrackers through the open door. Allen Ginsberg and I went outside to the sidewalk to cool them out. One young man was

You are cordially invited

to the grand reopening

of the

PEACE EYE BOOKSTORE & GALLERY
celebrating Ed Sanders' recent court victory in the
Fuck You/ a Magazine of the Arts case.
tuesday june 27

5-10 pm

383 East 10 th Street

The gallery exhibition will feature
literary relics & ejaculata
from the culture of the
Lower East Side

featured will be the entire outspew of
the Fuck You/ press, and the entire
14 issues of Fuck You/ a Magazine of
the Arts,

also several of Allen Ginsberg's autographed
cold cream jars fresh from sensual
spurt scenes.

for information, call Ed Sanders

Gr 3-4555

Bill Binzen's photo of the Peace Eye Victory Party, June 27, 1967; from left to right: Tom and Angelica Clark, Ed Sanders, Julius Orlovsky.

Spain Rodriguez's fine poster for the Community Defense Fund
benefit, June 28, 1967.

brandishing a wide-tipped hunting arrow. It was another flashlight into
Allen's personality as he sank to his knees on the sidewalk in front of the
wide-eyed youth and made his hands together in the shape of a mudra. The
young man raised his arm back high over head, the arrow trembling, and I
was very afraid he was going to hurl it into the bard's neck, but Allen's calm
words at last caused him to put it down to his side. It was another emblem of
conduct by a great poet.

The day after the Grand Reopening of Peace Eye, The Fugs did a concert with the Mothers of Invention, Allen Ginsberg, and others at the Village Theater to raise money for the "Community Defense Fund." Spain Rodriquez did a fine poster.

Flaming Creatures Resurfacing in DC

In mid-1967 LBJ nominated Abe Fortas for chief justice of the Supreme Court. Right-wing nuts were able to attack the nomination because of Justice Fortas's liberal views on erotic art.

A print of Flaming Creatures had been seized by the fuzz in Ann Arbor, and Senator Strom Thurmond had it flown to DC, where copies were shown to fellow senators. One U.S. senator said he couldn't even get aroused by Flaming Creatures, "it was so sick."

The Trouble over Virgin Fugs

When the owner of ESP-Disk basically bootlegged a sequence of tunes from the first two Fugs sessions and called it Virgin Fugs, it went against my principles of Apt Artistic Flow—that an artist should be able to select what created items get to be placed before the world. Allen Ginsberg didn't like the use of "Howl" lines in the song "The I Saw the Best Minds of My Generation Rock." I didn't like it. And the bootlegger stole all the income derived. Stole Stole Stole. Because of our being dumped by Atlantic Records, Virgin Fugs became the only Fugs album to appear during the crucial Year of Love.

The Summer of Love in the Lower East Side

The 1967 clampdown in the Lower East Side had similarities to the 1964–1965 clampdown on movies, theaters, and coffeehouses. This one was more about stomping down the urban and rural commune movement and the so-called problem of runaways than art and words.

All summer long just as soon as Groovy and his cohorts, such as a young man named Galahad, would set up a commune, the police would kick in the doors and shut it down. There was a centuries-old dislike of even the concept of communes on the part of the square überculture. Everybody—

the police, the city government, the churches, social workers, the media, and puritanical socialists—all wanted to stomp down communes. The media tended to view communal sleeping zones of current youth from the perspective of the ideal middle-class family.

One such crash pad/commune was set up by Galahad at 622 East Eleventh. He was determined to keep it alive in spite of continued police harassment during the Spring and Summer of Love. The *East Village Other* covered the clampdown under the headline "Cops Crush Communes," citing invasions by the police, over and over during the late spring of 1967, as the Ninth Precinct sought to squash the network of crash pads set up to accommodate the roaming youth who came to the Lower East Side in search of a New American Dream.

The era of the protest button, well under way by '67.

The Psychedelicatessen

An archetypal business located on Avenue A, not far from where Miriam, I, and Deirdre lived, was the Psychedelicatessen. It flourished for about two years, 1966–1968. The Psychedelicatessen provided employment and fit in well with the Lower East Side community. The place DID serve as a deli for the psychedelic community. You could pick up an extra hash screen for a pipe or get a new tube for a water pipe. If the peacock feather in a vase in the living room accidentally broke, a Lower East Sider could head for the

Psychedelicatessen to get an inexpensive replacement. We regularly stopped by to check out its displays of incense, body lotions, body-revealing gowns, black lights, ever-burning candles, cases of love beads and moiré patches, standing close to fellow visitors sporting pantaloons, early tie-dyes, and Afghan vests.

The Psychedelicatessen helped bring burning incense to the Lower East Side streets as barefoot Hippessas from Brooklyn or the Heartland bought sandalwood wands, lit them, and then carried them down to Tompkins Park to listen to free concerts by The Fugs, the Grateful Dead, the Blues Project, and other bands performing on the hard-won outdoor stage. There was plenty of cultural conflict on the Lower East Side during those years. When the deli was busted for psychedelic drugs in late June '68, it was thriving. The owners were adding a "Trip Room" and a room for free rock shows and jams. The two rivers of commerce, that of pot and acid and that of incense, power sticks, and flavored candles, were a bit too commingled at the Psychedelicatessen for it to survive, even in 1968, so it faded into the flow of history.

The Riots of July

While the streets of the Lower East Side were strutting with people holding burning incense sticks in their hands and leaving them burning in the cracks of the sidewalks, there were riots in various parts of the nation. The armored scenery of a long, hot summer clanked into place. The uprisings began in late June in Buffalo and then ignited in Newark July 13–16, where 26 died, 1,500 were injured, and 1,000 were arrested (in the dry statistics of printed insurrections). Then Detroit caught fire on July 23 in a surge of destruction that killed 43 and left many blocks destroyed for the rest of the century and beyond.

On July 24 LBJ ordered 4,700 troops to Detroit, and for two days soldiers and uprisers traded gunfire. The battle had the taste of Vietnam, with headlines such as "Tank Crews Blast Away at Entrenched Snipers with 50-Caliber Machine Guns" splattered across newspapers until the riots were quelled.

On July 27 Johnson spoke to the nation to announce the formation of the National Advisory Commission on Urban Disorders, to be headed by

Governor Otto Kerner of Illinois and Mayor John Lindsay of New York City (who had been instrumental, I'm sure, in suppressing the oppression of artists and filmmakers in the city). (The commission's 1,400-page report, issued a few months later, attributed the uprising of blacks to white racism. The United States, it said, was at risk of becoming "two societies, one black, one white—separate but inequal." It seemed clear what was causing the unrest: poor housing, hostility from surrounding white communities, inferior schools, unemployment, lack of money.... *Boom!*)

The FBI and Army Intelligence Not Buying It

The U.S. military viewed the situation with alarm. U.S. Army Intelligence tallied riots and looting in one hundred cities that summer. The FBI thought that commies and other "subversives" were helping to create the riots. So did the U.S. Army.

The head of U.S. Army Intelligence in '67 and much of '68 was a human named Major General William P. Yarborough, who was a counterintelligence and psychological warfare specialist. Yarborough thought that rioters were "insurgents" manipulated by the Communist Party. When Detroit began to boil that summer, General Yarborough announced to his staff, "Men, get out your counterinsurgency manuals. We have an insurgency on our hands."

The Questioning of Black Men in Detroit

Agents of the U.S. Army's Psychological Operations Group, in civilian attire (in conjunction with something called the Behavior Research Institute of Detroit), brought 496 black males arrested for firing weapons during the Detroit riot to a warehouse to the north of Detroit and asked each black man dozens of questions.

Of the 496, 363 gave astounding answers to the question "Who is your favorite Negro leader?" Was it Stokely Carmichael? No. Was it Huey Newton? No. Was it H. Rap Brown? No. It was Martin Luther King Jr.!!!

Linda and Groovy

Late in the Summer of Love Groovy began to hang out with a young woman from Connecticut named Linda Fitzpatrick. Linda came from wealth in the suburbs—a thirty-room house with nine bathrooms and ten fireplaces, where she had her own painting studio. She'd saved money from the hundreds of days—birthdays, name days, play days, holidays, days her field hockey team had won at boarding school. She even owned enough stock that she could have lived on the dividends. Her mother sent her a monthly check, and fresh-cut flowers were put in her painting studio each morning at the mansion.

During the early weeks of the Summer of Love Linda commuted back and forth between the mansion and the Village. There were many things unspoken. Her family didn't pry, and she even went through a few family-soothing moves toward preparing for college. She plunked down money for sweaters, pleated skirts, a trunk, a bookcase—as if she were headed for the ivy. Dad didn't dig her long hair and kept asking her to chop it. Finally in August she went to Saks Fifth Avenue for a Sassoon snip.

Then, returning from New York in early September, she told mom she wasn't going to college. She wanted to be a painter. Mom and Dad groaned but gave their permission, and Linda left for Groovy's world of the Lower East Side the next day. A search for art was something her liberal family would not squash. Her mother understood her restlessness and hunger for renown. She had wanted to be a dancer when young and was a well-known model. Somehow from mother to daughter had passed this cloudlike hunger for performance, for runway lights and fascinated stares, for the smells of a painter's studio, for drifts of powder across rows of dressing room lights, for the devotion of gallery-goers, and, now during a year of Love, for thrills and forbidden fun. She told mom she would be rooming at a hotel off Washington Square with a secretary friend named Ronna, a twenty-two-year-old from an acceptable family who would be Linda's guide in the weirdness zone. Ronna, it turned out, was really Ron, and she began to hang out with her newfound love, Groovy.

Groovy and Linda—phantoms of the Summer of Love.

Zip Gun Cisco

Meanwhile, a young neighborhood kid began to hang out at Peace Eye. I called him Zip Gun Cisco. His face reminded me of Desi Arnaz. He would get angry with me for refusing to let him use my tools to work on his home-made pistols. Occasionally he would come into the store and point a crooked zip gun at me with a thick rubber band as part of the firing mechanism and a metal barrel, plus a wooden handle that looked as if it had been carved from a chunk of two by four.

Cisco was a fairly good drummer, and he had formed a band with some neighborhood kids. I arranged with Manny Roth at the Café Wha for Cisco's band to play one weeknight. Band members were very eager to succeed. One of their tunes stood out; it was The Beatles' "I'm Down." They sang that tune with fervor.

I probably should have helped them record, but it was a time when The Fugs were themselves without a label, and we ourselves were groveling in the abyss of possible failure.

The Fugs at the Players Theatre

I was still aiming at putting together a perfect band, to make a landmark album, fresh with The Fugs' vision of poetry, satire, and antiwar fervor. We had a very good band, even though the excellent musician and singer Jake Jacobs left The Fugs in the summer. We replaced him with Danny Kootch (Kortchmar), who had been in a band with childhood friend James Taylor called the Flying Machine. The Flying Machine was breaking up; I caught one of their final gigs at the Night Owl, and Kootch had talent! Dan Kootch was soon doing great work on guitar and violin. Maybe I should have also tried to hire James Taylor, who was soon off to England. A young man named Geoff Outlaw was our bass player. Later he appeared in the Arlo Guthrie/Arthur Penn movie *Alice's Restaurant*.

RULES FOR FUGS CONCERTS

1. during performances the audience should be faced as much as possible

2. yawning, narcolepsy, sleeping, bored sighs should be repressed. The FUGS must put on at every instance an energetic outspew. Energy, interest, & excitement are important keys to successful performance.

3. immediately following the tuning after songs, unless inspired by irresistible urge to create genius, instrument playing should be either very low or not at all. This will cause the show pace to be much more brisk.

4. The ending of songs should be very precise, many of the Fugs songs sort of end in trailing stages, so that the audience doesn't quite know when a number is over. This should be remedied.

5. drum practice should not occur during intermissions.

6. performers should be prepared to play precisely at the minute scheduled for the show to begin, in tune, & on the stage.

7. when it is agreed that a certain vocal arrangement will be used, an attempt should be made at every performance to sing said arrangement, loudly, into the microphones, with energy.

8. Perfection should be worshipped. Arrangements should should proceed thru slight & ever-improving modifications toward the Absolute Arrangement

Semisatiric rules for performances at the Players Theatre, 1967.

The Fugs, Players Theater, MacDougal Street, 1967; left to right: Ed Sanders, Geoff Outlaw, Jake Jacobs, Dan Kootch, Ken Weaver. Photo by Lanny Kenfield.

Theater in Boston

The Fugs took the week of July 17–24 from the Players Theatre to perform at the Back Bay Theater in Boston. It was an exhilarating week until it came time to receive our final $2,000 due ($2,000 had been paid in advance) at the end of the engagement. When our managers asked for the money, they were greeted with "How'd you like your legs broken?"

After the week in Boston we returned to the Players Theatre. Country Joe and the Fish came to town at the end of July. Joe wanted a place to rehearse, so I turned over The Fugs set at the Players Theatre for the band, as it prepared for a week's run, August 1–6, at the Cafe Au Go Go.

Signing with Reprise Records

Thanks to the outreach of our managers, Charles Rothschild and Peter Edmiston, The Fugs had offers that summer from two prestigious record labels: Elektra Records, home of The Doors, and Reprise, home of Jimi Hendrix. I was, for the first time in months, feeling as if a giant minus sign WAS NOT following me around in my polka dot sports jacket.

The manager of Janis Joplin, Bob Dylan, Richie Havens, and Peter, Paul and Mary—Albert Grossman—recommended signing with Jac Holzman's record label, Elektra. I met with Paul Rothschild, producer of The Doors and later Janis Joplin. He'd liked "Morning Morning" on the second album and suggested I give him the songs we had already written and recorded—some demos, plus the Atlantic material—to listen to.

Instead I decided to go with Reprise. I felt it was a better, more liberal fit for a controversial band with raw material. The contract was signed on September 1. As Tom Clark once noted, I ran a tight ship, and I wanted control of the production. Unfortunately our managers demanded to sign their own production deal with Reprise, so that The Fugs (Tuli, myself, and Ken) signed with our managers' production company. Unlike earlier, when Gene Brooks, Allen Ginsberg's brother, advised us on our original management contract with Charles Rothschild and Peter Edmiston, I did not get an attorney. I still don't know to this day what sort of contract was signed with Reprise, nor have I ever seen a royalty statement.

I insisted that we record again under the creative graces of Richard Alderson. I decided to record all future music projects, if at all possible, with Alderson. He had the touch and the skills to bring out the best in a session. We began recording what would be *Tenderness Junction* in the late fall, and we more or less kept recording constantly with Alderson, through *It Crawled into My Hand, Honest*, until the early fall of 1968. We did some research on why we had been thrown off Atlantic, and we were told by Albert Grossman that Warner Brothers was negotiating to purchase Atlantic and the pooh-bahs at Atlantic were afraid having The Fugs aboard would lower the selling price. Learning that, we surged forward and opened negotiations with Warner Brothers, and Reprise signed us! *Heh Heh Heh.* There was a slight consolation in being signed by the company that was purchasing the company that had tossed us.

Mo Ostin, the goodwilled president of Reprise Records, told me that before Reprise could sign The Fugs, he played the Atlantic album tape to label founder Frank Sinatra. He, to our lasting gratitude, okayed the deal! He said, "I guess you know what you're doing." New York, New York!

At last we were back on a major label, although our managers insisted we re-record the entire abandoned Atlantic album, so the final four months of '67 were a whirl.

The CIA's "Operation Chaos"

Meanwhile, the underground press, including the *East Village Other*, three blocks down A from Miriam's and my pad on the corner of Twelfth, was thriving across the nation. The underground newspapers were about to have a first gathering in DC just prior to the upcoming massive antiwar demonstrations and civil disobedience at the Pentagon on October 21, the one where The Fugs would help exorcise the Pentagon. The undergrounds were supporting the drive for massive social change, the use of psychedelics, the legalization of grass, and the giving of aid and comfort to the Black Panthers and antiwar groups. The insolence of the underground press movement! the energy! the treason! It was riling the minds of the military-industrial surrealists, and so in early August the CIA began an enormous and mostly still-secret program called Operation Chaos for spying on and looking for ways to stymie the antiwar left.

A telegram was sent out to a slew of CIA field stations setting up a "Special Operations Group" to be run by counterintelligence head James Jesus Angleton. He selected a human named Richard Ober to lead what would not long ahead be called Chaos or Mhchaos. Because it was illegal for the CIA to try to destroy domestic newspapers such as the underground press, Chaos grew into one of the most secret of all secret programs. LBJ knew full well about Chaos because Ober's reports were sent to his desk (and later to Nixon's). Ober was given a staff of ten at first, and they all set out to "disrupt the enemy."

The CIA fed the National Security Agency a "watch list" of 1,700 dissident Americans in 1967 so that the NSA could monitor phone calls and other communications—a monitoring that went on until 1973. Thank You, O Twerps of Chaos.

Abbie Hoffman

I became aware of activist Abbie Hoffman, who had begun organizing in the Lower East Side. I was impressed with his zeal, creativity, and ability to think in the fun-filled realms of Guerrilla Theater, Street Action, and what had to be called the Performance Art of Immediate Social Change. For a few years in the time track Hoffman was the Jim Thorpe of social action— he never seemed to sleep; could engage in fifty projects at the same time; was an adroit writer, whether of leaflets or books; and had an uncanny ability to get the attention of the media.

He was born November 30, 1936, in Worcester, Massachusetts. He grew up there and then went to Brandeis, graduating in '59 with a degree in psychology. That fall he entered graduate school at the University of California at Berkeley. He began to demonstrate. On May 1, 1960, Abbie and others, including Shirley MacLaine and Marlon Brando, went to San Quentin for an overnight vigil prior to the morning execution of Caryl Chessman. On May 12 the same year the House Un-American Activities Committee opened hearings into putative subversive activities in the Bay area. There were demonstrations outside the federal building in downtown San Francisco. Police with waterhoses and Plexiglass visors attacked the protesters. There was a riot. The '60s had begun.

He married Sheila Karklin, and the couple had two children in the early 1960s. They lived in Worcester and became active in the Black freedom movement. Abbie went to Mississippi for Freedom Summer in 1964. He returned to Mississippi in the summer of '65, teaching at a Freedom School in McComb. In 1966 Abbie started getting stores in New England to sell handcrafts made by the Poor People's Corporation in Mississippi. PPC was a network of rural cooperatives making an assortment of leather and cloth items.

That year Abbie and Sheila were divorced and Abbie moved to an apartment in the Lower East Side. He opened a double storefront in the West Village, which he named Liberty House, and operated on behalf of SNCC. Late that year and early in '67, because of the rise of the Black Power movement, all whites were purged from SNCC. Stokely Carmichael and others advised Abbie to turn Liberty House over to black management and to spend his time organizing to end the war in Vietnam—advice Abbie took. By early '67 Abbie had rented an apartment on St. Mark's Place near Second Avenue with a woman, Anita Kushner, who worked at Liberty House. That June Abbie and Anita were married in an outdoor be-in-style wedding in Central Park, attended by 3,000 celebrants, which was featured in *Time* magazine.

Abbie and the Burning of Money at the Stock Exchange

On August 24 a group tossed money down at the New York Stock Exchange. Abbie and Jim Fouratt organized the action under the umbrella of an entity called the East Side Service Organization, which was just being incorporated. The group received permission to tour the Stock Exchange. Group members viewed themselves as Diggers espousing the Politics of Free.

According to an article in the *East Village Other* by editor Walter Bowart, when Hoffman and Fouratt entered the visitors' gallery, above the active trading floor, a "guard stopped the Diggers, saying 'You're hippies and you've come to burn money.'"

Hoffman insisted, "That's not true. I'm Jewish," and Jim Fouratt shouted, "I'm a Catholic."

"The confused guard backed down and the Diggers were admitted."

Several went to the balcony and tossed money down on the busy trading floor. Bills floated in the greed-spasm zone. Some stockies booed, but others groveled on the floor like eels of greed to gather the cash.

Guards tossed the flutter forces. Outside Hoffman and Jerry Rubin, who had come from California to work on a big antiwar demonstration at the Pentagon upcoming in the fall, burned money.

Abbie later gave me a half-burned dollar bill from the demonstration. It was a creative action that struck a nerve and became one of the most inspiring actions of the late 1960s.

The Community Breast Concert for the Free Store

The Community Breast concert at the Village Theater on Second Avenue on August 16 raised $1,000 for a Lower East Side version of the Digger's San Francisco Free Store. The Fugs performed, as did Tiny Tim, Judy Collins, Richie Havens, Paul Krassner, Hugh Romney (soon to become Wavy Gravy), and Timothy Leary's sitarist, Peter Walker.

T.E.A.T . (To Each All Things)
Benefit For The Community
Wed. - Aug. 16 - 8 P.M.
Breast Board ...
Paul Krassner
Bob Fass
Hugh Romney
Walter Bowart

The Pearls Before The Swil
Ritchie Havens Bob Fass
Judy Collins Tiny Tim
Hugh Romney
Paul Krassner
The Fugs
Peter Walker
The Others

Village Theatre   105 2nd Ave.   Seats $3.00   Phone 228 8640

The money raised indeed went to the establishment of a free store, set up on East Tenth, just around the corner from the offices of the *East Village Other.*

Just a few days later The Fugs performed our annual free outdoor concert on the stage in Tompkins Square Park. It was the third free concert we did that summer, in addition to our regular full run Off Broadway at the Players Theatre.

The Fugs will perform free on Tuesday, August 22, at 8.30 p.m. in Tompkins Square Park. Avenue A and East 7th Street. The concert will be presented by the Lower East Side Civic Improvement Association (LES CIA).

(*Above*) Poster for the Community Breast concert, Village Theater on Second Avenue.

(*Left*) Quick ad in *EVO* for the August 22, 1967, annual free Fugs concert in Tompkins Square Park.

The Rise and Sad Fall of the Digger Free Store

The Free Store opened at 264 East Tenth, just off A, on September 21 with all the hope and energy that the era could summon. It represented the Spirit of Free and echoed the lines from Allen Ginsberg's great poem "America": "When can I go into the supermarket and buy what I need with my good looks?"

Underground comic artist Spain Rodriguez made the groovy sign above the door at 264 East Tenth, a one-story building just down the street from the red-brick St. Nicholas Carpatho-Russian church on the corner at Avenue A.

The Free Store grew out of a similar store created in San Francisco a few months earlier by Diggers. Two key San Francisco Diggers, Peter Berg and Emmet Grogan, visited the Lower East Side in the spring of 1967, where they inspired Abbie Hoffman, Jim Fouratt, Marty and Susan Carey, and others to organize one.

It was another of the trend-setting ideas from the West Coast such as the be-in, forty-five-minute guitar breaks, Digger free food in Golden Gate Park, the Haight-Ashbury communes, indecipherable rock posters, head

The Free Store in its first florescence, with a love banner above the entrance. Photo by Bill Binzen.

shops, fear of oil spills, anger against nuclear power, concern for the safety of sea lions, and necklaces for guys.

Everybody around the park was talking about the Free Store. In the summer The Fugs and other bands had done the Community Breast benefit that had raised over $1,000 for the Free Store. The LBJ administration had announced that poverty was to be banished in America, so a New York City antipoverty agency slipped the organizers of the Free Store another $1,000.

The first few weeks of the Free Store were a time of bounty. The dailies wrote stories, and a wide assortment of poets, novelists, artists, radicals, anarchists, actors, nuns, and those sympathetic to socialism brought tons of clothing and household items down to Tenth and A. Soon the store was packed with Ukrainians, Puerto Ricans, Blacks, and Hippies mingling politely, trying on shoes and working through the bins and shelves. In addition to duds, they took home hundreds of useful kitchen utensils, toys, appliances, and things like reading lamps!

There was a satiric sign, "If you break it, you take it." Writer Paul Goodman worked as a volunteer sorting clothes. Writer and publisher Paul Krassner reportedly offered to pay a year's rent for the store.

The store seemed to attract trouble. It was a hyperagitated era, of course, not to mention the difficulty of setting up a Network of Free when so many were busy Staring at the Universe on psychedelics. There was also a fine line between burning out for the Social Good and just plain old burning.

Right away owners of used Hippie clothing stores began plundering the Free Store, filling up their bags with largesse to stack on their own shelves. This caused a few freak scenes and confrontations, but there was no structure in the Free Store to deal with the concept of the spiritual parasite and the hip capitalist mooch.

Somehow the baton of leadership for the Free Store passed from its original organizers to local Hippies to bikers. Motorcycle Ritchie, a biker who'd run the San Francisco Digger store assisted by a guy named Clyde, began running the Free Store. Both wore iron cross earrings and leather jackets. Ritchie worked on his motorcycle on the sidewalk outside the Free Store, with parts spread out here and there. Ritchie and pals spewed forth an "aura of violence." Ross Wetzsteon, an editor and writer at the *Village Voice*, lived on Tenth near the Free Store and wrote an article that mentioned how the biker managing the store had smashed and beat up a kid on the block.

Within a short time the Free Store's image changed from Love to Threat. Part of it had to do with racism. In an eyewitness account of the Free Store, author Naomi Feigelson wrote of an angry guy named George who came into the store swinging a chain and complaining, "All these spades around here are just bad news. You see signs all over, 'Wanted, ride to California.' You don't see anything in California about wanting a ride to New York."

I lived just three blocks from the Free Store, and the rumor at the time was that amphetamine- and methedrine-heads had brought aimless frenzy and "'noia" to the store. (Methedrine, the trade name for methamphetamine hydrochloride, was always known just as "meth.") Chattering, jittery methheads could really suffuse a project with excess confusion and fear.

The Murder of Linda and Groovy

It was Saturday, October 7, just after midnight. Linda Fitzpatrick and Groovy Hutchinson were together in a basement furnace room at 169 Avenue B, near the Annex bar, which had the words FREE LOVE written on the front of the door. There were dark blue halls in the building.

Her black panties and clothes were neatly stacked in a corner, as was Groovy's jacket, and they were on a mattress. During the night Linda was raped four times, according to *Time* magazine. They both were murdered by being smashed with a boiler brick.

They were found at 9:00 AM by Fred Wright, "assistant superintendent" of the building, who slept on a cot in an adjoining room in the basement.

Groovy, on the right, joking with his pal Galahad in Tompkins Square Park just a few hours before his murder behind the FREE LOVE door in a basement on Avenue B. Photo by Nathan Farb.

He had been out all night and found the bodies. He was arrested on Monday, October 9, for raping and robbing a young woman in the cellar several hours before the murders.

Monday, October 9, Donald Ramsey, twenty-five, was charged with the murders. He lived with his wife, Anaya, in a three-room pad upstairs from the FREE LOVE basement on Avenue B. The *New York Times* reported that a green sticker reading "Black Power" and a drawing of a black panther were affixed to Ramsey's front door.

His attorney told the judge, "He belongs to the Yoruba religion. He . . . wants permission not to shave or cut his hair because of his religious scruples."

Groovy helped people by the score find places to crash during the Summer of Love. He operated a crash pad with Galahad at 622 East Eleventh, but the police crushed it. Groovy told his friend Galahad a plan he had. He wanted to open a nonprofit café called the Thing Shop. Everyone would do their thing in the Thing Shop, whether they had the money to pay or not. It would be a restaurant.

I needed to wall off the grief that was coursing through the Lower East Side. I was beginning to feel as old as Methuselah as I mourned for Groovy and Linda. The FREE LOVE basement was situated along the Sacred Via—Tenth to Twelfth, home of the Charles Theater, the Annex, and Stanley's Bar. Right then—in a flash—Avenue B between Tenth and Twelfth went from Street of Glory to *Via Terroris*—waypath of terror and desolation.

I felt a great amount of guilt that I had had to shut Groovy out of Peace Eye when my landlord complained about the karate lessons in the courtyard, the class in tightrope walking, the fifteen or twenty mattresses in the three rooms, plus the recruiting activities of Jade Companions of the Flowered Dance. In a better world Groovy Hutchinson, spreader of goodwill, warder off of Burns and Bad Acid, and finder of a sleeping space for the partisans of Love, might have gotten a Great Society job to help locate housing or temporary communes in the tenements.

I never really got to mourn Groovy and Linda completely. The hits on the soul came without respite from '67 on. Groovy, MLK, RFK, d. a. levy, Kerouac—*ping ping ping,* until early 1970, with the passing of Charles Olson. In the late 1960s death became quick calls and gossip, after which we moved on quickly, without respite, from scurry to hurry to worry.

The Free Store love sign, which had turned to hate in just a few weeks. Photo by Bill Binzen.

We were just about to start planning the Exorcism of the Pentagon. And then Carl Sandburg passed away the same month! and the CIA murdered Che Guevara in Bolivia. In mid-November Motorcycle Ritchie split from the Free Store back to California, after being invited to become a member of the Hells Angels. By December 16 the Free Store was closed, not even two months old.

But the Spirit of Free was hard to rub out, as evinced by the Community Switchboards that were being set up around the nation, the Free Clinics here and there, the Free Stores in places like Woodstock, and, of course, the Great Free Food for 400,000 by the Hog Farm at the Woodstock Festival up ahead.

Che

Two days after Groovy and Linda were smashed to death behind the FREE LOVE door, Che Guevara was hunted down and murdered by a pack of CIA operatives in Bolivia. His assassins lashed Che to the right skid of a helicopter at La Higuera. The CIA sleaze (Felix Rodriguez) who was in charge of hunting down Che stole Che's Rolex watch as if the assassination were a mugging in a New York City alley. The CIA guy wrapped the tobacco from

Che's final pipe and stole that, too. Another CIA off-oid who helped kill Che stole a swatch of his hair, took pictures, and smeared Guevara's fingerprints on some cards that forty years later he peddled for $100K.

Somehow a photo of the face of the murdered Che was released. A horrified CIA endured a Jesus/Martyr image of him being placed on the walls of huts and houses around the world. It was a powerful image that not even millions of rubles from the Marxist-Leninist-Black Panther-Left-Wing-Hippie-Conspiracy could have purchased.

A Fugs Movie Project with Barbara Rubin and Shirley Clarke

Films were in the wind. The Group Image, a well-known Lower East Side artist-musical collective, was, according to *Time*, shooting a "full-length psychedelic western titled *Indian Givers*," in which Tim Leary was going to play a sheriff.

I began talking with Barbara Rubin about a movie on The Fugs. We had discussed such a project as far back as '65 when she took me to the Café Bizarre on West Third to see a throbbing new act called the Velvet Underground.

She teamed up with Shirley Clarke, a bright force in the avant-garde movie world. Clarke had won an Oscar in 1963 for her documentary on Robert Frost. In 1962 she'd filmed the Living Theater's production of Jack Gelber's *The Connection*. She was a cofounder, with Jonas Mekas, of the Film-Makers' Cooperative.

For a few months in late summer and fall we worked very hard on The Fugs movie project. There was a party at Shirley Clarke's place at the Chelsea. Her friend Archie Shepp was there. Weaver and I practically begged him not to sign with ESP Records. It worked, and Shepp was saved.

Weaver wrote pages of ideas, and Tuli and I did, too. My idea was to begin filming in war-tense Saigon; my thought was to have a chamber orchestra playing when our plane landed, a "salute to mortar and small arms fire."

In my archive is a typed page listing "possible titles for Fugs movie" as follows: "The Golden Door, Eagle Shit, Eagle, Aluminum Sphinx, Electric Forest, Arbitrary Madness, Oxen of the Sun, America Bongo; Unh! Unh! *Ahh!* Vampire Ass, Grail Gobble, Winnow'd in Fate's Tray, No Reality; Bend Over, Earthling! All Is Skush, Blob Tissue, Mystery at Cabin Island, On-

```
Saigon Fugs do concert in French Opera House.  Press
conference to end war.  Fugs march to front.  William
Burroughs dressed as Carrie Nation attacks opium den
with axe.  Black market supply house selling Joan Baez
records.  fugs do work in rice paddy.  napalm freak
flesh.   goon soldiers.   fake generals in power room.
total freak-scene in power room.   vietcong watermelon.
LeRoi Jones as homosexual cia agent.   naked viet cong
orgasm donuts suck off gi's with poisoned teeth.  Fugs
filmed naked at dmz waving white flags.  ken weaver
i,n trench jacking off with military uniform on.
mongolian cluster fuck in fox hole during mortar attack.
horny priests disguised as penguins fight savagely for
captured viet cong grope boy.  buddhists discover the
third eye of gautama ensnared in a spurt-web in saigon
brothel.  Shower of candy canes comes from sky over
us headquarters in Saigon, each with message attached
, pants down earthlings.  Allen Ginsberg is led thru
the streets of Saigon as the reincarnation of the Heavenly
Leader.  William Burroughs is the prime minister.
Fugs and 50 bare breasted gropers have statue licking
orgy .  cia intrigue scenes.  scenes denoting murderx
--- worship service for new religion: Rodney.
```

The Fugs Go to Saigon, a movie treatment from 1967.

ward, Forward March! Hemorrhaging Frog, Gobble Gobble, Primal Substance, Moon Brain, It's Eating Me! Useless Passion, and Hemisphere Gimme." All wonderful movie titles from the fall of 1967, and now I pass them on to all filmmakers to use.

Meanwhile, I worked with Tuli and Ken on a film script. I was interested in somehow linking it to the Eleusinian Mysteries, those ancient myths about the goddess Demeter and her search for her daughter, Persephone, seized and taken to the underground by the god Ploutos. I intently studied C. Kerényi's very scholarly *Eleusis—Archetypal Image of Mother and Daughter* and George Mylonas's equally scholarly *Eleusis and the Eleusinian Myster-*

ies. Both books rekindled my thirst for scholarly pursuits. We also had brainstorm sessions on western themes. Shirley Clarke tried to raise money. We met with potential money source Dan Selznick at Shirley's pad at the Chelsea. For almost any film project there's a treatment prepared. I assigned myself to come up with a one-page treatment, starring William Burroughs, LeRoi Jones (prior to becoming Amiri Baraka), Allen Ginsberg, and, of course, The Fugs. I liked the idea of presenting a new religion called "Rodney." For his part Weaver brought in ideas of adding western themes, so for a while our film had the general title of *Badass.*

Finally we had around 150 pages of ideas, scene descriptions, songs, vignettes, and the like. What I needed were a few weeks of calm in our groovy marble-fireplaced floor-through on Avenue A to type a final version. But that was not to be. We were wiggling in the space-time continuum, and the continuum was itself wiggling in wild whirls and moiré patterns of Bacchus and the ole Beatnik sense of Gone!

Planning for the Exorcism

All throughout the history of The Fugs in the '60s, the war in Vietnam throbbed like an ever-seething soul sore. However much we partied, shouted our poetry, and strutted around like images of Bacchus, we could never quite get the war out of our minds. It was like that Dada poetry reading that Tristan Tzara gave in 1922 in Paris, with an alarm clock constantly ringing during the reading. The war was THE alarm clock of the late '60s.

It seemed as if the war might become permanent, so there were big demonstrations planned for October to surround the nerve center of the war—the Pentagon in Washington, DC. Somebody came up with the idea of holding an exorcism of this mystic pentagonal citadel of napalm and incineration.

I was in charge of coming up with a structure for the Exorcism. For the actual Exorcism/Levitation of the Pentagon, I consulted with my authority on all things magic—Harry Smith. As long as we were ACTUALLY going to exorcise demons, I figured that we might as well prepare a structure that, at least in the theories of actual Mageia, might do the job. Harry advised consecrating a circle around the Pentagon and using the alchemical symbols of Earth, Air, Fire, and Water. He also suggested adding Egyptian elements to the Exorcism, such as a cow, to represent the goddess Hathor. (We

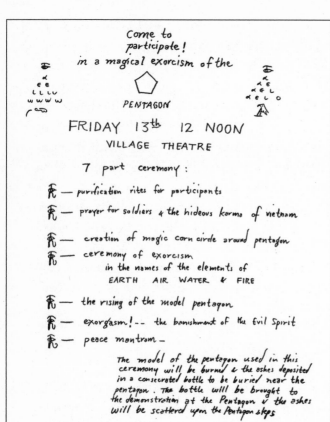

Come to
participate!
in a magical exorcism of the

PENTAGON

FRIDAY 13th 12 NOON
VILLAGE THEATRE

7 part ceremony:

— purification rites for participants

— prayer for soldiers & the hideous karma of vietnam

— creation of magic corn circle around pentagon

— ceremony of exorcism
in the names of the elements of
EARTH AIR WATER & FIRE

— the rising of the model pentagon

— exorgasm! -- the banishment of the evil spirit

— peace mantram —

The model of the pentagon used in this
ceremony will be burned & the ashes deposited
in a consecrated bottle to be buried near the
pentagon. The bottle will be brought to
the demonstration at the Pentagon & the ashes
will be scattered upon the Pentagon steps

(*Left*) Leaflet for mock Exorcism, October 13, 1967.

(*Below*) A letter in *EVO* by Abbie Hoffman, writing under the name George Metesky, making a rather fanciful prediction about what would occur during the Exorcism.

PAGE 2
Dear Mary Prankster:

On October 21st, a mighty Exorcism of the Pentagon will take place. Pentagons, as you know, are a symbol of evil in almost all religions. We plan to encircle that evil building with waves of beautiful people. We will play "Ring-Around-the-Pentagon-a-Pocketful-of-Pot." On October 12th (Columbus Day) a peace caravan called "Wagon Wheels East" left San Francisco. It was complete with real live Indian scouts and medicine men, compliments of Chief Rolling Thunder of the Shoshone Indian Tribe. Junk cars, stolen buses, motorcycles, rock bands, flower banners, dope, incense and enough food for the journey. The caravan will pass through some very hostile territory, and many will die on the trip. On Friday the 13th, a mock exorcism of the Pentagon took place in the Village Theater. On the 15th, a benefit to provide free buses will occur again at the Village Theater. In Washington, all religious fanatics, and your fellow merry pranksters, will meet at the Jefferson Memorial at 11:00 a.m. -- or, rather, everyone will bump into everyone else there. A few mobile sound trucks will be around, and rock groups such as JEFFERSON AIRPLANE, THE FUGS, STEVE MILLER'S BLUES BAND, MOTHER EARTH and many more, will play for a while. Then a massive swarm will begin. We will hurl everything we've got. We will dye the Potomac red, burn the cherry trees, panhandle diplomats and try to kidnap LBJ while wrestling him to the ground and pulling his pants off. We will attack with noise makers, water pistols, marbles, bubble gum wrappers and bazookas. Girls will run naked, and piss on the Pentagon walls. Sorcerers, swamis, priests, warlocks, rabbis, gurus, witches, alchemists, medicine men, speed freaks and other holymen will join hands and encircle the Pentagon -- 1200 people for each ring. Rock bands will play "Joshua at the Battle of Jericho." We will fuck on the grass and beat ourselves against the doors. Everyone will scream "Vote for Me," and we shall raise the flag of nothingness over the Pentagon. We shall all join in the mighty OM, and the Pentagon will begin to tremble and, as our magic grows stronger and stronger, the Pentagon will rise in the air. A great cry of liberation will echo through the land. "We are free. Great God Almighty! Free at last."

Love,
George Metesky

PS: October 21st: (1) Meet in NYC at Tompkins Park at 6:00 a.m. Free bus tickets at Digger Free Store, 264 E. 10th St, on Oct. 18th, or (2) Meet in Washington 11:00 a.m. at Jefferson Memorial.

Donations to Council of Love, Box 81, Village Station, NYC 10014.

If people have car room available, they should assemble at Tompkins Square Park for the caravan.

AWAKENING OF THE PENTAGON

did have a cow prepared, painted with mythic symbols, but the police prevented it from getting near the Pentagon.) Tuli and I also purchased dozens of daisies to toss upon the Pentagon from a plane.

By the second week of October I began to pay attention to the Exorcism of the Pentagon. On October 13 there was a demonstration of the Pentagon Exorcism for the press at the Village Theater. Exorcists constructed a model of the Pentagon, with wires attached, so that it could actually elevate during the mock Levitation. I printed a leaflet announcing the mock exorcism for Friday the Thirteenth.

I purchased some cornmeal and consecrated a circle around the mock Pentagon. After a singsong chant the "Pentagon" was elevated high above the stage.

The Trial for the Killers of Schwerner, Chaney, and Goodman

It sure seemed like Slow Justice! My generation had been horrified at the evil murders of the three participants in Freedom Summer, whose murderers, now more than three years after the fact, were going on trial. The week of October 15 leading to the Exorcism, Cecil Price and others went on trial for the June 1964 murders of Michael Schwerner, James Chaney, and Andrew Goodman. Published pictures in *Time* magazine on October 20 showed Price chewing tobacco and snickering like a small-town bully in the courtroom.

Back in December 1964 nineteen men had been indicted for the Freedom Summer slayings. They were charged not with murder but with conspiracy to violate the constitutional rights of the three murdered heroes under an 1870 statute. After many twists and injustices that flung dirt on the Feather of Justice, seven were found guilty on October 20, nine were acquitted, and the jury was hung on three. The seven fought jail on appeal but finally entered federal prison in 1970.

The Exorcism and Levitation of the Pentagon

The Fugs flew down to Washington on Friday, October 20, to perform at a psychedelic theater Friday and Saturday evenings. Shirley Clarke and Barbara Rubin filmed the arrival of our plane at the airport. Clarke also filmed the Exorcism. She was on the flatbed truck parked in the Pentagon parking

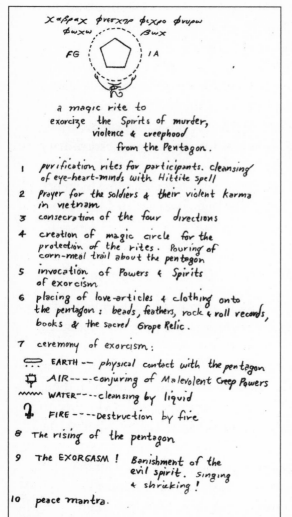

Χαββαχ φνεσχπ φεχρο φυυρω
Φωχω ⋯⋯⋯⋯ βωχ
FG 〈 ⬠ 〉 I A

a magic rite to
exorcize the Spirits of murder,
violence & creephood
from the Pentagon.

1   purification rites for participants. cleansing
of eye-heart-minds with Hittite spell

2   Prayer for the soldiers & their violent karma
in vietnam

3   consecration of the four directions

4   creation of magic circle for the
protection of the rites. Pouring of
corn-meal trail about the pentagon

5   invocation of Powers & Spirits
of exorcism

6   placing of love-articles & clothing onto
the pentagon : beads, feathers, rock & roll records,
books & the sacred Grope Relic.

7   ceremony of exorcism :

    ⊑⊒ EARTH -- physical contact with the pentagon

    ⚡ AIR----conjuring of Malevolent Creep Powers

    ∿∿∿ WATER----cleansing by liquid

    🔥 FIRE----Destruction by fire

8   The rising of the pentagon

9   The EXORGASM !   Banishment of the
evil spirit. singing
& shrieking !

10   peace mantra.

Leaflet I drew and printed on the Peace Eye mimeograph, following the advice of Harry Smith on the structure for the Exorcism of the Pentagon.

lot, where we chanted, "Out, Demons, Out!" Fellow film-maker and magician Kenneth Anger set up a magic ritual underneath the flatbed truck.

The issue of the Exorcism, as always, was about Good and Evil and the Egyptian Maat, the Feather of Justice. I had been raised in Missouri to believe in the threat of actual Evil. That the Devil was actual evil. Accordingly, I created as serious an Exorcism as I could.

There were at least 200,000 demonstrators who marched across the Memorial Bridge from the Lincoln Memorial, as well as a flatbed truck containing a generator, a sound system, The Fugs, and a group of San Francisco Diggers (including Michael Bowen), plus filmmakers Shirley Clark, Barbara Rubin, and Miriam Sanders (magician/filmmaker Kenneth Anger also was there) to exorcise the Pentagon. Anger claimed he had buried something magical inside the Pentagon days previous.

Tuli Kupferberg and I had paid for, out of our earnings that weekend from The Fugs' appearance at a psychedelic venue in DC, the

Button: the Pentagon Rising, October 21.

rental of the flatbed truck, the generator, and the microphones and speakers through which to intone our Exorcism ritual. We positioned ourselves on the edge of a parking lot a few hundred feet from our target, while tens of thousands of marchers walked past, and I intoned a singsong litany of Exorcism after which we all began to chant, "Out, Demons, Out!" over and over for about fifteen minutes. Rubin and Clarke filmed the chanting, while Anger positioned himself beneath the truck and performed his own ritual of exorcism. It was quite an afternoon. (Thanks to Bob Fass of WBAI-FM in New York City, a tape of our Exorcism survived [we put a good part of it on *Tenderness Junction*].)

Up near the Pentagon itself the 200,000 assembled and 250 were arrested, including Norman Mailer and Dave Dellinger. I stood up at the microphone on the flatbed truck at the Pentagon and began to chant:

> In the name of the Amulets of Touching, Seeing, Groping, Hearing and Loving we call upon the powers of the Cosmos to protect our ceremonies. In the name of Zeus, in the name of Anubis, God of the Dead, in the name of all those killed for causes they do not comprehend—in the names of the lives of the dead soldiers in Vietnam who were killed because of a Bad Karma, in the name of Sea-borne Aphrodite, in the name of the Magna Mater Deum Idea, in the name of Dionysus, Zagreus, Jesus, Iao Sabaoth, Yahweh the Unnameable, the Quintessential Finality, the Zoroastrian Fire, in the name of Hermes, in the name of the Beak of Thoth, in the name of the Scarab, in the name of the Tyrone Power Pound-Cake Society in the Sky, in the name of Ra, Osiris, Horus, Nephthys, Isis, Harpocrates, in the name of the mouth of the Ouroboros, we call upon the Spirits to Raise the Pentagon from its Destiny and Preserve it. In the naaaaame—in all the names!
>
> Out, Demons, out! Out, Demons, out! Demon out! Out, Demons, out! Out, Demons, out! Out, Demons, out! Out, Demons, out! Out, Demons, out! Out, Demons, out! Out, Demons, out! Out, Demons, out! Out, Demons, out! Out, Demons, out! Out, Demons, out! Out, Demons, out! Out! Out! Out! Out! Out! Out, Demons, out!
>
> For the first time in the history of the Pentagon, there will be a grope-in within a hundred feet of this place. Seminal Culmination in the spirit of Peace and Brotherhood. A real Grope for Peace. All of you who want to protect this rite of love may form a circle of protection around the lovers. Circle of Protection!

These are the Magic Eyes of Victory! Victory for Peace. Money made the Pentagon, melt it! Money made the Pentagon.... In the name of the generative powers of Priapus, in the name of Ourouriouth Iao Sabaoth Ereschigal, we call upon the malevolent Demons of the Pentagon to rid themselves of the Cancerous Tumorous War-Death.... Every Pentagon general lying alone at night with a tortured psyche—Out Demons, out! Out Demons, out! Out, Demons, out! Out, Demons, out! Out, Demons, out!

Out, Deeeeemoooon! Out, Deeeeeemooon! Out, Demons, out! Out, Demons, out! Out, Demons, out! Out, Demons, out! Out, Demons, out! Out, Demons, out!

In the name of the Most Sacred of Names, Out, Demons, out! Out, Demons, out! Out, Demons, out!

I spotted Kenneth Anger. He was being hissily dismissive of Shirley Clarke, who was filming the Exorcism. "Our magic is stronger than yours, Kenneth," I chanted at him through the microphone. A reporter for *Newsweek* peered under the flatbed truck, where Anger was burning a sacred card surrounded, it looked like, by a pentagon-shaped angularity of pieces of wood. He, too, received a hiss from Anger.

After the conclusion of the Exhortation and Levitation of the Pentagon, we walked over to the big demonstration. Some of us were carrying the daisies we'd purchased for the flyover and daisy tossdown that had been thwarted at the airport. Soldiers with fixed bayonets stood in rows guarding the entrance to the Pentagon, and a few of us stuck the ends of the daisies into the rifle barrels of the nervous young troops. Tuli missed the show at the Ambassador Theater that night in DC because he was among those hundreds who were arrested.

It was at this demonstration, I've read, that an upset Lyndon Johnson first heard the kids chant, "Hey, hey, LBJ, how many kids did you kill today?"

It was a famous thing we did, and people praised us for our audacity, yet the Vietnam War went on for another seven years. So much for "Out, Demons, Out!"

I sometimes tell interviewers that, yes, we DID elevate the Pentagon from its pediments, but we neglected to rotate it, and so the war continued.

The problem that remaineth.

Meanwhile, Out in Topanga Canyon by the Pacific

Meanwhile, not many days after the Great Exorcism, there arrived out in Topanga Canyon, California, a black school bus with the words "Holywood Productions" on the side. The people in the bus decamped at a ramshackle countercultural location called the Spiral Staircase. They were a roaming band of youth more or less led by a would-be musical star named Charles Manson. They weren't communards. They were clearly under the spell of this small ex-con with a guitar. There was a lot of pot, LSD, and sex sex sex, and they mingled at the Spiral Staircase with a satanic cult from England. The black bus had brought their leader to Los Angeles to try to get his brains on tape: that is, to record an album for Uni Records. Some of them were starting to believe that Mr. M had religious meaning. Some of their subsequent problems, I would partly blame on Acid Lingus, or even on Theolycergicolingus—cunnilingus on acid with a Deity.

Publishing Some "Cantos" of Ezra Pound

Back from the Exorcism I became involved in the strange literary history of Ezra Pound, a poet I had once held in awe but whose anti-Semitic broadcasts, some of which I read at the Library of Congress the day of the Great March back in '63, had caused me to rethink my fascination with his poetry. At the end of October I began work to publish an edition of unpublished "Cantos."

Here's how it happened. I ran into fellow bard Tom Clark on St. Mark's Place one afternoon in late October. I had purchased a new Gestetner electric mimeograph machine, plus a Gestefex electronic stencil-cutting machine, the only one in the Lower East Side, and I was looking for stuff to publish. They were valuable, and because Peace Eye had been broken into several times, I kept both in our apartment on Avenue A.

Clark mentioned that he had a clean copy of a book of unpublished "Cantos," numbered 110–116, by Ezra Pound that he had acquired from poet Donald Hall. There was a rumor, I was told, that Pound's wife, Dorothy, was blocking publication. So why not put out an edition for the world through the Fuck You Press? Tom gave me the manuscript, and we asked artist Joe Brainard, who lived nearby, to come up with a cover.

How did this manuscript wind up in Tom Clark's possession? Donald Hall had interviewed Pound in Rome in 1960 for a series in the *Paris Review* called "Writers at Work." Hall was then poetry editor of the *Review.* Pound had requested payment, and rather than break the tradition of not paying for "Writers at Work" interviews, George Plimpton, the editor, chose to buy rights to publish new material for the *Review.* Pound gave Hall "Cantos 110–116"—and Hall was to choose for publication those that related to the interview. Hall made his own typescript of the "Cantos."

Meanwhile, Donald Hall lent a carbon copy of the "Cantos" to student Tom Clark, who had a friend retype the poems (it was pre-photocopy), a copy of which remained in Clark's hands. For four years, beginning in 1963, Clark had studied Pound's poetry at Cambridge, England. He had returned to New York in 1967 and by now was himself poetry editor of the *Paris Review.*

Being a Greek major, I corrected the Greek, and I did my best to reproduce the Chinese ideograms. In a way the "Cantos" project paid for the renting of the flatbed truck and the sound system for the Pentagon Exorcism. It turned out that the very days in which I was having the printing paper delivered to our house on Avenue A, drawing the adornments for the edition,

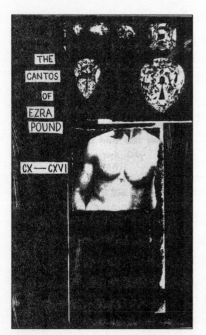

Joe Brainard's cover for *The Cantos.*

and cutting the stencils for *Cantos 110–116,* Allen Ginsberg was spending time with Ezra Pound in Venice. On October 28 Pound's longtime companion, Olga Rudge, told Ginsberg during lunch in Venice that Pound now had enough new poems for a fresh book of the "Cantos." Little did they know that I was on that very day hard at work on an edition of them!

Pound, of course, had been deliberately silent for a number of years (since '61), but the voluble Allen Ginsberg, who had studied intently Pound's *Cantos* for the better part of a month, looking around Venice for specific places mentioned in the poem, managed to spur a historic conversation with the bard of Rapallo. That was the afternoon that Pound, depressed and remorseful over his life's work, rubbing his hands together, told Ginsberg that his writing was "stupidity and ignorance all the way through." He then opened up to the core element of the Pound question, saying, "But the worst mistake I made was the stupid suburban prejudice of anti-Semitism. All along, that spoiled everything." It was the first public statement of the remorse he felt for his radio broadcasts in World War II.

I didn't learn of Allen's conversation with Pound until a bit later, but at the time I was not that impressed. I recalled vividly scanning the anti-Semitic elements in his World War II radio broadcasts at the Library of Congress just an hour or two before Martin Luther King delivered his great "I Have a Dream" speech at the Lincoln Memorial and then filming the Nazi's on the edge of the crowd making "Jewish noses" signs at those trying to listen to the music and speeches.

CANTOS 110–116

Ezra Pound

printed & published by the FUCK YOU/ press at a secret location in the lower east side New York City USA 1967 cover by Joe Brainard

The FUCK YOU/ press

peace peace

in the name of GASH COW

The E.S. Year of Love D.C. (adapted from one of his shrine doors).

All I knew at the time was that Pound had given the Fascist salute not long after he had been released from the asylum in Washington. And that he supposedly was intransigent in his World War II beliefs. I remember how back in 1963 Pound had allowed one of his poems to be published in the right-wing *National Review.* And so it went. Another project crowded into late 1967 was the so-called Gash Cow edition of *Cantos 110–116* of Ezra Pound.

The Gash Cow drawing on the title page was a riff on one of my favorite Egyptian images, my version of Hathor, the Divine Cow, which is found in gold on Tut-Ankh-Amun's famous burial shrine.

King Tut's Divine Cow.

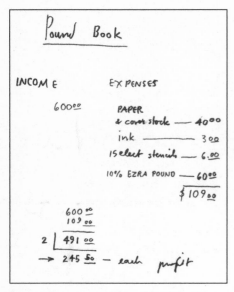

Accounting statement for publication of
Cantos 110–116.

We sold one hundred copies to the Gotham Bookmart for $6 each. And then we gave a hundred or so free to friends. Tom Clark and I split the money 50/50, after mimeo paper and stencils, so that each of us made $245.50, as the accounting sheet I jotted back in early November indicated.

The book caused a bit of a stir in literary circles. My Gash Cow edition seemed to spur the powers that be into action and caused James Laughlin, owner of New Directions, to publish all the known "Cantos." I agreed to meet Laughlin at the Russian Tea Room several months later to discuss the publication. Laughlin seemed worried about control of the copyright, and I assured him I had no intention of publishing any further writings of Pound.

I had already responded to a huffy letter from an attorney from Covington and Burling, a big wheel DC law firm, stating the firm was to leave me alone or I would summon a Green Toad to appear in the letter writer's dreams and ejaculate in his throat. No further inquiries arrived after my response.

A Robbery on Avenue A

Miriam and Deirdre had been invited to visit old friend Bill Szabo and his mate Marianne at their pad down the street. When Miriam and Deirdre returned home, they surprised robbers in the house, who fled out the back. I returned shortly thereafter to find the house a shambles and a box of our possessions resting on the sill of an open window that led out on the rear fire escape.

I searched nearby stairwells and found my typewriter on the window behind the stairwell on Twelfth Street around the corner. But some important items were missing. They'd ripped off Miriam's wedding ring, which

she had left by the kitchen sink. (It had been a gold band with golden orchids, but when we went over to the wedding ring store on Eighth Street
near the 8th Street Bookshop, it no longer carried the orchids ring, so we
purchased one featuring roses, which she still has over four decades later.)

The burglars also had taken my sacred Bell and Howell 16 mm camera!
Veteran of many an underground session, even though all of my footage
had been stolen by the police in a raid over a year before. I remember watching Jimi Hendrix filming backstage in San Francisco; if only I had also
filmed during 1968 and 1969! But I was disheartened after the police had
raided my Secret Location and taken every piece of my films! And now my
beloved Bell and Howell was stolen!

It was devastating. I immediately closed off our gritty second-floor
porch and patio with a heavy iron gate and put in a police lock on the front
door. I'd thought we'd have dinners and soirées out there in warmer
weather, but now it had to be blocked with a junkie-warding metal gate.

So long to the moving image. I always felt that The Fugs WERE their
sounds. They were their audios. After my camera was stolen from our Avenue A apartment, I knew that I could take care of Sound. The Fugs were
their Sound. Words, melody, poetry, tape recordings, and my hand-drawn
designs I called glyphs: These were to be the items of my art for the rest of
my career.

Completing *Tenderness Junction*

I turned to ultracreative Richard Alderson to save The Fugs' recording career from careening down into atonal masochism, angst, metaphysical distress, and failure. I adjusted the band that fall, adding a young bass player
from New Jersey, Charles Larkey, who had been in the Myddle Class, a
band managed by writer Al Aronowitz. Also joining The Fugs was a brilliant
guitarist named Ken Pine, also from New Jersey, who had been a member
of The Ragamuffins, a band led by singer/songwriter Tom Pacheco. It was a
lineup that played well together—very well. Weaver, Sanders, Kupferberg,
Kootch, Larkey, and now Pine.

As I indicated, our managers wanted me to record the entire album
over—something about threats from the earlier engineer, Huston, to sue
over production rights. I resisted redoing the album entirely new but

compromised. I added and subtracted. I kept "Aphrodite Mass," "Knock Knock," "Hare Krishna," "Wet Dream," "Dover Beach," and "Fingers of the Sun." And I added a bunch of new material, such as "War Song," which we created in the studio, to make the Reprise album substantially different from the Atlantic one. The great Bob Fass of WBAI gave us a copy of "Exorcising the Evil Spirits from the Pentagon," to which we overdubbed chants of "Out, demons, out." In addition we added Tuli's excellent tune, "The Garden Is Open," while taking out "Coca Cola Douche," "Carpe Diem," and

---

The Atlantic Album	The Reprise Album
1. Knock Knock	Turn On, Tune In, Drop Out
2. Wet Dream	Knock Knock
3. Wide Wide River	The Garden Is Open
4. Dover Beach	Wet Dream
5. Aphrodite Mass	Hare Krishna
6. Carpe Diem	Exorcising the Evil Spirits from the
7. Hare Krishna	Pentagon Oct 21 1967
8. Fingers of the Sun	War Song
9. Nameless Voices Crying for	Dover Beach
Kindness	Fingers of the Sun
10. Turn On/Tune In/	Aphrodite Mass (in 5 sections):
Drop Out	I—Litany of the Street Grope
11. Coca Cola Douche	II—Genuflection at the Temple of Squack
	III—Petals in the Sea
	IV—Sappho's Hymn to Aphrodite
	V—Homage to Throb Thrills

Ed Sanders: Percussion, vocals
Tuli Kupferberg: Percussion, vocals
Ken Weaver: Drums, vocals
Danny Kortchmar: Guitar
Charles Larkey: Bass
Ken Pine: Guitars, vocals
Allan Jacobs: Sitar ("Hare Krishna")
Allen Ginsberg: Vocals ("Hare Krishna")
Maretta Greer: Vocals ("Hare Krishna")
Gregory Corso: Harmonium ("Hare Krishna")
Producer: Ed Sanders

"Nameless Voices Crying for Kindness." It was a good album. Too bad it couldn't have come out in the spring of 1967.

We had lost a crucial year; we should have had an album out in the Year of Love to join *Sgt. Pepper, Light My Fire, Somebody to Love,* and all the other melodies of be-in. Our second album had made it onto the charts, and there was no reason the next album couldn't have done so if it had come out, say, a few weeks after I was on the cover of *Life* magazine. It was the year in which we were the hottest. In rock-and-rock chronology it was about ten years!

I wanted to do a great album. I felt we had it in us. And so almost immediately we started work on the album that would become *It Crawled into My Hand, Honest.*

Richard Avedon Overseeing Design of The Fugs Album

I asked my friend famous fashion photographer Richard Avedon to design the album package for *Tenderness Junction* and to take pictures of Tuli, Ken, and me for the cover. He agreed, and we went to his studio for a photo session. He assigned the actual album design to a guy named Marvin Israel.

Richard Avedon gave me a series of sheets from his photo shoot of The Fugs.

Meantime, we kept going out to do gigs.

Tenderness Junction, front and back covers. Photos by Richard Avedon.

Richard Avedon proof sheets, September 25, 1967. Ed Sanders collection.

The Fugs in Cleveland

We traveled to a club called Le Cave in Cleveland, where Linda Ronstadt and the Stone Poneys used to perform, for gigs on November 3 and 4. It was our first visit back to d. a. levy's home city since the benefit for him, with Allen Ginsberg, back in May. Le Cave was packed; every table was filled. levy attended one of the concerts.

Backstage at Le Cave Ken Weaver offered a reporter covering the gig for a local newspaper a hit on his rum and coke. "Have some," he said. "Drink it in remembrance of me." The reporter lifted the glass to his lips, and, as he reported, everybody in the back room cheered. "You've just consumed 2000 micro-grams of LSD," Weaver informed me.

Fugs co-founder Ed Sanders didn't offer much help when I asked him, in desperation, how an acid-user could avoid having a "bad trip."

"My advice is always carry in your billfold polaroid pictures of those with whom you copulate."

Before I could establish to my satisfaction whether or not these psyche-delic song-wailers had really impregnated my mind with a hallucinogenic, they ran off to begin their second set.

The reporter sat and listened to our singing. He noted:

A thousand colors began to flash. The music sounded distorted. My skin was getting wet and clammy. Then I caught sight of someone manipulating switches in a light booth, discovered that I was sitting on a beer-soaked chair, and that the music—that god-awful wild music—was SUPPOSED to be that way. As an electric guitar squealed and groaned at the hands of a musical sadist, d. a. levy appeared out of nowhere and nudged me in the arm.

"'Great, huh?' he said, nodding his approval.

I nodded back. Who needs LSD, I thought, when you've got the Fugs?

No doubt we felt it hilarious to josh and kid the reporter about LSD in his rum and coke. I wouldn't think it so funny at a gig at the same club in 1968 when bikers actually did spike my backstage drink with STP.

The following week we did a gig at Cornell University in Ithaca.

The Fugs in Detroit

We flew to Detroit just after Thanksgiving—Ken Pine, Danny Kootch, Charles Larkey, Tuli Kupferberg, Ed Sanders, Ken Weaver—to play two days, November 24 and 25, at the beautiful Grande Ballroom, a huge place able to hold over 1,500 humans. It was located at 8952 Grand River Avenue, in Detroit, an old theater but elegant, built in 1909.

Praise for *Tenderness Junction* from Robert Shelton

Eminent *New York Times* music critic Robert Shelton listened to *Tenderness Junction*, comparing it to the extremely successful *Hair*, which had opened back in late October at the Public Theater:

> We are predictably entering a new era in which the challenging cynicism that American youth had exercised toward all Establishment products and life-styles will be turned toward the popular-culture scene. When that day arrives, "Hair" will get trimmed and The Fugs will be philosopher-kings. The musical show has simply borrowed the external trappings of The Fugs' super-hippie outrages at convention and dull normality and turned it into a commercially acceptable cliché of musical and social inconsequence.
>
> The work of The Fugs is by no means of an even consistency. Heaven help the protest poets if they ever do get to be polished. But their latest album, *Tenderness Junction* (Reprise 6280), is their most musical work yet. After some false starts on Broadside and ESP, The Fugs are ready here to do battle in the commercial marketplace with their anticommercial rants, their satirical slashes that draw blood, their Lenny Bruce—isms that hit the conventional middle-class right between its myopic, suburban eyes. The contrasts and comparisons between "Hair" and The Fugs could make a long article but this is a record column merely calling attention to the sextet's hymnology to an American cultural revolution on its best album yet.

Late 1967

The Fugs went back to the Players Theatre on MacDougal for our final run in December 1967. We recorded the final two nights, thanks to Richard Alderson, who brought in and set up recording equipment. We did our final performance at the Players Theatre on New Year's Eve and closed a run of a year and a half (with time off for touring) and around seven hundred performances.

Still Searching for the Perfect Band

As good as the current Fugs lineup was, Frank Zappa suggested we add to our lineup a young woman he'd dubbed Uncle Meat. He said she was very talented. She not only was performing with the Mothers of Invention at the Garrick Theater on Bleecker Street that year but also Frank Zappa let her open for them, performing her own songs accompanied by the piano. Her real name was Sandy Hurwitz. I met her and thought seriously about adding her to the band, but in my mind the current lineup was very strong, so I decided against it. That decision may have been a mistake; it would have been good to get a woman's fine voice into the mix and to open up the variety of song themes for The Fugs. Meanwhile, I was busy recording the tunes that would become *It Crawled into My Hand, Honest* at Richard Alderson's Impact Sound up on West Sixty-fifth Street.

The year had passed like one of those whip-you-around carnival rides, and now it was 1968. From the Year of Love we rushed into the year during which the War Culture would win the struggle, at least for the next few years. We could not have known that on New Year's Eve when The Fugs performed their final concert at the Players Theatre. This I did know: We had to confront not only the war but also the War Party. So I was ready to spend more time struggling against the Democratic Party and against the war that would not end.

1968

‹❧›

The Indictment of Dr. Spock and Others

In the fall of 1967 and into 1968 a fairly powerful Resistance movement against the military Draft arose. The government didn't dig the Resistance, didn't dig it at all. The day before the Exorcism of the Pentagon, there was a demonstration outside the Justice Department against the military Draft and then four Americans activists took inside what their later indictment called a "fabricoid briefcase" packed with Draft cards (which all Draft-age young men were required to carry with them at all times) and handed them back to the war machine.

The military and the CIA did not dig the well-planned turn-ins of Draft cards around the States that October. The four, not long thereafter indicted, were Yale theologian William Sloan Coffin, writer Mitchell Goodman, famed baby doctor Benjamin Spock, and Marcus Raskin of the Institute for Policy Studies. I viewed them as heroes in the struggle against evil. There was a candlelight vigil in honor of the just-indicted Dr. Spock in New York City in early January 1968.

The Fugs played the Psychedelic Supermarket in Boston the weekend of January 20. (It's a place long since gone; it's now, I'm told, a biomedical research facility for Boston University—in a way, it was a research facility in early '68 also.) That same weekend in London (on January 20) actress Sharon Tate wed director Roman Polanski. They were there for the premiere of *Rosemary's Baby* and soon returned to LA, where they stayed for a while in a fourth-floor apartment at the Chateau Marmont Hotel.

Ed Sanders and Allen Ginsberg, candlelight vigil for Dr. Spock. Ed Sanders collection.

From January 22 to 27 The Fugs were in Montreal at a club called the New Penelope. I asked Jake Jacobs to rejoin us for the gigs. He had a beautiful voice. Few things are as thrilling as singing with another person whose voice interweaves with yours to form that mantram-seed cloth so cherished by the Muses of Singing. The Fugs drove to farmland outside Montreal in their psychedelic garb, rented snowmobiles, and raced crazily through the Montreal snow, howling and growling, in long curving arcs, for a couple of hours of peace.

On January 28 The Fugs played a club called the Trauma in Philadelphia, always a good party town. The place was so packed with half-clothed bodies we could barely get on stage. We returned to the Lower East Side in time for the Tet Offensive on January 30.

The Viet Cong planned the Tet Offensive from a huge tunnel complex northwest of Saigon containing 150 miles of tunnels on three levels, about two feet wide and two feet high dug during the decades of struggle. There were even underground rooms that served as hospitals for wounded VC. On January 31 the Viet Cong entered the presidential palace and the U.S. Embassy in Saigon, holding it for six hours.

Watching Tet unfold on television, we realized that the war was far from over and in fact might soon be "lost." It was time to announce a "festival of life."

A Festival of Life in Chicago

In early February I helped write a press release signed by Abbie Hoffman, Jerry Rubin, Paul Krassner, and myself for the birth of the Yippies (dubbed the Youth International Party by Rubin) and a festival of life to be held in Chicago during the upcoming Democratic National Convention in August. Arlo Guthrie, Country Joe and the Fish, The Fugs, and Allen Ginsberg were so far the biggest draws, but the idea was to get The Beatles, The Rolling Stones, and Bob Dylan to sign on.

At first it was a triumphant idea—a festival of life in a city where LBJ was coming for his crown—to rouse up a six-day festival where be-in and love-in turned left. The spirit of the Digger Free Store would suffuse it—free food, free music, free pot, and loitering love.

I liked it. We planned a daily newspaper. There'd be a night where 100,000 people would burn their Draft cards, with the words "Beat Army" written in flame. "We demand

Poster, The Fugs at the Avalon Ballroom.

the Politics of Ecstasy!" our leaflets shouted. "Rise up and Abandon the Creeping Meatball!"—though it was a tactical error, analyzed in retrospect, to announce up front that 500,000 people were going to make love in Chicago parks. Most Americans didn't want kids balling in the streets.

On February 3 The Fugs flew to San Francisco to play the Avalon Ballroom with Electric Flag, Mad River, and a band called 13th Floor Elevator. Poster artist Victor Moscoso drew the flier.

The Death of Neal Cassady

On February 4, the very day we were playing the Avalon in San Francisco, oh no! Beat hero Neal Cassady passed away in Mexico! Cassady had gone to a wedding in San Miguel de Allende. He'd left his bag at a railroad station a few miles away, and after he left the party drunk and high, he died on the tracks walking back. He was the first of the Beat Generation pentad (Burroughs/Ginsberg/Huncke/Corso/Cassady) to pass.

Ginsberg was at his apartment on East Tenth off Avenue C when one of Neal's women friends telephoned. The great bard's "Elegy for Neal Cassady" laid down beautifully the grief of someone who'd lost a soul buddy, with memories of discourse, Spirit to Spirit, as in these lines:

I could talk to you forever,
The pleasure inexhaustible,
discourse of spirit to spirit,
O Spirit

Kootch's Departure

Right around the time of the Avalon gigs our brilliant guitarist and violinist, Danny Kootch, master of the just-invented wah wah pedal, announced he was leaving The Fugs! It was another huge hole to fill. He told me he was going to join a newly forming LA-based band, The City. Our bass player, Charlie Larkey, also announced he was leaving, though he would stay on through our upcoming Scandinavian tour in the spring.

Kootch and Larkey were set to form a group with none other than famous songwriter Carole King! She had met her future husband Gerry Goffin at Queens College in New York, and beginning in the late '50s they created hit tunes such as "Will You Still Love Me Tomorrow" for the Shirelles, "Take Good Care of My Baby" for Bobby Vee, and the great Drifters recording, "Up on the Roof." King by early 1968 had split with Gerry Goffin and would soon marry Charles Larkey, with whom she would have several children. King went on to write the huge hit for James Taylor "You've Got a Friend," and then after The City she started her own sequence of albums, including her vast-sales-of-vinyl *Tapestry*.

Danny Kootch was very creative. He also played the violin (such as on "The Garden Is Open"). Not long before he departed The Fugs, Kootch sang for me a tune called "Steamroller" and suggested we place it on what would be called *Tenderness Junction*. It was the following set of lyrics that turned me off to the tune:

Now, I'm a napalm bomb, baby
Just guaranteed to blow your mind
Yeah, I'm a napalm bomb for you, baby
Oh, guaranteed, just guaranteed to blow your mind

I was a bit horrified, knowing too well what napalm was doing to the scorched backs of Vietnamese villagers fleeing their villages, so I gently turned it down, without really explaining to Kootch. Just over a year later Kootch's coplayer in the Flying Machine, James Taylor, put "Steamroller" on his megaselling album *Sweet Baby James.* Luckily for The Fugs, we already had a fine guitar player aboard—Ken Pine—so we could continue without any lineup lurch.

An Exorcism of Joseph McCarthy's Grave

I took part in a panel discussion on the New Journalism at Dartmouth College in New Hampshire in late '67. On hand to discuss the new techniques of presenting information were Jack Newfield, Richard Goldstein, Ellen Willis, Robert Christgau, and Paul Krassner. I told Newfield that The Fugs were going to give a concert in a few weeks in Appleton, Wisconsin, the hometown of Senator Joseph McCarthy, the famous right-wing Red-baiting politician who had wrecked careers through falsehoods. He was buried there. Jack Newfield suggested that we exorcise McCarthy's grave. I thought it was a great idea and made preparations. Allen Ginsberg was also going to perform at the same venue in Appleton, and he agreed to help in the Exorcism.

Our concert February 19 with Ginsberg was held at the Cindarella (*sic*) Ballroom in Appleton. It went smoothly, except at the intermission an officer with the local sheriff's department came up to me backstage. He wasn't happy. He said, "I don't care what you sing, but if you jack off that microphone one more time, I'm going to arrest you."

That night, and early in the morning, I prepared the Exorcism. A serious one, because if my hero Allen Ginsberg actually thought he could lecture the ghost (or the summoned apparition) of the Red-baiting senator for his homophobia, who was I not to pour all my energy into the project? So I actually wrote out a ceremony of Exorcism and Summoning.

Sanders reading the Exorcism text at the grave of Joseph McCarthy, Appleton, Wisconsin, February 20, 1968. Ed Sanders collection.

The next morning The Fugs and Ginsberg, plus maybe fifty to seventy-five friends, gathered at Senator McCarthy's grave on a chilly winter hillock and performed the Exorcism, which enraged right-wing commentators. I chanted a singsong conjuration of deities and power words, similar to what I had done at the Pentagon Exorcism. With Allen commenting on the Great Red-baiter's homophobia, he led forth with an invocation to bisexual Greek and Indian gods. We tried to be dignified and respectful.

The Fugs exorcising Joseph McCarthy's grave in Appleton, Wisconsin; top: Ken Weaver and friend; above: Ken Weaver, Ed, Allen Ginsberg with harmonium. Ed Sanders collection.

Allen recited a Hebrew prayer and an invocation to Shiva, and we recited the Prajnaparamita Sutra. Then the entire crowd sang, "My Country 'Tis of Thee" and a few minutes of "Hare Krishna," after which I chanted the final words of Plato's *Republic* in Greek. A young woman agreed to array herself atop the senator's stone as an offering.

We asked those present at the Exorcism to place a gift on McCarthy's stone. I looked back as we left and saw a very interesting visual gestalt atop the granite: a bottle of Midol, a ticket to the movie *The War Game*, a Spring Mobilization Against the War leaflet, a stick of English Leather cologne, one stuffed parrot, one candy bar, a ChapStick, one dozen red roses, one dozen white geraniums, one dozen yellow geraniums, one "Get Fugged" button, some coins, sugar wafers, coat buttons, and two seeds of marijuana. "So long, Joe," Tuli said as we walked down the hill.

Right-wing radio man Paul Harvey growled enormously about the Exorcism on his show, just as right-wing columnist Jim Bishop had railed against the *Marijuana Newsletter* from Peace Eye two years previous. These right-wing guys are always railing, wailing, and trailing after our scents.

Dawn Protest Concert at Stony Brook

We were barely off the road and back on the Lower East Side when we were called to perform at dawn outside the front gates of the State University of New York at Stony Brook, out on Long Island. It was a protest, sponsored by the just-founded Yippies, against a dawn raid by the police a few weeks previous to arrest marijuana smokers in the Stony Brook dorms.

So we set up our amps and microphones in the chilly dawn of February 27 and sang. Also performing were Country Joe and the Fish, the Pageant Players, and a group called Soft White Underbelly. The *Daily News* ran a picture of me from the demonstration, in my chilly long gray coat, and our guitarist, Ken Pine, while the *New York Post* noted that "Timothy Leary predicts that 100,000 dancing, joyous yippies will swarm over Chicago's airports so the Presidential plane cannot land at convention time."

The afternoon of the Stony Brook concert I signed a lease to take over the *East Village Other* office at 147 Avenue A, near Ninth Street, in order to move the Peace Eye Bookstore there from its prior location next to Tuli Kupferberg's building on Tenth Street between B and C.

The Fugs at the Anderson Theater, March 6, 1968. Photo by Elliott Landy.

Meanwhile, More Benefits

On March 6, just a few days after the McCarthy Exorcism and the dawn concert at Stony Brook, The Fugs, Country Joe and the Fish, Bob Fass, Paul Krassner, and Light Show creators Joshua and Pablo did a benefit for the War Resisters League at the famous Anderson Theater, home to many a Yiddish production, at 66 Second Avenue. I wrote a new song for the concert, a country and western satire titled "I Cried When I Came in Your Best Friend's Mouth." I could hear the gasps from the front rows of the Anderson Theater as we sailed through the tune. It was the only ditty in the history of The Fugs that any band member objected to, so I dropped it from the repertoire.

A young rock photographer named Elliot Landy was just beginning his career. One of his first concerts was The Fugs/Country Joe gig at the Anderson. This Landy photo of The Fugs on the Anderson Theater stage captured marvelously the grooviness of the stage ambience during those times.

Time to Complete a Major Album

Meanwhile, we were recording what would be our triumphal album of the 1960s, *It Crawled into My Hand, Honest.* I worked very closely with Richard Alderson in producing it. It cost a fortune in 1960s money, around $25,000, with weeks and weeks of recording at Impact Studios on West Sixty-fifth (soon to be torn down to make the Lincoln Center parking garage). I created a lengthy "Magic Rite," which we recorded. Ken Weaver wrote "Aztec Hymn," which we also recorded. And I worked with jazz composer Burton Greene on another long work, "Beautyway," based on a Navajo ceremony. We also recorded a song about poet William Blake walking naked with his wife, Catherine, while reading Milton's *Paradise Lost* in their garden in 1793. None of these tunes would wind up on the album.

Before he left to join Carole King's new group, Dan Kootch had strongly urged me to hire a second drummer, as Frank Zappa had done for the Mothers of Invention. This created considerable dissension with our original percussionist, Ken Weaver, though it freed him to come frontstage more often to sing and perform his famous routines.

Alderson brought us great singer and arranger Bob Dorough, who sang and arranged various tunes for *It Crawled*, such as "Marijuana," "Johnny Pissoff Meets the Red Angel," "Ramses the 2nd Is Dead, My Love," and "Life Is Strange." Alderson also brought aboard Warren Smith to arrange "When the Mode of the Music Changes."

Idea for Recording a Single During a Parachute Jump

I had an excellent idea early in 1968! We'd record a Fugs single during a group parachute jump from a plane. Richard Alderson would join us, holding a tape recorder, which would be connected to me, Ken, and Tuli, each outfitted with broadcast mikes. We'd be in communication with Alderson by means of headphones. He'd count it off, and then we'd record! Tuli balked, so another good idea hit the basket.

Moving Peace Eye to Avenue A

After the landlord forced me to take back Peace Eye from the Jade Companions of the Flowered Dance in the spring of '67, I had left it fairly dormant, caught in the pleasant pincers of carousing, recording, and fame. I had re-opened Peace Eye in the summer and fall of '67 after winning my court case. But then I allowed it to close in late '67 until the spring of '68, when I was determined to bring the bookstore back to power. So the afternoon following the cold dawn concert at Stony Brook I signed a lease on Avenue A for the place that had once housed the *East Village Other*. I gave the *Other*

Spain Rodriguez's design for the Peace Eye Bookstore. Photo by Ed Sanders.

owners $500 in key money and hired people to get the space ready—scraping, painting, putting in shelves.

Artist Spain Rodriguez, who'd painted the groovy sign for the Digger Free Store around the corner, did the new Peace Eye sign—chrome yellow letters on red and a fine Eye of Horus.

I was determined to get Peace Eye, in its new location, on a better business footing, and I brought in Joe Arak, who had worked for The Fugs, to manage it. And then my thanks to the guys who worked there during the next two years, including Doug Hasting, John Matthews, Burt Kimmelman, Vince Aletti, and Jim Retherford.

Life During the Glory Years of the Great Society

Underneath the Goof, of course, lay the skree of weirdness, calamity, and secret police. The theremin fill, *oo-oo-oo-oo* in the Beach Boy's "Good Vibrations" and the *oo-ee-oo* in Krzysztof Komeda's soundtrack for *Rosemary's Baby* were always there in the sounds of '68 (along with the throb of tall stacks of amplifiers, the sizzle of napalm, and the sky-groaning vowels of lysergica).

The secret police were always there also, like puking drunks in a phone booth, hung up on manipulation, looking for evidence of rubles, racist,

Miriam and Deirdre in 1968 on Ave A with the bugged phone. Photo by Larry Fink, used by permission of Marc Albert-Levin.

pretty much right wing and hating the left. Miriam's mother would call Avenue A, and there'd be no ring. Then all of a sudden she could hear everything in the room. We were pitiably easy to monitor.

(Later, from reading my FBI files I realized how closely surveilled we were. I was shocked to learn that the FBI at least twice forwarded actual Fugs records to the U.S. attorney "for prosecutive decision," to use the bureau's own icy language.)

But the streets were safe. Miriam and Deirdre, then not quite four, could go out at 3:00 AM to the vegetable store called Three Guys from Brooklyn on First Avenue and do so without undue fear.

The heroin started arriving, and the violence, after Nixon took office in early 1969. It's not clear if there was a connection, but we would notice it, and it would become a factor in Miriam's and my deciding to depart from the Lower East Side.

A Mantram to Chant in Chicago

I had written Charles Olson in Gloucester for a mantram we could chant in Chicago to quell the violence. I also asked poets Ed Dorn and d. a. levy. My request came from the chanting The Fugs and the Diggers had done at the Pentagon, "Out, Demons, Out! Out, Demons, Out!" and the ceremony we had performed at Senator McCarthy's grave. I figured it was worth a try to see if a great bard's sung seed syllables could help end the war.

Backstage at the opening of the Fillmore East, March 8, 1968, with Janis Joplin and band. Ed on the left. Photo by Elliott Landy.

On March 14 Charles Olson called Avenue A and recited his mantram to Miriam:

Plann'd in Creation, Arouse the Nation
Blood is the Food of
Those Gone Mad
Blood is the Food of
Those Gone Mad
Blood is all over already the Nation
Plann'd in Creation, Arouse the Nation
Blood is the Food of Those Gone Mad

Olson then mailed us the chant from Chicago on the way to deliver some lectures entitled "Poetry and Truth" at Beloit College.

Blown Away by Sly

The Fugs played in Detroit at the Grande Ballroom, with the MC5 and the Psychedelic Stooges on March 29–30. There was an opening act I'd never heard of, Sly and the Family Stone, who performed just before The Fugs. Sly and the Family Stone proceeded to arouse the audience to incredibly high ecstasy, leaving everyone limp. It was a Blowout by Sly so that when The Fugs went on, it was impossible for us to rouse the audience back to the Sly Frenzy. I vowed to try never to get caught in the "Blown away by Sly" mode ever again.

Martin Luther King

We knew that Martin Luther King was working on a huge Poor People's Campaign that would bring tens of thousands to camp out in Washington, DC, for Peace, Justice, and Jobs. Then suddenly, on a motel balcony in Memphis on April 4 he was gunned down. It was quickly reported that the putative rifleman was a guy named James Earl Ray.

I remembered so intensely standing beneath a big tall elm by the Lincoln Memorial that hot day in August '63 to hear King give his "I Have a Dream" speech, and now I hated the guy who killed him, just as I hated the scampering men with swastika armbands I filmed that day on the edge of the huge crowd by the Memorial.

Bacchus, as ever, pushed into the Grief, and The Fugs flew the day after King's death to Cincinnati for an arts festival. I remember how someone at Frank O'Hara's funeral had asked if there was a party afterward. Sitting next to me on the plane was a pretty young woman who claimed she was returning from a tour as a courtesan for one of Ohio's senators.

For a city that later persecuted photographer Robert Mapplethorpe, there was a glut of fun in Cincinnati. For instance, a party in our motel where a Fug (not I!) frolicked with a fan, after which they watched a Mexican vampire movie while his toe was moving gently in and out of the entrance of Venus.

Meanwhile, big riots began in DC, Baltimore, Chicago, Detroit, Boston, and 125 other places, where 46 died, with over 20,000 arrested and 55,000 troops sent to quell the disorders. In Chicago, for instance, 5,000 federal troops and 6,700 Illinois National Guardsmen were dispatched to assist police. Mayor Richard Daley soon criticized the Chicago Police Department "for having failed to take more aggressive action when the riot started."

On April 11 The Fugs flew to Denver to play a version of the Avalon Ballroom that had opened there. Then we flew the next day to San Francisco to play the main Avalon, April 12, 13, 14. Jim Morrison was backstage

The Fugs at the Avalon Ballroom, April 1968.

one night in his snakeskin pants, swigging from a Jim Beam bottle. He was a bit too wasted to ask him to sing in Chicago. I had gone to Frank Zappa, and others including Janis, to try to get them to sing at the Festival of Life during the upcoming Democratic Convention in Chicago in August.

We stayed in San Francisco until April 17, with a few extra days to party. My mentor Charles Olson was in town for two weeks (he had a gig to experiment with other poets in the new medium of video) and staying with editor/publisher Don Allen on the pullout sofa in his apartment on Jones Street.

One morning I visited Janis Joplin. I told her the great poet Charles Olson was in town and would she like to meet him? I thought maybe Olson could write some songs for her, and, well, both were single and maybe there could be some eros between bard and blues.

We went to a restaurant in Chinatown, and because Don Allen was the famous editor of *New American Poets* and the *Evergreen Review,* the party was paid for by Grove Press! Afterward we crowded into a booth at Gino and Carlo's in North Beach. Olson was talking about Sutter's Mill, and the word "Donner Party" entered the quick flow of his words. Around then Janis went to the back to shoot pool, and my plans for a blues/bard romance were racked up on the green.

On April 17 The Fugs flew to Los Angeles and stayed once again at Sandy Koufax's Tropicana at 8585 Santa Monica Boulevard, just a few blocks from the Troubador bar. During our two weeks in LA jukeboxes everywhere were singing out with the seething/soothing of Leonard Cohen's "Suzanne." We performed on April 19 and 20 at the Cheetah, a place built on piers at the beach in Venice.

It was like playing Coney Island. There seemed to be a glut of bikers backstage, some of them Straight Satans, who lived nearby. I had no idea that a couple of them would become involved in the Manson family at the Spahn Movie Ranch.

Janis came to one of the gigs and later visited one of The Fugs at the Tropicana. At 2:00 AM she decided to take a swim. She was topless, and at first the place was desolate, but then, in minutes, the poolsides came awake! As if it were daytime, a dog walker arrived and stood by the bougainvillea near the pool. People were holding drinks and chatting with vigor.

The front desk rang my room, "Mr. Sanders, I'm sorry, but The Fugs will have to leave if Miss Joplin continues to swim bare-breasted."

A Possible Career Mistake

I used to take a cab over the powdered granite hills and down into the San Fernando Valley to Burbank to visit Warner/Reprise, The Fugs' recording label. Fresh in my mind was all the work we did trying to do a film with Shirley Clarke and Barbara Rubin. And, of course, my career as an underground filmster even though my footage had been stolen by the police.

I'd talked with people at Reprise about a movie idea I had starring Jimi Hendrix and Janis Joplin. They'd be marooned together on a Mississippi riverboat in a flood. They'd be romantically involved, as they say, and they'd sing together.

It was a good idea. Just the concept of Janis and Jimi singing together, even their harmonies woven together or maybe in call and response with Jimi's genius guitar, would have been a marvel. I could hear her voice and his guitar and voice make hieroglyphics in my Egyptian-sensitive mind.

At the Warner Brothers complex I was introduced to Ted Ashley of the Ashley Famous Agency. I ran down my idea of a Hendrix/Joplin riverboat film project. I got a call when The Fugs returned to New York.

The agency wanted to sponsor it! I'd get my own office and secretary, but I'd have to move to LA. I probably should have done it, but, well, I was working hard on the new album at Alderson's studio, plus I'd just reopened Peace Eye on Avenue A, so I reluctantly turned the offer down.

Photo Shoot

We had a memorable photo shoot for our album cover at the Warner Brothers movie lot in Burbank. We had our pick of costumes from the Warner Brothers wardrobe department. We ordered anything we wanted from movies we'd seen. Larkey, for example, perhaps under the influence of Carole King, ordered the attire of a nineteenth-century Viennese fop. Weaver was transformed into a horn-headed ninth-century berserker.

Ronald Reagan was then the right-wing governor of California (and we would have sneered and bet big money in the spring of '68 that he'd never be president), so I ordered Reagan's old Gipper #32 football uniform from the *Knute Rockne Story*, a tuxedo from a Fred Astaire–Ginger Rogers movie, and an Errol Flynn D'Artagnon Renaissance puff-sleeved outfit with a sword.

We went to some Warner Brothers sets. The place where the TV series *F Troop* was shot, with its famous falling tower, and the sets of Camelot, and, I think, the Alamo (the Mission church on the back cover of the album). Reprise supplied some limber-limbed damosels, who frolicked with us for the session, clad in scantness and breasts exposed in the *F Troop* air.

We learned that the week of April 22 had been designated "D for Decency Week" in Los Angeles by the LA County Board of Supervisors. We noted a groovy "Stamp Out Smut" poster.

We couldn't let that pass by without some fun. We selected a supervisor named Warren Dorn for our focus. He had been particularly vehement against erotic literature. We were scheduled to play a large psychedelic club, with a rotating stage, called the Kaleidoscope the weekend of April 26–27. The press release from the Kaleidoscope was headlined:

FUGS PERFORM MAGIC RITE
FOR WARREN DORN
DURING DECENCY WEEK

... The Fugs will lead a gathering of gropers, chanters, lovers and toe freaks in a magic ceremony to be performed in a 1938 Dodge, the back seat of which is an important symbol of the American sexual revolution.

In the parking lot of the Kaleidoscope, where they are currently engaged, the Fugs will declare National Back Seat Boogie Week and will conduct a magic rite to sensually refreshen and testicularly juvenate Supervisor Warren Dorn.

The club had rented a searchlight the night of our rite, which beamed white tunnels of psychedelic allure up toward Aquarius. There was an anarcho-bacchic Goof Strut parade into the parking lot of the club behind a mint-condition '38 Dodge (similar to a Kienholz work at the Los Angeles County Museum of Art).

A woman volunteer in a green gown lay supine in the backseat holding a carrot, waiting to erotomotivate into the dreams and mind of Dorn and ball him. It had a kind of pizzazz—the visual of the woman in rustling green through the backseat window as we spread a line of cornmeal around the Dodge. Just as at the Pentagon and Senator McCarthy's grave, I tried to give the rite my finest singsong C chord, chanting such sizzling lines as "I exorcise the circle in the name of the Divine Toe" and

Arise ! Arise! Eye of Horus! Arise Toe Freaks!
Arise! Sir Francis Dashwood! Arise Tyrone Power!
Arise! Arise! Spirits of heaven! Arise William Blake!

The green-gowned deva then suck-licked the carrot in oneirophalloerotic mimesis as she was "telechanted" into Dorn's Decency Week dreams.

Afterward I lead the crowd in a few minutes of "Ommmm," and then we sang "My Country 'Tis of Thee" before retiring to the Tropicana to party. I was getting very tired of exorcisms and did no more after the carrot-licking woman in the green dress.

We flew up to Portland, Oregon, May 3 after our fun in LA for a gig there and the next day drove to Eugene, the very day protesting students were occupying the streets of Paris. We played at a club called the Lemon Tree, located next to a beaver pond. Before the performance I walked out to water's edge, where I experienced a great transmission of Peace. I had to go back in my mind to the lakes of my Missouri youth or to Elvis Presley's rendition of "Peace in the Valley," which helped me through the grief from my mother's death in '57, to find such consolation as I had during those moments. The beaver pond by the Lemon Tree was the best time for me in '68.

A Tour of Sweden and Denmark

The Fugs, accompanied by my wife, Miriam, went on a tour of Sweden and Denmark, May 6–13, where we performed with the bands Ten Years After and Fleetwood Mac. Fleetwood, which later filled hockey arenas, was our opening act. Monday, May 6, we did a tour-opening press conference at Jazz House, Montmartre in Copenhagen. Tuesday, May 7, we put on two concerts at the Falkoner Centret Copenhagen. At the end of the shows the audience rhythmically clapped. I was so inexperienced that I didn't realize people were clapping for encores!

Wednesday, May 8, there was another Fugs press conference, this time in Gothenberg. Then, that night, a concert that was shocking to me was given by Bill Haley and the Comets at the big city auditorium. The crowd chanted, "Ve want Beill Haley! Ve want Beill Haley!" I was amazed that Haley performed almost the SAME SET as when I had seen him at the Municipal Auditorium as a junior in high school in Kansas City in 1956! Rudy got up on his standup bass and rode it during "Rudy's Rock," just as he had in KC!

Thursday, May 9, we did two concerts at Liseberg, Gothenberg. On May 10 we flew to Stockholm for a TV show, plus a public meeting with American Draft resisters and two performances at Congress Hall. In Paris the same day the group known as Le 22 Mars invaded a class on Nietzsche and demanded participation in the General Strike. The faculty voted to strike, and demonstrators took over the Latin Quarter by midnight.

On May 11 The Fugs flew up near the Arctic Circle to Umea to sing at the university, and on May 12 we flew south to Copenhagen for two gigs at the Studenterforeningen. The next day we took the hydrofoil across the harbor from Copenhagen to Lund, Sweden, for two concerts at the university and a visit to a famous pornographic art show. In France on May 13 there was a day and night of nationwide strike by hundreds of thousands, and on May 14 students occupied the Sorbonne as The Fugs boarded their SAS flight back to the United States.

Trying to Finish an Album

After the Scandinavian tour Charles Larkey was off to join Carole King and Kootch in Los Angeles. After an upcoming two-day gig at the Fillmore East, we replaced him with Bill Wolf, who brought us excellent playing, plus a fine harmony voice. For the final months of The Fugs' 1960s incarnation we stayed the same: Pine, Mason, Wolf, Weaver, Kupferberg, and myself.

Right away I leaped back into sessions for the album. As usual I was making long lists of possible album titles. It got down to where the title was either *Rapture of the Deep* (Miriam's idea) or *It Crawled into My Hand, Honest.*

Producing the album was getting expensive. I didn't like a number of the tunes we had recorded back in the early part of the year, and I had shifted directions toward more of a concept album. I wanted one whole side to run as a single flow without separations between numbers.

The Fugs at Fillmore East

We appeared at the Fillmore East with Moby Grape and Jeremy Steig on May 31–June 1. I decided to record the gigs for a live album, so we hired Warren Smith to conduct an ensemble consisting of the regular Fugs (Weaver, Wolf, Pine, Mason, Sanders, Kupferberg), with additional musicians, all of whom were conducted by Warren Smith. He was brilliantly arranging "When the Mode of the Music Changes" and other pieces on the soon-to-be-released album.

A few months later I carefully went through all the takes and selected the following flow of live tunes:

Slum Goddess 3:10
Coca Cola Douche 2:50
How Sweet I Roamed 3:21
I Couldn't Get High 4:08
Saran Wrap 3:45
I Want to Know 2:39
Homemade 5:18
Nothing 4:54
Supergirl 2:42

We recorded live at the Fillmore East, May 31 and June 1:

Ed Sanders: Vocals, routines
Ken Weaver: Drums, vocals
Tuli Kupferberg: Vocals, skits
Kenny Pine: Lead guitar, vocals
Bob Mason: Drums
Charles Larkey: Bass
Richard Tee: Organ
Howard Johnson: Tuba, saxophone
Carl Lynch: Guitar
Julius Watkins: French horn
Producer: Ed Sanders
Orchestra leader: Warren Smith

Warhol and Solanas

A writer named Valerie Solanas had visited me at Peace Eye with a twenty-one-page manuscript she asked me to publish called the *S.C.U.M. Manifesto*. SCUM was the Society to Cut Up Men. The manifesto began, "Life in this society being, at best, an utter bore and no aspect of society being at all relevant to women, there remains to civic-minded, responsible, thrill-seeking females only to overthrow the government, eliminate the money system, institute complete automation and destroy the male sex."

I'd had the manuscript a while. She'd stopped by Peace Eye a couple of times wanting to know if I were going to print it. Then she'd left a note in late May. She wanted the manuscript back. I got the impression from the store clerk that she was miffed.

Solanas had a part in Andy Warhol's *I, a Man*. She'd submitted a film script that Andy had turned down and then somehow, building up toward June, came to believe he was stealing her intellectual property.

That spring Warhol had moved his famous Factory from Forty-seventh Street to a fourth-floor place at 33 Union Square on the north side of Union Square Park. Late Monday afternoon, June 3, Valerie Solanas took the elevator to the fourth floor. Warhol was there, as were Paul Morrissey, Fred Hughes, and Mario Amaya, the publisher of an English art magazine.

It may have been an error for Hughes to greet Solanas with "You still writing dirty books, Valerie?" The telephone rang, and Andy was on the phone with a writer known as Viva, star of *Nude Restaurant* and *Chelsea Girls*.

Solanas slid a .32 automatic out of her trench coat and aimed it at Warhol, who shouted, "Valerie! Don't do it! No! No!" and she pinged him. She then chased Mario Amaya and shot him also. Amaya fled bleeding into the other room and held the door while Solanas shoved against it, apparently intent on further pinging.

The author of the *S.C.U.M. Manifesto* next sought to ping the young man named Hughes, who had punched the elevator button while she was trying to push open the door the wounded Amaya was holding shut. Hughes dropped to his knees and proclaimed his innocence, and he was still in a beseeching mode when the elevator opened and Solanas fled downward and away.

I learned of the shooting at home on Avenue A and became sorely alarmed about my own safety. I was afraid she might come to Peace Eye or, worse, to our apartment, with her smoking .32, demanding the return of the *S.C.U.M. Manifesto*. I hid behind the police lock at 196 Avenue A until she turned herself in to the police on Times Square a few hours later. *Whew!*

The Shooting of Robert Kennedy

I didn't care what the Yippies thought about Robert Kennedy. I was a big fan. His words quoting Aeschylus just after hearing about Martin Luther King's assassination had kept total despair at bay.

The success of Robert Kennedy's campaign for the presidency had caused the Yippies to scale back their plans for a huge festival of life in Chicago. Instead Jerry Rubin told me that the Yippies were planning a caravan of Keseyesque buses, based on the Hog Farm's, to wend to Chicago. That was fine with me because I had my hands full, completing The Fugs record, overseeing the Peace Eye Bookstore, and spending time at home on Avenue A.

It was on Avenue A where we had watched Robert Kennedy's triumphant June 5 speech at the Ambassador Hotel in Los Angeles. We still had the television lit when the gun by the ice machine fired in the dark hotel kitchen and Robert Kennedy fell, mortally wounded.

I was devastated. I remembered how just a few days before at The Fugs concert at the Fillmore East, Weaver had referred to RFK as an "amphetamine wolverine." For a few days I thought seriously about changing my life, even going to law school and then putting myself into the service of the Public Good. I considered entering a Catholic Worker type of life. Part of me missed the spirit of the 4H, of the Future Farmers of America, and the Grange—the orderly rural life. But even when I grew up in Midwest farm country, I had become cut off from the earth. The farmers in the town where I was raised began, even when I was in high school, to sell off their land to commuter subdivisions in and around Kansas City until almost all of the orchards and farms were gone. And now I was stuck on gritty Avenue A. What to do? was very much on my mind in the post-RFK convulsions of grief.

A Hunger to Study

I recalled my experience with Al Fowler and the possible visits of Lee Harvey Oswald to Greenwich Village in late 1963. Then the Jim Garrison investigation into possible CIA involvement in the assassination of John Kennedy. Now it was June 1968, and something just didn't seem right.

That one night by the ice machine in that hotel changed the direction of my life. It began to push me back to my scholarly roots, studying ancient languages. And to push me toward what I later termed "Scholar Activism," toward studying every day, reading, reading, and reading, trying to understand the Real Story. What was really going on.

In Anton Chekhov's story "Rothschild's Fiddle" a dying coffin maker named Yakov plays a tune for Jewish musician Rothschild, who later performs the melody "so passionately sad and full of grief that the listeners weep." All that night after RFK's shooting the strings of Rothschild's fiddle trembled my soul. It was the kind of night that made one want to join an intentional community.

Drear morn droned drear on a destiny day. I awakened in a pit of ashes, forlorn and bereft, out of sorts with America and wanting a different life when Jerry Rubin called around noon.

"Did you hear the good news?" he asked.

"What good news are you talking about?" I replied.

"About Bobby," he said. "Now we can go to Chicago!"

I let what he said pass by in silence, though I felt more alienated than someone crawling for miles in a Samuel Beckett novel.

Jerry Rubin probably wasn't the only one exulting over RFK's death. Although there are no smoking stockings, of course, I picture J. Edgar Hoover rewarding himself with a little lipstick, some rouge, a wig perhaps, pulling his garter belt on his freshly shaved legs and maybe strutting in joy around his bedroom in spike heels to some records he'd gotten as gifts at an organized crime casino.

Still Recording The Fugs Album

Less than a week after the assassination of RFK The Fugs began seven long and exhausting days, June 10 to 16, recording at Richard Alderson's Impact Sound on *It Crawled into My Hand, Honest*.

I wanted the second side of the record to be like a long collage. I was working with composer Burton Green on a long piece, with words, called "Beautyway," named after a Navajo ceremonial. We were recording the song, but it did not wind up on the album.

I abandoned the long, complicated "Magic Rite" that we had recorded early in the year because I was getting disgusted with the fake shortcuts promised by Mageia that substituted for real change. (I finally used a short snippet of it on the record—the "Irene (Peace)" section at the end of side two.)

And I also gave up a tune called "The Vision of William Blake's Garden" (a version of which can be heard on our CD *Fugs Live from the Sixties*, from our spring '69 concert at Rice University). We'd planned to use Olson's mantram "Plann'd in Creation / Arouse the Nation / Blood is the food of those gone Mad!" as a chanted preamble to "The Vision."

Prague Spring

In Czechoslovakia there was the Prague Spring, when Alexander Dubček loosened the authoritarian grip on his nation but "remained a devoted communist" and wanted to keep in place single-party rule. Nevertheless during Prague Spring he allowed greater freedom of expression. Once humans escape a cage, it's not that easy to get them back inside.

The Communist authorities allowed rock and roll over the state-run radio! The Beatles arrived! They were a huge influence! and had a vast impact on students and the young, creative generation. "All You Need Is Love"! "Sgt. Pepper"! "Norwegian Wood"! Records by the Velvet Underground, Frank Zappa and the Mothers of Invention, and even The Fugs were allowed into the country during the Prague Spring. A group called the Plastic People of the Universe would soon form and actually perform Fugs songs!

Years later I helped raise money to smuggle musical instruments into Czechoslovakia. This was after the crackdown that began August 1968, with Soviet tanks invading Prague. This was not long before the military, with fixed bayonets, patrolled the streets of Chicago during the Democratic Convention.

World Poetry Conference

At the State University at Stony Brook (where we'd done the dawn concert early in the year), there was the World Poetry Conference, June 21–23, organized by Louis Simpson, Jim Harrison, and Herbert Weisinger. I was invited to deliver a statement at a panel discussion on politics. Some of my friends, including Anselm Hollo and George Kimball, were there, as were Donald Hall, Louis Simpson, Nicanor Parra, Zbigniew Herbert, Eugene Guillevic, and many others.

There was a party on Saturday, June 22, at Louis Simpson's house in Bell Terre, Long Island. It was a thronging, well-done event, both indoors and out. Donald Hall, that brilliant poet, was very drunk and in fact was about to pass out. I myself had drunk so much that my liver was feeling like a Rudi Stern neon.

Drunk as I was, I overheard a discussion between a male professor and the wife of another professor. He taunted her, "You're nothing without your husband."

I laughed at him and then began to taunt him that he was a nothing also. (After all, Tuli Kupferberg's "Nothing" had become one of The Fugs' most popular tunes.) A poet pal, George Kimball, came up from behind and broke a bottle of champagne over his head. The result was a broken glass-topped table on the outside patio.

Uh oh, what to do? Should we confess to the owner of the pad, Louis Simpson? It was then, noticing the *zzz*-zoned Donald Hall, future Poet Laureate of the United States, that we hatched a scheme to say that it was Hall, a good friend of Louis Simpson's, who had broken the table. It was years before the gentle bard found out he hadn't bacchus'd the broad glass table.

During the World Poetry Conference a number of us stayed in the dorms. I recall Anselm Hollo trying to toss a typewriter out a window, but the glass was too tough, whereupon he hurled it down some stairs, a piece of typed-on paper around the roller. It was a battered relic I couldn't resist retrieving. I took it back to Avenue A and kept it for many years as a Literary Relic First Class. I wish I still had it.

The Summer of 1968

That summer I divided my time in slices of too many commitments: being in our pad on Avenue A, running the Peace Eye Bookstore, recording *It Crawled*, working on the Chicago demonstrations, and hanging out in the many bars of the counterculture: Rafiki's and PeeWee's on Avenue A and Stanley's, the Annex, and Mazur's on Avenue B, plus Slugs, the Old Reliable, the Cedar, and many West Village places (such as the Lion's Head). What a toke of ruination for the liver! Dr. Nemhauser of Tompkins Square North told me to stop drinking, that my liver was enlarging. It was something I wouldn't heed until 1973 after my sojourn writing my book on the Manson family.

A few times I helped soldiers fleeing the war. They arrived in their uniforms and slept in the back room at Peace Eye. They changed into civvies, and the next day I tossed away their uniforms here and there in the garbage cans of Tenth and Twelfth.

At Peace Eye I printed hundreds of leaflets and fliers free, including many for the Motherfuckers, even though they'd been mean to me, one of them accusing me at an early Yippie meeting of having a Swiss Bank account!

I strolled around the scene in my red boots or my white boots, attired in necklaces, striped pants, Tom Jones shirts, and lacy finery that helped rinse away what Kenneth Rexroth once called "the light from Plymouth Rock" from my Midwest Protestant roots.

Miriam and Didi went just about every day to the playgrounds at Tompkins Square Park. Didi had a little bell from the Psychedelicatessen she sometimes wore around her wrist. The park was where all the races, cultures, and factions came together. There was very little open strife, and the streets were safe enough, especially if you knew which part of which block—as all longterm residents did—had spots where it was not safe to stroll.

Working with Bob Dorough

On July 7 I took a bus from New York City to Stroudsburg, Pennsylvania, where I was picked up by well-known composer Bob Dorough and went with him to his rural spread in Mt. Bethel. I brought with me my autoharp so that I could play some tunes I wanted him to arrange and perform on for the new Fugs album. Dorough back in '62 had written a famous tune with Miles Davis called "Blue Xmas." Richard Alderson had recommended him. Dorough had coproduced an album by Spanky and Our Gang at Impact Sound in '67. Dorough also had a remarkable singing voice, which reminded me of when I was a kid in Missouri and saw Hoagy Carmichael sing "Buttermilk Skies" on television. Dorough prepared lead sheets and oversaw the recording of Tuli's marvelous tune "Life Is Strange" and my "Johnny Pissoff Meets the Red Angel." I also had the idea to combine a poem Tuli had written that listed a good number of different names for hashish/marijuana with a kind of Gregorian chant on the word "marijuana." Dorough jumped aboard this project with gusto.

Dorough sang lead while performing a magnificent piano part on "Life Is Strange," and he did harmonies on "Johnny Pissoff." On "Marijuana" Dorough outdid himself, leaving behind a deathless track.

Late July

The Fugs went back to the Psychedelic Supermarket in Boston to sing and party from July 25 to July 27 as best the Chicago summer allowed. By late

Bob Dorough's lead sheet for "Marijuana in Nobis-Pacem Eternam."

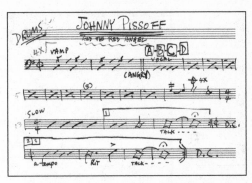

Bob Dorough's drummer's lead sheet for "Johnny Pissoff Meets the Red Angel." Note the instruction "Angry" for the drummer's lead-in to the tune.

July/early August I was desperate to finish *It Crawled into My Hand, Honest* before the Chicago convention (because I thought I might be jailed, or worse) and before our upcoming European tour. I also was writing the liner notes and designing the foldout album.

We went to Cleveland to play Le Cave. We were there from July 30 to August 1. During the mornings of July 31 and August 1 I flew back to New York to mix the album at Alderson's studio and then flew back later in the day to the gig in Cleveland.

Designing the Album

On Wednesday, July 31, I went to Ivanhoe drafting supplies to get a drafting board and t-square, which I carried back on the plane to cut and paste the inner foldout sleeve of *It Crawled*. I also drew an ink glyph to use in the liner notes.

Bard d. a. levy came to one of the gigs in Cleveland. I tried to interest him in coming to Chicago. (He was one I'd asked to send a mantram to chant in the streets.) He'd been publishing the *Buddhist Third Class Junkmail Oracle*, a mix of his brilliant collages, his poems, and the usual look of a tabloid underground paper. He'd just printed his August issue, in which he announced he was giving the publication up because of no financial support from the community.

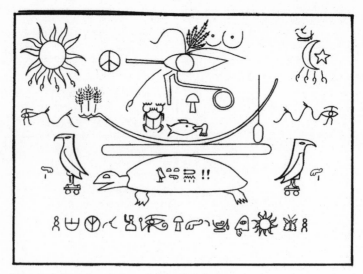

The glyph for *It Crawled into My Hand, Honest.*

August 2–3

From Cleveland we flew to Chicago to play a psychedelic auditorium called the Electric Factory. I rushed back to New York City to do the final sequencing for the album, and then, at last, it was done! The mixed master reels and the boards containing the design were airmailed to Reprise Records in Burbank.

On August 7 a bunch of us (myself, writer Richard Goldstein, Paul Krassner, Abbie Hoffman, and Jerry Rubin) flew to Chicago for a meeting with Al Bougher and David Stahl of Mayor Richard Daley's office. I found myself paying for Rubin's ticket. It was scorching hot. They didn't dig Abbie smoking pot in the mayor's office. We continued to beg for permits for our Festival of Life in Lincoln Park, but they kept up their balking at giving any permits whatsoever.

The staff at the underground newspaper the *Chicago Seed,* fearing bloodshed in the streets during the Convention, wanted the New Yorkers to cancel activities in Chicago and issued an editorial to that effect.

The Telegram

Chicago wasn't Selma. I just couldn't believe that the police, even with the help of provocateurs, would turn Chicago into pizza. Nor did I believe that

Abbie and Jerry and their hard-core Yippie cohorts would actually stir up bloodshed. So when the *Seed* called for demonstrators not to come to Chicago, I sent an upset telegram in reply. I thought the *Seed*'s change of mind was more because of a dislike of Abbie's and Jerry's personalities and media tactics than any actual perceived danger to demonstrators coming to Lincoln and Grant parks.

The Fugs' Tompkins Square Park Concert

It was our annual concert in the park. We had a new tune, which we performed with straw hats and canes and delivered in a kind of Al Jolson watery-mouthed vocal, "Up Against the Wall, Motherfucker" (borrowed from a famous Amiri Baraka poem). The tune also satirized the group called the Motherfuckers, whose leaflets I'd often printed gratis at Peace Eye, whose logo on their publications was UAW/MF. A young man named David Peel was in the audience. I don't know for sure, but soon he was singing a song with a similar title, and it helped make him famous on an album for Elektra, later that very year, *Have a Marijuana.* Later Peel approached me to ask if he could put a medley of Fugs tunes on a recording or in his act. Didn't say yes, didn't say no. I wanted to hear first what he came up with.

Getting Ready for Chicago

The Fugs were in California during the several weeks leading to the Chicago demonstrations. The cab from LAX to the Tropicana Motel on Santa Monica Boulevard in those days cost $7.30.

The Fugs played Friday and Saturday, August 15 and 16, at the Bank in nearby Torrance, California. It was one of the few times I performed barefoot. I was continuing my experiments in rinsing my Puritan heritage out of me by being the first performer on Warner/Reprise to dance barefoot. I did this during "Kill for Peace," wearing gold-flecked toenail polish, which Miriam had graciously painted on just before I got on the plane.

The Fugs in Torrance, California, just before the 1968 Democratic National Convention.

Thursday, August 22

Early in the morning on August 22 two teenage hippies near Lincoln Park in Chicago (where we planned the following week to hold our Festival of Life) were stopped by the police. One was a Native American from South Dakota named Dean Johnson. Police officers said he pulled a gun, so they killed him with three shots.

It was on my mind when I arrived in Chicago from LA later that day to work on whatever music we could get together for the Festival. The Fugs had remained behind in Los Angeles while I looked for a safe place for them to stay. I checked into the Lincoln Hotel, located just off Lincoln Park. Miriam and Deirdre would soon fly to Chicago to join me.

Saturday, August 24

That afternoon there was a big planning meeting at the Free Theater at
1848 Wells near Lincoln Park. I learned that the police, not only were not
going to allow protesters to camp out in the Park, but they also were going
to toss people out at 11:00 PM.

The issue was, what to do? Abbie predicted "fifty or sixty people in a
band going out from the park to loot and pillage if they close it up at 11." I
didn't dig the L and P words, so I exploded, "I'm sick and tired of hearing
people talk like that. I don't want some kid who hasn't been through it all
and doesn't know what it's all about going to get his head busted. You're urging people to go out and get killed for nothing. Man, that's like murdering
people." We decided not to urge people to sleep in the park overnight,
though clearly that what thousands were going to try to do.

After Saturday afternoon's meeting wherever Miriam, Didi, and I went
in Chicago we were followed by two plainclothes detectives. All the so-
called demonstration leaders had surveillance teams. At the time I didn't
think much of it. I'm more angry about it now, decades later, than then. That
night Miriam, Didi, and I walked from the Hotel Lincoln to a Mexican
restaurant while the police followed us, then waited outside to save Western
civilization.

Sunday, August 25: The Festival of Life

I'd found a safe place for The Fugs to stay during the Chicago demonstrations, but one of them phoned from his room at the Tropicana in LA. They
were worried about violence in Chicago. He said they'd seen a report on
TV that Country Joe had been punched out in a motel in Chicago by a
member of a conservative Democratic delegation. They were hesitant to
come.

I was upset, but I let them off the hook. Everybody flew back to New
York, except Tuli Kupferberg, who showed up for the fun in Chicago.

Sunday was also the "Day of the Honey." Abbie introduced me to a guy
who was dipping into jars of hash-oiled honey with a spoon, which he
would swirl on our tongues. It was very, very, very powerful, and shortly after getting my mouth of honey, I looked up through the tear-gas sonata of

Lincoln Park, and the Universe from the edge of the Lake up across the wide Midwest sky was made up of pulsing, writhing mountains and vistas of spinach. It was literally that: spinach! Cooked spinach. It was as if I had awakened in one of my Kansas City aunts' Thanksgiving dinner bowls!

I was not alone. Tuli had taken a tongue of the honey and immediately passed out. Paul Krassner was on his knees nearby holding on to the grass very tightly; he later wrote, "so that I wouldn't fall up."

I found my police surveillance team, told them I wasn't feeling well (I did not mention the universal sea of Ultimate Spinach in which we were standing), and the officers helped me back to the Hotel Lincoln, where Miriam, just as she had done during my psilocybin trip with Charles Olson in Gloucester almost two years in the past, talked and soothed me back into normalcy.

That night the police drove out those who were trying to camp in Lincoln Park. I walked about with Allen Ginsberg, who was singing long "Oms," singing along with him as we tried to lead the young people out of the park around the deadline of 11:00. Police used tear gas and billy clubs to disperse the campers.

The next day when Miriam and I tried to take Deirdre from the Hotel Lincoln across Lincoln Park to the zoo, the tear gas still lingered in the grass, and Deirdre, being very short, wept with the pain of it.

In our trip to the Lincoln Park zoo our plainclothes detectives kept on following us. That afternoon I went with Miriam and Didi to the sporting goods section at Marshall Field department store at North State Street at Randolph, where I was trying on football helmets. I wanted one with a face guard in case my police escort should wax face-bashy. I was wearing a football helmet when a tall plainclothes guy approached. He said, "Mr. Sanders, we've been following you for twelve hours, and the next shift is scheduled to take our place. I've called them. They'll be here in a few minutes. If we miss them, it could be another six hours before we're relieved."

I chuckled and told him we'd wait. Early in the evening I went back into Lincoln Park, and noticed, with a shudder, that my police escorts were lifting billy clubs out of their unmarked car.

That night when the Yippies tried to march on the Loop from Lincoln Park, a line of army troops stopped them after a few blocks with an armored vehicle wrapped in barbed wire. Barricades were built in Lincoln Park to defend the right to sleep there. At 12:30 AM the police clubbed and attacked the barricades.

Famous French writer Jean Genet was in the park! He had no visa and had sneaked in from Canada. Allen Ginsberg was acting as his interpreter. Genet had an assignment for *Esquire* magazine (along with Ginsberg, William Burroughs, and Terry Southern) to cover the convention. All four had press passes to attend.

It was just about time for the invasion of the fuzz. Tonight they marched behind a street sweeper truck whose water tanks apparently had been converted to hold tear gas! I'll never forget the sight of Jean Genet, dressed in leather, peering into the paranoid darkness of the park just before the tear-gas truck began spraying. He strode into the darkness and was gassed himself.

Allen and I left the park to return to the Hotel Lincoln, but there were snout-nozzled cops there lobbing tear-gas grenades that plomfed near our feet. We crouched down and dashed through the hostile molecules, heads low, knees high, as if we were halfbacks on a junior high football team, toward the lobby.

Tuesday, August 27

At dawn on August 27 Ginsberg came back to the park, singing various mantrams for several hours until his voice became hoarse and whispery. As a result Allen was the only bard in the history of Western civilization to have over-ommed, that is, he'd uttered the seed syllable "Om" for so many hours trying to quell the violence that he peace-pained his voice and was omming, at the end, like Froggie the Gremlin.

That night the protesters threw a sixtieth Unbirthday Party for Lyndon Johnson at the packed Chicago Coliseum. Six thousand people were there while Phil Ochs sang "I Ain't Marchin' Anymore." A guy burned his Draft card, and then in one amazing sequence of seconds there was a sudden poof-up of maybe a hundred blazing Draft cards pointillistically patterning the Coliseum audience.

Ginsberg's voice had not yet returned from his many hours of over-omming to quell the violence, so he passed me a note to read to the audience: "Introduce me as Prague King of May—Ed—in my turn, you explain

I lost my voice chanting Aum in park—so please you read my piece—then I'll do 3 Minutes of Silence Mind consciousness & belly breathing."

Wednesday, August 28

That afternoon Daley allowed a single rally at the bandshell in Grant Park sponsored by the Mobilization (one of the sponsoring groups in Chicago, whose formal name was National Mobilization Committee to End the War in Vietnam). Around 10,000 to 15,000 showed up. About 4:30 Dave Dellinger addressed the crowd through a portable bullhorn to announce a nonviolent march to the Democratic Convention, four and a half miles from Grant Park.

Grant Park is connected to downtown via a series of bridges across railroad tracks to the west. Lines of soldiers prevented the marchers from leaving over any of the bridges, and many of us sat down in front of the troops while U.S. Army helicopters circled overhead.

It was very scary. There were fixed bayonets and jeeps with barbed-wire Hippie-sweeping screens, plus the *whoppa whoppa* of helicopters mixing with the songs Phil Ochs sang to calm us: "We're the cops of the world, boys, / We're the cops of the world." And then, through a bullhorn someone was holding to his face, Ochs sang "Outside of a Small Circle of Friends."

Then Allen Ginsberg, still hoarse from singing seed syllables in the rings of violence, chanted "The Grey Monk" by William Blake through the bullhorn. All of us who were sitting and waiting were chatty and restless, yet by the time he chanted (from memory) the final verses of the poem, all grew silent except the ghastly helicopters:

Thy Father drew his sword in the North,
With his thousands strong he marched forth;
Thy Brother has arm'd himself in Steel
To avenge the wrongs thy Children feel.
But vain the Sword & vain the Bow,
They never can work War's overthrow.
The Hermit's Prayer & the Widow's tear
Alone can free the World from fear.
For a Tear is an Intellectual Thing,

And a Sigh is the Sword of an Angel King
And the bitter groan of the Martyr's woe
Is an Arrow from the Almightie's Bow.
The hand of Vengeance found the Bed
To which the Purple Tyrant Fled;
The iron hand crush'd the Tyrant's head
And became a Tyrant in his stead.

A few of us had pushed fresh daisies into the rifle barrels at the Pentagon just ten months ago. But now, even though I again had fresh white flowers, I knew that this was a different type of event and that I would likely have been bayonetted and shot pushing petal in metal. Finally, after hours of negotiations, the protesters found a way of getting out of Grant Park, and they surged across a bridge and gathered in front of the Hilton on Michigan Avenue at Balbo.

In the lobby where the Democrats were preparing to go to the convention hall four miles away, soldiers with helmets and guns marched past the plush divans and the potted trees. Then, without warning, a throng of police charged the demonstrators at 7:56, smashing, macing, beating, apparently to clear the avenue.

Jeeps with machine guns mounted to them arrived at the Hilton. "Wahoo! Wahoo!" an officer on a three-wheeled motorcycle shouted as he mashed into the crowd, sounding like the bomb-riding cowboy at the end of *Dr. Strangelove.*

Thus began hours of bloodshed. In the streets outside the Hilton and Convention Center and in the surgery-room glare of the television lights, thousands took up the chant "The Whole World Is Watching. The Whole World Is Watching."

Volunteers for Senator Eugene McCarthy set up a first aid station on the Hilton's fifteenth floor at his suite. They gave up their passes to get the injured to the rooms. Hubert Humphrey was on the twenty-fifth floor. An aide opened a window and complained of tear gas.

On the nominating floor four miles from the Hilton CBS-TV's Dan Rather gave a live report, "A security man just slugged me in the stomach," to which Walter Cronkite, the dean of American broadcast journalists, replied, "I think we've got a bunch of thugs here, Dan."

Inside the convention that horrible night Senator George McGovern was a last-minute peace candidate after McCarthy refused to lead a floor fight against Humphrey. Senator Abraham Ribicoff was giving his nominating speech: "With George McGovern," said Ribicoff, "we wouldn't have Gestapo tactics on the streets of Chicago."

Mayor Richard Daley, his face reddened with malevolence, shouted, "Fuck you, you Jew son of a bitch! You lousy motherfucker, go home!"

Daley was seated in the front. Ribicoff looked down at Red Face and said, "How hard it is to hear the truth."

Allen Ginsberg leaped to his feet in the balcony and began shouting, "OMMMMM" for about five minutes. Meanwhile outside in the television lights, the teargassed, terrified, and angry crowd continued its own version of ommmmm, chanting, "The Whole World Is Watching! The Whole World Is Watching!"

The next day, Miriam, I, and Deirdre flew from Chicago back home, where I immediately began plans for the release of our new album.

The Two Albums for 1968

We tried to make up for lost time with two albums in 1968—*Tenderness Junction* early in the year, and now, our greatest production, in early September, *It Crawled into My Hand, Honest*, just in time for our fall tour to Germany and to London.

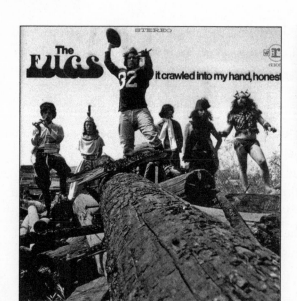

Tenderness Junction. Photos by Richard Avedon.

The cover of *It Crawled into My Hand, Honest*.

My liner notes for *It Crawled into My Hand, Honest.*

Side A

Crystal Liaison: Ed Sanders, Ken Weaver, Ken Pine (3:11)

Ramses II Is Dead, My Love: Ed Sanders (2:50)

Burial Waltz: Ed Sanders (2:27)

Wide, Wide River: Lionel Goldbart, Ken Weaver (2:53)

Life Is Strange: Tuli Kupferberg (2:41)

Johnny Pissoff Meets the Red Angel: Ed Sanders (4:33)

Side B

Marijuana: Bob Dorough, Ed Sanders, Tuli Kupferberg (1:36)

Leprechaun: Ken Weaver (:11)

When the Mode of the Music Changes: Tuli Kupferberg (3:55)

Whimpers from the Jello: Ed Sanders (:21)

The Divine Toe, Pt. 1: Ed Sanders (:37)

We're Both Dead Now, Alice: Ed Sanders, Ken Weaver (:15)

Life Is Funny: Tuli Kupferberg (:14)

Grope Need, Pt. 1: Tuli Kupferberg, Visited by the Ghost of Plotinus/
  More Grope Need (:38)

Robinson Crusoe: Ken Weaver (:17)

Claude Pelieu and J. J. Lebel Discuss the Early Verlaine Bread Crusts:
  Ed Sanders (4:27)

The National Haiku Contest: Ed Sanders, Ken Weaver (:24)

The Divine Toe, Pt. 2: Ed Sanders (:47)

Irene: Ed Sanders (1:11)

For backup harmonies, we used some fine singers who had worked as Harry Belafonte's harmonists. You can hear them, say, on "Wide, Wide River" and "When the Mode of the Music Changes."

Ed Sanders: Vocals
Tuli Kupferberg: Vocals
Ken Weaver: Drums, vocals
Ken Pine: Guitar
Charles Larkey: Bass
Bob Mason: Drums
Engineer and music talent coordinator: Richard Alderson
Recorded at Impact Sound, New York City
Vocal arrangements (except "Wide, Wide River," "Johnny Pissoff,"
and "Life Is Strange") by Doug Franklin
"When the Mode of the Music Changes" arranged by Warren Smith,
Ken Pine, Dan Kootch, Ed Sanders
"Burial Waltz" arranged and conducted by Warren Smith
"The Divine Toe (Parts 1 and 2)" arranged by Arthur Jenkins
"Claude Pelieu and J. J. Lebel Discuss the Early Verlaine Bread Crusts"
arranged and conducted by Randy Kay
"Ramses II Is Dead, My Love," arranged by Al Schactman
"Johnny Pissoff Meets the Red Angel," "Life Is Strange," and "Marijuana"
vocals and instrumentals arranged by Bob Dorough
"Crystal Liaison" arranged by Ken Pine, Dan Kootch, Richard Alderson,
Warren Smith
Thanks to the Fugs Chorale: Leslie Dorsey, James Jarvis, Kenneth Bates,
Jennifer Brown, Marlys Trunkhill, Barbara Calabria, Bob Dorough,
Bob Hanson

An Apartment for Doc Humes

Late that summer I located an apartment on Ninth Street for legendary novelist H. L. "Doc" Humes, one of the founders of the *Paris Review*, around the corner from Peace Eye. A few of us paid the rent. The building was owned by Sam Scime, the landlord for Peace Eye. (Doc Humes was known for his generosity, so it was time to help him. Back around 1960 he had given around six months rent money to future Fugs producer/engineer Richard Alderson to rent a loft on Sixth Avenue.)

Of course, it was an era of 'noia, and fear of the government. Part of it was caused by the cosmic revelations of acid and psychedelics. But that was only a part of the Era of Fear: the revelations about the CIA; the suspicion it had killed JFK; the bugging of my home phone. It was in this context of 'noia that Doc Humes began to hang out at the Peace Eye Bookstore. I'd been friends with Doc through most of the '60s. It was through him I first met Harry Smith, who produced the first Fugs album.

He had the 'NOIA. He thought there was a huge and benevolent network of computer scientists who ran a network called FIDO. He would stand in Peace Eye up against the bookcases and talk in a low voice, certain that FIDO satellite-based monitoring equipment was picking up his words. He also thought the CIA was spreading low-grade infections in the counterculture. He told me he thought a friend of his was a CIA officer who had tried to strangle Sirhan Sirhan in the Ambassador kitchen after Kennedy was shot. Doc was very magnetic, and young people would come into Peace Eye to hear him talk about FIDO and the Great Fear.

A Yippie Pot-Mailing Caper

I drew Doc Humes into a clandestine Yippie project that September. It involved the mailing out of thousands of rolled joints, along with a Yippie flier, to a random list of New Yorkers.

My responsibility was around five hundred joints. We were given envelopes with stamps and addresses. I recruited Doc Humes and a volunteer named DAK. All of us wore rubber gloves as we rolled the joints and stuffed them into the envelopes, along with the Yippie salute, sitting in the Secret Location studio (where once I had shot my underground films) I still rented on Avenue A.

Floor of the Secret Location in 1968 during the time we mailed the Yippie joints.
Photo by Ed Sanders.

On *Firing Line* with Kerouac, September 3

I appeared on William Buckley's television show *Firing Line* with Jack Kerouac and sociologist Lewis Yablonsky, author of a book called *The Hippie Trip*. I was in the elevator going up to the studio when a guy came aboard wearing a checked sports coat with two friends. I didn't recognize him at once. All of sudden he said, "You look like Ginsberg, you talk like Ginsberg, and you write like Ginsberg."

I had spoken with Allen Ginsberg before the show and agreed not to respond to any Kerouacean hostility. He was one of my heroes whose novels, especially *Big Sur*, *Dharma Bums*, and *The Subterraneans*, had been like religious texts when I was in college.

I knew he'd swung to the right, as they say, and had supported Buckley's run for mayor of New York City. One of the first things Allen Ginsberg had told me when I first met him in person in early '64 was that Jack couldn't handle fame.

He'd ridden to New York from Lowell with two pals, Joe Chaput and Paul Bourgeois. They'd had a couple of drinks on arriving in the city, then checked into the Delmonico Hotel. William Burroughs was also at the Delmonico, finishing his piece on the Chicago riots for *Esquire*. At the Delmonico Jack had chugged and smoked pot into the zonk mode. Burroughs urged him not to go to the show.

The audience for the September 3 *Firing Line* comprised Allen Ginsberg, plus students from Bernard Baruch College, Columbia University, and Hofstra University. The film that aired lasted fifty-two minutes.

Kerouac wasn't very friendly. His face was very florid, and his forehead vein popped out when he stroked above his nose with a hand that held a Coronella-sized cigar. I told him before the show that I respected his writing too much and that I wasn't going to fight with him on camera, even though my years steeped in controversy as a poet, publisher, and Fug had trained me well to give back razory raillery.

During the show I was very tempted to mention his daughter Jan, who'd come to many Fugs shows. I remembered how the owner of the Astor Place Playhouse had come on Jan and a Fugs guitarist making it on the drum riser one midnight.

I remembered how Kerouac would call me now and then and recite little poems, which I would write down. I remembered other things that Peter

Orlovsky told me in Peace Eye after Kerouac visited Allen's pad just up the street at 408 East Tenth, but why tell all just because Tell tells you to tell? So I mostly kept silent in front of the author of *Mexico City Blues*, as the filming began and he tried to jab at me.

William Buckley: Our topic tonight is the Hippies, the understanding of which we must, I guess, acquire or die painfully. We certainly should make considerable progress in the next hour because we have a professional student of hippies and also someone who is said to have started the whole Beat Generation business, and finally a hippie type who can correct us, ever so gently please, if we're wrong.

Mr. Lewis Yablonsky is a sociologist who studied at Rutgers and took his doctorate at New York University and teaches at San Fernando State College in California, where he is chairman of his department. His first book, which focused on teenage gang life and drug addiction, prepared him for his magnum opus, which is called *The Hippie Trip: A Firsthand Account of the Beliefs and Behavior of Hippies in America*.

Mr. Jack Kerouac over here became famous [the camera pans on Kerouac, his eyes closed, his right hand holding a small cigar and pushed against his face] when his book *On the Road* was published. It seemed to be preaching a life of disengagement, making a virtue out of restlessness. The irony is that when the book was belatedly published in 1958, seven years after it was written, Mr. Kerouac had fought his way out of the Beat Generation, and is now not exactly orthodox, at least a regular practicing novelist, whose thirteenth book, *The Vanity of Duluoz*, is widely regarded as his best.

Mr. Ed Sanders is a musician, a poet, and a polemicist. He is one of The Fugs, a widely patronized combo. He has published four books of poetry and has vigorously preached pacifism for a number of years. I'd like to begin by asking Mr. Sanders if we have serious terminological problems. Are you a hippie, Mr. Sanders, and if not, wherein not?

[I was attired in a white, ruffle-fronted shirt, fresh new black jeans, and white boots, and I was wearing a recent birthday present from Miriam on my thumb, my silver "runic thumb ring," adorned with runes, which I played with during the program.]

Sanders: Well, I'm not exactly a hippie. I have certain sentiments toward that, quote, hippie movement, unquote. I would say that I differ from hippies in that I would have a more radical political solution to the problems of this part of the century. And I have my roots more strongly in, say, the classical tradition and in poetry and literature rather than in dope and street sex.

[I was presenting my bifurcated roots: my studies in Greek, Latin, and modern poetry, versus my experiences in the wilder reaches of the counterculture.]

Kerouac [breaking in]: And you published that magazine called what?

Sanders: Called *Gutter Expletive/ A Magazine of the Arts.*

[Round of laughter from audience]

[I should have blurted out the real title: *Fuck You/ A Magazine of the Arts.*]

Buckley: Do I understand from this, that we are supposed to make the inference that the hippies don't have a highly developed political schedule, a highly developed political ideology.

Sanders: The problem with the term like "hippie" is that they have a definition foisted upon it by the media, and that the word "hippie" has been limited by the necessities of the type of journalists that promote it. You can't rely on the name "hippie" to include a human being, everything about a particular human being. It's a bad term, I think, because it has no meaning; you might think of hippopotamus. It has no other connection, spiritual or emotional, like, say, the Beat Generation title has. It has other implications. The word hippie, you immediately think of—you don't have any good connections....

Lewis Yablonsky [breaking in]: I kind of disagree with that. I spent last year traveling around the country to various communes, to various—Haight Ashbury, the Lower East Side, various city scenes—and there was an identifiable—define a hippie as generally a young person: in several categories. There's kind of a priestly type; I would include Allen Ginsberg and Timothy Leary, and individuals like that in that category. People searching for some loving solutions to society's ills, trying to tune into the cosmos, whatever that means, we can explore that. Generally using psychedelic drugs.

[Kerouac flashes thumbs down sign at the phrase "psychedelic drugs."]

And then there's a whole cadre of individuals [Kerouac breaks in with a short blurt, "Cadré."] whom I term novices, who are attempting to achieve a certain transcendental state. Then there are teeny bopper kids who are sort of hanging on, and there are some ancient folks like Kerouac here who . . .

Kerouac: What do you mean ancient?

Yablonsky [to Kerouac]: Why couldn't you have kept quiet while I was talking? I'll keep quiet while you talk.

Kerouac: You said cadres; it's cadrés,

Yablonsky [a bit mockingly]: I apologize for my semantics.

Kerouac: And I showed my thumbs down to Ginsberg over there in the back.

[Kerouac flashes thumbs down sign.]

Yablonsky: He's a nice fellow.

Kerouac: We'll throw him to the lions.

William Buckley: Well, what about it, Mr. Kerouac? You're exercised about something, by something. . . .

Kerouac: Restless, it's true. You had the right word, restless.

Buckley: What is it that in your judgement distinguishes the hippie? . . .

Kerouac [breaking into Buckley's sentence]: Nothing.

Buckley: What distinguishes the hippie movement from simply an orthodox radical, say, Adamite movement?

Kerouac: Adamite? Adam and Eve?

Buckley: Now, Jack Kerouac, what I wanted to ask is this: To what extent do you believe that the Beat Generation is related to the hippies? What do they have in common? Was this an evolution from one to the other?

Kerouac: The older ones. I'm forty-six years old. These kids are eighteen. It's the same movement. It's apparently some kind of Dionysian movement, in late civilization, in which I did not intend, any more than I suppose Dionysus did, or whatever his name was. Although I'm not Dionysus [unclear], I should have been.

Buckley: That's a point.

Kerouac: It's just a movement which is supposed to be licentious, but it isn't really.

Buckley: Well, licentious in what respect?

Kerouac: The hippies are good kids. They're better than the Beats. The Beats, Ginsberg and I, we're all in our forties. He started this, and the kids took it up, and everything, but hoodlums and communists jumped on our backs.

Buckley: Un-huh.

Kerouac: Well, on my back, not his [waves with cigar toward Ginsberg, in the audience], Ferlinghetti jumped on my back and turned the idea that I had that the Beat Generation was a generation of beatitude and pleasure in life and tenderness, but they called it in the papers the Beat Mutiny and Beat Insurrection, words I never used. Being a Catholic, I believe in order, tenderness, and piety.

Buckley: Well, then, your point was that a movement which you conceived as relatively pure has become ideologized and misanthropic and generally objectionable.

Kerouac: A movement that was considered what?

Buckley: Pure.

Kerouac: It was, in my heart.

Buckley: What about that Mr. Yablonsky? Do you see that as having happened somewhere between the Beats and the hippies.

Yablonsky: I thing there's in early '67 going back to around '64 or '65, there were a lot of people trying to return to sort an Indian-style of life, or to relate to the land differently, [Kerouac breaks in with a sotto voce "ya-oo." Buckley shushes him.] trying to love each other, to communicate and be more open with each other, and I think recently it has taken a turn in a violent direction. A lot of the responsibility, I think, is due to drugs like methedrine and amphetamines. And perhaps the overuse, it's been around quite a while now, of drugs like LSD....

Kerouac: How about herring?

Buckley: What is herring? Is that a kind of drug?

Sanders: Cherry Herring.

[Big laughter]

Yablonsky: Kerouac is still on alcohol. There are other drugs now.

Buckley: What about it, Mr. Sanders, is that out of tone?

Sanders: You mention misanthropic and objectionable. Many of the so-called misanthropic elements of this generation are due to the war, in that you have a surly generation of draft eligible but literate and articulate people who are confronted with the hideous probability of having to go to an Asian land war.

So they have to go to war, and they're faced with this looming, gloomy future, [A hissing sound here, probably from Kerouac] and that rather than die in Vietnam, they'd rather prepare themselves to articulate a lifestyle in the streets and in the open that really reflects something they really want to do, rather than this other thing they have to do later on which they don't believe in, but they will do, because push comes to shove most kids go to war.

Buckley: It doesn't account, for instance, for the restlessness in, say, Paris, where they don't have that particular problem.

Sanders: That's the Up Against the Wall...

[This segment ended, after which Kerouac's chair fell off the studio riser, and it was obvious he was stumbly-drunk. The producer wanted to substitute Allen Ginsberg, who was in the audience, for Kerouac, but we all protested and on it went.]

William Buckley: Mr. Sanders, I'm interested in trying to pin this point down, because a lot of us heard that the restlessness of so much of American youth which has contributed to the growth of the hippie movement has to do with the trauma of Vietnam, but then all of a sudden a while ago in France it seemed like the entire student population exploded even though that particular provocation was singularly and conspicuously absent, France having been officially very pro–North Vietnam, very anti-America. How do you account for that, and has it caused you to perhaps to look into more generic sources?...

[I had read that Madame de Gaulle, wife of Charles de Gaulle, had taken a strong hand in controlling and censoring French culture following the May '68 uprising.]

Sanders: I think it's the nefarious occurrence in French civilization of Madame de Gaulle.

Buckley: Madame de Gaulle?

Sanders: Because she has exercised a noxious influence on French television, sitting up and personally censoring it....

[Outbreak of laughter]

No, that's absolutely true, and I think that when you have a type of obnoxious matriarchy that's evident in France, plus an encrusted, boring, boorish university structure, and the old man himself, there's a huge structure there to revolt against.

Buckley: Madame de Gaulle is roughly equal to Vietnam.

Sanders: She's Madame Nhu.

Buckley: Professor Yablonsky, what would you say if a student of yours told you that?

Yablonsky: I think in the United States, the hippies, with all the difficulties of defining them, come from the middle/upper social economic situations. These are generally people who have tasted the best that American society seems to have to offer, they have access to all the goodies, and they're turned off by it, and they feel it's kind of a plastic society, there's no room for political change. I'm talking about the pure hippie. A pure hippie isn't particularly involved in politics, he retreats from that, he's withdrawn from it, and he's involved in Cosmic Consciousness. There is an experience one seems to get under LSD, that a lot of people talk about, as putting them in touch with all things, with all people. There's a kind of extremist effort at love which seems to dominate the hippie scene, a retreat from politics.

Buckley: Is there a causal relation between their adopting these attitudes and the Vietnam War. Or do you reject the Vietnam War as the proximate cause of the movement?

Yablonsky: I think the Vietnam War is part of it.

Buckley: If we had had no Vietnam War, we might have had the identical thing, is that your point?

Yablonsky: I think there's no single cause for a particular movement. I think part of it may have been the assassination of JFK. I think that people on the left felt that through the establishment, through political devices, the society could move in other directions.

Buckley: In what direction was it moving in 1963 that was pleasing to them?

Yablonsky: There was a movement toward greater welfare programs; resolving in some way the civil rights issues. There seemed to be some hope, and then this seemed to be snapped off, and a lot of kids who went to Mississippi...

Buckley: It's precisely the movement that didn't get passed in 1961, '62 and '63, the time you just enumerated, were passed in '64, '65 and '66. So it seems there was almost a negative correlation between the civil rights legislation and welfare passages and the growth of the movement.

Yablonsky: I think you can cross-compare the limited JFK administration and the rather lengthy LBJ administration. I think the LBJ situation has been going through the motions of doing something. I feel and a lot of people have told me this, in the country.

There seemed to be a bit of a revival with Bobby Kennedy, and to some extent the McCarthy involvement. I think a lot of people are turned off from the political establishment, because they don't see any hope for changing it. They use terms like "plastic," and more severe words about it; they are disengaged; they're uncommitted to it.

Buckley: What about it, Mr. Kerouac, does that make sense to you?

Kerouac: I lost the entire train of thought.

[Kerouac is red-faced, with his right fist pushed up against his face.]

Buckley: Well, the train of thought has to do with whether in the last few years people have ceased to look at the political process as possible in terms of bringing on the kind of world we want to live in, and maybe that has nothing to do with the assassination of Kennedy, and that kind of thing....

Kerouac: No, that was an accident. I refer back to Count Leo Tolstoy, who wrote *War and Peace*, who said that at one time the hourglass, that's the sand that's coming down from one top of the hour glass onto the other, and that will be the end of war. I think that war will be over fairly soon, although I don't know for sure. [Kerouac huffs.] That's what Tolstoy said. The guy who taught _____, and Henry David Thoreau.

Buckley: Taught them a lot of foolish things.

Kerouac: I didn't get the full context of your question.

Buckley: Well, the full context of the question is, are a significant number of Americans precisely [amazed?] when we enunciated the Great Society?...

Kerouac: Oh, Great Society!

Buckley: I.e., the society that was actually going to introduce politics.... Are they disillusioned, and does this have to do with the growth of the hippie movement?

Kerouac: I think the Vietnamese war is nothing but a plot between the North Vietnamese and the South Vietnamese, who are cousins, to get jeeps from the country.

[Big laughter from the audience, applause from me]

Buckley: They're not very good plotters, are they?

Kerouac: But they got a lot of jeeps! [Another round of laughter] I think they're pulling the wool over our eyes. We're American lambs.

Buckley: They turned out to be more expensive than Sears Roebuck jeeps.

Kerouac: That's what I really think there. As for the Russian takeover of Czechoslovakia, that showed the world what they're like, what the Communists are really like; they're really fascists.

Buckley: Mr. Sanders. [I was holding up my hand.]

Sanders: It was a terrible thing. If I were in Czechoslovakia, a student in Czechoslovakia, I would be putting out an underground newspaper, and doing my best...

Kerouac: Called what?

Sanders: *Gutter Expletive/ A Magazine of the Arts.*

[Lots of laughter, including from Kerouac, who guffaws, stamping his foot]

Buckley: Since you aren't in Czechoslovakia, Mr. Sanders, what do you think it's appropriate to do in the United States?

Sanders: During the presidential campaign?

Buckley: By way of protest against the Czechoslovakian situation?

Sanders: Well, I recommend sit-ins in front of the Russian mission. ...

Kerouac: What for?

Sanders: To vigorously and more forcefully yet nonviolently to witness against it. I would advocate writing articles, and I would advocate maybe going to Czechoslovakia. The Fugs are going to Europe in a couple of weeks.

Kerouac [breaking in]: Bring your carbines?

Sanders: We are going to the Essen Song Festival in Germany, and we may just try to freak across the border into Czechoslovakia to visit Kafka's birthplace. So we may have a homage to Kafka with our band.

Buckley: Do you draw any generalities on the basis of the behavior of the Soviet Union which instruct you in assessing other political situations?

Sanders: Yeah, like Mayor Daley in Chicago.

Buckley: What are those?

Sanders: Well, those are when you attempt to essentially get together to press a point about a war, about a freedom, or freedom of journalism; when you're confronted by people like the Soviet leaders and like the leaders in Chicago, namely Mayor Daley and Mr. Stahl and Mr. Bougher of the Chicago municipal office, that you're confronted with essentially the same position, you're not allowed, you're clubbed, you're maced, you're gassed, you're freaked, zapped, pushed over. If you're an old lady you're thrown through a plate glass window; if you're a cripple, you're thrown against a streetlight; if you're a peaceful, long-haired, loving protester, you're smashed and knocked down; if you're a cameraman, you're bricked, and your camera is destroyed, and your blood is splattered all over you. It's a nefarious thing, and there's all kinds of correlations. And the lesson you would draw, would be to prepare yourself, in the sense of, if you're nonviolent as I am, and if you believe in pacifism, you would attempt to create a body of love and life, so that that thing can't happen, that there will be so many loving people there, that you *will* have a Festival of Life and all its attributes, and you can do that by praying together, by loving together. [I point over to Ginsberg in the audience.] Allen was singing Om in the streets, which is the Hindu benevolent word. By getting together and creating love, I think it's a great force, at least in allowing you to demonstrate in the United States against Daley. You know, it's Al Capone.

Buckley: Yeah.

Kerouac [looking over at Ed Sanders]: Beware of false prophets, who come among you dressed in sheep's clothing, and underneath they are ravening wolves.

Sanders: Who's that?

[End of second segment]

Buckley: Mr. Yablonsky, I would like to ask you this, because you have studied the whole hippie mentality. I was in Chicago, and so were a lot of people who would not really have recognized what happened on the basis of Mr. Sanders' description. But I do think that Mr. Sanders means it; I think that he really thinks the cops were looking for old ladies and gentle people to savage. And I think that the fact he thinks it is interesting. I would like to hear your analysis that they seem to feel that it is compulsive to believe a Daley, who was after all is a hero of John F. Kennedy and Bobby Kennedy, whom you associate with the best of the aspirations of the youth, how come they feel this way, what is it in their creed that requires? ...

Yablonsky: First of all, I wouldn't hook Daley in with JFK. He's a big city boss. I just observed you and others on television in Chicago.

Buckley: Nothing bellicose about me. ...

Yablonsky: I think that if the people were involved, the hippies, the Yippies, had been permitted to sort of do their thing, and to chant, and to have a peaceful march ...

Buckley: Their thing involved the assassination of a few Democrats, wouldn't it?

Sanders: Absolutely not!

Yablonsky: I think there were around maybe ten thousand young people who would have sung peace songs in the park. I think there was apparently a lot of frustration of their efforts to do something. . . .

Buckley: Wait a minute. You know Tom Hayden. You know Rennie Davis. You know these characters. Everybody here knows them. And we know these are not sweet little old flower children. They went there intending to make a scientific, ideological point, which is to engage the police in violence in order . . .

Sanders [breaking in]: Not at . . .

Buckley: Be right with you. In order to try to produce a wave of sympathy which they succeeded and they are absolutely elated; it would have been impossible for the police to withdraw in such as a way to satisfy them, because the only way they could have been satisfied is by forceable encounter.

Yablonsky: You asked me about the hippies and the Yippies, and what they would have done. I tend to agree with you that there were other segments of the population, possibly including the Blackstone Rangers, and other groups who were prepared to stir something up if it didn't happen, but I think there was such an overreaction, such a trigger-finger kind of situation, that these kids began to open the thing up, and before anything could get going, there was a lot of smashing. And then the others moved in. I think there would have been kind of a love-in type of scene in Chicago by a large segment of the young people.

Buckley: If you could have separated the two.

[I'm holding up my hand to speak.]

Sanders: They were very clearly were separated. There were two movements operating in Chicago. The Yippies wanted Lincoln Park, which is many miles away from the Amphitheater, and is many miles away from the Hilton. They wanted to have a Festival of Life with rock music in the park, with theater classes, with guerrilla theater, with like various poets and people coming together for a Festival of Life.

Buckley: What is guerrilla theater?

Sanders: Guerrilla theater is a bunch of people who don't need props and who don't need a regular stage.

Kerouac: Crucified chickens?

Sanders: No, that's not guerrilla theater. But guerrilla theater just need themselves, and their own body makeup, and a few props like that. Anyway, we wanted Lincoln Park, and to use the beach to swim and sleep at. And the

Chicago authorities continually thwarted us throughout a whole six months of negotiations, refusing at any point to allow any demonstrations, so they literally drove Allen, Jean Genet, William Burroughs, and even Clive Barnes of the *New York Times*—driven out of the park at night by tear gas.

Voice [maybe Kerouac's]: Good.

[Laughter]

Sanders: So all these people were forced into the streets, with no place to go, except for the benevolence of a couple of churches, to sleep. There was a bus strike in Chicago, there was a cab strike, and there was no live TV coverage of anything, so they were forced into the street. The police attacked, pushed, pulled, maimed; it's really what happened. Now the other Movement was the Mobilization movement—they wanted to march upon the Amphitheater [where the Democratic Convention was being held]. And that's Rennie Davis, and that's Tom Hayden, but also Dave Dellinger, who's an avowed pacifist, and benevolent leader of some standing. And they wanted to have a peaceful march on the Amphitheater, split up into groups, and those who wanted to march on would march on, and those who wanted to sit down would sit down. But there was never any violent confrontation planned.

And when the Chicago people thwarted and frustrated constantly anybody's attempts to have peaceful demonstrations, naturally frustration, it mounted. But the amount of brick throwing was so negligible compared to the number of peaceful people there for peaceful purpose, namely, to protest with their loving bodies what was going down at the alcoholic Amphitheater.

Buckley: What were you saying, Mr. Kerouac?

Kerouac: I said there are people who make a rule of creating chaos so that once the chaos is under way, they can then be elected as the people who take care of the chaos.

Buckley: And you think this applies to the Chicago situation?

Kerouac: No, I don't know about Daley. I don't know anything about him, I wasn't there. I'm talking about his idea [points over at me] of protesting and running around and making noise all over the place. If you create chaos, you can become the commisaaaar, of the control of chaos.

Yablonsky: I think there was a situation that was operative there. To go back to Prague, maybe to the thirties, a guy named Kapek wrote a book called *RUR*, a great writer, related to the Universal Robot; what he was doing was making a statement that man is turning into kind of a machine, that there's no love, there's no communication, no humanity, and in Chicago we had a Political Machine which was airtight, plastic, solid as a rock, and here were some antagonists, but not really antagonists. They were people who were trying to be spontaneous, to do something else, to loosen the situation up, and we had these forces, kind of at opposite ends of the continuum, and a clash took place. I think this was part of the problem.

Buckley: I think that's an interesting theory, but I'm not sure how convincing it is in light of the fact that the Democratic Party was by no means airtight. It may have been airtight up against People who want to storm the Amphitheater and burn it down, but it was certainly not airtight in terms of the tussles going on with it. There was very spirited debate and there was a very high permeability for ideas that were fired in from about every Democratic philosopher in America In other words, this was not a Tito-like neat little culminating session. . . . A lot of people had decided that they wanted Humphrey, and they were not shaken.

Sanders: But you do not have to stack the galleries with "We Love Daley" signs; you don't have to shake down Mrs. McCarthy, and search her purse when she's surrounded by four Secret Service guards; you don't have to run people up to the wall, and smack them down.

Buckley: A lot of people say you don't have to publish the sort of stuff you publish in order to love people.

Sanders: Well, you know, then why don't we just unite with the Russians and dance around?

Kerouac: You know what my mother calls Humphrey?

Buckley: I don't know.

Kerouac [singing]: Fat Fake floogie with a floy floy.

[Laughter]

Buckley: I'm surprised he wasn't nominated vice president.

Kerouac: And you know what Agnew's real name is? I not nostopolis, which means the son of the reader. In Messina, in ancient Greece, the Turks have taken over ancient Greece, Messina, and they said, Don't read. You're censored. And his father read all the books. Very proud name.

Buckley: I say some day you'll become vice president.

Kerouac: My father, my brother, and my sister, and I always voted Republican. We voted for Hoover. I was six years old, voting for Hoover.

[Laughter]

Sanders: The only thing that that type police state repression forces upon us—the next convention we're going to have to take ten thousand of us and run naked through the streets smeared with strawberry preserves.

Kerouac: Maybe I can lick it!

Sanders: My wife, maybe. They force you into an incredible position in the world when you want to protest, or you want to make your voice known in a benevolent way, and yet at the same time, you're pushed and clubbed....

Kerouac: You make yourself famous by protest.

Sanders: Who does? Not me. I make myself famous by singing smut.

Kerouac: I made myself famous by writing songs and lyrics about the beauty of the things that I did, ugliness, too.

Sanders: You're a great poet.

Kerouac: You made yourself famous by saying, "Down with this! Down with that!" Go exit this; go exit that.

Sanders: I hope not. That's not what I want.

Kerouac: Take it with you. I cannot use your abuse; you can have it back.

Sanders: You're a great poet, we admire you, in fact it's your fault.

[Segment ends here.]

Buckley: Now, Mr. Yablonsky, in your book, you list what you call the psychedelic creed. I take it that these are articles of faith to which most hippies would adhere. I think it would be interesting to check them out with Mr. Sanders and Mr. Kerouac. For instance, you say that "the hippie movement is a spontaneous evolution, it is not a heavy workout plan."

Yablonsky: I would say that those creeds are kind of summarizations based on several hundred interviews with people on the scene, and what they say, and it's not ...

Buckley: It wasn't handed out on some tablet; you infer it. Now then you say, "Drugs are a key to the Gods in men, drugs are sacraments for a greater knowledge of the universe, drugs are a vehicle to a cosmic consciousness." Is there a considerable [unclear] on this point?

Yablonsky: A lot of people in the movement do take the position that every man is a god, and it's a very individualistic kind of a movement; each individual should be free to do his own thing. It's rather anarchist actually....

Buckley: How are standards arrived at in hippie culture? On the basis of what one decides is somebody's thing?

Yablonsky: I saw someone assaulting someone in a commune up in Northern California. And I started to intervene, and several people rather gently said, "Well, he's just going through his violence bag; let him do his own thing." And I said, "What if he kills him?" Their position was that everyone should be free to do their own number. I don't share this view. . . .

Buckley: Do you endorse that particular impulse, Mr. Sanders?

Sanders: I've seen a lot of communes, and I've never seen a commune that really tolerated violence. I think that's one of the chief characteristics of a community of free people, that they're there to get away from violence. And when there's like drug-induced violence or other types of violence, in my experience it's generally quelled.

Yablonsky: Every commune I went to I saw some degree of violence, anarchy, and chaos, and they would tell me about another one, and I went to around four. The last one I was way back in the hills, and I was rather frightened, because there was a rather high degree of violence; there were a lot of people freaked out on drugs. It was a rather chaotic scene.

Buckley: And how do victims of this violence characteristically act?

Sanders: Ouch.

[Laughter]

Buckley: They have no mechanisms to which to appeal.

Yablonsky: This was one of the few times in my life that I wish police were around. It was the black flag of anarchy.

Buckley: Would you say their leaders are "spontaneous" and they're not pushy leaders who are self-appointed. They are selected by hippie constituents, because they are "spiritual centers." How are they selected, and what authority, once selected, do they have?

Yablonsky: The philosophical theme would be that certain individuals are purer, more loving, more tuned into nature than other people and that people seek them out.

Buckley: What power do they have?

Yablonsky: They deny they have any. And claim to have no power.

Buckley: So that a victim in one of these situations would get no way by addressing his complaint to the quote "leader." Because the leader would have no authority to address those grievances?

Ed Sanders [breaking in]: Are we talking about reality or not? I've never seen such a situation. He's talking about say a desert commune, or a commune that's isolated from the fabric of the police. And I'm familiar with the communes in New York City, for instance, where you're constantly reacting and relating to the so-called other world, and you're never really without police protection. You usually have a phone.

Yablonsky: Up in Big Sur and places like that...

Kerouac: I was at Big Sur.

Yablonsky: When were you there?

Kerouac: Oh, get off it!

Yablonsky: Were you there lately?

Kerouac: When were you ever there?

Buckley: Is it okay for a hippie to call the police when he needs help, or is that considered anti-something?

Sanders: Sure, you got some snuffer that's going to get you, call the police, of course. Why not? You're attaching all these theoretical tags. That's the problem with using the word hippie. They all have middle-class equipment, a lot of them, and they can plug right back in. It's easy, gee, let's see, police, you dial them. You know, 9–1–1.

Yablonsky: Isn't one of the goals of a lot of people on the scene to turn off all middle-class values, and tune into some other sense of reality?

Kerouac: Nixon's the middleman. Man for the middleman, and Agnew.

Sanders: What we're really involved in is the definition of the word "dropout." I think that thinking "hippies" are involved in a new interpretation of what dropping out means. You naturally retain some connection to the police, the fire department, the hospital.

Yablonsky: Isn't this a negative retention of things your parents laid on you?

Sanders: I'm glad they laid hospitals on me.

Kerouac: Hey, Ed.

Sanders: Huh?

Kerouac: Ed. I was arrested two weeks ago. And the arresting policeman said, I'm arresting you for decay.

[Big burst of laughter]

[End of segment]

[Questions from the audience]

Voice [unclear]: I'm interested in what kind of future you see for the hippie movement.

Yablonsky: I think a lot depends on American society. If it becomes more open, and less plastic, and more loving, and a lot of the rigidified institutions that have developed like a lot of our families and whatever, if things begin to change, there won't be any need for people to react in a rather extreme form, looking for love. It will be found in the regular social system, in that case it will disappear, or it may grow if things become more rigidified, if Nixon gets elected....

Buckley: I'd like to comment on that. [laughter] It may very well grow to the extent that we all encourage (a) intellectual irresponsibility, and (b) personal irresponsibility. It may very well be that the psychologists are correct who say that what precisely has encouraged the hippie movement to be irresponsible is a complete lack of leadership. Maybe when we start writing books about them, we ought even to muster up the courage to say certain things they do they ought not to be permitted to do.

Question: Would any of you regard the hippie not only as a reflection of the inadequacies of the society as a whole, but also as a manifestation of the psychological inadequacies of the individual hippies themselves?

Yablonsky: Well, there's such freedom within the framework of the movement, that people who society would classify as "psychotic" are allowed to do their thing and they live and eat and are taken care of by others and appreciated. In fact, to a great extent this is one of the interesting facets of the hippie movement, that there's a humane approach to certain people who society would label in an extreme fashion, and so there are a lot of young people who don't make it through the usual channels that find a life for themselves on the hippie scene.

Buckley: The question itself poses a methodological challenge, doesn't it, because it's hard to establish by mutually agreed upon means what normalcy consists of. Maybe Mr. Sanders is normal, for all we know.

Kerouac: Maybe I am, too.

[Laughter]

Yablonsky: If people get nude, as Ed described, and put strawberry jam on, and run through the streets ...

Kerouac: Scatological there, Sanders.

Yablonsky: It's a movement; if one guy does it, he'll get arrested in a moment.

Kerouac: Why do you want followers?

Buckley: Did you want to comment on that, Mr. Kerouac? Sorry.

Kerouac: I was asking why he wants followers.

Buckley: Who? Mr. Sanders?

B Abramowitz, or whatever his name is. [Laughter]

Yablonsky: Don't get anti-Semitic with me. I happen to be Jewish. My name is Yablonsky.

Kerouac: I called you by your name.

Yablonsky: Why did you call me Abramowitz?

Kerouac: What is it?

Yablonsky: Yablonsky.

Kerouac: Oh, Yablonsky.

[Laughter]

Buckley: You didn't mean to be rude, did you? Come on, Kerouac.

Kerouac: No. No. I forgot his name.

Buckley: Did you want an answer to that question?

Kerouac: Which question? Yes, I'll answer that question over there about the methodological.

Sanders: What about emotional paraplegic.

Buckley: Here's one for you.

Voice: Hippies and those who live in a commune, are they making it a lifetime occupation? Are they going to sit down and watch the world go by?

Sanders: Everybody sits down part of the time and watches the world go by.

Voice: Are they adding anything?

Sanders: It's like there are certain religious movements, like the Brethren or the Quakers, who don't believe in proselytizing but live by example. And you'll never get any queries from the Church of the Brethren to join their beliefs, but at the same time they try to live an exemplary life, and that's probably the main motivation behind a commune life. Rather than say, "Come here and join us," they would show an example and hopefully accrue . . .

Voice: Do you plan to be a Fug when you're fifty?

Sanders: When I'm fifty, I plan to be an emotional paraplegic smoking peace-herbs.

Kerouac: Neurasthenic psychotic.

Buckley: Do you think that would be an improvement, Mr. Kerouac?

Kerouac: No, no. I was just kidding.

Buckley: Why should this particular impulse ever last? Why when you get around thirty or thirty-five you think, oh I'm going to put my youth behind me and go to work for the First National Bank?

Yablonsky: A lot of the young people who are in this movement, they look up and see their fifty-year-old father, who did everything, has all the goodies, 2.89 cars and three houses, and whatever, and he's kind of miserable, and he's not communicating with his wife and whatever. And they say, well, if I go to the right schools, and do all these things, this is what is going to happen to me. I'm going to try something else. And I think that the hippie movement is partly this, kind of a social experiment.

Buckley: Partly a social experiment that understands the likelihood of its own futility. Will anybody be thinking about the hippies ten years from now other than in the sort of hula skirt sense?

Sanders: By then, the hippies will be in the command generation, and all the pot-smoking law students and all the young legislators who are introducing legalization of pot bills and all the young professionals who are "turned on" and articulate and who are aware of Mr. Kerouac's and Mr. Ginsberg's great contribution to American Civilization.

Kerouac [breaking in]: You hope. I'm not connected to Ginsberg. Don't put my name next to his.

Sanders: Okay, Mr. Kerouac's contribution to American Civilization, those people will be quote "command generation," and hopefully retain some of the humane . . .

Kerouac: Command generation!

Sanders: Well, that's what it's going to be. That's what *Time Magazine* calls it.

Then the program ended. Things were quite friendly once the cameras clicked off. Afterward we all went out to a bar in Times Square to light up the neon liver. I never saw Jack again. I think he was buried, a little more than a year later, in the very checked jacket he was wearing on *Firing Line*. Allen Ginsberg was soon off to his farm in Cherry Valley, in upstate New York, where he would set a group of William Blake poems to music, using a large old Victorian-era ornately wooded pump organ.

"Win a Fug Dream Date" Competition

Reprise Records ran an ad in various newspapers announcing a "Win a Fug Dream Date" Competition.

Ad for Fug dream date.

Here were a couple of entries into the contest.

I haven't heard the album but I like the cover; I think Ed Sanders looks foxy. In fact it doesn't matter so much what's inside the jacket; it is in itself fine to hang on the wall as contemporary art. The songs you can always hear at a party.

By the way, I want Ed (as a date). I've heard about his tattoo.

Lyndhurst, N.J. 07071

Hi Reprise!

To approach this nonsense at a different angle + as your main object is to push the new album:

You give me one of the Fugs, TULI or KEN (whichever is most compatible with a genuine, 100% Piscean), and I promise — cross my heart (Remember, Piscean integrity) — to buy a Fugs album for ten (10) of my straightest friends so to convert and lead them to the road of salvation (the crooked one).

As all new converts, they will, in turn, want to turn-on THEIR friends — and soon... we'll have a crusade going, to out-crusade Billy Grahm.

And maybe, just maybe, ol' Billy might even get the message one day; and with a real Fug-y smirk on his face, he'll testify to the doubting world + relate the experience of how he caught his first glimpse of the what-ever-it-was that really freaked him out:

"It crawled into my hand, honest",

Is it a deal, Reprise?

N.Y.C. 10024

Pigasus to the U.S. Embassy in Montreal

We flew to Montreal to play a week at a club called New Penelope. We also brought the Yippie candidate for president Pigasus, to the U.S. Embassy in Montreal, accompanied by a television crew from Canadian Broadcasting. I put out a press release at the time.

Crackdown on the Underground Press

The CIA set up a domestic program to suppress what it called "Underground Newspapers" for their "almost treasonous anti-establishment propaganda." Around October a CIA Chaos agent (Chaos was a disruption program against the antiwar movement) whacked out a memo that noted "the apparent freedom and ease in which filth, slanderous and libelous statements and what appear to be almost treasonous anti-establishment propaganda is allowed to circulate" in underground papers. The CIA smut sleuth then suggested a strategy for silencing the underground: "Eight out of ten," he wrote, "would fail if a few phonograph record companies stopped advertising in them."

The CIA of course denies it directly carried out the proposal. Instead the FBI did it. In January '69 the San Francisco office of the bureau wrote to headquarters that Columbia Records, by advertising in the underground, "appears to be giving active aid and comfort to enemies of the United States."

The memo suggested the FBI persuade Columbia Records to stop advertising in the underground press. It worked. By the end of the next year many record company ads had been pulled and a number of undergrounders had folded.

The great Allen Ginsberg sniffed this crackdown out and spent years researching it, finally supervising a book, based on his research, for the PEN American Center called *The Campaign Against the Underground Press.*

The FBI on Avenue A

On September 24 two FBI agents visited our house on Avenue A. I allowed them to enter but restricted the questions. Later when I got my files, I saw

```
                                    for release September 20
            AMERICAN CONSULATE ACTS TO SUPPRESS FUGS FILM FOOTAGE
            SHOT BY CANADIAN BROADCASTING COMPANY IN MONTREAL


                During their recent engagement (Sept 9-14) in Montreal
        The FUGS, an American rock group advocating sexual street-splashing,
        visited the United States Consulate with J. Edgar Pigasus, the
        Yippie presidential candidate, a pig.  Accompanying The Fugs was
        a film crew from the Canadian Broadcasting Company.  The Fugs,
        with Mr. Pigasus, walked to the front door of the consulate
        where they were filmed for several minutes.  Subsequently, according
        to Jason Harris, a member of the CBC film crew that filmed the event,
        American officials pressured the CBC to suppress the footage which
        was scheduled  to be shown in Canada this week alongside a Moral
        Rearmament program.  Mr Harris reported that the American officials
        lied to CBC officials, saying that the FUGS brought the Pig to the
        consulate wrapped in an American flag.  In actuality, however,
        candidate Pigasus was brought to the consulate covered with a mod
        gunny sack.  It must be noted that Pigasus at every moment behaved
        in a continent and peaceful manner.

                Below is the text of a letter from The FUGS to the American
        Consulate in Montreal:


                        To the hip pot-smokers of the American Consulate
                        (there must be some of you there):

                        Recently we visited you with our honored Pig.  You took
                        pictures of us from the second story  window.
                        You also lied to the Canadian Broadcasting Company in
                        that you said we brought the Pig to the consulate wrapped
                        in an American flag.  The pig was not dead, so how
                        could we have had it wrapped?  We brought it, in fact,
                        safe inside a potato sack.  The next time we visit you,
                        we shall bring the yippie cabinet in full, 16
                        homosexual albino porcupines.
```

Press release complaining of suppression of Fug/Pigasus footage.

what they wrote: "Outside of his personal belongings the only items he took with him to Chicago were five dozen daisies and a gas mask."

Perhaps they were looking for the origins of the psychedelic honey, or maybe they felt I would break down sobbing and admit I had hauled in a crate of bazookas packed in grease from a Black Panther camp in the mountains of Cuba.

My FBI files indicate bureau awareness that The Fugs were thinking of trying to visit Prague. A single entry remaining on a page otherwise totally

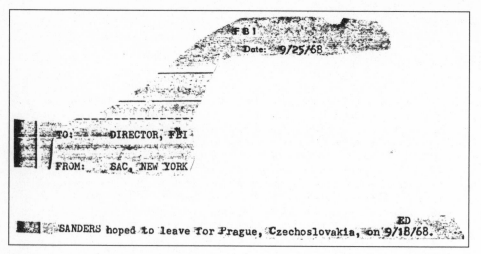

Heavily censored FBI report, September 25, 1968.

censored, dated September 25, 1968, to Director, FBI from SAC, New York: "Ed Sanders hoped to leave for Prague, Czechoslovakia, on 9/18/68."

Perhaps they felt I might be going to pick up my rubles from the KGB.

A Visit to Europe, with Pigasus

And so Miriam and I and The Fugs flew to Europe for the second time this year, first to the Essen Song Festival, September 25–29, with Frank Zappa and the Mothers and many others. Once again we held a press conference with Pigasus, this one in the central square of Essen. The Fugs did a concert or two, appeared on a political panel, and then did what we hungered to do: tried to sneak into Czechoslovakia.

We rented a car and drove toward Czechoslovakia—Ken Weaver, Miriam, myself, and Peter Edmiston, of Edmiston-Rothschild Management. We couldn't go through East Germany, so we drove southwest into Bavaria to the Czech border. In a restaurant in Bavaria I wrote much of a song called "Jimmy Joe the Hippybilly Boy" which I later recorded for my solo album *Sanders Truckstop*.

It was potato-harvesting season, and we spotted big carts of potatoes in distant fields right at the border. We heard that at harvest farmworkers cross back and forth across the border along farm roads, so we thought we might be able to sneak along a potato lane, then streak to Prague.

We had some vague concept of shooting an album cover lying down in front of the Soviet tanks and visiting the house of Franz Kafka, whose texts seemed keys to quelling the fear at the end of an endless year.

We tried going in by one of the paved roads. Border guards were stopping even the milk trucks. While we waited, Miriam walked out into a field to pick some small light yellow wild violas next to the border guard. We pressed some little blue harebells, clover, and a few violas in a poetry book. The harebell-viola glyph is still resting in a bound copy of my book *Peace Eye.*

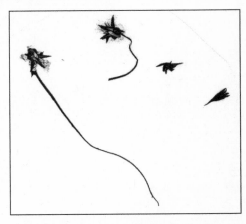

Flowers Miriam picked at the Czechoslovakian border.

Then we drove along the potato wagon border looking for a guardless path to Czechoslovakia. We thought we had found one. A few more yards and we'd have been on the way to Prague, but then we spotted a single guard with a machine gun hanging down his back off a shoulder strap.

"*Halten sie!*" he shouted, holding out his weapon, and then gave forth a stream of German ending with "*demonstrazionen.*"

Miriam was asleep beneath a blanket in our rented BMW, and the guard, when he pulled away the blanket, thought we were trying to smuggle her in! Thus came to closure our search for an album cover with Soviet tanks, and we drove back to Essen.

On Monday, September 30, The Fugs flew to England for television and some concerts. That day we had a press reception at the Arts Laboratory on Drury Lane. Tuesday, October 1, we were on the BBC TV show *Twenty Four Hours* at Lime Grove Shepherds Bush. Before filming, I received a note that the BBC producer was fairly eager to discuss our "programme content."

Friday, October 4, The Fugs did a live show on the BBC TV show *How It Is* and then did a gig at the Roundhouse in London. It was the new theater of the Institute of Contemporary Arts and a good place to play. The Doors and Jefferson Airplane had been there not long before; our opening act was the Hare Krishna singers.

(*Left*) Ken Weaver, Ed. All three photos in the Ed Sanders collection.

(*Below*) Stonehenge in '68.

(*Below Left*) Miriam at Stonehenge.

It was the last time I saw poet Harry Fainlight, who came to the gig. The next day we rented a double-decker bus for a trip to Stonehenge. We packed it full of friends and were ready to head for that re-markable circle of stones, but there was a bit of a delay because a poet friend, Michael Horowitz, had a toothache, so we took the bus to his dentist until Michael was repaired.

We flew back to New York and then almost at once to Toronto for an October 7 concert at Massey Hall, one of the best Fugs concerts of '68, but I've never seen a tape of it in the bootleg catalogs. We were guests at the Rochdale Commune. It was the last time in the '60s that I wasn't unhappy or dissatisfied after a Fugs gig.

An Underground Comic Show

I began gathering original art from some underground comic artists whose work I admired for a show at Peace Eye, which opened November 7. I think it was the first underground comic art show. The walls were packed with great works—pages from R. Crumb's notebooks and original strips by Crumb, Art Spiegelman, Kim Deitch, Bill Beckman, and Spain Rodriguez (who drew the invitation).

I sent out a press release that included this text:

These comic strip plexi are high energy spew-grids which at their best discharge intense power & beauty in to the brain as the eye slurps across their surface. The jolt of such immediate energy creates in the beholder profound sensations of mirth, anarch, poetry, sodomy-froth, Hideum apparitions and somehow, faith. It's not easy. These artists live & work together, constantly comparing a million ideas and anecdotes, cackling & chortling over the pushy violence of the world, annotating with their tense disciplined rapidographs the terror in the wall.

Invitation drawn by Spain Rodriguez.

Peace Eye was packed that night—even Robert Frank showed up!—and so were the fine-drawn walls.

Ed Sanders standing in Peace Eye with the comic art on the wall.

A Book Party for *Revolution for the Hell of It*

The phone always rang. Abbie told me he had conditioned himself to be fully awake and ready to discuss anything the moment he picked up the phone at 4:00 AM. I was impressed how in one weekend after Chicago he'd slaved around the clock to finish his book called *Revolution for the Hell of It*. I thought the title told a great deal about his psyche, but I was under the sway of his brilliance, so I worked with Dial Press and threw a publication party November 22, the anniversary of JFK's death, at the Peace Eye Bookstore.

Abbie signed a copy for me on a bookplate tree whose roots clutched a book:

To Ed Sanders
There are
but few that get
to fuck the world
Abbie

(There was another Abbie signature from around that time that helped set his legend: Movie rights to *Revolution for the Hell of It* were bought by MGM with an initial payment of $25,000. Abbie signed the check and gave it to the Black Panther bail fund.) During Abbie's party at Peace Eye I went down the street to get more wine. There'd been a stickup and a shooting at the liquor store just a hundred feet from the party. It was one of those *400 Blows* moments, a frozen image of an elevated heap of burbly blood on the pavement, reminding me of the mound of chicken fat by the feather sizzler in Peace Eye when I first opened it and was painting the floors. I stepped over the burble on Avenue A to get into the store to purchase some Bacchus.

November 22 was also the day The Beatles' double White Album was released. In Death Valley, in a lonely old dry upper desert ranch, the Manson group listened to the White Double on a record player powered by a gasoline-generator and began to believe the words of black-white war were hidden in the vinyl grooves.

d. a. levy's Suicide

And then on November 24 came a dreadful telephone call notifying me that my friend d. a. levy had shot himself in the third eye while sitting lotus on a mattress in a nearly empty pad in Cleveland using his childhood .22 and triggering the shot with his toe. Since we'd talked during The Fugs gig in Cleveland in August, he'd begun to give away his things and he'd broken up with his wife. In the fall he'd gone to Madison to be the poet in residence at the Free University.

He taught a course in telepathy at the Free U, which he did not attend, though the class met anyway and focused on levy from afar. He made some brilliant collages in Madison, and then in November he returned to Cleveland.

He wrote a final lengthy poem, with its haunting lines:

> i don't know
> poetry seemed like such
> a good idea
> a way to communicate
> pretty pictures
> or to see things that exist now. But the people want blood.

I had heard he was moving to the West Coast. I think he hated to be driven from Cleveland, but the poverty that had haunted Hart Crane smashed levy without mercy. The issues of economic justice, LeMar, and personal freedom that wore out the good bard levy have not yet been addressed in America so that a shyer and less-pushy genius can flourish a proper span.

This was the year Lord Byron finally got his plaque in the Poets Corner at Westminster Abbey. It sometimes takes centuries to sort out a poet, and so it may be for darryl allan levy of Cleveland.

On November 27 Eldridge Cleaver fled to Europe on the day he was to surrender for parole violation. The CIA followed him as a fascinating threat to national security. The Fugs played the Kaleidoscope Theater at 4445 Main Street in Philadelphia for $2,700 on November 29–30. The place was outfitted with hundreds of sofas upon which the audience toked and erotically disported during our gig.

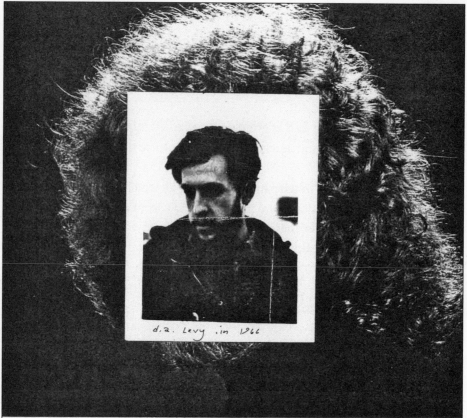

Photo of d. a. levy atop a later ad in a Cleveland paper.

December 15

Ted Berrigan wrote me from his job teaching poetry at the University of
Iowa in Iowa City:

> Dear Ed,
> thanks for the poem, and the records, and papers. The
> new album is inspirational. Sandy likes Crystal Liaison
> best, not knowing it's RC ... and I
> like all of it, especially Ramses II is daid and
> the last cut on side one whose name I don't recall.
> There's a real feeling for quietness, sepulchralness
> (is that a word) and death throughout. A kind of awful
> hush filled with song that's fitting and so saying the
> critic took another pull on his stogie and then nodded
> out
> Levy's suicide was a kick in the gut. A terrible
> disappointment, tho not in him of course ... what's it
> all about ... is what it released in my heart awfully. . . .
> If you do his book, you might try to get some of his collages
> The few I've seen were quite nice and
> and quite beautiful in some ways.

Another Visit to the Galactic Spinach:
Miriam Once Again Helps Me to Land Softly

Just as during the hashish honey experience during the Chicago riots, when
my police surveillants helped me back to the Hotel Lincoln and Miriam's
uncanny ability to talk me down, once again I telephoned in the middle of
the night as if she were the Avenue A Control Tower. It began the day after
Christmas when The Fugs flew to Cleveland for a three-day gig at Le Cave.

Some bikers came backstage at Le Cave and spiked our drinks, maybe
with STP. Whatever it was, it was another one of those Ultimate Spinach
trips, which I had to experience in an orange-and-green-hued Howard
Johnson motel. I called Miriam to have her talk me down from the spinach.

Things didn't turn out as well for our bass player, who was almost para-
lyzed the next day when we had to take the train to Chicago because a

snowstorm had closed the airport. At the Chicago gig we told him just to hold his bass and not to try to play. (A few days later he was hauled in at JFK, trying to get back to London, convinced he was Paul McCartney! He had a beautiful voice, and he soon returned from the Visionary Other and stayed with us for the remaining months of the 1960s Fugs.)

Our gig in Chicago was at the Aragon Ballroom with Wilson Pickett! We couldn't wait to hear him sing his hits "In the Midnight Hour" and "Mustang Sally." Unfortunately Pickett was kept by the snow from coming to Chicago, and The Fugs, one of our players in a stupor, faced a rather upset audience, whose members not only were told the lead act wasn't there, but also they weren't getting their money back.

It was in this context that when I called Mayor Richard Daley a motherfucker, the restless crowd of 5,000 didn't take it well. A woman directly in front of me tossed a container of Coca-Cola in my face, and we fled to our hotel, the fancy Astor Towers, to party.

Next we hopped up to Detroit to play the Grande Ballroom once again, December 30, and the next day flew to LaGuardia and back to 196 Avenue A, in time to celebrate New Year's Eve with Miriam at Pee Wee's Bar, just up the street from our house.

Becoming a Social Democrat

One thing seemed increasingly clear—no set of groups or combinations of individuals working even more-or-less together in '68 had the strength, the time to commit, the grit and drive, the genius, the Vision to open the doors of the United States to the structure of sharing. Even so I came to the realization that I was a democratic socialist or a European-style social democrat. In the years just before World War I there were 70 socialist mayors in 24 states and 1,200 socialist officeholders in 340 cities. And socialist Meyer London was in the House of Representatives working on behalf of the very apartment where Miriam, Didi, and I were living! Eugene Debs in 1912 got 6 percent of the vote for prez. My mentor Allen Ginsberg had once sought to become a labor lawyer, and there were even a few good overtly socialist poets, including Carl Sandburg, and so I joined the not-that-large cadre of the democratic left. What that would mean in the upcoming decades was checking in to Heartbreak Hotel each election night when the votes were counted.

1969

The Fugs were becoming a huge and, to me, overwhelming burden. It was just too much to do. The Peace Eye Bookstore was my exit. It was a popular destination for literary tourists. The location on Avenue A near Ninth was perfect. It had a groovy past as the home of the *East Village Other*. One reason I had kept it open was that, in a crunch, I could run it myself and make more than enough for Miriam, Deirdre, and me to live on.

Maretta Greer Barefoot in the Snow

It was a snowy January day. I was at Peace Eye. All of a sudden a cab stopped, and Maretta Greer stepped out, fresh from JFK airport. There she was, barefoot in the snow, the cab speeding away. She'd been deported from India. She was trembling with excitement, quite beautiful. The same woman who had helped sing "Hare Krishna" with Allen Ginsberg on finger cymbals, Jake Jacobs on sitar, and Gregory Corso on harmonium for *Tenderness Junction* at Bob Gallo's Talent Masters recording studio. The same woman sitting on stage, January 14, 1967, in Golden Gate Park with Michael McClure and Allen Ginsberg as Gary Snyder blew through a ram's horn to begin the Great Human Be-In.

She was trembling and distraught. I invited her into the store. She was hallucinating. She pointed at the store desk and said, "They are caught in the Transylvanian Transvestite Time Trap!" It was a line I used a few months later in "Are You a Vampire, Melvin Laird?" a song against the antiballistic missile system that Nixon and his secretary of defense, Melvin Laird, were hotly proposing. The ditty wound up on my solo album, *Sanders Truckstop*.

Allen and Maretta at one point were a love couple. It was rumored they might be seeking to have a baby together. I recalled that when Allen took me to various literary parties in 1964 after he returned from India, he would point out various women he had made it with. He said that they liked it that he never lost his erection, even after coming. I called Allen on Tenth Street, and he came to retrieve Maretta and took her back to his pad.

Miriam recalls me telling her that Maretta told Allen she was pregnant with his baby, but it was not true. Allen then told Peter that he and Maretta would be a couple. Distraught that he was no longer the wife, Peter cut his long hair in anguish.

Baleful Words from Charles Mingus

On January 8 there was a benefit for the *New York Free Press* at the Fillmore East. There was an excellent lineup, featuring Norman Mailer in his triumph for *Armies of the Night*; Charles Mingus with David Amram and Jeremy Steig; Nico; John Hammond; and the Joshua Light Show. The Fugs performed, even though it would kill any paid performances at the Fillmore East for about a year. I was the master of ceremonies.

When it came time to introduce Charles Mingus, I shouted into the microphone, "Ladies and gentlemen, Charlie Mingus!"

Big applause. He didn't come on. I trotted off stage to find out why.

He was glowering and sulky. He said, "Young man, you go back out there and introduce me as CHARLES! Mingus."

Yes, sir. So I went back before the microphone, and said, "Ladies and gentlemen, our next performer is CHARLES Mingus."

More "Win a Dream Date with The Fugs"

Reprise Records continued its "Win a Dream Date with The Fugs" ad campaign in the trades and in the underground papers as well. Included was one in *Billboard*:

The Reprise VP in charge of these "campaigns" was Stan Cornyn, who had a humorous streak and wrote film scripts as well. He was very blunt, but fair, and always supportive of The Fugs. In his memoir, *Exploding: The*

The Fugs at the Fillmore East, January 8, 1969.

Highs, Hits, Hype, Heroes, and Hustlers of the Warner Music Group, which he wrote with Paul Scanlon, Cornyn filled us in on who won the Dream Date competition. Here is her letter:

> Dear Sirs (or whoever you are)
>   I would like to go out with Tuli because I would like him to fuck me.
>   —Barbara
>   P.S. Even if I don't win, I would still like it.

(*Right*) Dream date reply from Reno, Nevada.

(*Below*) Dream date ad in *Billboard*.

Dear Sirs. (Or whoever you are:)
I would like to go out
with Tuli because I
would like him to
fuck me.

[redacted]

Reno. Nevada
89502

P.S.
Even if I don't
with I would still
like it.

Pacem
In
Terris

Brand new contest! It's our

"Win a Fug Dream Date" Competition

Choose one:

TULI   ED   KEN

Imagine: a dream date on the town with your favorite Fug, and all that can imply. It could be yours.

Just tell us what you think of the latest Fugs album, "It Crawled Into My Hand, Honest." In from one to 100 words. Or more words, if you insist. Or, if you've got something classier than words, fair enough.

We of course reserve the right to make up more rules as we go along. But for now, that's all. This is a pretty loose contest.

Along with your entry, be sure to name your fave Fug, the one you want for your once-in-a-lifetime Dream Date. We'll plow thru the mail and then let you know if you're the big winner. Honest. Even if you don't win, your chances are pretty good: the 99 runners-up will get a free copy of the *next* Fugs album, whenever that's ready.

But till that's ready, we're zeroing in on "It Crawled Into My Hand, Honest."

To give you an idea of the competition — what other folk have written about "It Crawled Into My Hand, Honest" — we offer this sampling:

"Undoubtedly from under a rock."
— *Portland Maine Press Herald*

"Consistently entertaining."
— *Playboy*

"A beautiful record. The album is actually their best."
— *Rolling Stone*

You can do better, can't you? Those reviews are pretty dull reviews. What we want is *your* thoughts, in any form that'll get thru the mails. (Caution: don't think by doing a naughty, you'll captivate our judges. They read all that years ago. They much prefer urbanity.)

If, to prepare your entry, you want to buy the album, we have no objection.

Then, once you get it all together, mail your joy to:
Room 208-A
Reprise Records
Burbank, Calif. 91503

So do it. You have little to lose; maybe something to gain. Of that, we're pretty sure.

In fact, we *know* it.

We, in case you wondered, are Reprise. We make Fugs albums. To sell, but also to take home and corrupt the neighbors.

Make your entry. Slip it to us. We'll get back to you.

And remember (when you get a chance) that The Fugs are on where they belong.

DESCRIBE ME

Gig with the Velvet Underground and the Grateful Dead

February saw the final Fugs concerts of the 1960s. On February 7 we performed with the Velvet Underground and the Grateful Dead at the Stanley Theater in Pittsburgh. We used the Grateful Dead's sound system, and I was determined that the words to Fugs tunes be heard, so I kissed the microphone very closely. There was a party at the Grateful Dead's various rooms at the hotel afterward, although after a few initial elevators full of partyers, the hotel called a halt to further fans.

On February 20 we performed at Rice Memorial Center, Rice University, Houston. Luckily for us, the concert was recorded fairly well, and we have used various tunes from that reel-to-reel tape on several Fugs compilations. There was further nonstop partying, and then we traveled from

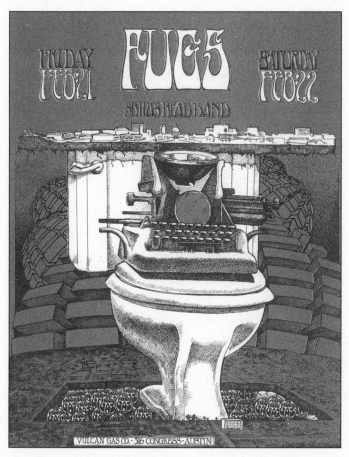

Poster for The Fugs by Jim Franklin, well known for his armadillo motifs.

Houston to Austin for concerts at the Vulcan Gas Works, Friday and Saturday, February 21–22.

In Austin I stayed with my friend Bud Shrake and his wife, Doatsy. Shrake was already a well-known writer, a member of a group of Texas authors who called themselves the Mad Dogs and included, besides Bud Shrake, Bill Brammer, Larry L. King, and Dan Jenkins. At the time Shrake was a staff writer for *Sports Illustrated*. He spent considerable time in New York and used to come to openings and book parties at the Peace Eye Bookstore. One was the previous November's party for the release of Abbie Hoffman's *Revolution for the Hell of It*. The six-foot-six-inch-tall Shrake sat on a stool by the cash register for hours, then invited us up to Elaine's for further partying. Back in '63, at the time of Kennedy's assassination, Bud was writing a column for the *Dallas Morning News* and going out with a woman named Jada, a stripper at Jack Ruby's Carousel Club. He wrote a well-received novel, *Strange Peaches*, set in Dallas during the era of the assassination.

He told me an anecdote about Nelson Bunker Hunt. He was writing a piece for *Sports Illustrated* on Hunt's involvement with thoroughbred horses. Hunt was a famous right-wing activist and had paid for a hostile anti-Kennedy ad in the *Dallas Morning News* the morning of the assassination. There were rumors that he knew quite a bit about the how and why of the hit.

It turned out that while working on the Hunt piece, Shrake had Hunt in a car with him while driving back into Dallas from Hunt's horse farm. They were on the very roadway past the Dallas Book Depository in the exact location of John Kennedy's limousine when the shots killed him. "We stopped at a red light in Dealy Plaza," Bud Shrake told me, "right by the School Book Depository, and I said, 'Okay, Bunker, after all this time, you can go ahead and level with me, who really did it?' And Bunker just kind of chuckled, but didn't say." It was a question that took guts to ask—Shrake had the writer's Prime Rule in mind: Never let the opportunity to ask a choice question pass you by.

Shrake took me around to the sights of Austin during The Fugs' visit. We drove past the sight of an automobile accident. Nearby, in a liquor store window, was a woman who stood weeping, holding a baby. Was it alive? It looked injured. She must have been waiting for an ambulance. It was a stunning reminder of the fragility of all our paths.

Retiring

The gigs at the Vulcan Gas Works in Austin were the last shows of the 1960s Fugs. There wouldn't be another one for over fifteen years. Ahh, I was so weary of it! That image of the woman holding what surely looked like her dead baby in the liquor store window, the wrecked autos outside on the street, stayed with me.

I decided to break up The Fugs. Part of me just wanted to write poetry and be a regular ole Beatnik. Running a rock band was a fifteen-hour-a-day job. Each morning after I woke up, the first thing I thought about was how to promote The Fugs, maybe flesh out a press release for the day, call up our managers to see what gigs were being lined up. It was a lot of worry and stress and not as satisfying as it once had been. I also had an opportunity, as an official Reprise Records producer, to produce my own album. I thought of doing a satirical "Out-There" electro-punk country-and-western album, with elements of proto-environmentalism. My plan to keep the Peace Eye Bookstore open paid off because it had kept up its popularity and was a steady source of income.

An Art Show for Claude Pelieu

Ever since I had published Claude Pelieu's *Automatic Pilot* back in early 1965, we had been friends. I had also been friends with his wife, Mary Beach, an outstanding artist and translator of his poetry. (Mary would translate into French the novel I was working on during 1969, *Shards of God*.) Pelieu was one of the outstanding collagists of the era, and so I organized an exhibition of his glyphic art, which combined images and text, at Peace Eye.

You are invited
to a party & exhibition
of collages
by the immortal poet
Claude Pelieu
Friday
Midnight
March 28
1969
Peace Eye Bookstore
147 Ave A

ARMED

ĀN--FUCK

Invitation/poster for Claude Pelieu's show at Peace Eye.

Mary Beach, Miriam Sanders, Claude Pelieu, Deirdre Sanders at Peace Eye. Photo by Ed Sanders.

Red Boots on Avenue A

Even though I was breaking up The Fugs, the rest of '69 flamed past, as full of projects as any other year of the decade. I kept the Peace Eye Bookstore open throughout the year and minded the store on many days.

One early April evening I walked up Avenue A from the store to our apartment. I unlocked the door, and then I was rushed from behind by two guys who tossed me to the floor and pushed a knife against my throat, chanting, "Where's the amphetamine—where's the amphetamine?" with an insistence that portended arterial insert. Someone had burned them for some uppers.

I told them I never used amphetamine, much less traded in it, and I swore to God I wasn't the one who'd burned them. Finally one of them, wearing a blue trench coat, said, "Hey, man, the guy that burned us didn't have no red boots on." And so my stylish red rock-and-roll boots may have saved my life.

Recording *The Belle of Avenue A*

Our longtime producer, Richard Alderson, who had coproduced *Tenderness Junction* and *It Crawled into My Hand, Honest* (our Reprise albums), had gone off to study Mayan music in the Yucatan and had closed his studio.

Frank Zappa had been doing sessions at Apostolic Studio on East Tenth Street, which was outfitted by its owner, John Townley, with the scene's first twelve-track recording equipment. Townley had been in the Night Owl house band, the Magicians, with future Fug Jake Jacobs. Our engineer at Apostolic was David Baker, a veteran of the civil rights movement who had done field recording in the South during Freedom Summer in 1964.

I ran an ad in the *Village Voice* looking for a guitarist to help me work up songs. A young man named Dan Hamburg answered, and we began a fruitful collaboration, starting with *The Belle of Avenue A* for The Fugs and then my solo albums for Reprise, *Sanders Truckstop,* and *Beer Cans on the Moon.* Hamburg had just been fired as a caseworker at a foster care agency "because," as he later told me, "I was complaining about how I thought that too many 'difficult' kids in my caseload were being summarily diagnosed with 'schizophrenia-undifferentiated type,' ejected from foster homes, and warehoused in Creedmore State Hospital, where they were zombified with thorazine and stellazine." Later Hamburg spent thirty-one years teaching in New York's inner-city junior high schools. But in 1969 he was all creativity and élan, and he helped us immensely.

Hamburg played guitar on Tuli's "Bum's Song" and on my tunes "The Belle of Avenue A," "Queen of the Nile," and "Yodeling Yippie." The Fugs performing ensemble—Ken Pine on guitar, Bob Mason on drums, and Bill Wolf on bass—recorded Weaver's two tunes, "Dust Devil" and "Four Minutes to Twelve"; "Chicago" by Country Joe McDonald and myself; "Mr. Mack"; and Tuli's "Flower Children" and "Children of the Dream."

Bum's Song	3:06
Dust Devil	3:18
Chicago	2:14
Four Minutes to Twelve	5:40
Mr. Mack	3:51
The Belle of Avenue A	5:42

Queen of the Nile	2:46
Flower Children	4:25
Yodeling Yippie	2:19
Children of the Dream	5:54

Dan Hamburg, guitar backing up Tuli's vocal on "Bum's Song"

"Dust Devil," Ken Pine, guitar; Bill Wolf, bass; Bob Mason, drums; vocal,
Ken Weaver

"Chicago," written by Ed Sanders and Country Joe McDonald for the Yippie
film in the fall of 1968. Sung by Ed Sanders, Bill Wolf, Ken Pine; Ken Pine,
guitar; Bob Mason, drums

"Four Minutes to Twelve," Ken Pine, guitar; Bill Wolf, bass; Bob Mason, drums;
Ken Weaver, vocal

"Mr. Mack," Ken Pine, guitar; Bill Wolf, bass; Bob Mason, drums;
Ed Sanders, vocal

Dan Hamburg, guitar backing up Ed Sanders' vocals on "Yodeling Yippie,"
"The Belle of Avenue A," and "Queen of the Nile"

"Flower Children," Jim Pepper, flute; Ken Pine, guitar; Bill Wolf, bass;
Bob Mason, drums; vocals, Tuli Kupferberg, Bill Wolf, Ken Pine

"Children of the Dream," Ken Pine, lead and rhythm guitar, stylophone;
Bob Mason, drums; Bill Wolf, bass; vocals, Tuli Kupferberg; harmony,
Bill Wolf, Ken Pine

Producer: Ed Sanders

One of my contributions to *The Belle of Avenue A* was based on my experiences at the Chicago riots, commingled with my newfound skill at yodeling:

Yodeling Yippie
I ride the left wing airlines
stirring up trouble at night
Secret signs and secret deeds
I'm just a Yodeling Yippie
kai-yippie yodelaydie ... etc.
I went to see Mayor Daley
Drove into Chicago town
Mayor Daley that porcomorph

The lettering: "The Fugs: Messages of Love, Peace, Social Concern, Poesy, Rectitude, Honor, and Spiritual Salvation."

Radio spots for *The Belle of Avenue A.*

> He chopped down his yodeling friends
> Hodelaydie Hodelaydie Hodelaydie . . . etc.
> I ride across the U.S.A.
> Stirring up peace-creeps at night
> We'll ride high and we'll ride low
> I'm just a yodeling Yippie
> kai-yippie yodelaydie . . . etc.
> I went to see Mayor Daley
> Rode into Chicago town
> Mayor Daley that porcomorph
> Chopped down his yodeling friends
> hodelaydie hodelaydie hoo

For much of 1969 I kept recording at Apostolic Studio, with outstanding engineer David Baker. I mixed and sequenced *Golden Filth*, The Fugs live at the Fillmore East, which we had recorded the weekend before RFK's assassination. I also recorded Lionel Goldbart's album *God Loves Rock and Roll* there and my own solo album *Sanders Truckstop*. Later in the year I turned Allen Ginsberg onto Apostolic, where he recorded his album of his musical settings of William Blake poems.

Saying Good-Bye

My formal duties as a Fug were over. It had not been an easy time. We were very, very controversial. We were always on the verge of getting arrested. We had bomb threats. We were picketed by right-wingers. Someone sent me a fake bomb in the mail. Someone called once and said he was going to bomb, first me, then Frank Zappa. We were investigated by the FBI, by the Post Office, by the New York District Attorney's Office. We were often encouraged not to try to perform again at the same venue. We were tossed off a major label. All of this took bites out of our spirit. I was getting weary— four years had seemed like forty and I felt as if I'd awakened inside a Samuel Beckett novel.

Running a rock band is a quick and hasty thing, and however much long-term planning gets done, improper and impolite decisions are sometimes made—and they haunt a bandleader into midlife and beyond. And so The

Fugs of the 1960s were no more, and I put a few boxes of live concert tapes into my archives and did not pay attention to them for twenty-five years.

As everyone knows all too well, everything flows, frays, rots, and rinses. For instance, the building that had once housed the Peace Eye Bookstore on East Tenth Street is no more, so that the exact spot where The Fugs shouted out "The Ten Commandments" and "Swinburne Stomp" at the opening party was for years a summertime vegetable garden. *Tempus fugorum fugit.* (Now the site of the "Swinburne Stomp" has been turned into a housing project.)

The Fugs were lucky throughout those years in attracting quality. The musicians who played with us—Lee Crabtree, Ken Pine, Bob Mason, Dan Kootch, Jake Jacobs, Bill Wolf, Stefan Grossman, Jon Kalb, Geoff Outlaw, Charles Larkey, John Anderson, Pete Kearney, Steve Weber, and Peter Stampfel—were among the finest of their era. We also attracted quality engineers: Richard Alderson, Chris Huston, and David Baker. We are lucky to have found Mo Ostin, then the president of Reprise Records, who always supported and encouraged us and never censored us.

The Resist Tour

Just a few days after completing *The Belle of Avenue A*, I went on a tour of the United States with a group of poets protesting the Draft and the ever-continuing war in Indochina. From April 25 to May 3 there were one-nighters in Iowa City, Minneapolis, Chicago, Boulder, Detroit, Pittsburgh, and Milwaukee. I was honored to be included with such poets as Gary Snyder, Robert Creeley, Galway Kinnell, Robert Duncan, Clayton Eshleman, Morgan Gibson, Muriel Rukeyser, and Barbara Gibson.

During one of the flights I sat with my friend Robert Bly, who had a year before received the National Book Award for *The Light Around the Body*, but in the awards ceremony in New York City he handed the $1,000 award check to a representative of the Draft Resistance, saying, "I ask you to use this money … to find and to counsel other young men, urging them to defy the Draft authorities, and not to destroy their spiritual lives by participating in this war." (It was a brave thing to say in public because he said it just weeks after Dr. Benjamin Spock, William Sloan Coffin, and other anti-Draft activists had been indicted.)

Poster for the May 3, 1969, Resistance Read-In at St. Boniface Church in Milwaukee.

In our conversation on the flight Bly told me about flying saucer publications he had been reading, particularly about peculiar outer-spacelings that had been observed who had "I-shaped mouths." That inspired me in writing *Shards of God*, where I placed in the story line some I-mouthed saucerlings.

God Loves Rock and Roll

In the spring of 1969 I produced an album of Lionel Goldbart's songs, with the great title *God Loves Rock and Roll*, for Douglas Records. David Baker of Apostolic Studios was the engineer. We completed the album, though Alan Douglas never released it.

Lionel Goldbart signed a contract with me, dated March 1, 1969. The album had a budget of $5,000, which was substantial for 1969. I gave him a $500 advance against 90 percent of all royalty moneys received from Douglas Records.

The album was arranged by Dan Hamburg and by Randy Kaye, both of whom had done work on *It Crawled into My Hand, Honest*. Kaye oversaw some sessions on *God Loves Rock and Roll*, with Miroslav Vitous on bass, Kaye on marimba and vibes, Perry Robinson on clarinet, Richard Youngstein on sitar and bass, David Izenson on bass, and Rusty Clark on electric viola. The basic studio setup for takes was overseen by Randy Kaye: vibes, clarinet, viola, and two standup basses.

I turned in the completed album to Douglas Records.

Side A
God Loves Rock and Roll
Teeny Bopper Song
Sun Is Hole in Sky
The Kabbalah Gang
Space Cadets
City of Clay

Side B
Jack o' Lantern
Piggy Wiggy's Back in Action
In My Lives
Little Tripper
Brain Girl
Kasoundra

One of the mysteries of the 1960s: What happened to this album? Is it somewhere in the vaults of Douglas Records?

Shards of God

I had been in negotiations with Grove Press about a novel I was writing in 1967 called *The Hairy Table*, which was a very fictionalized semiautobiographical account of my operation of the Peace Eye Bookstore and the adventures of The Fugs. Richard Seaver, one of the main editors at Grove, had written me in October '68, "I wonder if you've made any progress on THE HAIRY TABLE since we last discussed it about a year ago? If you'll remember, you gave us an outline and we were wondering if we could get a little more to go on. It occurred to me that you may now have some further material and in that case I'd like very much to see it." A chapter of *The Hairy Table* was published in the summer–fall '68 issue of *San Francisco Earthquake*, edited by Jan Herman. The chapter created a stir, as we shall see, when it won a National Endowment for the Arts literary prize, but then was censored by George Plimpton from an NEA anthology on the grounds that its inclusion might endanger the entire NEA budget, which is voted on by Congress.

Like Phil Ochs, I had been wounded by the Chicago police riots and the thuglike conduct of the Democratic Convention, so I decided to set aside *The Hairy Table* and with my oodles of free time (now that The Fugs were disbanded) to concentrate on a satiric novel set inside the Chicago riots and the partisans of the Yippies. I added a sci-fi theme—the I-mouthed saucer people and their visits to earth.

July 20

Miriam and I watched the moon landing at our apartment on Avenue A. It seemed like a great gift from a slain president, who had set the moon voyage in motion. Meanwhile out in Los Angeles in a hillside home on Cielo Drive, Sharon Tate, eight months pregnant, and her father, Lieutenant Colonel Paul Tate, watched the moon landing. She had asked Abigail Folger and Wojtek Frykowski to stay at the house until her husband returned from London.

Out at the Spahn Movie Ranch on the edge of the San Fernando Valley, just at that moment, young Snake Lake and a few other followers of Charles Manson gathered in the "bunkhouse" on the make-believe western town movie/TV ad set to listen to "That's one small step for a man, one giant leap for mankind" on Straight Satan biker Danny DeCarlo's radio.

In the days before her death Sharon was seen in local department stores purchasing baby supplies. Her white Rolls Royce was on the way home from London. The nanny would come as soon as her papers cleared immigration.

Sharon was bubbling with happiness over the impending birth of the baby. She was exercising in preparation for the delivery. She bought books on childcare and supplies for the nursery, which was being built in July in the north wing of the house. Everybody had plans in motion. I was trying to finish my novel about the Yippies in Chicago and was wondering, what was the deal with Chappaquiddick? What the hell was going on?

We were enjoying the summer. People were talking in the Lower East Side about some sort of huge rock festival being planned in upstate New York for August.

Ten Years for Two Joints

On July 28, two and a half years after poet John Sinclair's arrest for rolling a couple of joints from a brown cookie crock to give to an undercover cop in Detroit who was pretending to be a volunteer for the Committee to Legalize Marijuana, he was sentenced to ten years in prison! It was the ultimate punishment for taking part in LeMar. I wrote an article, "The Jesus Christ of Marijuana," for *EVO*. It began:

> It makes one weep that a man like John Sinclair is imprisoned when criminals like Kenneth Conboy, the board of directors of Minneapolis Honeywell (the fragmentation bomb company) and Melvin Laird [then secretary of defense] are allowed to roam about destroying the noble spirit of humanity.
>
> John Sinclair was sentenced to 10 years in the Southern Michigan Prison for passing out free, two joints to a bearded undercover agent who with a policewoman posing as his wife, was running a psychedelic candle shop in the Detroit poetry-rock-publishing community. 10 years for 2 cigarettes of marijuana, the benevolent herb of Ra. 10 years! One ought to be given awards for turning on a cop. Instead he may be forced to tithe one-seventh of his allotted earthly time for dispensing 2 items of pleasure!

East Village Other, August 6, 1969.

The article continued tracing Sinclair's heroic career running the Artist-Writers Workshop in Detroit and managing the MC5 rock group. I mentioned a big campaign ahead to free him. Indeed several years would pass before John Lennon and others would mount a successful drive to free Sinclair, with John Lennon performing in December 1971 at a sold-out Free John Sinclair rally at Crisler Arena in Ann Arbor.

Sanders Truckstop

I had an okay from Mo Ostin, head of Reprise Records, to do my own solo album. Yay! For some reason I decided to do a modern country-and-western/East Village/truckstop project. I went forth to record stores and purchased about eight albums of Hank Williams—all I could find. He was a fixture of my Missouri childhood. I also bought Jimmy Rodgers, Buck Owens and his Buckaroos, a Porter Waggoner and Dolly Parton album, plus Dave Dudley trucker albums. I listened to them over and over. I also spent time practicing my yodeling to Williams and Rodgers. It was dawning on me, finally, that I was the only Beatnik who could really yodel, as I had shown on The Fugs tune "Yodeling Yippie." Slowly I was forming my "Theory of Truck," working up a sequence of my melodies on my autoharp at home on Avenue A.

I went to a Linda Ronstadt concert at Town Hall in August. There she was, barefoot and belting a kind of country-and-western uptempo hipster-saturated music that was amazing! She had put out a remarkable album in the spring, *Hand Sown . . . Home Grown*, for Capitol Records. *Hand Sown* brought country music to rock. Her voice could soar and had great subtlety. I had known of her since her days with the Stone Poneys when we played at the same club in Cleveland.

I was astounded by her marvelous voice, belting out tunes from the stage of Town Hall. Wow. I also liked the upfront quality of her drummer, John Ware, and the bass player, John London. I learned they were going to be in town for a few days, so I hired them for *Sanders Truckstop*.

I moved quickly, booking Apostolic Studios, where in two days, September 20–21, we recorded "Home Sick Blues," "The Plaster Caster Song," and "Johnny Pissoff Meets the Queer" (what the American Federation of Musicians forms that were filled out that day called "The Iliad"), "The Maple

Court Tragedy," "Breadtray Mountain," "The Heartbreak Crash Pad," "Banshee," "ABM Machine," and, finally, "Cutting My Coffin at the Sawmill."

Guitarist Dan Hamburg was a big part of the musical ensemble I put together for the *Sanders Truckstop* sessions at Apostolic. Dan came to my house, and we worked on a bunch of the tunes, such as the Johnny Pissoff tune, "The Iliad."

Jay Ungar: Fiddle
Bill Keith: Banjo and pedal steel
Dan Hamburg: Guitar
John Ware: Drums
John London: Bass
Dave Bromberg: Dobro
Patrick Sky: Guitar

It was a good group. *Sanders Truckstop* was released in spring of 1970.

Jimmy Joe, the Hippybilly Boy 5:14
The Maple Court Tragedy 2:31
Heartbreak Crash Pad 4:02
Banshee 3:00
The Plaster Song 2:58
The Iliad 4:05
Breadtray Mountain 2:20
The ABM Machine 2:25
Cutting My Coffin at the Sawmill 3:12
Homesick Blues 2:33
Pindar's Revenge 3:25

Off to LA

I flew to Los Angeles in September to work on the album design and to bring the mixes to Reprise Records. I stayed at the Landmark Motel. Janis Joplin was also there. We had a chance to catch up one afternoon when I visited her room. She was waiting for a ride and was very upbeat. She joked about how she was becoming so wealthy she was going to be able to purchase her hometown, Port Arthur, Texas. She talked about two recent lovers, Joe Namath and Dick Cavett. She said Cavett was better. She blew Cavett, she told me. He contended it was his first time. Her tone of voice indicated to me that maybe she thought he was fibbing. On her arm were about twenty narrow bracelets. I thought later they might have been obscuring her shoot-up marks.

The murders of Sharon Tate and three of her friends in Los Angeles were all the gossip. My friend poet Allen Katzman (also editor of the *East Village Other*) had returned from his own trip to LA right after the murders, and he told me excitedly about some things he had heard about the killings he said he'd gotten from Dennis Hopper. Dennis Hopper—director, author, and one of the stars of the recently released *Easy Rider*—was on top of the film world at the time of the murders. And he was then living with Michelle Phillips of the Mamas and the Papas, the source, Hopper told Katzman, of what he had heard.

Katzman was in San Francisco the weekend of the murders and decided to go to LA, apparently as the guest of *Los Angeles Free Press* publisher Art Kunkin. Hopper called Kunkin, Katzman later wrote in his autobiography, *The Perfect Agent, an Autobiography of the Sixties*, and offered to supply an inside story he had learned. Kunkin and Katzman met with Hopper at Columbia Studios. They then went to a restaurant, and Hopper explained that he and Michele Phillips were then living together, and "through her he had recently been caught in the maelstrom of the Tate murders," as Katzman recounted it.

"He explained that the four murder victims had been involved in a sado-maso club run out of Mama Cass' house. A coke dealer had 'burned' Sebring and Frykowski for a large amount of money, and as revenge he was kidnapped by them, taken to Mama Cass' where in front of 25 prominent rock and movie stars he was 'stripped, whipped and buggered.'" Hopper implied his source was Michele Phillips. After that, the tale went, vengeance occurred.

Katzman wrote a piece on the murders in the *East Village Other*, which he edited. (It turned out that the dealers had alibis and went free.)

When I was in Los Angeles to hand in the mixes of *Sanders Truckstop*, Andy Wickham, then an executive at Warner/Reprise and a longtime friend of The Fugs, had heard a lot of the same gossip about the murders as Katzman had.

An idea was forming. I was looking for something to do—maybe I should look into these strange murders. The Fugs were in the past. *Sanders Truckstop* was done. I probably should have put together a band and prepared to tour to back up the album. Indeed, I was doing some performances with Dan Hamburg of songs from *Truckstop*. I rented a country-and-western shirt and cowboy boots from Nudie's. Then at dawn I drove out with a photographer to Bakersfield, looking for a proper "truckstop" location for the album cover for *Sanders Truckstop*.

In Bakersfield at dawn, September 1969, in my country outfit rented from Nudie's.

The Harsh Reality of Airplay

Reprise Records sent "The Iliad" and "Jimmy Joe, the Hippybilly Boy" to Frank Zappa, who praised them. Reprise VP Stan Cornyn pointed out that because the word "jockstrap" was used in "Jimmy Joe," it would never get airplay.

Signing with Grove

After I completed my novel *Shards of God*, set in the milieu of Chicago '68 and Yippiedom, I signed a contract with Grove Press in September. So I had three post-Fugs careers lined up: (1) running Peace Eye Bookstore, (2) working as a novelist, (3) recording solo with Reprise.

The Chicago 8 Trial

On September 24 the Chicago 8 went to trial: David Dellinger, Rennie Davis, and Tom Hayden of the National Mobilization to End the War in Vietnam; Abbie Hoffman and Jerry Rubin of the Yippies; John Froines, a chemistry teacher at the University of Oregon; Lee Weiner, a grad student at Northwestern University; and Bobby Seale, chair of the Black Panther Party. All were indicted for the rider placed on the 1968 Civil Rights Act—

the so-called Rap Brown amendment—crossing state lines for the purpose of civil disruption.

Bobby Seale demanded to represent himself and to cross-examine witnesses. (His attorney, Charles Garry, had to have surgery, but the judge wouldn't postpone the trial.) Seale kept interrupting the proceedings until finally Judge Julius Hoffman ordered Seale bound and gagged, and there he was in court like someone shackled in a ship's hold. (On November 5 Hoffman finally severed Seale from the trial, and the Chicago 8 became the Chicago 7.)

Richard Nixon weighed in with his usual sour-souled analysis on one of his secret tapes: "Aren't the Chicago Seven all Jews? Davis is a Jew, you know." When someone told Nix that Davis wasn't Jewish, Nix noted that, well, Abbie Hoffman was Jewish.

The Passing of Kerouac

The night of the second anniversary of Exorcism of the Pentagon, October 21, Allen Ginsberg was at his farm in Cherry Valley, just about to leave for a poetry tour beginning with Yale and then a teach-in about Vietnam at Columbia. Gregory Corso had come for a visit.

That evening the phone rang. Gregory answered. It was writer Al Aronowitz. Corso turned to Ginsberg. "Al! Jack died."

Kerouac had been watching a cooking show called *The Galloping Gourmet*, eating some tuna and sipping whiskey in his living room, jotting in a notepad, when the blood burbled up his throat. He never regained consciousness.

Early the next morning Ginsberg and Corso walked through the early snow to the woods up the hill and carved Jack's name in a tree.

Allen wrote a beautiful poem, "Memory Gardens," after Jack's funeral. Here are some lines:

I threw a kissed handful of damp earth
　　down on the stone lid
　　　　& sighed
　　looking in Creeley's one eye,
Peter sweet holding a flower

The poem ends with these words:

Well, while I'm here I'll
        do the work—
and what's the Work?
        To ease the pain of living.
Everything else, drunken
                dumbshow.

Those lines became the watchwords of the late 1960s and beyond.

The fall saw John and Yoko's Bed-In for Peace in Canada. Allen was mentioned in "Give Peace a Chance," so he called Lennon during the Bed-In to give good wishes.

Learning About the Manson Group

In October I was back in New York City when I received an issue of an environmental newsletter called *Earth Read-Out*. This issue contained the first mention of the group that soon would be known as the Manson family, reprinting a story from the *San Francisco Chronicle* dated October 15, 1969:

> The last survivors of a band of nude and long-haired thieves who ranged over Death Valley in stolen dune buggies have been rounded up, the sheriff's office said yesterday. A sheriff's posse, guided by a spotter plane, arrested 27 men and women members of the nomad band in two desert raids. Deputies said eight children, including two babies suffering from malnutrition, were also brought in. Some of the women were completely nude and others wore only bikini bottoms, deputies said. All the adults were booked at Inyo county jail for investigation of charges which included car theft, receiving stolen property and carrying illegal weapons. Six stolen dune buggies were recovered, deputies said.
>
> Deputy Sheriff Jerry Hildreth said the band lived off the land by stealing. He said they traveled in the stolen four-wheel-drive dune buggies and camped in a succession of abandoned mining shacks. The band previously escaped capture by moving only at night and by setting up radio-equipped lookout posts on the mountains, he said. "It was extraordinary the way they covered up their tracks and would make dummy camps to throw us off," Hildreth said. "They gave us a merry chase.... This is probably one of the most inaccessible areas in California."

Earth Read-Out commented favorably on the roaming Hippie commune. Then, six weeks after I read those two paragraphs, the front pages of newspapers were filled with glaze-eyed pictures of Charles Manson, the accused murderer, and his band of choppers. He was depicted all at once as a Hippie-Satanist-car-thief-cult-leader-sex-maniac-bastard butcher. His followers—a few young men and around twenty girls—were depicted as "Satan's slaves," willing to do anything, anytime, anywhere for him. Out of all the headlines and stories, no consistent set of facts seemed to emerge that explained in any depth how a group of young American citizens could develop into a commune of hackers. It seemed possible at this early stage of the case—from my perspective of just reading the frenzied news accounts and hearing rumors—that the whole thing was a setup and that they might even be innocent.

Meanwhile, there were two big demonstrations that fall in DC, called the "Moratoriums." The first was on October 15, with coordinated activities across the nation. The Second Moratorium occurred on November 15, when at least 250,000 came to Washington. I was there, and the memory is exquisite of clanging the Justice Department doors while chanting, "Bring out your dead! Bring out your dead" and looking up to see wasp-eyed Nixonites staring from the upper windows.

Establishment figures such as Senators Charles Goodell, George McGovern, and Eugene McCarthy were on hand, as were Peter, Paul, and Mary, Dick Gregory, and Leonard Bernstein. While the 250,000 sang John Lennon's "Give Peace a Chance," Nixon ignored the message. He was watching a football game as 40,000 walked back and forth in front of the White House, each holding a card with the name of an American who had died while fighting the war.

Nixon pooh-poohed any thought that the Moratoriums would change his course, yet in his later *Memoirs* he wrote how they made him stop scheming for a wider war: "I knew, however, that after all the protests and the Moratorium, American public opinion would be seriously divided by any military escalation of the war."

I wrote a satiric article on the Moratorium, describing the thrill of clanging on the doors of the Justice Department, which I submitted to *Esquire* magazine. The editors decided not to publish it, but then in early December the Manson case broke, and I spoke with an editor at *Esquire* about doing an article on the Manson group for an upcoming issue that would feature a section on the theme of "California Evil."

Becoming a Clipper

I had learned from Allen Ginsberg to clip articles. I mean oodles of articles. He'd started in the 1930s during the Spanish Civil War and the rise of Adolf Hitler. Allen sent me lots of clippings during the 1960s, often on the struggle to liberate pot from the grouches of the überculture. Late in 1969 I started clipping everything I could find on the Manson group and what the press called the Tate-LaBianca murders. You know how it is when you read the same clippings over and over—the questions start to pile up.

I was set to fly out to California and do some research, utilizing my extensive connections in the music world and in the counterculture to get the inside story. Then I learned that *Esquire* had decided to give the Manson assignment to writer Gay Talese. I had already clipped oodles of articles on the Manson group, so I gulped and decided to write a book, thinking it would take about six months, after which I could return to a quiet life of poetry and peace.

Of course, poetry and peace were not what 1970 had in mind. Because I was well known, it did not take much effort to get a book contract. I acquired a top-rank agent, Carl Brandt (who at the time represented Jerry Rubin, who had recommended Brandt). Hal Scharlatt, editor in chief of E. P. Dutton, offered a contract, and I picked up an assignment from *Esquire* to write an essay on the upcoming trial. In order more easily to acquire information from the remnants of the Manson group, I secured a position on the staff at the important underground newspaper the *Los Angeles Free Press*, agreeing to write a weekly column on the case.

Olson's Float-Away

My mentor Charles Olson had landed a teaching job at the University of Connecticut that fall. Then his health began to deteriorate. By late October he checked into a local hospital, and then during his third week there came the diagnosis—liver cancer. On December 18 Harvey Brown, longtime Olson supporter, brought him in an ambulance from Manchester to New York

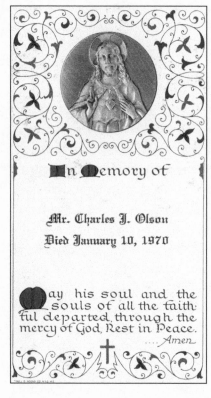

CHARLES OLSON
DEC. 27, 1910
JAN. 10, 1970
BETTY OLSON
NOV. 3, 1925
MAR. 28, 1964

Olson's winged skull stone.

Charles Olson's funeral card.

Hospital. The slim hope was for a liver transplant, but tests in New York showed the cancer had metastasized and a transplant was not an option.

Visitors by the score showed up, including a prominent book dealer who brought a thick stack of Olson's books to sign. I brought an Egyptian painted plaque, which went up on a nearby table. Olson told me because he felt that a woman's liver could regenerate, then he wanted to have his sex surgically changed and to be given injections of "female hormones."

There were the indignities of failing fast, such as when they lost his dental plate in radiology. His eighteen-year-old daughter, Kate, stayed with him to the end. I recall a roommate sharing Olson's room, also a cancer patient, who checked his stocks each day in the *New York Times*. Early in the morning of January 10, 1970, Olson passed away. It shivered through my life like an icy scimitar! In a way it seemed as if my entire youth, especially the 1960s, had also passed into the void.

I flew to Boston with Allen Ginsberg and George Kimball, then to Gloucester for the funeral. As I helped carry Olson's coffin from the

Catholic church on the way to Beechwood Cemetery in Gloucester, I felt as if a close relative had passed away. During the viewing of Charles's open casket, a local Gloucesterman paused and exclaimed, "Charlie, you're beautiful."

An era had closed. There was an indirect line from helping carry his coffin to the limousine all the way back to discovering Olson's great poem, "Maximus from Dogtown—I" in 1959 at the 8th Street Bookshop when I was an NYU student. Only eleven years separated the two, but it seemed like an eternity.

Final Recording Session of the 1960s

The final recording session of the 1960s occurred in early December with Ken Pine at Apostolic. I recorded "Six Pack of Sunshine," "While My Moog Gently Weeps," "I'm Just a Tired, Lonesome Street-Punk," and "We Don't Allow No Robots at Sunday School," all tunes I was thinking of using on the follow-up album to *Sanders Truckstop*.

An Award for "The Hairy Table"

At the end of 1969 I became involved in a censorship issue over my short story "The Hairy Table," which had been published in 1968. A panel of judges, including Joyce Carol Oates, had selected it to be in a prestigious anthology to be published by Viking Press. Furthermore, it had won a $1,000 prize from the National Endowment for the Arts.

My Lower East Side congressman, Leonard Farbstein, sent me a letter of congratulations dated December 2, 1969.

Dear Mr. Sanders:

I was indeed pleased to learn that you have been granted an award in the amount of $1,000 by the National Endowment for the Arts for your short story, "The Hairy Table."

May I take this opportunity to extend to you my warmest congratulations and wish you the very best in the future.

Leonard Farbstein, Member of Congress.

```
LEONARD FARBSTEIN                                                          NEW YORK OFFICES:
   19TH DIST., NEW YORK                                                     276 FIFTH AVENUE
                                                                            2121 BROADWAY
       COMMITTEE:                Congress of the United States           MUrray Hill 4-2200
   FOREIGN AFFAIRS
                                   House of Representatives              WASHINGTON OFFICE:
CHAIRMAN, SUBCOMMITTEE                                               2455 RAYBURN HOUSE OFFICE BLDG.
     ON EUROPE                        Washington, D. C.                 WASHINGTON, D.C.  20515
                                                                     TEL.: AREA CODE 202, 225-5635
SUBCOMMITTEE, STATE DEPARTMENT
ORGANIZATION AND FOREIGN
       OPERATIONS

SUBCOMMITTEE ON NEAR EAST



                                                    December 2, 1969



                    Mr. Ed Sanders
                    196 Avenue A
                    New York, New York 10009


                    Dear Mr. Sanders:

                          'I was indeed pleased to learn that you have been
                    granted an award in the amount of $1,000 by the National
                    Endowment for the Arts for your short story, "The Hairy
                    Table".

                          May I take this opportunity to extend to you my
                    warmest congratulations and wish you the very best in the
                    future.

                          With kind regards, I am

                                         Sincerely yours,

                                         Leonard Farbstein

                                         LEONARD FARBSTEIN
                                         MEMBER OF CONGRESS

          LF:bs
```

"The Hairy Table" had originally been published by Jan Herman in his magazine *San Francisco Earthquake*. It was a section of a novel I was writing back in 1967–1968. The *Kansas City Star* described the story this way: "The short story deliberately carries obscenity to an absurd extreme." I was exploring the outer limits.

I also received a letter of congratulations from Nancy Hanks, who was appointed by Richard Nixon to be the head of the National Endowment for the Arts:

Dear Ed Sanders:

   You have been selected to receive a National Endowment for the Arts award under the American Literary Anthology program for your short story: 'The Hairy Table,' in THE SAN FRANCISCO EARTHQUAKE.

It will appear in THE AMERICAN LITERARY ANTHOLOGY/3, to be published by Viking Press in January 1970.... I congratulate you on this award and wish you every success in your future work.

Sincerely yours, Nancy Hanks, Chairman, National Endowment for the Arts

There was pressure on me to proof the galleys and get a short bio to the publisher. It looked like a dollop of glory was to come my way as I headed off to Los Angeles to write about the Manson group.

Then Nancy Hanks was given the galleys and read "The Hairy Table." She reportedly actually fainted. The piece consisted of a highly fictionalized series of erotic encounters at the Peace Eye Bookstore while I was printing the second edition of *The Toe-Queen Poems*. It also involved various ancient Greek and Egyptian elements.

I spoke with George Plimpton when I was already in Los Angeles. He was staying at the Beverly Hills Hotel. He said that if they left "The Hairy Table" in the NEA/Viking anthology, the entire NEA budget, in the first year of Nixon's reign, would be in danger. Did I want the entire National Endowment for the Arts, a glory of American democracy, to fail because of my story? I was already at work on my investigation of the M group, and so I agreed, reluctantly, to the excision.

In a later letter to me Plimpton noted that "Nancy Hanks, who is the director of the Endowment, told me that she honestly felt that a one-word poem ('Lightght') by Aram Saroyan [published in the NEA/Viking anthology, volume 2] had, in the hands of certain 'Neanderthal' congressmen, cost the endowment five **million** dollars."

I decided not to protest too much. I was getting tired of being a modern-day American Bacchus. Instead I purchased a dark blue Gucci blazer with brass buttons to wear at the upcoming Manson family murder trial and set aside Bacchus while I spent two years investigating a murder case.

Then 1970

It may be late-1960s 'noia, but the amount of heroin in the Lower East Side jumped drastically with the advent, in early 1969, of the regime of Richard Nixon. I was mugged that spring, and Miriam and I had that winter witnessed a woman knifed to death in the street outside our second-story window. She staggered among the cobbles, screaming for help, then died, as we called the police. The man who ran a sewing machine repair shop across the street was murdered by someone wielding a brick.

The streets seemed more and more dangerous. We placed Deirdre in kindergarten at the Emmanu-el Midtown YM-YWHA, up on Fourteenth Street. But for the first grade she was going to have to attend a school on Avenue D, involving dangerous walks each morning and afternoon.

Through poet Joel Oppenheimer we learned of a brand new loft building for artists and the creative located in the West Village—it was called Westbeth. The National Endowment for the Arts had given a matching grant back in '68 to the J. M. Kaplan Fund to set up the nonprofit Westbeth Corporation, which purchased the old Bell Telephone Laboratories on West Street for renovation into artists' studio/living quarters. There were some 384 units, ranging from efficiencies to three-bedroom apartments, and ample room for studio space in the basement, plus exhibition galleries. The building was a product of the Great Society of the 1960s!

Westbeth was about to open in early 1970, and I learned that there were a few apartments still available, at a very modest rental, which was to be adjusted according to income. I pulled strings and landed us a new pad—a beautiful duplex for $186 a month! Peter Orlovsky helped us move our stuff from Avenue A to the West Village.

Closing Peace Eye

I decided to close Peace Eye Bookstore. I'd thought of keeping it open, or bringing in a partner, but in the end I just gave away thousands of books. Wow, did they flock into the store to get free stuff! It was like the old Digger Free Store, but only for a couple of days. I brought Spain Rodriguez's Peace Eye sign to our new loft at Westbeth. (I still have it, in our garage in Woodstock, forty years later.)

My Testimony at the Chicago 7 Trial

I paid for my own ticket from New York to Chicago to testify at the Chicago 7 trial before Judge Julius Hoffman and twelve jurors. I was given a prep talk by Tom Hayden just before my testimony was to begin on January 8. The way I interpreted what Tom Hayden was saying to me was that I was to come on weird, as if to show the sort of person who WAS NOT indicted. I did my best to fill the bill.

To my disappointment, Judge Hoffman refused to allow into evidence a large Yippie flag I had brought to court with the inscription "Abandon the Creeping Meatball." This referred to a song I had written back in early '68 to celebrate the birth of Yippie. The tune's opening lines were

Rise up and abandon the Creeping Meatball
in Nixon's land
We're going to sing and dance in Chicago
for the Festival of Life

I had purchased brand-new shiny blue suede shoes for the testimony, so at the outset of my testimony, the defense thought of a game whereby I'd pretend I was waiting for my shoes.

Mr. Weinglass: Your honor, without excusing the jury, our next witness is waiting for his shoes, and if I may have a few minutes.

The Court: Well, I have seen people come here almost without shoes so he may come in without his shoes. I will excuse him.

Mr. Kunstler: I just want to see if they arrived.

[I came in to the courtroom wearing just my socks, and then my spanking new blue suede shoes were brought to me, and I put them on.]

Mr. Weinglass: Do you recall what it was that brought you from Jackson County, Missouri, to New York?

The Witness: Reading Allen Ginsberg's "Howl" in shop class in high school in 1957.

Mr. Weinglass: Mr. Sanders, could you indicate to the Court and to the jury what your present occupation is?

The Witness: I am a poet, songwriter, leader of a rock-and-roll band, publisher, editor, recording artist, peace-creep.

Mr. Schultz: What was the last one, please?

The Court: Peace-creep?

The Witness: Yes, sir.

The Court: Will you please spell it for the reporter?

The Witness: P-E-A-C-E, hyphen, C-R-E-E-P.

The Court: Peace-creep, Mr. Schultz.

The Witness [continuing]: and yodeler.

Mr. Weinglass: Now in connection with your yodeling activities—

Mr. Schultz: Your Honor, this is all very entertaining but it is a waste of time. We don't have to do anything in connection with his yodeling to get to the issues in this case.

The federal judge would not allow me to demonstrate my yodeling abilities. I was disappointed, for verily I was and am the only Beat who can yodel. However, I resisted the dramatic impulse to weep and show trembling agitation in front of the judge at this restriction on my yodeliferous genius. Why? Six-month jail term and maybe a $1,000 fine for insulting the dignity of the court. I had to get to LA and start investigating the Manson family.

The Court: You may finish your question.

Mr. Weinglass: Mr. Sanders, can you identify these two items?

The Witness: They are two phonograph records. The records were produced by me, by the group, The Fugs, of which I am the leader and head fug, so to speak.

Mr. Weinglass: Now, Mr. Sanders, have you also written a book about the Yippies?

Mr. Schultz: Leading, objection.

The Witness: Yes.

The Court: I sustain the objection. Mr. Witness, will you wait when there is an objection so that I can indicate my view of the objection? Will you do that?

The Witness: I'll try.

Mr. Weinglass: Now, directing your attention to the latter part of November in the year of 1967, did you have occasion to meet with any of the defendants seated here at the counsel table?

The Witness: I met with Jerry Rubin. There was a conference at the Church Center for the UN in New York City.

Mr. Weinglass: And at the time of that meeting did you have a conversation?

The Witness: Yes. I mentioned the Monterey Festival, which was a free festival featuring all the rock bands in America. Mr. Rubin said it was inspirational that some of the major rock bands in America were willing to play for free at a large tribal-type gathering of people, and I said it was really great and that we should consider convening something for the following summer or in the following year of a similar nature, that is, a free rock festival composed of all the major rock bands in America.

Then Keith Lampe said, "Why don't we hold it next summer, you know, sometime in August?" And it was agreed-at that point everybody decided it would be a wonderful idea to have a free rock festival denoting the new life styles emerging, and that we would get in touch with Abbie Hoffman and other people and have a meeting right away.

Mr. Weinglass: Now, directing your attention to the evening of January 4, 1968, do you recall where you were that evening?

The Witness: Yes. I went to Jerry Rubin's house in New York City to get briefed on a meeting that had taken place.

Mr. Weinglass: What took place at that meeting you had with Jerry Rubin?

The Witness: Well, first we had a period of meditation in front of his picture of Che on the wall for a half hour.

The Court: Picture of whom?

The Witness: Che, Che Guevara. Che, the great revolutionary leader.

The Court: Oh. Would you spell it for the reporter.

The Witness: Well, he said that he was very—he had gone to Chicago and that they had placed a petition for a permit, filled out the necessary forms with the necessary officials in Chicago.

Then I said to him, "I hear that you're thinking about nominating a pig for President, an actual pig, oinky-oink, you know, Pigasus, the Immortal."

Then I said, well, I let it be known, as a pacifist and a vegetarian, I had heard there was a faction within the hippie hemp horde that was advocating a big pig roast after election at which point the pig would be made into bacon, lettuce, and tomato sandwiches, and that I was a spokesman for the vegetarians and I was opposed, philosophically opposed to this.

And so it was agreed tentatively at that point that there would be no bacon, lettuce, and tomato sandwiches made of our presidential candidate.

Mr. Weinglass: Now, directing your attention to the date of August 7, at approximately nine o'clock that evening, do you recall where you were on that date and at that time?

The Witness: Yes, I was in an interior office somewhere near Mayor Daley's office for a meeting with Al Baugher, David Stahl, Richard Goldstein, myself, Jerry, Abbie, Krassner, I guess.

Mr. Weinglass: Do you recall what was said at that meeting?

The Witness: I addressed Mr. Stahl and Mr. Baugher, saying that for many months we had planned a Festival of Life with the basis of free music and that I had negotiated with rock groups and singing groups to come to Chicago on that basis and that we needed permits, and we needed the use of the park for our various festival activities.

Mr. Weinglass: Now, what, if anything, were you doing during the course of that meeting?

The Witness: I was making notes for a document that had been requested by various editors and people about the Yippie program for the Festival of Life. You know, poetic rendering of it.

Mr. Weinglass: Now, I show you D-252 for identification, and I ask you if you can identify that document.

The Witness: Yes. I wrote it. I mailed it out to various editors and publishers who had requested me for a statement.

Mr. Weinglass: Your Honor, the defense offers Defendants' Exhibit D-252, identified by the witness.

Now, how many paragraphs appear on that document?

The Witness: C-H-E.

Then we practiced for about a half hour toughening up our feet walk around in Baggies full of ice, and then Jerry informed me about the circu stances of the meeting that had taken place, forming the Youth Internatic Party, and that it was decided to hold a free rock festival in Chicago dui the time of the Democratic National Convention, and that the conven would be a convening of all people interested in the new politics, guerr theater, rock and roll, the convening of the hemp horde from all over various tribes in the United States. I was asked by Jerry if I would help co dinate since I knew the major rock groups in the United States, if I wo contact them and ask them if they would play.

I said I would be happy to and that I would proceed forthwith in c tacting these major rock groups, and that I did.

Mr. Weinglass: Now, had you ever discussed with either Jerry Rubin Abbie Hoffman in person your contacts with these major rock groups?

The Witness: Yes.

Mr. Schultz: Your Honor, would you please ask Mr. Weinglass not ask leading questions, not to lead the witness?

We keep on getting up and getting up. It becomes embarrassing. F people who don't know the legal rules, it looks very bad for the Gover ment to constantly be getting up.

The Court: I appreciate that, Mr. Schultz.

Mr. Schultz: I am begging—I am begging defense counsel to ask que tions properly.

The Court: Don't beg.

Mr. Schultz: That is what it is.

The Court: Don't beg. You needn't beg. I will order them not to as leading questions.

Mr. Weinglass: Now, directing your attention to March 27, do you re call where you were in the evening of that day?

The Witness: I was at my home in the Lower East Side.

Mr. Weinglass: What, if anything, occurred while you were at hom that evening?

The Witness: I received a phone call from Jerry Rubin.

Mr. Weinglass: Could you indicate to the Court and to the jury what the conversation was that you had with Jerry Rubin on the telephone that night?

The Witness: Eighteen.

Mr. Weinglass: And could you read to the jury those paragraphs which are marked.

The Witness: "Predictions for Yippie activities in Chicago:

"A. Poetry readings, mass meditation, fly casting exhibitions, demagogic Yippie political arousal speeches, rock music and song concerts will be held on a precise timetable throughout the week, August 25 to 30.

"A dawn ass-washing ceremony with tens of—"

The Court: I didn't hear that last.

The Witness: Excuse me.

"A dawn ass-washing ceremony with tens of thousands participating will occur each morning at 5:00 AM., as Yippie revelers and protesters prepare for the 7:00 AM volley ball tournaments."

Three-oh, no, five, excuse me.

"The Chicago offices of the National Biscuit Company will be hi-jacked on principle to provide bread and cookies for 50,000 as a gesture of good-will to the youth of America.

"The Yippie ecological conference will spew out an angry report denouncing Chi's poison in the lakes and streams, industrial honkey fumes from white killer industrialists and exhaust murder from a sick hamburger society of automobile freaks with precise total assault solutions to these problems.

"Poets will rewrite the Bill of Rights in precise language detailing 10,000 areas of freedom in our own language to replace the confusing and vague rhetoric of 200 years ago.

"B. Share your food, your money, your bodies, your energy, your ideas, your blood, your defenses. Attempt peace.

"C. Plan ahead of time how you will probably respond to various degrees of provocation, hate and creep vectors from the opposition."

Mr. Schultz: I didn't get that. Creep what?

The Witness: It is a neologism. Creep vectors.

"D. Learn the Internationale.

"E. Bring sleeping bags, extra food, blankets, bottles of fireflies, cold cream, lots of handkerchiefs and canteens to deal with pig spray, love beads, electric toothbrushes, see-through blouses, manifestos, magazines, tenacity.

"Remember we are the life forms evolving in our own brain."

Mr. Weinglass: Now, August 27, at two o'clock in the afternoon, do you recall where you were?

The Witness: Yes, I was at the Coliseum.

Mr. Weinglass: How long did you stay at the Coliseum?

The Witness: From approximately 2:00 P.M. to approximately midnight. I was the master of ceremonies at the Johnson birthday festivities, and I was in the process of coordinating the program and introducing people.

Mr. Weinglass: Do you recall what time you introduced Abbie Hoffman?

The Witness: Approximately. It must—about 8:30, quarter to nine.

Mr. Weinglass: Were you present when he spoke?

The Witness: I was.

Mr. Weinglass: I have no further questions.

The Court: All right. Is there any cross-examination of this witness?

Mr. Schultz: Yes, your Honor. Now, you said, I think, that on January 4, 1968, you went to Rubin's house, is that right?

The Witness: Yes.

Mr. Schultz: And that you meditated before a picture of Che Guevara, is that right?

The Witness: Yes.

Mr. Schultz: Is this the same Che Guevara who was one of the generals of Fidel Castro in the Cuban revolution?

The Witness: Yes.

Mr. Schultz: How long did you meditate before his picture?

The Witness: About a half hour.

Mr. Schultz: In Mr. Stahl's office on August 7, did you hear Hoffman say the Festival of Life that you were discussing with Deputy Mayor Stahl and Al Baugher would include nude-ins at the beaches, public fornications, body painting, and discussions of draft and draft evasion? Did you hear that?

The Witness: Nudism, draft counseling, the beach thing, but he didn't use the word "public fornication."

Mr. Schultz: He didn't use that word. What word did he use in its place?

The Witness: Probably fuck-in.

Mr. Schultz: This was a very important meeting for you, was it not, because if you didn't get the permit, there was a possibility that your music festival would be off, isn't that right?

The Witness: The concept of the meeting was important; the substance turned out to be bilious and vague.

Mr. Schultz: And you wanted those permits badly, did you not?

The Witness: We sorely wanted them.

Mr. Schultz: While you were writing this document, you were also listening to what was going on at the meeting, weren't you?

The Witness: I was keeping an ear into it.

Mr. Schultz: Will you read number four of that document, please.

The Witness: Four. OK. "Psychedelic long-haired mutant-jissomed peace leftists will consort with known dope fiends, spilling out onto the sidewalks in porn-ape disarray each afternoon."

Mr. Schultz: Would you read eight, please?

The Witness: "Universal syrup day will be held on Wednesday when a movie will be shown at Soldiers Field in which Hubert Humphrey confesses to Allen Ginsberg of his secret approval of anal intercourse."

Mr. Schultz: Will you read nine, please.

The Witness: "There will be public fornication whenever and wherever there is an aroused appendage and willing aperture."

Mr. Schultz: Did you read thirteen?

The Witness: You want thirteen read? "Two-hundred thirty rebel cocksmen under secret vows are on 24-hour alert to get the pants of the daughters and wives and kept women of the convention delegates."

Mr. Schultz: Did you ever see these principles, or whatever they are, published in any periodical?

The Witness: Yes, a couple.

Mr. Schultz: They were published before the Convention began, weren't they?

The Witness: Right. Before.

Mr. Schultz: I have no more questions, your Honor.

The Court: Ladies and gentlemen of the jury, we are about to recess until ten o'clock tomorrow morning.

Ladies and gentlemen, good night. You may go.

[Jury excused]

The Chicago 7 Convicted

The Chicago 7 trial at last came to a clamorous closing on February 14 after five and a half months of mishugas, and the jury went away to deliberate. There was a kind of collective "Whew!" that the defendants could have uttered just then except that as soon as the jury had departed, the ghastly and arbitrary Julius Hoffman sentenced the seven defendants, and attorneys William Kunstler and Leonard Weinglass as well, to jail terms of up to four years for contempt of court.

On February 18 all seven were acquitted of "conspiracy" to incite riots, but the jury convicted five of the seven—Dave Dellinger, Rennie Davis, Tom Hayden, Abbie Hoffman, and Jerry Rubin—of violating the so-called Rap Brown amendment to the 1968 Civil Rights law, that is, crossing state lines to foment a riot (John Froines and Lee Weiner were acquitted).

Then on February 20 Judge Hoffman added five years to the five for Rap Brown. (Bobby Seale was tried and convicted separately.) By February 27 all were out on bail and began to appeal their convictions. (Ultimately none would have to serve time. *Whew*.)

The Invention of the Term "Punk Rock"

I provided the first-known use of the term "punk rock" in an interview in the *Chicago Tribune*. "Self-honesty entails an admission," wrote Robb Baker in that article, published on March 22, 1970, "even if that heritage has been rejected. Sanders does this particularly well in his first solo album for Reprise records, 'Sanders' Truckstop,' which he describes as 'punk rock—redneck sentimentality—my own past updated to present day reality.'"

No one sent a check for coming up with the term.

Changing Directions

Sanders Truckstop was released in the spring. When the members of the Manson Family heard it out at their Spahn Movie Ranch, they invited me to lead them in singing one evening after a garbage-run dinner—an offer I turned down.

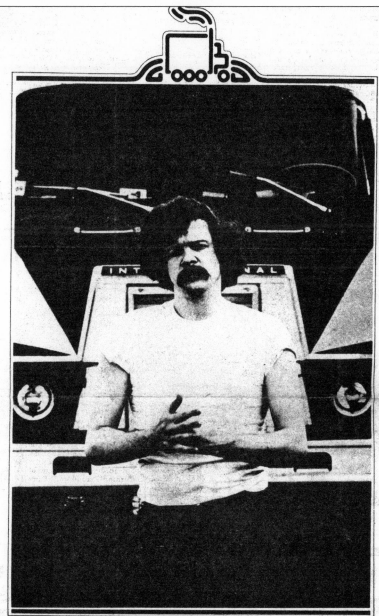

Ed Sanders invites all those who have been discomforted by the Mexican border war to "Get out there like any other red blooded American and start a Victory Garden today! I'm sick and tired of bra-less mini-skirted school teachers talking about ecology at the country school!!" After a long and sordid stint as an undercover Fug, Ed Sanders has found truckhood and has gone country . . . and mountain . . . and Great Plains . . . and Western in an effort to become the mayor of Bakersfield, California.

SANDERS' TRUCKSTOP

Full-page ad for *Sanders Truckstop* in the *Village Voice*.

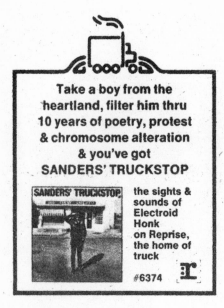

I got to design my own ads.

Also appearing in 1970 was my novel about the Yippies, *Shards of God*, from Grove Press. And from Reprise records came *Golden Filth*, The Fugs live at the Fillmore East. When in August Lou Reed left the Velvet Underground, The Fugs already seemed like a distant fantasy.

Setting Aside Poetry to Study "The Family"

I stopped writing poetry as the Manson case consumed my life for almost two years. I neglected touring for *Sanders Truckstop*. I had planned to put together a band, but that never happened. I more or less withdrew from the counterculture.

I arranged to get on the staff of the *Los Angeles Free Press*, the premier underground weekly, to cover the upcoming Manson trial. During 1970 I wrote about twenty-five articles for the *Free Press* on the Manson Family trial.

Miriam and I, with Deirdre, flew to Los Angeles, where I began the quest for data. I went out to the Spahn Movie Ranch to visit the remnants of the

Manson family. It was eerie. I'd thought at first they might have been set up or that there was a bigger story than had been published in *Life* or the *New York Times.* I became swept up in research for *The Family.* I'd been raised to ponder the real presence of evil. Now I was about to come up close to its clear and present manifestations.

Something was over. But "Over" was not over. Writing a book on the Manson group helped me to grow up. Helped me to get to know, and even become friends with, police officers. Helped me to measure evil more acutely, to appreciate the sense of right and wrong given to me by my parents, especially my Sunday-School-teaching mother, Mollie.

As for The Fugs, I quickly forgot they were of any importance at all. Years were to go by, all the way to 1984, until I realized The Fugs had an unfulfilled destiny of songcraft and I would rebegin their voyage with regular reunions and the issuing of new CDs.

The 1960s had ended, and Miriam and I were still together. We had survived the Revolution. I was very grateful for that. The war was still going on like a sore that wouldn't heal. But still I was feeling vim and energy. The Future was there, ready to savor.

INDEX

❧